DATE			
JY 17 '98			
AUG 1 4 03			

THE PSYCHOLOGY
OF INFANCY AND CHILDHOOD

Evolutionary and Cross-Cultural Perspectives

CHILD PSYCHOLOGY

THE PSYCHOLOGY
OF INFANCY AND CHILDHOOD

Evolutionary and Cross-Cultural Perspectives

Harold D. Fishbein
University of Cincinnati

LAWRENCE ERLBAUM ASSOCIATES, PUBLISHERS
1984   Hillsdale, New Jersey   London

Lawrence Erlbaum Associates, Inc., Publishers
365 Broadway
Hillsdale, New Jersey 07642

Library of Congress Cataloging in Publication Data

Fishbein, Harold D.
  The psychology of infancy and childhood.

  Bibliography: p.
  Includes indexes.
  1. Infant psychology. 2. Child psychology. 3. Child
psychology—Cross-cultural studies. I. Title.
BF719.F57 1984   155.4   84-4041
ISBN 0-89859-416-2

Printed in the United States of America
10 9 8 7 6 5 4 3 2 1

This book is dedicated to all who have helped me to learn—both young and old, in past and present.

Contents

Preface

This book unknowingly received its start during the Fall of 1977 while I was on sabbatical leave from the University of Cincinnati. I had convinced the National Science Foundation, the National Institutes of Mental Health, and the University to support me for two years of study at the Philadelphia Child Guidance Clinic. Salvador Minuchin, my sponsor and one of my teachers, helped me learn about child development in the family context. I believed that families were the most potent and persistent shapers of children's lives, and my understanding of these effects was dependent upon two factors: (1) acquiring access to families and (2) developing skills for studying them. Minuchin and I believed that these goals could be accomplished by observing family therapists at work and learning to be one myself. Bernice Rosman, Director of Research at the Clinic, worked closely with me during this time in order to increase my understanding of research methods in this extremely complicated area.

The Clinic is conveniently located across the street from the University of Pennsylvania Anthropology Department and down the block from the Department of Biology. A number of people from both departments befriended me and allowed me to audit their courses. Bill Skinner, then a visiting anthropologist from Stanford, enlightened me about cultural influences in family formation and child development. Ward Goodenough, Chairman of Anthropology, my most frequent luncheon companion, helped me to see the parallels between the culture of families and of societies, and between cultural change agents and family change agents, e.g., family therapists. John W. Smith, social ethologist and naturalist, helped me to deepen my understanding of behavioral ecological systems.

Except for having to awaken at 5:30 A.M. on Tuesdays, I recommend bird watching to budding developmental psychologists.

Shortly after returning to Cincinnati in the Fall of 1979, Dave Ricks and Ed Klein, whose offices were adjacent to mine, approached me with this proposal: since many book companies were looking for "life-span" developmental psychology texts, the three of us could collaborate on writing this type of text. We had previously organized a three quarter life-span course which was going well, and we might readily put together a book based upon our teaching experiences. This idea appealed to me. We agreed to write three highly related books which could be put under either one or three separate covers, and to work together closely to ensure maximum continuity and minimum overlap. I started work on this collaborative effort in 1980; by 1982, however, my contribution to the project had taken on a life of its own as an independent work.

Basically, the present book begins where my first one–*Evolution, Development, and Children's Learning* (1976)–ends. The *Evolution* book presents many of the technical arguments for an evolutionary perspective of human psychological development. Thus, they are not repeated in the present work. By page count, the two books have a 5% overlap. So, virtually everything in the present work is new–particularly the emphasis on culture. My anthropological friends showed me that despite the existence of canalized behavior owing to our evolutionary design, cultural influences were also powerful, especially in the realm of social interactions. Because the *Evolution* book focused on cognitive development, I was not so sensitive then to the impact of culture. In the present book cognitive development issues are presented, as well as personality, social, and socialization issues.

Although I am by nature a very planful person, my research and writing rarely reflect this characteristic. I can't outline a work and follow that outline. Instead, I start with a broad plan, cut out a specific aspect of it, and keep working until I sharpen it. I then move on to the next part, follow the same procedure, and continue in this way until the work is finished. The present book is no exception to this pattern. I began with the idea of presenting material for a one quarter psychology course in infancy and childhood which would be accessible to sophomores and upper classmen. This book would present the effects of evolutionary and cross-cultural influences, tie in with courses in adolescence, and provide a strong research emphasis. As the work evolved it became clear that the most likely group of readers would be upper division undergraduate and graduate students in psychology and education. I hadn't planned in 1980 to include so much education-related research, but as the shape of the book emerged, it became necessary to include material on schools, reading, mathematics, and IQ. How can you write about child development without including these topics?

My colleagues tell me that the book has a cohesive shape and clear perspective. It presents my view of the essentials of the psychology of infancy and childhood.

Harold D. Fishbein

Acknowledgments

I am very grateful for all the assistance I received from two of my friends and colleagues at the University of Cincinnati, Edward Klein and Dave Ricks. They helped shape the content of the book so that it would conform to a life-span perspective, they spend many lunches discussing developmental issues, and they provided encouragement. Dave wrote Chapter One, and closely edited chapters Two and Three. Ed edited every chapter in the book except "Recapitulation." His favorite statement was "There are too many details." Marv Schwartz and Gwenn Briscoe of the University of Cincinnati read and commented on chapters 6 and 7. Thank you both. Lorna Volk, secretary and editor, was tremendously helpful with parts of Chapter 6 and 7, and all of Chapter 8. Thank you. Dave Palermo of Pennsylvania State University read a near final draft and made a number of helpful suggestions concerning content and organization. He was very encouraging.

Jack Burton of Lawrence Erlbaum Associates "signed me" to do the book. He was pleased by the opportunity to publish a developmental text that included substantial evolutionary and cross-cultural work. Bob Stutz and Bill Dember, Department Head and Dean, respectively, gave me a quarter off from teaching commitments to make headway with this project. Alex Fraser has continued to stimulate my thinking about and understanding of canalization processes. And my wife and children, Diane, Jeremy, and Aaron, continue to teach me about child and family development. I thank all of you. Finally, I thank all those scholars whose hard work, dedication, and publications made this book possible.

THE PSYCHOLOGY
OF INFANCY AND CHILDHOOD

Evolutionary and Cross-Cultural Perspectives

1 Theories and Methods of Developmental Psychology[1]

THE DEVELOPMENTAL ORIENTATION

Developmental psychology is one part of psychology and shares many methods with experimental, social, and clinical research.

But some of the concerns of developmental psychology are like those of a novelist working out the trajectory of an individual or a family. At other times a developmental psychologist might most resemble a sociologist or anthropologist working to explain kinship systems and their effect on the developing person. In this chapter we try to describe the main characteristics and uses of a developmental orientation to life, the goals of developmental psychology, and some of the ways of studying the context of development. We then describe levels of knowledge, which will involve us in distinguishing between common-sense observation, clinical case studies, and systematic research. Developmental psychology differs from the study of subjects such as astronomy and cell physiology because its subject matter—how we grow up—is already familiar to us before we begin systematic study. Reading about development, and thinking about the implications of what you read for your own life, involves you in a kind of dialogue with the writer of this book. At times you will disagree, and at

---

[1]This chapter was written by David F. Ricks, Department of Psychology, University of Cincinnati.

times you may find your own experience does not support the conclusions reached. Science has developed in just such situations. When we write about the methods of developmental research we describe ways of settling controversy, of appealing to observations and so settling differences of opinion on the basis of empirical fact. Personal experience is the starting point in the quest to understand development. But appreciation for the observations made by experimental pioneers like Piaget, and clinical pioneers like Freud, can help you broaden your own awareness. As you learn more you will see new dimensions in the homely details of life: a baby and mother engaging in a cooing dialogue can take on all the stately regularity of a formal dance; a girl and mother engaged in the push and pull of separation can be as powerfully engaging as a Greek tragedy.

Students often come to a field of study with a hope for facts, each of which is really the answer to a question. Most research scientists believe that it is harder to find the right questions than it is to find the right answers. The developmental orientation to life is first of all a way of asking questions.

Imagine, for example, that you are a camp counselor faced for the first time with a group of 9-11-year-old boys or girls. What would you want to know about them, beyond the obvious things like names and bunks? You might find yourself wondering about skills, interests, friendship groups, who was lonely and who was glad to be at camp, and so on. If you were dealing with girls it would help to know that the physiological events of puberty would already have been well launched in some girls, while others would lag on that developmental path. What main ideas would a developmental psychologist be concerned with?

Change Through Time — Sequence and Stage

Look closely at that question of puberty. Notice that the concern is with change, not static characteristics. In the study of development we will be working with ideas like path, trajectory, and sequence. All of these are ways to describe events through time. The most general goal of developmental psychology is discovery of *invariant sequences*, so that we identify where an infant or child is on a given developmental path and make predictions about the sequence and timing of coming changes. For example, a child who has developed reasonably secure bowel and bladder control, and who can take some interest in other children and engage in the beginnings of peer play, can be considered ready to begin nursery school

(Freud, 1965). We can predict for such a child a growing ability to control bodily functions, a flowering of interest in other children in an environment rich in peer stimulation, and increasing ability to tolerate separation from earlier objects of attachment. In biological sequences, like puberty, the order of physiological changes is highly predictable. Yet children may differ by as much as 3 or 4 years in the age at which they begin or end the process. In general, we might expect that psychological sequences will show the same pattern: relatively unpredictable times of entry and exit from a sequence, but strong predictability in both the order and timing of events once the sequence starts. While this invariance of sequence is most clearly shown in physiological development, it is a questionable characteristic of the stages of cognitive development. Are stages of development really there, or are they only convenient labels that we apply to sections of a growth process that is really continuous? Every junior high boy is likely to notice, for instance, that some of his peers, and particularly some of the girls in his class, have embarked on a growth spurt. Subjectively, a boy may feel like a different person after a growth spurt at 14 has added 6 inches to his height (see Fig. 1.1). But on a long-term chart of his growth, that 6 inches that feels so large is only a small perturbation on a long-term succession of inches added per year. He may take an interest in sports like basketball, where his new 6 inches gives him a gratifying advantage, or he may "discover" girls. All of this may make him feel that he has passed through some kind of portal, and that he is in a new stage of life. The test, for a developmental psychologist, is that of organization. Is his personality organized in a new way? Have old interests been dropped and new interests developed? If growth has resulted in a qualitative reorganization of personality and of relationships—for instance a move from dependence on parents to reliance on peers—we are probably accurate in speaking of a new stage of life. If the change has been continuous—with small quantitative changes gradually accumulating, but with no major reorganization—it is more accurate to speak of a process of growth, or a continuum, than to make arbitrary breaks along the developmental trajectory and call them stages.

Another controversial issue is the direction of change. Is there only one direction, as in physical height, in which we grow fairly continuously until adolescence ends and then stay much the same until the minor shrinkage of old age? Or is change in both directions possible? One of the most valuable ideas in the Freudian approach to development is *regression,* a con-

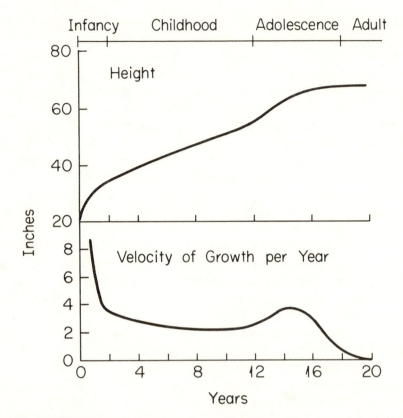

FIG. 1.1 Linear growth of one boy, expressed as increments per year (below). Note the rapid rate in infancy and adolescence with rather consistent rates in between. (Source: Smith, D.W. & Bierman, E. L. *The biologic ages of man.* Philadelphia: W. B. Saunders, 1973.)

cept Freudians use to describe the way a person under stress may fall back to ways of life that had been abandoned earlier. Those who believe in regression may point out how a child who has long since given up sucking a thumb may once again adopt that comfort when a baby sister is born, or how a young man who is frustrated in his sexual life may find comfort in a secret orgy of eating. Those who do not believe in regression may explain these behavior patterns in terms of reinforcements, but the Freudian theory in this instance has the advantage of greater simplicity and clarity.

Trajectory Types

If our concern is with change and sequence, how do we describe differences between people? Much of psychology is concerned with this question of individual differences. Usually, these are described by the adjectives of common sense: John is more intelligent than Bill; Pete is more active than Jerry. The result is a psychology of traits, which are generally thought of as stable. A developmental approach, on the other hand, conceives of people as moving along developmental paths, or trajectories. It asks why people differ at a given time, whether those differences have been characteristic in the past, and whether they will continue in the future. Block (1971) has called the classifications we might make when we take the pattern of development into account *trajectory types*, consistent patterns of development. In people that Block calls "cognitive copers," for instance, a pattern changes that shows a slowly cumulative growth of competence. For example, compared to other girls in junior high school, cognitive copers show many characteristics that suggest tension and self-criticism, but by young adult life they are doing spectacularly well. When we talk of individual differences in development, we are concerned with such consistent patterns of development, not with static differences at any one time.

Consider a representative question that has generated a great deal of interest, as the mean life span has increased and new policies regarding retirement age have been debated. Does intelligence decrease with age? If so, which aspects of intelligence decrease and which remain intact? To answer such a question, we must look at changes in intelligence, by age, in groups whose intelligence is at different levels. (Some further questions are taken up later, in relation to developmental research designs.) Most generally, the answer proves to be dependent on the shape of the growth curve in early life. When age changes in intelligence are studied empirically (Baltes & Schaie, 1973) it turns out there are different trajectories for intelligence, with different consequences in old age. Those who develop high intellectual ability in early life have ways of continuing to learn, and in old age their intellectual abilities (particularly general knowledge and vocabulary) continue to grow rather than decline. Those whose abilities are less developed in youth level off sooner and show more decline in old age. Differences that were apparent in early life not only continue in age, they actually increase. We should not be surprised to see the brilliant scientist or the highly motivated lawyer continue to learn and to lead in old age, for in such people abilities are still growing.

People become less like each other over time; on measures of ability, interest, and so on we find increased dispersion rather than increased similarity. But, with age, each person becomes more consistent, more predictable, and at the extreme, more rigid and resistant to change. One way to think of this is that as we age we become less like other people, but day-to-day and year-to-year, we become more like ourselves. We develop a style, and in time people come to know us by that style: hurried or gracious, narrow or broad-reaching, incisive or vague. How early does a style develop? In extensive studies of American presidents, Barber (1972) has shown the characteristic presidential style could be recognized in adolescence. Hoover was early recognized as a hard-working, steady, reliable plodder, a man who could solve problems given to him but who had trouble recognizing problems when he had to define them for himself. Barber was able to predict the troubles of the Nixon presidency well before they developed. (However, careful study of Barber's work by Jimmy Carter did not prevent troubles in his presidency – perhaps a style as definite as Carter's could not be changed a great deal after middle age.)

GOALS OF DEVELOPMENTAL PSYCHOLOGY

At this point our discussion may appear to have moved well beyond the confines of developmental psychology. Nobody expects us to help presidents govern the country. But, what are our goals? At the simplest level, we are concerned with *description* of development. When do processes start? What sequences do they follow? How do they fit together into patterns of development? Everyone has noticed, for instance, that infants are attached to their mothers, and that mothers reciprocate this feeling. But when does attachment start to develop? What can we do to study the stages of attachment? Are securely attached babies more able to relate to strangers, or do babies who develop less attachment reach out to others more readily? All of these questions are descriptive issues. They tend to be answered by a mixture of field research and experimental work. This research results in a tremendous number of discrete facts being discovered – nowhere else in psychology are there so many detailed bits of knowledge as in developmental psychology. It is hard to remember all of these details, but they have great importance. For instance, a developmental psychologist working with pediatricians might be presented with a child of 28 months, whose only words are "Mommy," "Daddy," and "eat." Is this child developmentally slow? What are the normal patterns of speech development, and what amount of vocabulary and structured speech should we expect at 28 months? Diagnosis, treatment, and advice to the parents will depend on our answers to each question.

It is an enormous help to understanding that observations do not stand alone but fall into patterns and sequences. As soon as we can describe a developmental sequence and locate a child on that sequence we can begin to make some reasonable judgments about his rate of development, whether behind or ahead of other children, and to make some predictions as to what to expect next. When we have physical growth curves and other trajectories laid out and enough data about the person in front of us, we can often estimate what his options are going to be. Suppose that a boy in the 9th grade, asked about his vocational plans, says that he wants "to be either a doctor or a forest ranger." Is he vocationally mature for a 15-year-old, or ought he to recognize that these two vocations require quite different kinds of preparation and he should be making some choices? Research (Jordaan & Super, 1974) indicates that he is a typical 15-year-old, but that by 18 he is likely to make judgments like "either a doctor or a dentist." If he is still thinking like a 15-year-old, while other 18-year-olds have matured, he is likely to flounder more than his peers before he finds himself vocationally. In sum, if the first goal of developmental psychology is to describe developmental facts, the second is to fit them together into *descriptive patterns*, both patterns that occur together and sequences over time.

The third goal is to look beyond the immediately observable patterns and explain why they develop. This question has at least two parts: why does a sequence start to develop and why does it continue to develop? Suppose an 8-year-old boy is slow to learn school work, is restless and rebellious, cannot be taken to the supermarket because he gets into every attractive display, and has no friends. According to one theory, such a child is likely to have a neurological disorder called minimal brain dysfunction, and the appropriate treatment is continued maintenance on amphetamines. Other theories emphasize faulty learning history, and a therapist who holds this kind of theory would work toward training such a boy in tolerance for delay, concern for consequences, and other components of skilled living with other people. Still other therapists, noting how this pattern of restless searching and dissatisfaction resembles certain types of behavior after loss, might inquire into the child's history – has he lost a parent, a brother or sister, or a treasured grandparent? If we can put our facts together into patterns, and if we can find a reason for them, we can feel that we understand development. So great is our need to understand, in fact, that we seem to typically overgeneralize theories. Children like the boy just discussed can be understood only if we consider the biological facts of minimal brain dysfunction, the psychological facts of loss behavior, and the social facts of changing family patterns and increasing frequency of divorce. A student looking for reasonable theories for why things happen as they do in development is likely to find the various "authorities" in good agreement about observable facts, in fair agreement about the patterns and sequences that unite those facts, and in rather poor agreement on the level of causal theories. The development psychologist cannot afford to ignore genetic, psychological, or cultural factors, and in this book we try to give due attention to all three.

Developmental Theory as a Guide to Action

Why are the theories important if we can agree on the facts? Students are often bored by theory, or feel it is unnecessary. But it is theory that guides any action we might make to intervene in a developmental process. If our theory is that learning disabilities are basically matters of brain physiology, we will at least begin our treatment of the 8-year-old with stimulant drugs. On the other hand, if we think that minimal brain dysfunction is a myth (Schrag & Divoky, 1975), we might emphasize the weaknesses in teaching methods that require children to be quiet and unresponsive for extended periods. If we have an adequate grasp of the facts, of their developmental pattern, and of their causes, we can set reasonable goals for intervention. Perhaps our best approach will be to build on strengths, and to help the person optimize development. Or we may want to help the person catch up in some area of neglected development. There are several current programs in prisons to help offenders learn to read. A psychological theory of the effects of the person's own felt competence (further achievement) or feelings of incompetence (frustration, anger, and delinquency) suggests that these programs ought to be helpful in preventing criminal careers after discharge. The most important value of a good developmental theory is that it may allow early intervention and prevention of outcomes generally agreed to be bad. For instance, we have good reason to suspect that certain kinds of early physical and psychological damage make children vulnerable to schizophrenia. From this follows a theory of schizophrenic development that has many practical implications for early intervention and prevention (Ricks, 1983).

The Importance of Context

Every period in history has had its own theories of child development. Comparative studies of child development in third world and industrialized countries have emphasized the overwhelming importance of certain social factors, such as adequate nutrition and clean water, if the child is to normally develop both physiologically and psychologically. The American "baby boom" that peaked in the 1950s – resulting in a large group of young people who competed for places in college and are now competing for jobs – led to intense interest in cohort differences. A *cohort* is defined as a group of people who are born in a given environment at a given time. All American children born between 1955 and 1957 would be considered a cohort, the crest of the baby boom. Even though only a few years passed between the time these young people applied to college, in the mid-1970s, and now, life conditions for their cohort and current applicants to college are very different. They faced a situation of many people in competition for scarce places in college. Current students are likely to find colleges competing for them.

A somewhat more subtle effect is exerted by the history of ideas. Children born before Freud were not likely to have their psychosexual development investigated by psychologists or worried about by parents. In the last decade, a project on male adult development described in the Levinson et al. book *Seasons of a Man's Life* (1978) introduced into general use the idea of the male mid-life crisis. After this idea found its way into popular writing, it was hard for a psychologist to go to a party without being taken aside by one or more wives, with an inevitable question, "Do you think my husband is having a mid-life crisis?" The availability of the idea may have made it possible for some wives to become aware of changes in their husbands to which they had been blind. Or it may have suggested to some men that they could cover an interest in a sports car or in another woman with the appealing cloak of a personal crisis. The point is that every idea about human development has the potential to change the way we think about ourselves and those who mean the most to us. As our ideas change, we change. An extreme example of this is the changes in diagnoses in American psychiatry. In older manuals of diagnostic use, homosexuality was diagnosed as a mental illness, while there were no terms for abuse of common drugs like caffeine and tobacco. Current manuals, however, have removed homosexuality from the category of mental illness and have added a range of new addictions. We can summarize the effects of growing up in a given geographical area, in a given cohort, or in a given climate of ideas by seeing all three as contexts for development. The contexts in which a person grows up are certain to play a large role in the personality and skill patterns he develops. Our theories of development are one part of the context in which we and our children develop.

Because context is so important, developmental psychologists have a special concern for the robustness or *generalizability* of their observations. Some theories are attempts at universal laws, while others are attempts to explain limited issues. A given finding may be true only for a given area, or for a particular cohort, or for people who grew up in a period that emphasized permissive child rearing. But if the finding holds for people in different areas, in different cohorts, and in groups raised in different intellectual climates, then it has strong generalizability. A good deal of research is concerned with this issue. For example, it can be shown that as people age they lose their ability to hear high frequency sounds. Study of people who work under conditions of high noise indicates that they suffer more hearing loss than other people in their cohort. If further study finds that artillerymen, the men who help position jet airplanes in airports, and disco dancers all lose acuity for high notes, and that the loss is proportional to the amount of exposure to loud noises, the relationship between loss of acuity and noise exposure could be considered to have high generalizability. As another example, let us consider a prediction. In comparing adult outcomes of two groups of children, one popular and one unpopular with peers, Roff (1974) found that the unpopular children were more likely to later have adult psychiatric difficulties. Though this result held true in Minnesota, Ruff did not consider the results robust until he, Sells, and Golden (1972) had replicated the study in Texas. And even so the results have been shown true only for people in North American culture, which emphasizes sociability. There may be no long-term difference in outcome for popular and unpopular children in a culture like India or England, where civility and reticence may be more important than popularity.

COMMON SENSE AND SCIENCE
AS LEVELS OF KNOWLEDGE

We have just pointed out some of the limits of systematic research. Even with these limitations, however, systematic research involves a more reliable level of knowing, a better kind of observation, than common sense. It may be helpful to distinguish several levels of knowledge.

Consider this hypothetical situation: You see a person leaning against a lamppost. Is this person waiting for a friend, resting for a moment before jogging, or plotting an assassination? You may be able to seek out some particularly telling details. The person may be male, with messed-up clothing, and a strong smell of alcohol. Or the lamppost may support a young woman with extremely revealing clothing, on a street such as 42nd Street in New York. If there are details like this, you can make an informed guess as to why the person is there. You can make a good guess if you know the setting and know the history of that particular person. But your guess will have many limitations, and it would be hard for you to reach any general ideas about people-who-lean-on-lampposts without some sort of systematic sample and set of interviews with lamppost leaners. We cannot get very far, conceptually, on the basis of particular observations. You may notice the limits of particular observations the next time you try to make a general point and somebody answers with an opposite view, "I knew a person who. . . ." Unless your intended point was universal (e.g., all alcoholics are male) then one particular instance, either supportive or contrary, has little relevance. General ideas concern samples, or sets, of observations. Particular observations are instances of a general principle, or else their relevance is questionable.

Everyday observation is a mix of just such particular observations, of cultural stereotypes ("all old people are senile"), and of the personal history of the observer. We all are biased to see what we expect to be there when we look (Neisser, 1976). If you walked down 42nd Street, and you knew that the city had several policewomen out picking up men who accosted women, you might see the young woman on the corner in a different way. Most judgments in law rely on common sense, the test being what a reasonable person would think. But common sense is often wrong. A lawyer may go to the airport to meet a priest, and miss his connection because a reasonable man does not expect a priest to be with a woman. If the priest is travelling with his sister, the lawyer may be left waiting. The worst error in common sense is its reliance on traditional ideas, even when they have been shown to be wrong. Medicine has many examples of treatments that were continued long after they were known to be harmful, for example, bleeding the patient. We have to be wary of ideas that "everybody knows" to be true, for example that women are more emotionally variable than men. When Wessman and Ricks (1966) had people keep careful records of their moods, they found that women were in fact more stable, less "moody," than men.

If we cannot rely very safely on everyday observation, or on common sense, what can we rely on? We might begin with systematic observation of groups of people and begin making comparisons. In the previous example of the lamppost, we might start counting people who pass that lamppost, looking to see what ages, sexes, and races they represent. We might interview every tenth person who passes. Or we might hand out some sort of questionnaire. The method of giving a group, or several groups, a structured form of a data-gathering instrument (interview, questionnaire, test, etc.) is a main method of psychological research. With the results of these data the psychologist can often predict group behavior fairly accurately; e.g., a majority will vote for Candidate X. But predictions made from such data fit best on the group level. Unless the data are overwhelmingly one sided – e.g. 80% will vote for X – we do not have much basis for predicting the behavior of any given individual.

And our observations are likely to stop at the level of description of a pattern. We are often at a loss as to why our group prediction is correct. They will elect Candidate X, but there is no good reason for us to understand why.

Case Studies

To supplement group data, we often turn to case studies. In *epidemiological* research a given relationship may first be established on the group level, then studied in a series of cases to try to work out the mechanism of the relationship. For example, studies of the age of the mother at the time of birth of a baby have shown that there is an optimum period for childbirth, roughly 18 to 30, and that babies born to both young adolescents and to mothers in their late 30s are at high risk for various kinds of fetal damage. Once this is established, we must turn to individual *case control* studies to see why the relationship holds. What is it about 14- or 15-year-old mothers that makes them, physiologically or psychologically, ineffective reproducers of babies?

In clinical research we study individuals to try to find out what is constant, or consistent, in a given person across all of the times and situations of his life, and to find out how he adapts or fails to adapt. In one study (Ricks, 1972) a young man was found to have a characteristic work history that led to repeated vocational disasters. When first hired he would work hard, carry out all of his assignments conscientiously, and look like a model employee. He would begin to succeed. As soon as he tasted success, however, his behavior would change. He would become lazy and domineering, and he would soon be fired. It was found that he was repeating, over and over, a pattern first developed when he was an infant. He was a small, sickly, and much-favored child. His twin brother was domineering, and to his frail hard-working mother the domineering twin also seemed lazy. Yet he seemed to succeed. A therapist working with this young man helped him see that he was still trying, in adult life, to apply a pattern of living that he had learned as a child. He thought he had only two possible alternatives: to be dependent and conforming, or to be lazy and domineering. With help, he learned some other ways of approaching work.

A case study may be a rich source of hypotheses. Freud supported his general theories on less than a dozen published case studies. For many years Piaget based most of his ideas on systematic observation of his own three children. And case studies allow us to work out the mechanisms, the close connections, that explain the relationships we find in epidemiological and other large-scale studies. These are major uses. But as routes to reliable scientific data, case studies have serious limitations. Look again at the young man with the vocational problem. When we have devoted many hours to the study of his problem and have worked out, with his cooperation, a way to solve it, we have a kind of theory. But it is based on a strange kind of consistency between his childhood troubles with his brother and adult troubles with bosses. Will such a regularity apply to anybody else? Do we have a theory of human development after study of this person, or only a theory of one troubled young man? If we try to generalize, how should we go about it? A Freudian might look at this young man, for instance, and generalize that people who are fixated at a given stage in development, or who regress to it, may have difficulty with the demands of adult living. A humanistic therapist might argue that the young man's problem was learning to live in the here and now, rather than in the past. Will the study of individual cases allow us to resolve such differences of opinion?

Longitudinal Studies

Faced with the limitations in both large-scale survey research and in individual case studies, developmental psychologists have turned to the study of groups of individuals, in depth, over extended periods of time. What are the life patterns of the exceptionally able, the people among us who test out in the "genius" range of intelligence? In the 1920s Terman originated a series of "genetic studies of genius" that are still continuing (Terman & Oden, 1959). What patterns of behavior and feeling in childhood continue on into adult life, and which are changeable? The Fels studies (Kagan & Moss, 1962) and those of Olweus (1978) allow us to answer those questions fairly accurately. Intelligence, for instance, is quite stable, and so are most other adaptive characteristics. Using data originally gathered in the 1920s and 1930s in the Berkeley and Oakland growth studies, Block (1971) has been able to trace out in minute detail a set of male and female growth trajectories that combine some of the depth of understanding of individual case studies over time and the generalizability of data about groups.

Given the richness of these longitudinal studies, it would seem that many more such studies would be done. But it is extremely difficult to do a long-term, large-scale, in-depth study of a group of people. These studies put an enormous demand on the people studied. Labeled a genius as a child, Terman was not as alert as a current scientist might be about the effect of the experiment itself on the lives of its subjects. For example, a subject of the Terman studies felt guilty when she graduated only cum laude from Smith rather than summa cum laude. Later, with three small children and a husband immersed in his work, she was thrown into a near depression by a Terman follow-up questionnaire asking for lists of honors, publications, and scientific discoveries. Long-term longitudinal studies also make demands on the experimenter. When Mednick and Shulsinger (1970; Schulsinger, Mednick, & Knop, 1981) launched their series of studies of the origins of schizophrenia, they calculated their own ages and life expectancies and committed their remaining years to this series of studies. There is also a certain demand for altruism in setting up a study in which the original investigators may do almost all of the labor of data gathering, and later generations will harvest the returns.

Each new year that a long-term longitudinal study is continued makes it possible to compare that year's data with the data gathered in all previous years. The result is not a mere linear accumulation of information, but an exponential increase in the richness of possible analyses. The main frustration in working with the data bank established in such a study is that one works with the data the original investigator thought important. If the current investigator has new interests, the data may not be there to study them. But one has only to look at the richness of the descriptive data in the studies that have emerged from the Oakland-Berkeley growth studies to see that earlier investigators gathered much of the information we need now, even if they did not anticipate current interests such as need for and fear of achievement, androgyny, or learned helplessness.

Clinical investigators, interested in developmental issues such as the origins of schizophrenia, alcoholism, or delinquency, have used two main methods. The first of these might be called the *retrospective* method. In a representative study (Cohen et al. 1954), a group of 12 adult depressed patients were studied in a mental hospital. A research team was established, including the therapists of the patients. Working together, the research team tried to tease out the ways in which these patients were alike and the ways in which they were different. One way in which the depressed people proved to be similar was a rather subtle one. They were from families that had been marginal in their communities, families that had not quite fit in, because of race, religion, recency of family money (it was an expensive private hospital), or some other reason. Given their marginal status, the families turned to the children, and particularly the one who later became depressed, to try to show their right to a place in the community. This child had to achieve, to be a model, to make no mistakes. This kind of demand seems reasonably related to the kind of pefectionism often found in people who became depressed.

But there is a flaw in this method of study. The conclusions are based on what the patients report, in adult life, while in a mental hospital. Beck (1976) and his students have shown how biased the perceptions and reports of depressed people are – they systematically screen all incoming information, accepting anything that may reflect negatively on themselves and rejecting anything that might reflect positively. All of us, if we think about our moods, can observe that on low days everything depressing is only too easy to remember, while on up days it seems like nothing in the world can go wrong. A retrospective method might also be considered the main flaw in the Freudian corpus of work. In the long-term longitudinal studies such as the Berkeley-Oakland Growth Study (Block, 1971) the data on childhood were actually gathered in childhood, and records were made of play patterns, friendships, achievement, perceptions of parents, and so on. In the clinical retrospective method, we deal with memories, with all of their distortions. This makes the clinical retrospective method a good source for hypotheses, but nothing more. It can never prove a relationship between childhood and adulthood characteristics.

Follow-Back Research

The third main clinical research method makes use of existing records to try to trace out developmental pathways. Like the longitudinal methods of the Berkeley and Fels studies, it uses existing materials. Statements about what pre-schizophrenics were like in childhood are based on data recorded in childhood, not recalled in adult life. The materials are clinical records: the reason the child was referred for treatment, who referred him, what he said about himself, what the parents said, the child's feelings, and so on. Because of the relevance of the materials – what the child was actually worried about, his main symptoms, and his relationships with others, all reported over time to a trained listener who picked up

information and relationships that might pass by an untrained observer—
this design for research makes it possible to put clinical ideas to a
research test. Since many patients have repeated clinical contacts, over
many years, it is often possible to do what amounts to multiple long-term
case studies on large cohorts of people. The results of these studies, ably
summarized by Garmezy (1974) and by Neale and Oltmanns (1980) have
made it possible to trace out the origins of schizophrenia and other disorders, and in so doing, to find clues to early intervention and prevention.
To distinguish this method of research from the longitudinal/follow-up
studies and the retrospective clinical methods, it is called *follow-back*
research. The Henry Murray Center at Radcliffe College is establishing
systematic data banks for a variety of follow-up and follow-back studies.
Since such data are extremely complex, and approaching amounts of
material that would be hard for any person to remember, they are being
systematically recorded and computerized in ways that allow a variety of
analyses.

USING THEORIES — SHOPPING FOR A ROAD MAP TO DEVELOPMENT

Students are sometimes dazzled by a theory. It seems that Freud has an
answer to everything, or that Skinner points the way to a world in which
life can be a succession of reinforcements, with no restraints or pain.
Other students sometimes say, "That is only a theory," or "Well, that's
your opinion, but. . . ." The best use of theory is probably midway
between these extremes. A good theory is like a good road map. It tells
you how to get where you want to go. In order to do that, it describes a
part of the world, within certain boundaries of concern, and it defines
parts of the world as irrelevant. Anyone who wants to predict how two
people will get along on a date, for instance, might use a considerable
body of research on interests, social class, and so on. Those who think the
positions of stars at the time the two were born plays an essential role in
their relationship, have a good deal of work to do to prove that their data
are relevant.

The theories of developmental psychology are road maps for human
development. Not surprisingly, not all start at the same point or end up in
the same place. Long before you came to this book, you had such a model,
with yourself as its base and your own history as its limits. All of us have
such models. Beginning with simple sensory and motoric models of

ourselves-in-the-world, we develop from being able to grasp things with our hands to being able to grasp intellectually, from being able to dissect a piece of pie to being able to dissect a theory. With experience we take in more of the world, learn to use words and symbols to represent things, and make predictions about situations. A three-year-old can take one look at Daddy at the end of the day and make a good guess whether a request for a story will elicit a smile and a story or a request to leave Daddy alone while he watches the news. As you develop, you assimilate new experiences to your models, and as you do this your models change, accommodating to new aspects of reality. Science is just a very high development of such models, a more advanced way of thinking about how to operate with, and within, the parts of the world that it describes. Science differs from common sense mainly in its development of more systematic ways of making and recording observations, in its systematic ways for analyzing data and discovering errors, and in its dedication to criticizing its own operations and discarding ideas that tail to fit with observations. But even the highest level of theory is still a way of grasping the world, and it bears more than a slight resemblance to the infant's primitive model of grasping its rattle and making a pleasant noise.

Lewis Thomas (1974) has argued that the greatest accomplishment of 20th-century science has been the discovery of human ignorance. Our ignorance is probably also the greatest source of the anxiety we feel—a world in which there are no easy answers is mysterious and frightening. Our problem is not that there are no answers, but that there are too many, and often they are not in agreement. Achenbach (1978) has outlined the four main paradigms that people have used for understanding human development and described some ways of choosing among these theories. As you work to make your own ideas about development explicit and refined, you will find it useful to compare your ideas to these main theories: learning theory, psychodynamics, cognitive development, and ethology.

Historical Vignettes

Too much personal detail about the people who developed the theories can be distracting, but you may understand theories better if you look briefly at the person behind each theory. Imagine, for a moment, each of the following four situations in which you might have once found yourself:

1. You are a biologist trained in field observation and systematic observation of organisms. You conceive a grand project, no less than a

biological science of the origins of knowledge, an empirical, scientific developmental study of how human beings come to terms with their world and conceptually grasp it. Asked in this new way, the traditional questions of philosophy may be open to scientific answers that rise above traditional disputes. You will turn your biologist's mind to situations as diverse as a child playing with a rattle, a boy playing marbles with friends, and an adolescent studying a pendulum. In all of these situations you will ask the biologist's question, What is the nature of the interchange between this organism and its environment? Add to this picture some mountains, an interest in the answers which people come to but even more interest in the ways in which they reach those answers, and you would find yourself in the position of the Swiss scientist Jean Piaget, as he launched his studies in *genetic epistemology.*

2. You are a neurologist, have done original research on nerve conduction, and have worked with children not necessarily by choice but because you are poor and the job was available. You long for a career in medical research and dream of fame and discovery. But you also want marriage and a family. You are constrained by economic need to treat "neurotic" patients, and gradually you begin to discover some very disturbing things as they talk to you. Imagine yourself listening quietly as a long series of Victorian patients tell you their troubles, then thinking and reflecting and trying to see common patterns. You would be, if you do this, trying on the shoes of Freud as he launched *psychoanalysis.*

3. You are trained as a psychoanalyst, in a movement now grown into a world-wide collection of partially agreeing, partially competing schools of thought. Your own school, in England, emphasizes the development of human relationships. In a Europe torn apart by war, you turn your attention to the study of young people who seem "affectless," callous, manipulative. You find that what they have in common is that they did not have stable, affectionate mothering. Science has developed since Freud, and you have available a great deal of fieldwork on imprinting in animals, laboratory studies of how primates form attachments or fail to form them, and new computer-based models for human thought. You proceed to systematize what is known of human attachment and loss, beginning with the most intense attachment of all, that between mother and infant. If you can put yourself into this situaton, you can begin to see the world from the perspective of John Bowlby, who has created a modern synthesis of psychoanalytic and *ethological* perspectives.

4. Imagine that you grew up in a small town whose fortunes were on the decline as the railroad it served fell into bad times. Your mother is a

dreamer, full of illusions that you early reocgnized as false. Your father is a hard-working but easily depressed man. Your adored brother, whose warmth drew the family together, has died of a massive cerebral accident in his early teens. Would you, as an answer to your own doubts and depressions and desires to deal in only hard facts and avoid illusions, perhaps invent a very hard-headed, practical theory of how to manipulate environmental conditions in ways that will almost mechanically shape the behavior of organisms? If so, you would be rather like B. F. Skinner, the most influential modern *behaviorist*. You may still have visionary dreams of an ideal community, but it will be one based on hard facts and scientific concepts of human nature, not anything poetic or vague – or depressing.

The fact that different Freudian theorists do not always agree was mentioned above. There are also schools of behavior theory, some in agreement with Skinner, some strongly critical (Bandura, 1976; Herrnstein, 1977). Each theoretical paradigm covers a set of theories, more or less alike, but not identical.

It will help you to remember each theory, and to work with it, if you take some steps to actively grasp it yourself. Bandura (1976) has recommended three aids to this process. First, try to visualize the theory, or any parts of it you can. Erikson's (1963) theory, for instance, can be seen as an orderly series of steps, more or less like eight steps up to a porch, with a lively set of events going on below the stairs. Second, try to describe the theory verbally, in your own terms. What kind of theory is it, and why? Finally, find a good summary label for the theory. Freud called his theory of development *psychosexual*, to emphasize the role of *libidinal* development. Erikson, to show both his continuing reliance on Freud and his wish to deal with wider social realities than Freud took into account, called his theory *psychosocial*.

Criteria For Choosing Among Theories

How are we to choose between theories? There are several criteria. First, is the theory relevant? does it offer answers to questions that are important to you? Second, is the theory consistent and coherent? Does it all hang together, and is it free from internal contradictions? Third, does the theory lead to testable predictions, and are the predictions supported when the data are in? Since there are always several competing theories, and they sometimes lead to different predictions, it is sometimes possible to test the theories against each other. We will briefly describe several of these situations where paradigms clash, so that you can make up your mind between them.

Piaget, devoted to patient field study, has been content to describe invariable sequences of child development. In one of the most important of these, children learn conservation; e.g., the idea that water poured from a short wide glass to a tall thin one still remains the same amount, even though it now is higher – or that a ball of clay can be rolled out into a hot dog shape and still have the same amount of clay. When children have grasped the various kinds of conservation – mass, number, and so on – they are ready to move into the stage of thinking Piaget calls *formal operations.* You can think of these, for the moment, as operations like addition, subtraction, comparison of size, and putting things into order, e.g., from longest article to shortest. Although Piaget's original experiments were based on very few children, subsequent research all over the world has tended to confirm his description of cognitive stages. After the stages were confirmed, and traces of them were found in much younger children than Piaget had originally placed them in, a new question arose. Could progression through the stages be speeded up? Piaget, the European thinker, looked at the restless American psychologists, more doers then thinkers, and labeled this "the American question." Gelman (1969), for instance, reinforced children for ignoring irrelevant aspects of a stimulus and for paying attention to the relevant cues. Her method worked, and children were moved into conservation ahead of schedule! Has she proved that Piaget is wrong in supposing that these stages are an inevitable biological sequence? Are the Piagetian stages just learned behavior, open to endless manipulation by changes in environmental contingencies? Not really. The children were all at a stage where they were ready to move into conservation. One could repeat Gelman's studies with younger children, or with same-aged children who were intellectually retarded and so were slow to develop, or with Third World rural children who had no stimulus to think in the ways of school-educated people. If children who were not on the threshold of conservation could be moved there, the case for environmental influence would be much stronger.

A related issue is the invariance of sequence in Piagetian stages. Is it possible that a child, or an adult, might show in the cognitive realm the kind of regression that Freudians have described in emotional and social life? Voyat (1983) and his students have studied this question. Suppose a child is given a series of nails and asked to arrange them from the largest to the smallest. Then he is given a set of toy brass camels and asked to do the same task. He succeeds in both. This means that he is capable of *seriation,* arranging things in a rank order, or hierarchy. Suppose he is now given a set of paper dolls, some male and some female, and asked to make the same arrangement, from largest to smallest. Or he might be given photographs of members of his family. These tasks are much harder than arranging sticks or camels in order, and some children who were capable of seriation with impersonal materials now fail to make objectively correct orders. What does this mean? It may mean that when emotion enters into a person's thinking he may not be so rational as he is when dealing with purely cognitive materials. Voyat has found this kind of breakdown more frequent in disturbed children. This seems at least a fair beginning on the task of showing that there is cognitive regression that is quite comparable to emotional kinds of regression.

A paradigm clash occurs between learning theory and ethology over the issue of attachment. Learning theory holds that behavior that is reinforced increases in frequency, while behavior that is not reinforced gradually becomes extinquished. Ethological theory holds that certain kinds of behavior, including attachment, are programmed into our behavior by our evolutionary heritage. Most clinicians have observed parents who offer few reinforcements to the children, and who seem to deal with their children mostly with yells, prohibition, and occasional physical punishment. These children seem to cling much more than most children do, which would suggest that at least for abused children the ethological theory has more validity. Bell and Ainsworth (1972) studied the issue around a particular part of attachment, crying. Learning theories, like commonsense ideas of "spoiling" children, predict that mothers who respond to crying with cuddling, food, and warmth would reinforce crying, and hence would have babies who cried more than those of less responsive mothers. Ethological theory holds that crying is an innate response triggered by awareness of separation from the mother, and that responsiveness from the mother deepens the bond between mother and child, increases security, and should decrease crying. Bell and Ainsworth found the prediction from ethological theory to be the correct one – responsive mothers have babies who cry less. The finding seems to generalize well across species – Harlow found that battered monkeys raised by isolated mothers were especially clinging. The best test would probably be to look at mothering across many cultures, rank these for the closeness of mothering, and check to see if frequency of crying was inversely related to how close and responsive mothers were. Given these facts, would you choose learning theory or ethology as your framework for understanding development?

Comparison of psychodynamic and ethological viewpoints is more difficult, because in general they make rather similar predictions. Both psychoanalytic and ethological theories of development are based on the idea of an invariant sequence of biologically based stages. A fairly subtle comparison of psychoanalytic theory and ethology becomes possible, however, if we compare the viewpoints of attachment of Mahler, Pine, and Bergman (1975), fairly conservative child analysts, with the viewpoint of Bowlby (1969), who takes ethology into account. The question is a basic one in human life: What is the nature of the attachment of the infant to its mother, and what are the stages of separation? Both Mahler and Bowlby began by trying to understand a clinical problem. Bowlby's concern was with the affectless *delinquents* already mentioned. Mahler began with children who suffer a rare but fascinating disorder, *autism*. These children, who number only about 1 in 1000, seem not to think of themselves as human or to recognize the humanity of people around them. They may have no speech, or only an uncannily accurate parroting of television commercials. They do not play with other children, and may kick or scratch violently if another child intrudes upon them. If an autistic child wants something, and an adult is in the way, he may climb over the adult as if he were a chair or table, impersonally.

Study of these children led Mahler to conclude that there were two types: children who remained in their own autistic world, and those who emerged enough to form one powerful relationship, usually with the mother. These children Mahler called symbiotic. Mahler came to believe that all people begin life in a state of "normal autism," unrelated to others, and that all people then develop a normal symbiosis with the mother. To study this sequence, Mahler needed a new situation, a nursery school for normal toddlers, where attachment and separation could be observed. Mahler set up a room in which mothers would have to stay in one part, while toddlers were free to roam. She observed that children first remained with the mother, then ventured out to a place where they could inspect the whole of the room while still remaining in visual contact with the mother. Occasionally they might return to the mother for emotional refueling. Finally they would go into the part of the room furthest from the mother, play there, and then return. But this return had a new quality. The child had been where the mother had not ventured, and he could come back as a reporter on his new discoveries. Children at this point seemed to be struggling between attachment and freedom, and loving reunions might be alternated with angry "I can do it" kinds of statements. Mahler called this period rapprochement, a kind of vacillation between mother and world. Finally, the child developed individuality and a sense of the constancy both of himself and of the mother. He was free to explore the world on his own, and he could report back or not, as he chose.

It is worth examining Mahler's methods in some detail, before comparing her ideas to those of Bowlby. She has moved from the earliest method of clinical research—listening to patients as they talked about childhood—to direct observation of children. This frees her data from the distortions inherent in recalled events and feelings. She began with a clinical population and derived her main hypotheses from observing them, but she added to these observations the data gathered from observing "normal" mothers and their toddlers. Her style is deductive. She presents her ideas, shows how they hang together, and illustrates with particular observations and case studies. This is a familiar method in clinical research, and it is productive in the exploratory stages of research, what Reichenbach (1938) calls the context of discovery. But there are no hypotheses, no predictions, no systematic statistical analysis of the data. Since there is no clear way one can show the theory wrong, it is not really proved right. A good theory should be capable of being shown to be wrong. Mahler's methods produce fascinating possibilities, but it will remain for others to test her theories.

Putting all of her work together, Mahler has proposed that we all go through five stages of development: normal autism, symbiosis, separation, rapprochement, and consolidation of individuality as we develop object constancy. Her observations have focused on symbiosis, separation, and rapprochement, with the state of normal autism largely a hypothetical period based on the failures of development of autistic children. It is this period that Bowlby calls most into question.

Studying young people who never had the opportunity to develop secure attachments, reviewing Harlow's monkey babies raised clinging to terry cloth doll mothers with bicycle reflector eyes, and taking into account all we know of innate behavior patterns and their releasors, Bowlby concludes that there is no normal autism. We are born biased toward attachment. In this conception, symbiosis is a biological given. Secure attachment allows exploration of the environment, independence developing on the child's own schedule. What merits particular study is the life with no attachments, either because there is no mothering person, or more frequently, because there is some loss or separation before its time. From Mahler's perspective, autism is taken for granted and what has to be explained is the development of relationships. Bowlby sees life differently. We can assume, on the basis of our evolutionary history, a tendency to cling and to attach. What has to be explained is lack of relationships.

How can we choose between these theories? One test is to look at separation, and to see if it takes on the quality of push-and-pull movement away and rapprochement that Mahler describes, or more often resembles the protest, despair, and apathy that Bowlby finds in the loss syndrome. We can look at adolescent separation when people are articulate about the changes they are experiencing. But most directly, we can study infants and see whether they are unresponsive, unrelated, autistic in the first weeks. When we do this, we find that the infant is, even at birth, an alert, perceptive, actively choosing organism (Bower, 1977). Babies prefer complex designs like a cross to a simple dot, they prefer a human face to even a complex design, and they quickly come to prefer the face of the mother to any other possible design the world might take on. As the data on infancy accumulate, at an accelerating rate, they favor Bowlby's view over that of Mahler. More generally, the data support a modern form of psychoanalytic theory, informed by ethology, over the more classical psychoanalytic viewpoint of Mahler.

ORGANISM–ENVIRONMENT INTERACTION

Recent work on infancy (Bower, 1977) does not just call theories such as Mahler's into question. It also provides new evidence for the biological basis for learning and the biological limits to our capacity to change the ways of any organism.

The Skinnerian model for psychological development presumes an empty organism, shaped and prodded by an active environment. Readers of Skinner's autobiography (1976) will see that this is a deeply held belief, not just a convenient way of organizing data. But even Skinner's own students, such as Herrnstein (1977) have had to admit that there are biological limits to learning, that there are inherent behavior patterns, and that the organism is far from empty. In fact, the role of the environment is more often that of directing and constraining an inherently active organism than that of prodding and shaping an inert one.

As soon as we admit that the developing organism integrates its own environment, rather than being shaped by it, we are faced with a new complexity. It is clear that the effect of any environmental influence depends on the state of the organism at the time it encounters that influence. This has been worked out in grisly detail in regard to thalidomide and the development of the fetus. Pregnant women taking thalidomide two weeks apart had babies deformed in completely different parts of the body (see Fig. 1.2). Why is this so? Erik Erikson (1963) has introduced into psychology a principle from embryology, which he calls the "epigenetic principle." This holds that the organism does not develop in a uniform fashion. Rather, parts develop in order, with each part having a time when it is growing at its maximal rate, taking in material from its surroundings more rapidly than before or after, and so is maximally vulnerable to damage. Each organ, in turn, has its period of most rapid development. An adverse stimulus to the organism at a particular time will have its impact on the organ developing most rapidly. If conditions improve later, they will affect another organ, not the damaged one. To Erikson, development is a series of decisive encounters with the environment, each through a different bodily zone (mouth, anus, genitals). That part of the organism that is developing most rapidly is most vulnerable. In fact, as we show shortly, the part of the infant that is developing most

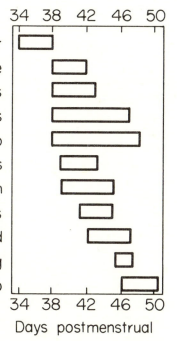

FIG. 1.2 The type of malformation produced by thalidomide in relation to the stage of pregnancy at which the drug was taken by the mothers. (Source: Saxen, L. & Rapola, J. *Congenital defects.* New York: Holt, Rinehart and Winston, 1969.)

rapidly during the oral/sensory stage is the brain, and it is far more vulnerable than the mouth or the digestive tract during infancy. But Erikson's principle would hold, even if his developmental physiology proved to be wrong in detail.

Critical Periods

Anyone who has read an introductory psychology textbook has probably seen one of the many examples of imprinting: a set of little ducklings walking single file behind a large, stooping, elderly scientist named Konrad Lorenz; a pigeon following a farmer as he hoes, ignoring the pigeons flying overhead; a crow signaling "danger" to a large human as a cat comes into a field, and so on. Lorenz (1956) and others have shown that birds and other animals will follow any large moving object that is near at the time of hatching or of birth. There seems to be a "critical period' for attachment of this sort. If one is around at the right time one is imprinted on the organism as "mother," but this has to happen at a specific developmental point or it will not happen at all. Hess (1962) describes a particularly illustrative film of this. A set of mallard ducklings has been imprinted on a decoy, and this decoy is towed behind a row boat. The ducklings swim in the usual row behind the decoy. A wild duck, with her own ducklings in tow, comes into view. She suddenly becomes agitated, swims over to the ducklings, and makes several efforts to separate them from their decoy. They take evasive action and rejoin their wooden-headed mother. Eventually the wild mallard gathers up her own brood and swims away. Attachment has an irrational component. It is clear that ducklings would be better off with a real mother. But once imprinted on a decoy or an elderly scientist or a family dog, the young organism will stick to it until maturation allows it to go free.

The physiological expression of the critical period is illustrated by perceptual development (Bower, 1977). A person born blind, whose vision is later restored surgically, has a long and difficult time learning to see. The infant, with intact eyes, very quickly develops the ability to discriminate patterns, to choose among them, and even to be bored by repeated exposure to the same stimulus pattern.

Bloom (1964) has given the idea of critical period its most elegant expression, in the form of growth curves for different psychological and physiological functions. The part of the curve where growth is most rapid, and where the curve is steepest, corresponds to a critical period. If we assume stable individual differences over time, then where measures of children correlate .75 with the measures of adults on a particular dimension we can say that 50% of the adult growth has been reached. For example, a child reaches about half of his adult height by the age of 2½ years. A child who is 3 feet tall at 2½ is likely to be a six-footer. And by age 2½ we can predict adult height fairly accurately in general, with a correlation between height at 2½ and adult life of .75. Clearly, if we want to influence the adult height of a population, the time to do so would be the first 3 to 4 years, including the three-fourths of a year when the child's nutrition comes by way of the placenta and the mother's own nutritional intake.

The critical period for brain growth is particularly interesting. It spans the 3 months before birth, and the 3 months subsequent to birth, which account for 50% of all of the brain growth the typical person will ever have. From this we can quickly see the enormous importance of the nutritional level of the mother, the drugs or medicines she might use, whether she smokes or not, early illnesses in the child that might affect brain growth, and so on.

There are four main criticisms of the idea of critical periods. First, most growth curves are smooth and do not show any sudden discontinuities. It is true that there are times when influences from such things as nutrition or good mothering can have their maximal impact, but this fact does not negate the possibility of influence either earlier or later than the critical period. While 50% of brain growth takes place in the 6 months just preceding and following birth, the other 50% takes place in the first 6 months of fetal life and in the 20 or so years following the first 3 after birth. Second, the idea of critical periods might be used to justify a fatalistic or apathetic approach to growth, the idea that the critical period is over and so nothing can be done. If attachment does not form, according to this interpretation of Bowlby and Harlow, a person will necessarily go through life as an affectless character. But Harlow's monkeys, raised without mothers, could be cured by continued contact with affectionate normal peers. Intervention can be maximally effective if it occurs at an opportune point in development, but it can still work later. A third, closely related criticism is that development sometimes seems to go in spirals or other patterns rather than in straight lines or growth curves—if a young child has a bad time with toilet training and comes away with lasting residuals of compulsive doubt, he may have a chance to work these out in grade school. A young child once said, "It is like I am a pencil, but the eraser is the most important part." He was working out his feelings over issues of compliance and conformity versus doing things his own way. Eventually he told his therapist that his first memory had been one of trying to draw a sailboat on the wall next to his crib, using his feces as materials. Today he is a successful set designer on Broadway. Fourth, the organism seems to have many built-in balance mechanisms, so that it automatically compensates for deficits. Kagan and Klein (1973) have shown that children raised with little stimulation may later catch up if they get adequate input from their environments. The most sophisticated research on the extent to which the developing person can make up for lacks suffered early has been done on the effects of chronic malnutrition (Birch, 1974). Malnutrition has its greatest effects early, as a critical period hypothesis would predict. If the period of malnutrition is not too severe or prolonged the organism will compensate later, getting back on the growth curve it had before malnutrition became severe. The difficulties of restoring both physical and cognitive growth, in children who have suffered severe prolonged malnutrition, provide a powerful illustration of the general principle that prevention is more effective than cure.

In one of the charming asides that make his books memorable, Erik Erikson (1963) commented "I came to psychology from art...the reader will find me painting contexts and backgrounds...I base what I have to say on representative description." Birch, whose work was described just above, came to the study of development from experimental psychology and the medical study of malnutrition. You, as a student of development, may find it useful at this point to put this book aside, and to make an effort at developing your own model for development, using the special strengths you bring to development from your own background as an older or younger child in a family, as a student of psychology or education or nursing or engineering, and as a person with a particular environment for learning. In the author's experience, people have been able to make use of computer backgrounds to invent models for development that emphasize how information is processed; medical students have been able to make use of their physiological training to develop innovative psychological models, and so forth. Try to name your model and describe its main features. One student, Dennis Schneider of the University of Cincinnati, developed the model shown in Fig. 1.3. It takes account of the spiral nature of many kinds of development, and it integrates Erikson with a much older description of polarities, the yin/yang of Chinese philosophy.

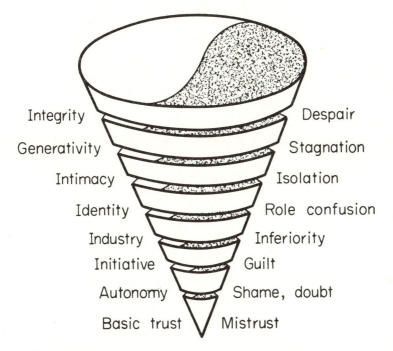

Integrity   Despair

Generativity   Stagnation

Intimacy   Isolation

Identity   Role confusion

Industry   Inferiority

Initiative   Guilt

Autonomy   Shame, doubt

Basic trust   Mistrust

FIG. 1.3   Opponent process theory of development.

Social Ecology, Designing Environments for Development

Suppose we have a systematic examination available for infants, one that will allow us to assess the social interactive capacities of the newborn child. Such an instrument has been developed by Brazelton and his colleagues (Als, Tronick, Lester, & Brazelton, 1970). Can we use this instrument to see whether children born in different cultures differ in systematic ways, and can examination of any differences we might find point toward ways of improving environments for development?

In a representative study (Brazelton, Koslowski, & Troneck, 1971), 10 Zambian infants were compared with 10 United States infants on the first, fifth, and tenth day of life. The Zambian families were from a semi-rural, urbanized slum area that surrounds the city of Lusaka. The mothers had had several pregnancies in rapid succession, at about 12–13 month intervals, and there were at least three children living at home. The American babies were first-borns, from middle-class families, and were delivered without anesthesia to the mother. All were normal and healthy by pediatric and neurological examination. The small sample sizes and selection of groups that differ on several variables at once (later child vs. firstborn, Zambian vs. American, poor vs. middle class) raise questions about what might cause differences in the babies. The differences in the samples, on the other hand, are clear observable facts, and these are what will concern us here.

Because of the Zambian mothers' undernutrition, their infants were severely depleted of fat and subcutaneous tissue, were dehydrated at birth, had skin that was wrinkled and dry, and appeared to American observers to require delicate handling. The day-old American babies were larger, longer, and initially more responsive; they had better muscle tone and better head control, and showed more capacity to respond to events in their environment. By the tenth day, however, Zambian babies showed improved muscle tone, high overall alertness, and strong interest in the examiner. Having been born behind the American babies, they seemed to catch up and even go ahead within a 10-day period. Why? The Brazelton team believed that this rapid development was due to a combination of nutritional improvement as the mother's milk restored the infant's depleted stores after delivery, and to the way babies were handled. The babies were taken home at Day 1 to get them with their family. The Zambian mothers actively played with their babies, as did everyone else in the family. The baby was breast-fed frequently and on demand. By contrast, the American babies were in the hospital for 3 days. At home the mothers generally fed the babies every 3 to 4 hours and did not play with them at other times. Between feedings the baby was usually kept in an isolated room, since the mothers wanted to protect them from possible infections and felt that babies would sleep better if they were alone.

American babies are not so frequently isolated as they were even a decade ago. They spend more time with the mother while they are still in the hospital, and less time staring at featureless ceilings. But experiments such as Brazelton's suggest that we are still depriving infants of human contacts, and that this deprivation has almost immediately observable effects.

Developmental psychologists, pediatricians, gerontologists, and others are involved in many similar kinds of studies. As our knowledge of human development grows and we learn more about the effects of different environments, we can work toward design of enviroments that are more attractive, calmer, quieter, more conducive to pleasant human contact, and more productive of healthy growth.

DESIGNS FOR DEVELOPMENTAL RESEARCH

Group Comparisons

Psychological research is one small part of scientific research, and developmental research is one part of psychology. In what follows we assume some general familiarity with scientific methods, particulary with the attitude that differences of opinion are to be settled by logic and appeal to observation. We also asume that the reader accepts the possibility of studying attitudes, feelings, and behavior systematically, as any other natural events are studied. We concentrate, then, on the special problems and solutions of developmental research.

The English empiricist philosophers, ancestors of modern psychology, worked from the principle that the baby was a *tabula rasa*, a blank slate on which experience wrote what was to be learned in life. Very gradually, as evidence accumulated, psychologists learned that the organism is active, that it does not have to be stimulated into learning, as old Stimulus-Response models held, but that beginning in infancy, the human being is at all times actively organizing information, experiencing a world and making it his own. This poses a problem for research. How can the psychologist put his measuring instruments into the ongoing stream of behavior and emerge with anything reliable? There have been two main answers, experimental control and statistical operations on the data. Both have their uses.

When Pavlov did the first great experiments on conditional reflexes (the response of salivation becoming conditional on a light or bell or any other stimulus being systematically paired with an unconditional stimulus such as meat) he found it necessary to put his dogs into restraining harnesses to control behavior unrelated to salivation. The ideal of experimental control is to keep all conditions except one constant, to vary that one condition systematically along some measurable scale, and to measure the resultant changes in a dependent variable. In Pavlov's experiments, for instance, one independent variable was the number of times a bell had to be paired with presentation of food in order to elicit salivation to the sound of the bell. Controlled experimentation gives us some assurance that the independent variable is systematically related to the dependent variable, often in a way we can specify exactly enough to write as a mathematical formula.

Physiological and experimental psychology are full of such formulas, expressing experienced brightness as a function of candlepower, memory for digits as a function of repetition, and so on.

A representative experiment in developmental psychology might be addressed to a problem that concerns many parents; does violence on television lead to violent behavior in children who view it? Two matched groups of children might be set up and Group A exposed to violent television for a short time. Meanwhile, Group B might watch some other type of television. Both groups might then be given a chance to choose between some kindly act or doing something that might hurt another person (who might conveniently be represented as being in the next room, hitched up to some apparatus, so that nobody is really hurt). Or both groups of children might be given a choice of gentle or violent toys with which to play. If the children who had watched TV violence behaved more aggressively, we would be hard put to find any reason for it other than our experimental exposure to television violence. This is what Liebert and Baron (1972) did. Their finding that children exposed to violent television for only 3½ minutes were more likely than controls to "hurt" another person, to choose more aggressive toys, and to assault playroom dolls all suggest that children exposed to violence learn by example—just as the rest of us do most of the time.

The problem with experimental studies grows out of their virtue, control. Life, in general, is not lived in laboratories. Was the 3½ minutes of televised violence that Liebert and Baron used representative of violence in other television shows, or of violence on the streets? Were the toys characteristic war and mayhem toys, or toys that appeal to kids for other reasons? A baseball bat might be used as a weapon, but it is also a major part of a peaceful game. The next step in answering the question of the effect of TV violence on aggression might be to see whether children who watch violent programs at home, over extended periods, are more aggressive on the playgrounds of school than children who watch other programs, or who do not have television. Or children who watch a great deal of violent television might be matched to a comparison sample that does not watch much TV, and both groups followed up to adolescence to see if the TV viewers are more aggressive. When several kinds of evidence converge, as they do on this issue, we can be quite sure of the answer. In this case the answer, amply documented by Achenbach (1978), is that television violence is one of the powerful causes of violence in its viewers.

The variables that interest developmental psychologists most are those involved in biological maturation, psychological development, and learning. How can we best design studies to look at these kinds of changes?

The simplest approach, and one that is often used as a first step in a program of research, is to look at a *cross-section* of people of different ages. If we were interested in changing ways of thinking about numbers, for instance, between the ages of 5 and 11, our design for a study might look like this:

Age Studied

Birth Cohort	5	7	9	11
1974				1985
1976			1985	
1978		1985		
1980	1985			

All of the children are studied in the same year, 1985, which allows us to do the study efficiently, in a fairly limited amount of time. If we can assume that there is no major difference between the cohorts, the sets of children born in different years, we can conclude that the differences such a design shows are due to age differences in the children, e.g., increasing cognitive complexity and computational skill.

But suppose that the school had introduced a new mathematics curriculum, then dropped it. We might find that the 11-year-olds had not been exposed to this new curriculum, the 7- and 9-year-olds had, and the 5-year-olds had not. This would introduce a cohort difference, one not intrinsically related to age. We could therefore conclude that the differences we found were due not to age alone, but to a confusing mixture of age and educational experience.

Or let us consider a larger issue, attitudes towards women and work. We might be interested in where people stand on issues such as affirmative action, equal pay for equal work, maternity leave, women in authority, and so on. And suppose we design our study to sample people who are 25, 35, 45, 55, and 65. Are the differences we find due to age? Clearly not, since these people come from different birth cohorts, were exposed to different kinds of role instructions in childhood, and had quite different role models as they were growing up. Problems like this have led people to look for a research design that does not mix, or confound, age and cohort effects.

Suppose we select one cohort and follow them up for several years, testing them repeatedly. If our interest is the way arithmetic and reasoning skills develop between 5 and 11, our design might look like this:

Age Studied

Birth Cohort	5	7	9	11
1978	1983	1985	1987	1989

This *longitudinal* design has several advantages. All of the people in the study were born at roughly the same time, so we do not have cohort differences that might mix with our age differences in confusing ways. But this design also has some problems. Children born in 1978 might possibly be a special group, not like those born before or after, so it might be difficult to generalize to other samples. And there are cultural/historical changes going on that might make the world of children in 1989 different from the world of children in 1983. The largest problem in long-run longitudinal designs, however, is the tendency of some people to drop out of the study. This drop-out group is seldom representative of the cohort as a whole. Those who remain in the sample therefore provide biased estimates of the total group characteristics. It is therefore extremely important, in longitudinal research, to keep the sample involved and intact. Thomas, Chess, and Birch (Birch, 1974) in their long-term studies of the outcomes of differences in temperament in infants, have provided medical care for the sample. Other investigators have sent staff members from Minnesota or Missouri to California to find one or two members of a given study, to visit them, and to see how they are doing. Problems such as these drive up the costs of longitudinal studies.

Suppose a psychologist with an interest in a topic such as "the changing American teenager" were to design a study to see if teenagers are changing over time. He might notice that in 1968 it was popular to regard school, work, and "the establishment" generally as corrupt and requiring some remedy ranging from mild reform to violent revolution. He might see, in 1982, high school seniors preoccupied with how to look preppy, worried about getting secure jobs, and wondering how one can combine a decent job preparation with an active social life. His design for a study might look like this:

Birth Cohort	Age Studied 18
1964	1982
1966	1984
1968	1986
1970	1988

Successive waves of high school seniors would be studied, in a *time-lag* design, over a period of 6 years. All are studied at the same age, 18, so there are no age changes in the design. The study is focused on social and historical change. Like longitudinal studies, time-lag studies take several years for data gathering. Their major problem is that the changes measured reflect both cohort differences and cultural/historical changes. Suppose the study is begun in a suburb of Los Angeles in 1982. The population of the suburb is largely native Angelinos. But in 1985 a factory is started in the suburb, using a technology developed in Pittsburgh, and a large group of people move out from Pittsburgh to work in the factory. The high school senior group in 1986 and 1988 will contain large numbers of these newcomers. The psychologist who designed the study wanted to measure only cultural/historical changes in what it was like to be 18, but he now finds himself with a group that will also show strong cohort differences. On the other hand, if the population studied has remained fairly constant, as it might in a Maine or Minnesota farm town, there will be little change in the cohort studied and differences found are likely to be due to changes over time in the culture of adolescence.

Cross-sectional studies, because they can be done rapidly, are often a first step in developmental research. Longitudinal studies, even though they are time consuming and demanding for both research subject and experimenter, give the developmentalist the kind of data of greatest interest, how the same individuals change over time. Time-lag designs are implicit in much of journalism and everyday observation, but they have not been used in developmental research as much as the other two designs.

Each of the three main designs measures change, and in each, two main kinds of change are confounded. Longitudinal designs confound age with time of measurement. Cross-sectional designs confound age with cohort effects. And time-lag designs confound cohort effects with time of measurement. Because of these problems, more complex designs that allow comparison of these effects and statistical manipulations to tease them apart are coming into general use. These all make use of the idea of *replication*, repeating a set of measurements in such a way that we can separate different components. One of these more complex designs is described here, in order to show how replication can be used.

Suppose we want to look at age changes, and to try to separate them from cohort differences. We want a design that will allow us to do this efficiently. The design we develop is called an *age-by-cohort plan*. It could look like this:

		Age			
		10	12	14	16
	1968				1984
	1970			1984	1986
Cohort	1972		1984	1986	1988
	1974	1984	1986	1988	
	1976	1986	1988		
	1978	1988			

This age-by-cohort, or cohort-sequential (Schaie, 1965) design, allows several kinds of comparisons to be made within the study. If we are interested in age changes, we have several to inspect: the 1972 cohort, for instance, can be studied through 4 years of change, as can the 1974 cohort. If the age changes show the same patterns in each of the cohorts, we can be safe in concluding that we have separated out cohort differences from age changes. If there are differences between different cohorts, and these are not too large, we might get a general picture of age changes by averaging changes seen in the different cohorts. Our conclusion would then have the form, "In the years between 10 and 16, this group changed in *x way* in general." We might then want to describe any differences observed between cohorts. The design also allows us to look at a 3-year period of cultural/historical change, the period of 1984 to 1988, as it affects four different age groups. If our concern were drug use, for example, we might find successive cohorts using drugs earlier, a cohort difference, and the inspection of cultural/historical trends might make it possible for us to understand the influences that led to earlier use.

Psychologists studying development make use of all of the standard statistics: measures of *central tendency* such as *means* to show the general character of a group of observations, measures of *variability* to show the tendency toward exceptions to the rule, and so on. A few statistics are used more in developmental psychology than in other parts of psychology. These are described briefly here. The reader interested in a more extensive discussion of these, and of developmental designs, may want to consult Achenbach (1978) or Baltes, Reese, and Nesselroade (1977).

Correlational Approaches

Probably the most widely used statistic, other than means and *standard deviations*, is *correlation*. A correlation coefficient is a measure of the relationship between two variables. Suppose we measure the heights of all of the pupils in a tenth-grade class on Monday, then again on Thursday. In spite of the fact that there may be small errors of measurement on both days, causing some small changes in measured heights, it is likely that the class will show exactly the same order of height on the 2 days. A correlation expressing this would have a value of 1.00. Suppose on the day we measure height, we also measure achievement in algebra. There is no reason why height and ability in algebra ought to be related, and we would probably find that they are not. A correlation at this level is likely to be near 0. Two variables that are opposed to each other in some way will have a negative correlation. We would find a negative correlation, for instance, between scales measuring political liberalism and economic conservatism.

Stability over time is often measured by the correlation between the arrays of people on a given variable at two points in time. If we measure at several points, we typically get a curve showing first fairly rapid decline, then slower. The curves for IQ stability and for aggression in males, for instance, are shown in Fig. 1.4 (based on Olwens, 1979).

Correlation can also be used to try to separate "the wheat from the chaff," the variables that make a difference in life from those that are less important. Suppose you are interested in what causes children to be bright or dull. You might suspect, from studies like the one Brazelton's group did in Zambia, that children who were given more attention and interest might develop higher levels of intelligence. Your hard-headed roommate might argue that intellience is inherited, and that the only

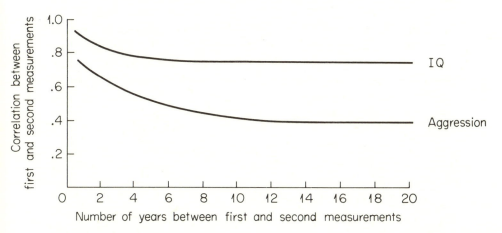

FIG. 1.4   Short and long term stability of I.Q. and aggression from childhood through adulthood.

thing you can do to raise it is to select bright ancestors. How do you decide who is right? Consider the following *cross-lagged panel correlation* set:

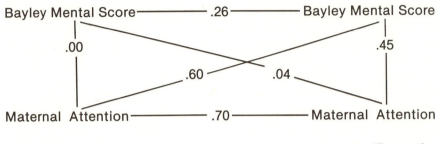

Bayley Mental Score ———— .26 ———— Bayley Mental Score

.00   .45

.60   .04

Maternal Attention ———— .70 ———— Maternal Attention

11 months   17 months

These correlations tell us that there is a fairly weak (r = 26) relationship between intelligence, as measured by the Bayley test, at 11 months and at 17 months. Knowing which children are "intelligent" at 11 months, we can improve our guess as to who will be bright at 17 months, but not very much. Maternal attention is much more stable than the baby's IQ. (Correlation between levels at 11 months and 17 months is .70.) The correlation between early maternal attention and later intelligence in the baby is .60. In the imaginary argument above, you are strongly right and your roommate is not really wrong. Your point of view is consistent with the correlation of .60, and you might go on to predict that if mothers were given training in how to pay attention to babies, they might well raise the intellectual levels of their children.

One of the main problems of developmental psychology is that our variables come in clusters. A psychologist asked to look at the effect of maternal smoking on the development of the baby soon finds that he is not dealing just with smoking, but with mothers who are very young, whose nutritional history contains more junk food than nutriment, who may well be using several drugs as well as tobacco, and so on. How do we decide, in all of this complexity, how many variables we have and what they are?

One of the best ways to do this, *factor analysis*, grew out of correlational methods. Factor analysis began when an English psychologist, Spearman, could not believe that all of the intelligence tests that were proliferating in the 1920s and 1930s were independent of each other. He developed some ways of correlating a set of tests with each other and extracting what they had in common. This factor, for intelligence tests, he labeled "g" for general intellectual ability. Each test had some parts independent of this main factor, and these specific parts could be put aside or examined in relation to special kinds of work, such as art or physics, which take some special talents as well as general intelligence. Cattell (1965), Stephenson (1953), and many others have worked to perfect and apply factor analysis, resulting in a method that allows us, currently, to identify in any given situation how many variables we have to deal with and their relationships with each other.

There are three main types of factor analysis. In the most widely used, *R-technique*, the question is how many dimensions are involved in a given problem. We might ask, for instance, how many types of intellectual ability would turn up in groups of people studied on a wide variety of tasks. Is there only one "g" or are there several equally important types of intelligence? Or we might ask how many dimensions there are to personality. We have a huge array of possible adjectives: strong, weak, active, passive, good, bad, and so on. Each of these pairs implies a dimension along which people might be arrayed. How many are necessary to give a comprehensive description of personality? Raymond Cattell found that he could summarize that whole universe of adjectives with 16 dimensions, so at least one answer is 16, the rest of the adjectives being mostly combinations of the 16 main dimensions. To do an R-technique factor analysis we give a large set of tests to a large set of people, correlate every test with every other test, and use factor analysis to extract the main dimensions. Any person can then be scored on the factors extracted, and we can describe him in terms of where he falls on the factors. If one factor is intelligence, we can say where he falls, relative to other people, on that factor. This method of factor analysis is useful for finding the dimensions along which people can be compared, their *individual differences*, and devising efficient tests to measure those dimensions.

What if our interest is whether we have types of people? Suppose that the welfare department of a major metropolitan government is interested in whether mothers on welfare are all alike or whether there are different types of mothers in this set. The author of this chapter was a consultant to the New York City Welfare Department on a study of this sort. To find types, the method used is *Q-technique*. Here our interest is comparing people, not tests. First, a large group of welfare mothers was interviewed, and statements gathered and transcribed verbatim; e.g., "I hate being on welfare and I cannot wait to get back to work," "I am a mother of little children and they need me so I cannot leave them to other people to raise." These statements were typed on index cards and sorted to eliminate duplicating ideas. Eventually a sample of 110 statements was assembled that seemed to sum up the range of possible feelings about work and welfare in this group. A new set of welfare mothers was gathered, and each woman was asked to sit down at a table and to sort the statements along a scale ranging from the two statements with which she agreed most to the two she agreed with least. The other statements were ranged in between. The statements she agreed with least were given a score of 0, the ones she agreed with most were given a score of 9, and the rest were given scores ranging from 0 to 9. After doing this, each mother's attitudes toward work and welfare were represented by her particular scores for all of the statements. These arrays of items were correlated with each other, with the correlation coefficient representing the degree of agreement between any two women. If they correlated .85, for instance, they agreed very closely on where they placed the different statements. If their correlation was −.45, they agreed on a few items, but mostly they disagreed. When the *matrix* of correlation coefficients was factored, we got sets of mothers. One set agreed with all of the items that expressed dislike of being on welfare, longing to work, feelings of boredom with housework, and interest in getting out of the house and into the work force. This set of mothers were mostly raised in New York, were young and had been through high school, were black, had not been on welfare long, and were physically healthy. This became an obvious target group for retraining and vocational guidance. Another group agreed with all of the items that emphasized motherhood and child care. These women were not interested in work so long as they had young children. They were mostly poorly educated, Puerto Rican in background, older, and not vocationally skilled. It seemed likely that vocational training for these women, until their children were older, would be a waste of time and money.

This study indicates that Q-technique factor studies can be extremely useful, and they are. Much market research uses Q-technique to divide up potential customers into market segments, so that advertisers and retailers can target their approaches to specific groups. These methods can also lead to spectacular failures—the market research that indicated to Ford Motor Company that there was a market segment that was longing for a Ford car comparable to the Oldsmobile led to that multimillion dollar flop, the Edsel.

To both of the methods above, clinical and developmental psychologists are likely to say something like, "OK, you can describe dimensions for arranging people, and you can describe types, but I am interested in what goes on inside the person, whether he gets angry and upset when he is under stress or how he responds to loss. Can your methods help me do that?" The factor analytic method that does this is called *P-technique*, and it involves changes within a particular person over time. Suppose you are interested in what is involved in headaches. There are some hints to causality already available: women are much more likely to have most types of headaches than men are; some people get migraines after eating certain cheeses or drinking red wine, and so on. But what feelings are involved? Are there tension headaches, and if so are the feelings that go along with them different from the feelings that accompany a migraine?

To answer questions like this we might have people who come to a headache clinic begin to keep records of their moods as well as of daily events, food intake, sleep habits, and so on. Since a headache that lasts through the day seems much more burdensome than one that merely occupies a morning, afternoon, or evening, you might ask people to keep records of headaches and moods three times each day, filling out their record forms at noon, 6:00 P.M., and just before bed. On days when there was no headache you might have a 0 score, and intervals in which there was a headache might be scored from 1 to 4, depending on the intensity of the headache. People with headaches talk a good deal about the issue of control, of being on top of things, or feeling like everything is getting out of hand and they cannot control their lives. You might design a scale to measure this feeling, and have the headache sufferer score herself on it each time she scored herself for her headaches.

The data produced by this method generate a set of curves over time. The headache curve, for instance, is usually at 0 to 1 levels, but from time to time it will rise to extreme pain, in the 4 range. Feelings of control range up and down, feelings of happiness come and go, and so on. In P-technique factor analysis all of these curves are correlated together, factored, and sets of feelings are separated out, one on each factor. Because P-technique factor analysis allows us to describe dynamic changes over time, and to find out which changes go together and separate them from independent changes, it can be particularly useful in developmental work. This method has not yet been applied to the problem of what psychological events accompany the physical event of puberty, but it would be the appropriate method for such a study.

Suppose you want to predict how people will do in some future task, and you have current data about them. A common problem of this sort is prediction of college grades on the basis of high school grades, SAT scores, and so on. The psychologist interested in prediction is likely to use *regression* analysis, a method that psychology shares with economics, weather forecasting, and other fields interested in prediction. If we have many possible predictors and many possible outcome criteria, regression analysis provides us with tools to decide which predictors are most powerful and which criteria are most predictable. Since the predictors are likely to group, we can reduce their numbers by factor analysis, then relate these sets to our outcome criteria.

Prediction of college grades can be used to illustrate the use of regression. We first correlate all of our predictor variables (say high school grades, SAT scores, parents' occupation, parents' education, etc.) with the criterion, college grades. To do a stepwise regression analysis we first select the variable with the largest correlation with the criterion, in this case high school grades. Regression procedures remove that part of the individual differences in college grades due to high school grades. Then we select the variable that explains the largest part of the remaining differences. We remove the part of the grades due to this and continue the process until we have nothing left to explain, or no variables left that contribute toward an explanation. Although all of this is in practice very easy if one has a computer available, it may sound quite complicated. But the process, though systematic, is really common sense. Imagine a bettor at a race track. He wants to predict which horse will be the fastest one in the race, which second, and which third. He first looks at the horse's past record (just as we do in predicting college grades from high school grades). Then he looks at the quality of the horse's previous competition (did the student go to a tough high school or a lax one?). He looks then at the jockey's record, the condition of the track, and so forth. Without quantifying his variables, he is following much the same logic as a multiple regression procedure.

To illustrate the outcome of a regression analysis, we can look at the outcome of a study of the kinds of high school students who are most likely to achieve success and satisfaction in the world of work by age 25, judged both by their own self-reports and by objective judges of their work history (Jordaan & Super, 1974). We do not have these data for women yet, so the following applies only to young men. He is likely to come from a middle-class home, get good grades, be active in school activities, have hobbies, have realistic goals, and know something about the occupation he hopes to follow. None of this is surprising, but regression analysis allows us to develop a full picture of the characteristics that contribute to success. If we eliminate any one of the characteristics mentioned in this group portrait, we lower our ability to predict vocational success.

Closely related to regression analysis is a method called *path analysis*. In this method we attempt to develop causal models and fit them to the data. The model that best fits the data can be considered preferable to other models, until something better is developed. Suppose our interest is predicting the level of a person's last job, on a scale made up of income, prestige, and so on. Our path analysis might look like this (Runyan, 1982).

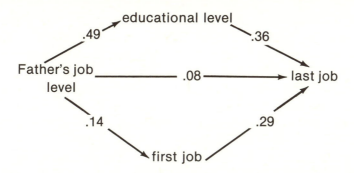

One way to interpret this set of paths to achievement is that the father's job level has no direct influence on the level one attains in one's own career. And the level of the father's job has little influence on the level one starts at—we all know children of successful parents who started their vocational career behind a quick-food counter or gas pump. But the father's educational level is quite powerfully determining as to the level of education one attains, and that in turn has quite a lot of influence on final vocational attainment. The route from successful father to successful son leads through college and other kinds of advanced training.

By this point you may be feeling that we have moved away from people and into some world of numbers. How do we get back to everyday application of what we find with these complicated methods? One answer is a simple method with a formidable name, the *risk ratio matrix*. This method is now coming into general use in medical work. Suppose you become pregnant and enter into prenatal care. The nurse who prepares your history will probably check for several *risk factors*, such as protein in the urine, high blood pressure, smoking, overweight, and diabetes. Those people who have several risk factors are given special attention, while the vast majority of people, who are free from these risk factors, are simply monitored while the natural process of pregnancy and birth takes its course. Knowing what the risk factors are, how they combine, and what levels of risk are associated with them singly and in combination allows the physician to make an informed guess as to how much intervention is needed, and when.

But can we use methods like this in psychology? Ramey and his colleagues (Ramey, Stedman, Borders-Patterson, & Mengel, 1978) have shown that readily identifiable risk factors, taken together, can select at birth the child at high risk for low academic achievement in the first grade. These factors are race (black) and a mother with a low level of education. Other risk factors, predicting other kinds of threats to competence, were lateness in birth order, low birth weight, litle prenatal care, and fewer weeks gestation. These factors can be used to select the children who need the most attention, and who, without that attention, are most likely to have difficulties in school and later life.

The combination of risk factors, and attention to periods of special risk often allow us to plan fairly specific times and methods of intervention to prevent poor outcomes. Educational intervention, for example, has to be early and has to involve both the home and school, if it is to be maximally effective. The optimal time for prevention of drug abuse is likely to be in the very early teens, the late grade school and junior high years; the population can be located by risk factors to be children growing up in crowded and highly stressed neighborhoods, and going to schools where drugs are readily available. In recent years *evaluation research* has been built into most large-scale intervention efforts. This kind of research can tell us which of our efforts work, which parts of complicated programs are most effective, and as a side effect, often tells us a great deal about the problems to which it is addressed. The two basic issues in *developmental psychopathology* are what makes a problem start and what makes it continue to develop. Research is our main hope for answering those questions.

SUMMARY

Developmental psychology is concerned with change, organized paths, trajectories, or sequences of development. Some changes are best conceptualized as continuous and irreversible, and can be plotted on regular growth curves. Other changes involve reorganization, and can best be understood as stages, each of which has its own internal consistency. If we study patterns of change through time we find that people become more diverse, less like each other, but that each individual becomes more consistent, more like himself. For some characteristics, such as visual integration, there are clearly critical periods for development. Other critical periods, for attachment, learning, and so on, are still being explored.

The goals of developmental psychology can be seen in a hierarchy, ranging from simple description of developmental facts, through description of integrated patterns and sequences, finally reaching comprehensive explanation of developmental patterns. If we can describe processes of development and can discover what causes them to start and what maintains them as they develop, we can sometimes find clues to intervention, aimed at maximizing positive developments and minimizing negative ones. Because of the importance of contexts for development, it is necessary to pay particular attention to generalizability or robustness.

The levels of knowledge involved in developmental psychology begin with everyday observation and common sense. Knowledge gained by systematic observation of groups and comparison of groups with each other provides a kind of knowledge that is more secure and less biased than common sense. Large-scale epidemiological methods provide powerful indicators of relationships between different influences on development. Case studies, or case control methods, provide detailed information as to mechanisms through which variables influence each other. The most secure knowledge in developmental psychology comes from large-scale, longitudinal study of groups of people over many years.

The sources of data in developmental psychology may be retrospective, data gathered in adult recall of childhood events. Because of the dangers of distortion in such recall, current research uses follow-back methods, studying records gathered in childhood by schools or child guidance clinics. The most useful source of data is the study designed from the beginning for long-term follow-up of its subjects.

How can you use a theory? It can be a road map, helping you get where you want to go. It can provide you with tools for seeing and hearing things you might have missed without it. You may find theories easier to comprehend if you learn something about each theorist, the problems he wanted to solve, and his own style of problem solving. To remember a theory, try to develop a visual image, to give the theory a label, and to describe its main features. And try to develop your own theory, comparing it regularly to the theories you are reading, and seeing if they have features you want to add to yours.

While you may want to adopt a theory simply because it appeals to you, it is more helpful to look at formal qualities of the theory such as internal consistency, relevance to important social issues, and the adequacy of the predictions you can make with the theory. Choice between theories is facilitated if you can find areas where the theories overlap and make different predictions. The theory that is correct in such situations is clearly superior to the incorrect theory.

Developmental knowledge can be used in intervention in individual lives, and it can also be used to help design better environments for development. A world-wide issue is hunger. Psychological study of the effects of hunger suggests that programs to reduce hunger can have important psychological as well as physiological effects.

There are many designs for developmental research. Developmental conclusions are most secure when they are based on converging evidence from several kinds of studies, with many populations. The quickest developmental design is cross-sectional, studying groups of people of different ages. A more difficult, but ultimately more useful, design is longitudinal, studying a group of people over a period of time. Time-lag designs study a set of people at a particular age, say high school seniors over several successive years, in order to find cultural or historical trends. Each of these designs has problems, and more complex combinations of designs are coming into use, allowing us to tease out cohort, age, and time of measurement differences from each other.

The statistics used by developmental psychologists are used to discover the degree of relationship between two variables or between sets of variables, to sort out of complex sets of variables the few that are most important, and to make predictions. If we can make predictions we can often estimate risk factors and combine them. This allows us to focus intervention efforts on those people who are at highest risk for disorder.

2 Evolution, Culture, and Socialization

In the course of describing development, we frequently return to a small number of important themes. These themes present a framework or context in which human development can be understood.

First, our species has an *evolutionary history*. Although many details are yet to be discovered, it is clear that we share common ancestors, structures, and behaviors with placental mammals and primates. Further, both biochemical and paleontological methods show that our closest living relatives from an evolutionary perspective are the Old World primates (monkeys and apes of Africa and Asia), and especially the chimpanzees and gorillas. Scholars still dispute the exact lineage of *Homo sapiens*—our species—but the available fossil evidence allows us to make some convincing statements about both the anatomy and the behavior of our ancestors and how these changed over time.

Why bother with evolution in a developmental psychology book? We share the view of the prominent sociologist, Alice Rossi (1977). In comparison with the millions of years of human evolution,

> ...the two hundred years in which industrial societies have existed is a short time indeed, to say nothing of the twenty years in which a few of the most advanced industrial societies have been undergoing the painful transition to a post-industrial stage. Our most recent genes derive from that longest segment of human history during which men and women lived in hunting and gathering societies; in other words, Westernized human beings now living in a technological world are still genetically equipped only with an ancient mammalian primate heritage that evolved largely through adaptations appropriate to much earlier times. (p. 3)

Second, all mammalian species create *cultures*. In any species there is a fair amount of variation in the social and physical environments of different groups. Some populations of rhesus monkeys inhabit Indian temples located in urban areas, some inhabit dense forests, and some inhabit American psychology laboratories. The psychological development of those raised in temples is different from those raised in forests or laboratories. We all know from our own experience that human cultural variation is enormous, and that children and adults reared in different cultures often differ from one another in important ways, e.g., beliefs and practices involving women's roles, family, abortion. Given this enormous cultural variation (which is part of the human evolutionary design) it is important to examine the cultural context when discussing psychological development.

Third, people living in the same culture – even identical twins – develop differently from one another. This fact is largely accounted for by the different *socialization* experiences everyone has. Socialization involves all the influences people have on one another through the whole life span. Certain kinds of socialization experiences, particularly those occurring early in life, have a greater influence on psychological development than do others. There is a fair amount of information about the most important influences. Four aspects are discussed in detail: family, peers, schools, and television. We defer most of our discussion about schools and all about television until Chapter 7.

EVOLUTION

Much of the following discussion is adapted from Fishbein's *Evolution, Development and Children's Learning* (1976). This discussion is also influenced by the recent work of Rossi (1977), Lancaster (1975), and Tanner (1981).

Evolution, Learning, and Adaptation

Genetic evolution and learning are the two major ways that members of a species become adapted to a particular environment. Adaptation has at least two related meanings. The first is the ability of a population of a species to survive and reproduce in a given environment. From an evolutionary point of view, we emphasize that populations (small or large), and not individuals, are adapted. Adaptation is not a fixed or unchanging condition—the population is constantly acting on the environment, and the environment is constantly acting on the population. For example, when members of a human gatherer-hunter group gather all the fruit in a given area, they dramatically change the environment. When there is a severe drought, this same group is forced to change its patterns of gathering and hunting, and many members may die in the process.

Adaptation is also defined as the set of processes through which a species develops the ability to survive and reproduce in a given environment. The two major processes are *genetic evolution* and *learning*. Three concepts are central to understanding genetic evolution: genotype, phenotype, and Darwinian fitness. The genotype of an individual is the collection of all the genes inherited from her parents. Each human being has about 500,000 genes distributed across 46 chromosomes. The genotype is set, more or less permanently, when the male's sperm unites with the female's ovum, forming a single cell called the zygote. The genotype can be thought of as a set of instructions for the possible ways in which the individual will develop and interact with her environment. It does not contain, as once believed, a preformed program directing the individual to "unfold" in completely fixed ways. For example, two identical twins (with identical genotypes), separated at birth, may develop language and motor skills at different rates and even quite different personalities, depending upon the environment they were raised in.

The phenotype of an individual is everything about him from birth to death except his genes and chromosomes. This includes his anatomy, e.g., height, weight, bone structure, muscle structure, brain size; his physiology, e.g., body temperature, heart rate, metabolism, brain activity; and his behavior, e.g., everything he says, perceives, thinks, feels, wishes, and does. The phenotype of an individual is constantly changing, usually more rapidly earlier than later in life. However, all aspects of the phenotype do not change at the same rate. For example, from birth to about age 6 the anatomy and physiology of the human brain are changing very rapidly relative to changes in the rest of the body. As another example, a child's ability to walk changes very slowly after age 2, but language ability changes very rapidly for the next decade.

Darwinian fitness refers to how many offspring an individual and her close relatives (who have similar genotypes) reproduce in a particular environment relative to other members of the species. Individuals who have many surviving offspring, or whose close relatives have many surviving offspring, are said to have high Darwinian fitness. Those with few surviving offspring, and no close relatives with surviving offspring, have low Darwinian fitness. Darwinian fitness is a measure of "natural selection," the term Darwin invented to indicate the weeding-out process of evolution. The core assumption of natural selection is that individuals best suited for life in a particular environment will, in the long run, reproduce more than those less suited. Thus, over many generations the genes of those best suited for survival and reproduction will be more plentiful in the species than those of less suited individuals.

It is very important to note that individuals might have high Darwinian fitness in one environment and low fitness is another. For example, millions of American buffalo roamed the West in a highly successful coexistence with native Americans and other predators. The environment changed dramatically when the "Buffalo Bills" arrived, shooting them at an extraordinary rate for their pelts. The buffalo became almost extinct in a very short time.

Learning is the other major adaptive process. Learning is a set of psychological processes that are set into motion when individuals interact with their environment. These processes organize and reorganize the ways individuals will experience their environment (e.g., feel about, perceive, think about it), and act upon it (e.g., learn to ride a bike). The long-range effects of learning enable individuals to improve their ability to interact with the environment. Learning doesn't always have this positive effect. A person may learn to be afraid of all animals after once being bitten by a dog.

Evolutionary processes and learning processes are interrelated in two important ways. First, learning processes are parts of the phenotype of any species. The way we learn and the extent to which we can learn are determined by our evolutionary history. Species differ tremendously in learning abilities. Humans obviously have great learning abilities, other primates (monkeys and apes) have somewhat lesser learning abilities, while reptiles, birds, fish, and especially insects have far less ability than the primates. Second, the greater the learning ability of a species, the greater will be the flexibility of its adaptation. In general, species with greater learning ability will quickly be able to modify their behavior to unexpected changes in the environment, and further, will be able to transmit this behavior to other members of the species. For example, if a new food source is found or a new way to protect the young is discovered, this information can readily be learned by other members. The human species is unique in its flexibility. We have been able to live in virtually every earthly environment without the necessity for genetic evolutionary change. None of the other primates even approaches us in this way.

Evolution as an Experiment in Design

One useful way to describe the above is that evolution consists of a number of unplanned "experiments." The experiments involve testing out various designs for living and reproducing in particular environments. Think about automobile racing, where the designs are planned. The goal of a driver is to win the race. In order to do so, a person has to be able to drive the car, the car has to be able to go fast, and it (and the person) have to be able to withstand the stresses and strains of the race. When a new fuel is invented, the engine, fuel tanks, and fuel lines have to be modified. The new fuel may respond differently to acceleration than the old fuel, and the driver has to learn to modify her driving to accommodate to this. Maybe the fuel heats up too much over the period of the race and becomes explosive. Precautions must be taken—another aspect of the design. Finally, you have a wonderful car. Now, how will it operate in the stop-and-go traffic in our cities? Terribly. It was designed for "life" on the track and not for city streets.

Konrad Lorenz (1969) has referred to evolution as a "trial-and-success" experiment. Each individual is a trial experiment in a particular environment. If the individual has high Darwinian fitness, the experiment is a success, and her genes are transmitted to the next generation. Those with low Darwinian fitness are experimental failures, at least in that particular environment.

Evolutionary designs are conservative. For example, the body plan of the vertebrates, which include fish, birds, reptiles, and mammals, is about 400 million years old. The hands of primates, including those separated by over 100 million years of evolutionary history, e.g., the New World (South America) and Old World (Africa and Asia) primates, are very similar. The color vision of all the Old World primates, including *Homo sapiens*, is apparently identical. The list of common characteristics among widely separated species is enormous. Evolutionary processes seem to operate on the principle "Keep it if you can, change it if you must."

One reason for this resistance to change stems from the fact that nearly everything in a design is connected with everything else. For example, one of the major changes in *Homo sapiens* during the period from about 5 million years ago to about ¼ million years ago was a tripling in brain size. Larger brained adults meant larger brained infants, which in turn meant larger brained fetuses. But bigger headed fetuses required big birth canals in order to emerge safely from the uterus and be born. Bigger birth canals required a larger and differently shaped pelvis. Changes in shape and size of the pelvis required different fittings with the vertebral column, legs, and all sorts of connective tissue. Apparently, at some point our heads got too big and the pelvis could change no more. So the brain changed in a new way. Brain size at birth did not increase, but doubled during the first year of life. This kept the human brain at birth small and immature, relative to the other primates. The head could pass through the birth canal, but this meant human infants were born far more immature than nonhuman primates. This immaturity had significant social consequences for the infant and its caretakers.

Canalization and Prenatal Development

Evolutionary processes operate on individuals throughout their entire life span. In order for individuals to reproduce, they have to "survive" prenatal development as well as the entire period of infancy and childhood prior to sexual maturity. They then must have the genetic, anatomical, physiological, and behavioral abilities to mate and reproduce. In addition, it is no accident that individuals live long after the period in which they are biologically capable of reproduction. If the end point of natural selection were only to give birth, as it seems to be for some fish and reptiles, then individuals would die off when they could no longer reproduce. It is likely that "grandparenthood" had high Darwinian fitness. That is, older members of a population kept their genes alive by aiding in the rearing and protecting of their children's children. We can summarize these ideas by saying that our evolutionary design is for lifelong development.

In the previous section we described evolutionary designs as being conservative. The genetic process that probably underlies this conservatism is called *canalization* (Waddington, 1957). Fishbein (1976) has described canalization as:

> ...a set of genetic processes which ensure that development will proceeed in normal ways, that the phenotypic targets will be attained despite the presence of minor abnormal genetic or environmental conditions. Canalization processes operate at each point in development to correct minor deflections from the sought-for phenotypic targets. Presumably canalization processes ensure that important phenotypic constancies will occur in all members of a species, e.g., in humans the presence of two eyes, one nose, two hands, language, bipedal locomotion. Canalization is a *collusion* of genes to keep the developing organism in balance. Not all characteristics of an individual are canalized, nor are those which are, equally canalized. (p. 7)

Thus, canalization processes compensate for moderately abnormal conditions either to keep development on a normal pathway or, if development has been knocked askew, to bring it back on target. For example, children who have been reared for short time periods in environments abnormal for either language development or brain maturation may show deficits in these characteristics. When placed in normal environments, their development will quickly "catch up" to that of their age group.

Figure 2.1 is a drawing of the image Waddington uses to describe the way canalization works. The rolling ball represents the individual's development of some characteristics, e.g., attachment to a caretaker. As the ball approaches a decision point, the characteristic (attachment) must move along one of two or more pathways. In the attachment example this means that a potential attachment figure must be present and responsive, and that a bond will develop between the infant and that person. The distance traveled and the depth of the pathway indicate the strength or degree of canalization of that characteristic. So, the greater the time spent in appropriate (evolutionary designed) ways with the caretaker/s, the greater will be the infant's attachment to that person or those individuals. If an attachment figure is not present when the ball (the developing infant) has reached the attachment decision point, then development will be abnormal.

What this drawing implies, then, is that at each decision point, some particular environmental stimulation must be present so that development can proceed normally. For strongly canalized phenotypic characteristics, it is likely that a wide variety of environmental stimulation (as opposed to very particular stimulation) will allow the characteristic to develop normally. For example, human infant attachment is a strongly canalized characteristic. The decision point extends from about 6 weeks to 6 months. Infants with appropriate contacts during this time period for as little as an hour a day will become attached to single or multiple caretakers. As we see in Chapter 3, a wide variety of situations are appropriate for attachment to occur.

There are other important implications of this figure. The times of greatest developmental instability are at or near the decision points. Once the organism has passed the decision point and has proceeded well along a pathway, it is difficult to disrupt its normal development. These periods of relative instability are called "critical periods." They are the periods where appropriate stimulation is absolutely necessary in order for development to proceed normally.

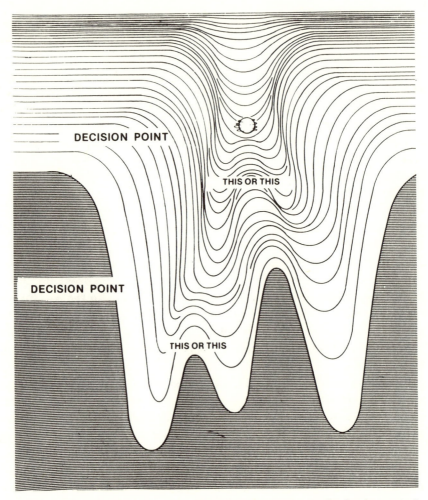

FIG. 2.1   The epigenetic landscape. The rolling ball represents the development of some canalized characteristic. At each "decision point" the characteristic is required to move onto one of at least two divergent pathways. As development proceeds along one of those pathways, the more difficult it becomes to move it into the alternative pathways (Drawn by Alex Fraser) (Source: Fishbein, H.D. *Evolution, development, and children's learning.* Pacific Palisades: Goodyear, 1976.)

If the individual has not reached a decision point for a particular canalized character, then environmental stimulation will have essentially no impact on how that character will develop. It doesn't make much sense, for example, to attempt to teach a one-year-old how to read or write. If the individual has gone well past the critical period without appropriate stimulation, then in all likelihood previously appropriate stimulation will be inadequate for normal development of that character. An appropriate caretaker, experienced for the first time when an infant is one year of age, will probably not lead to normal attachment.

The clearest illustration of some of these ideas can be seen in prenatal development. In Fig. 2.2 sensitive or critical periods in human prenatal development are highlighted. A teratogen consists of abnormal environmental stimulation, which canalization processes may or may not be able to buffer. Some examples of teratogens are x-rays, German measles, and certain drugs such as thalidomide, a tranquilizer that produced horrible anatomical abnormalities in the children of women who took it during pregnancy.

During the first 2 weeks of life, teratogens either have no effect on development or produce prenatal death—the woman miscarries. During the *embryonic period*—the third through seventh week of pregnancy—teratogens are either buffered by canalization processes, or produce major anatomical (in the figure the word "morphological" is used) abnormalities. For example, the most critical period for heart development extends from the middle of the third week to the middle of the sixth week. This is the period of most rapid heart development. If teratogens "break through" the canalization barrier during this period, the heart will develop abnormally. The heart is still being formed between the sixth and eighth week, and teratogens that are not buffered will produce minor anatomical and physiological abnormalities. Teratogens produce virtually no heart abnormalities if the fetus is exposed to them after the eighth week.

During the *fetal period*—the eighth through thirty-eighth week of pregnancy—most of the major anatomical structures are well formed. The slower developing structures, such as the brain, eyes, and external genitals, are still susceptible to teratogens during this entire period. The arms, legs, and heart are virtually immune to teratogens after the eighth week of pregnancy.

Probably one of the best tests of the effects of canalization processes on behavior development was carried out by Ronald Wilson (1978) with 10 sets of genetically identical twins. One of the twins of each pair weighed under four pounds at birth, and the other about two pounds more. It has been repeatedly shown that infants whose birth weight is under four pounds are "at risk" for a large number of behavioral deficits. Wilson measured the IQ of these infants at frequent intervals during their first 6 years of life. At age 3, there were substantial IQ differences in favor of the heavier twin. At age 6, on the average, the IQ difference between the

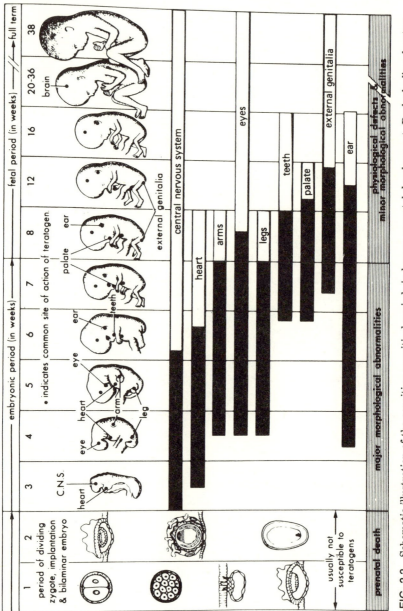

FIG. 2.2 Schematic illustration of the sensitive or critical periods in human prenatal development. Dark shading denotes highly sensitive periods; areas without shading denote less sensitive periods (Source: Moore, K. L. *The developing human.* 3rd Edition. Philadelphia: W. B. Saunders, 1983.)

two was only one point (out of about 100). This was exactly the same difference that would be expected for identical twins born with essentially the same birth weight. Hence, the canalization processes brought the "at risk" twins to the same developmental level as the "normal" twins.

Physical Development From Birth to Maturity

Evolutionary and canalization processes have played major roles in determining the course of physical development from birth to maturity. Each species has its own unique evolutionary design, but it is clear from comparisons with other species that the ways in which we mature follow the primate pattern (Tanner, 1978). The human variation of this pattern is shown in Fig. 2.3 (Tanner, 1962). Other primate species differ from this in two ways: (1) The "overshooting" of the lymphoid system is not seen; in fact, it may not be typically human. This curve sharply rises about age 6, the time that most children from industrialized societies start school (North American children tend to start earlier). The lymphoid system, largely involved with developing immunities and fighting disease, receives a massive attack at this time—the bacteria and viruses of other children. It grows in response. The decrease in size is associated with hormonal and other physiological changes occurring at puberty. (2) The brain and head of humans grow at a faster rate, reflecting relative immaturity at birth.

Tanner has summarized a great deal of information in this figure for the "average" person. We should point out that even within each of the four systems, various body parts and tissues grow at different rates. Of course individuals mature differently. When we say, for example, "He's physically immature for his age," that may be only partially true. The correlations in growth among height, weight, bones, and muscles are far from perfect. The correlations between systems, e.g., bones and teeth, are even smaller. Tanner (1978) suggests that the best single measure of physical maturity—the one that applies throughout this age range—is *skeletal maturity*. This refers to the shape, density, and relative positions of the bones to one another. The sequence of development for all individuals is the same for this measure, and everyone reaches the same relative end state.

All things being equal, the rate at which a person matures is largely under genetic control (Wilson, 1976). For example, Wilson found that at birth the correlation in height between dizygotic twins was .82, and for monozygotic, .58. By 6 months they reversed, and throughout development the correlations were higher for the monozygotic twins. Also, slow

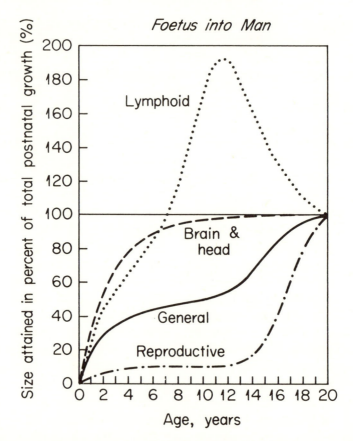

FIG. 2.3   Growth curves of different parts and tissues of the body, showing the four chief types. All the curves are of size attained, and plotted as percentage of total gain from birth to 20 years, so that size at age 20 is 100 on the vertical scale.
Lymphoid type: thymus, lymph nodes, intestinal lymph masses
Brain and head type: brain and its parts, dura, spinal cord, optic apparatus, cranial dimensions
General type: body as a whole, external dimensions (except head), respiratory and digestive organs, kidneys, aortic and pulmonary trunks, musculature, blood volume
Reproductive type: testis, ovary, epididymis, prostrate, seminal vesicles, fallopian tubes
(Source: Tanner, J. M. *Growth at adolescence.* 2nd Edition. Oxford: Blackwell Scientific Publications, 1962.)

maturing infants are usually slow maturing children and reach puberty at a relatively late age. Fast developers generally stay that way. These different growth rates have important psychological effects, as we see later.

We should also point out that Fig. 2.3 does not consider sex differences. From before birth until adulthood, girls mature faster than boys. They are nearly 1 month advanced at birth, reach one half of their adult height at 21 months (versus 2 years for boys), and are 2 years advanced in some systems at the beginning of puberty. There are few exceptions to girls' earlier development, but Tanner notes that "girls earlier" is clearly a primate characteristic, and perhaps mammalian as well.

If we looked only at height as an indicator of maturity, we would surely be confused. Up until about age 10, boys and girls lengthen at the same rate and, on average, are the same height. Girls in industrialized societies start their 2-year adolescent growth spurt at about that age, and become temporarily taller. Boys start their 2-year adolescent growth spurt at about age 13. There are two major consequences of this delay: (1) Boys ultimately become taller than girls because they stop growing at a later age. (2) Boys become longer-legged than girls, relative to their height, because during preadolescence the legs grow faster than the trunk. Most of the sex differences in body size, shape, strength, as well as metabolism occur during or after puberty. The anatomy and physiology that boys develop make them more capable than girls for highly energetic efforts, such as those associated with hunting and fighting.

One of the surprising findings about rate of maturity is that it tends to be correlated with intelligence. In Guatemala, Lasky et al. (1981) found that for infants between 6 and 24 months of age, body length and weight were correlated about .30 with measures of mental development. Head size (and presumably brain size) and nutrition were uncorrelated. In England and Scotland, Tanner (1978) reports that for children between 6 and 12 years old, height and IQ were correlated about .25. Although this is not a large correlation, the tallest 15% of children scored about 10 IQ points higher than the shortest 15%.

We said earlier that all things being equal, physical growth is under genetic control. In any given culture, or family, all environmental influences are not equal. Tanner (1978) summarizes the effects of many of these environmental variations. First, changes in height, rate of growth, and age of puberty onset have been observed in all Western industrialized countries over the past 120 years. For example, in Finland, onset of puberty in girls decreased from 16½ years in 1860 to about 13 years in 1970. In England, 10-year-old boys were on average 7 inches shorter in 1833 than in 1970. At age 18, they were about 6 inches shorter. Second, in nearly all urbanized cultures that have been studied (Sweden is the exception) the higher the family income, and the smaller the family size, the taller the children are, and the faster their growth rate. Bogin and MacVean (1983) have confirmed the family income findings in Guatamala in a 6-year longitudinal study. Not only did height vary with family income, but also weight and skeletal maturity. Third, during wartime conditions, children and adolescents often have markedly reduced growth rates. Tanner suggests that all these findings are explained by three factors: changes in nutrition; more proteins and calories in infancy; and a reduction in the length and severity of disease.

Although continuous, prolonged nutritional inadequacies can profoundly and permanently affect physical development, our systems are canalized against less prolonged external influences as well as hormonal ones. The hormonal case is illustrated in Fig. 2.4 (Tanner, 1978). The height curves for two brothers are presented, both of whom have human growth hormone (HGH) deficiences. Prior to the start of HGH treatment, the boys were growing at abnormal rates well below those expected for their genetic backgrounds. Treatment for the younger brother started at 2.1 years of age, and for the older, at 6.2 years. Growth velocity jumped dramatically for both, and the younger brother quickly moved onto his expected growth trajectory. The older brother never completely caught up to his expected adult height, but followed a low but normal growth trajectory once HGH treatments began. Tanner points out that disease or severe malnutrition early in life may not be completely protected by canalization mechanisms. They key considerations here are severity of the abnormality and its duration.

From both evolutionary and psychological viewpoints the anatomical structure of greatest interest is the brain. Among the primates, human brains are the least developed at birth, but at maturity have twice as many fully functional nerve cells as the great apes, our closest relatives (Tobias, 1970). The intellectual gains produced by such a large brain were enormous. One of the physiological byproducts of this evolutionary size increase—threefold over the past 3 million years—was a progressively delayed onset of puberty (Fishbein 1976). Fishbein argued that the larger the brain, the longer it takes to completely "wire it." He showed that among the Old World primates there is a strong relationship between adult brain size and age of puberty onset; but essentially no relationship between puberty and adult body size.

As with the evolution of other anatomical structures, that of the brain was highly conservative. The evolutionarily old parts were modified somewhat, and the new ones were added on. Paul MacLean (1967, 1973) has conceptualized this "adding on" process as shown in Fig. 2.5. In this view, the brains of higher mammals consist of three interconnected parts—a reptilian (the oldest part), an old mammalian (the limbic system), and a new mammalian brain (the neocortex). The reptilian brain is the basic foundation of the nervous system. It is concerned with the following

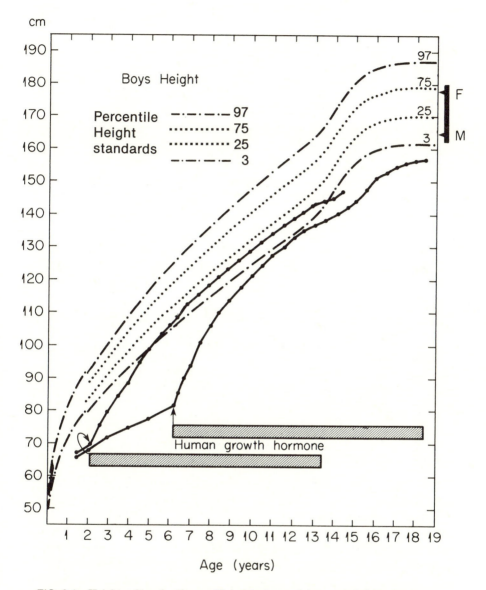

FIG. 2.4 Heights of two brothers with isolated growth-hormone deficiency treated with HGH from ages 6.2 years and 2.1 years. Catch-up of older brother is partly by high velocity and partly by prolonged growth and is incomplete. Younger brother shows true complete catch-up. F and M parents' height centiles; vertical thick line, range of expected heights for family. (Source: Tanner, J. M. *Fetus into man.* Cambridge: Harvard University Press, 1978.)

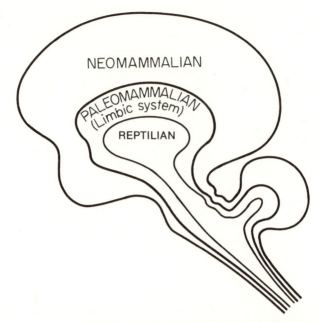

FIG. 2.5   Diagram of hierarchic organization of three basic brain types, which, in the evolution of the mammalian forebrain, become part of man's inheritance. Each type has distinctive structural and chemical features. Man's counterpart of the paleomammalian brain comprises the so-called limbic system which has been found to play an important role in emotional behavior. (Source: MacLean, P. D. The brain in relation to empathy and medical education. *Journal of Nervous and Mental Disorders*, 1967, *144*, 374–382.)

functions: alertness, consciousness, initial processing of environmental stimulation, digestion, breathing, and body metabolism.

The limbic system evolved about 100 million years ago and is very similar across a wide range of mammalian species. Apart from its absolute size, this brain is nearly indistinguishable among the Old World monkeys, apes, and humans. MacLean (1973) describes the limbic system as the emotional and motivational brain, which transforms "the cold light with which we see into the warm light with which we feel." As a consequence it is involved with all social interactions. One of the other chief characteristics of the limbic system is its function in memory, a topic we discuss in Chapter 5.

The neocortex evolved after and built upon the limbic system. It is relatively large in all primates, but huge in humans, comprising 99% of adult brain size. To a large extent the neocortex integrates and controls the activities of the two older brains through neural connections with nearly all their structures.

Figure 2.6 shows the surface of the left human neocortex. It is highly similar to that of the Old World monkeys and apes with two major exceptions. First, the human "interpretive" areas are larger than those of nonhumans. These areas are involved with interpreting sensory information, planning motor activities, reasoning, and thinking. Unlike those associated with specific functions such as the motor and skin sensation areas along the central sulcus (the top of Fig. 2.6), small amounts of brain damage have no noticeable effects. The interpretive areas expanded the most during the course of human evolution. Second, nonhuman primate brains do not have structures comparable to the three language areas (Broca, Wernicke, and the angular gyrus, which is not shown), located in the left cerebral hemisphere. Both human and nonhuman primates do have limbic system regions that affect vocalizations; but only humans have speech neocortex. In 3% of people, these speech areas are located in the right cerebral cortex.

Norman Geschwind (1972), a neurologist who has studied language extensively, presents the following model of its neural basis in normal hearing, reading, and speaking persons. Broca's area functions to control the muscles used in talking. People who have a damaged Broca area typically lose the ability to talk, but can still understand what others say and write. Wernicke's area functions both in understanding speech and in speaking meaningfully. Damage to this area results in the inability to

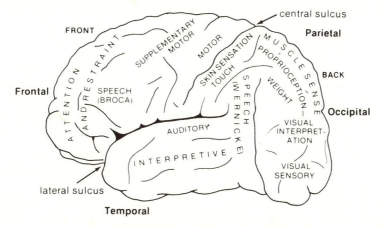

FIG. 2.6   The left (dominant) hemisphere of man showing various ages. Complex memories ("feedbacks") are evoked by electrical stimulation of the area marked "interpretative." There are two areas concerned with speech, one more anterior (Broca's area) and the other lying between the areas connected with the main receptor systems (Wernicke's area). (Source: Young, J. Z. *An introduction to the study of man.* New York: Oxford University Press, 1971.)

understand speech or to generate intelligible sentences. The angular gyrus, which lies at the border of the parietal, occipital, and temporal lobes, is involved with reading and writing. Damage results in a loss to both functions, but the person will still be able to speak meaningfully and understand the speech of others. In normal individuals, all these areas are interconnected and function smoothly. There is the possibility that some forms of reading disability, however, may be related to inadequate interconnections with the angular gyrus.

We saw in Fig. 2.3 that brain size reaches about 90% of adult levels at age 6, and 95% at age 10. This is misleading information, however, in that not all regions of the brain mature at the same rate. Of greatest interest is neocortex development. We are indebted to J. L. Conel, who painstakingly studied this and published his results in eight volumes over a 28-year period (1939–1967). As you might expect, the data are complex in that Conel used nine different criteria to determine the maturity of a given region. Conel's results can be placed into three groupings.

The first relates to the frontal lobes, which in Fig. 2.6 consist of the large region to the left of the central sulcus and above the lateral sulcus. The frontal lobes have close interconnections with the emotional portion of the limbic system and are important in attention and planning. Generally, as you move away from the motor areas toward the front of the brain, rate of maturity is slowest. In the motor area, maturation appears complete by about 4 years of age, whereas the interpretive areas are still developing at age 6. From birth to about age 15 months, the motor area is the most highly developed of the neocortex, underlining the importance of movement in early psychological development.

The second relates to the "primary projection" areas, which in Fig. 2.6 correspond to skin sensation, and auditory and visual sensory. These are the regions of the neocortex that are involved with processing touch, sound, and sight information. From birth to age 1 year, the skin sensation area is more mature than the other two, reflecting its close connection with movement, and the importance of touch in early development. From age 15 months to 4 years, the skin and visual regions develop at about the same rate, both more advanced than the auditory area. From age 4 to 6 years, all reach the same level of maturity.

The third group relates to the interpretive areas. In general, development is fastest the closer these areas are to either the motor or the primary projection areas. However, overall, the interpretive areas are the slowest to mature. The slowest of all appears to be in the region of the angular gyrus, which underlies language understanding. These findings strongly suggest that those psychological characteristics involving higher mental processes develop at very slow rates.

In looking at physical development piecemeal, we can lose sight of the fact that we are fully integrated systems, each anatomical structure and region intimately tied to the others. Moreover, our physical development is also linked to our social environment. Babies have limited physical capabilities, but enough to nurse and to let mother and other caretakers know of their needs. In evolution, changes in physical development that did not fit with the social environment did not survive. Each step along the road of physical development was finely tuned to the growing individual's social and physical environments.

The crowing achievement of human evolution is the brain. It incorporates nearly all that was essential in our evolutionary history, yet provides extraordinary opportunities for individual and collective creativity. This "achievement" takes a long time to mature, and along the route places limitations on our behavior and capabilities. To a large extent, the remainder of this book is an elaboration of these limitations and creative potentials.

Mammalian, Primate, and Hominid Behavioral Legacies

Canalization processes in the realm of behavioral development are closely linked with learning processes. Washburn and Hamburg (1965), two leading scholars of the evolution of behavior, have put the matter as follows:

> What is inherited is ease of learning, rather than fixed instinctive patterns. The species easily almost inevitably learns the essential behaviors for its survival. So although it is true that monkeys learn to be social, they are so constructed that under normal circumstances this learning always takes place. Similarly, human beings learn to talk, but they inherit structures that make this inevitable, except under the most peculiar circumstances. (pp. 5–6)

When the evolutionary record is looked at from the view of the human behavioral design, three broad classes of canalized social behavior appear. The first is mammalian, strongly canalized, and involves the emergence of mother-infant bonding. The second is primatological, probably moderately canalized, and involves the emergence of the social group. The third is hominid (i.e., the genus Homo, of which we are the only living species), probably moderately canalized, and involves the emergence of particular kinds of adult-adult and adult-children relationships.

About 200 million years ago the placental mammals evolved from reptilian ancestors. Apart from our physiological heritage, the most important mammalian characteristic is extensive and long-term maternal care of the young. Up until very recent times all infant mammals required a lactating mother in order to survive. The mother was her infant's sole source of food and a major source of its protection and socialization. Long-term maternal care requires that mothers stay very close to their nursing offspring, often in physical contact with them. Close proximity and physical contact appear to be the essential conditions for mother-infant bonding to occur.

The primates evolved about 75 million years ago from some common mammalian ancestors probably resembling contemporary tree shrews. Apart from obvious anatomical and physiological similarities, the key common denominator of nearly all the *Old World primates* (monkeys, apes, and humans) is that we are members of long-duration subsistence groups. The subsistence group provides food or opportunities for food, protection, reproduction, and socialization for its members. There are several important characteristics of these groups:

1. Mothers and their preadolescent offspring form the core of the group (infants are nearly always born singly). Relative to other mammals, mother-offspring involvement is very long, nearly always extending beyond the period of infancy. Not only does this produce strong mother-child bonding, but often strong bonding between siblings.

2. Members of these groups are all well-known to one another and, relative to outsiders, have strong bonds with each other. Group cohesiveness is essential in order for subsistence groups to carry our their essential functions.

3. Socialization occurs primarily by play, observation, and imitation. "Teaching" as we know it is uncommon. Play is typically more intense during the juvenile period of development and occurs among similar aged, same sex individuals. Socialization by observation and imitation occurs throughout the life span.

It is likely that 3–5 million years ago, the precursors of the human line of evolution, the Australopithecines, evolved in environments in which relative food scarcity was a regularly occurring event. That is, at times during the year there was not enough food in the nearby region to support a moderately sized subsistence group, e.g., more than 15 adults and children. The solution to this periodic scarcity involved a marked change in the social organization of these groups. Smaller groups of adult male/adult female/offspring subunits formed, which in times of food scarcity temporarily left the main group for days or weeks to fend for themselves. It can't be stated with any assurance whether these consisted of families, as we know them today, or as mother-offspring units and adult males who had affectional ties to the adult females. If these groups consisted of two or more adult males, or two or more females, it is likely that these adults formed closer ties to one another than they did to other adults in the main group.

Lancaster (1975) and Tanner (1981) have noted two other key features of the Australopithecines: mother-offspring food sharing, and maternal food gathering (as opposed to eating food on the spot). None of the living nonhuman primates either gather or share food to any significant extent, and it is clear that all living human groups do both. Sometime during our evolution these important behavioral characteristics emerged, and it is likely that they did so before hunting large game became part of the hominid way of life.

The above mammalian, primate, and Australopithecine social adaptations set the stage, and were probably a necessary condition, for the next period of hominid evolution. It is highly likely that about 1–1.5 million years ago male hominids started to engage in the collaborative hunting of large game for part of their subsistence. This form of hunting requires substantial cooperation among the hunters. But in order to cooperate, other changes had to occur. Male-male aggressiveness had to decrease and bonding had to increase. A second major social change brought about by collaborative hunting of large game was that male-female role differentiation increased regarding food-seeking activities, tool-making activities, and tool use. In most environments a gatherer-hunter group would starve if it depended exclusively on hunting success. In order for the males to have the opportunity to hunt, they had to depend on the food-gathering success of females, and the sharing of food among males and females. Sharing of food between adults now became obligatory.

If at this point in human evolution, subsistence groups were already comprised of single male/single female/offspring units, it is highly likely that this family structure was strengthened. If the family "design" was not yet in existence, then it probably came into existence then. The family was special in that greater bonding and reciprocity among its members occurred relative to other members in the group.

Given that future hunters and toolmakers had to be trained, this stage in human evolution brought about increased adult male involvement with offspring, especially with the male children. Fathers were identified as such, and were differentiated from "uncles" and male nonrelatives. Fathers became heavily responsible for their own offspring, with less responsibility for the offspring of their collaborators. Related to increased paternal involvement in offspring was the strengthening of cross-generational collaborative activities. Thus, parent/child reciprocities emerged such that parents were responsible for their young children and children became responsible for their old parents.

It appears from observation of contemporary gatherer-hunters that their society is largely democratic and without differences in rank among the adults. However, intermittently, work groups of various sorts have to be formed to carry out necessary subsistence, ritualistic, or political activities, e.g., arranging marriages. These work groups are usually hierarchically organized. The ability to form temporary groups of this nature, whose membership varies from activity to activity, is an enormous accomplishment. Where these groups are hierarchical, it is likely that the family is a model for their organization.

Thus, the gatherer-hunter behavioral design has been with us for at least one million years. This was the sole human design until only about 10,000 years ago when domestication and agriculture were invented. It is only in the last 5,000 years that these activities became widespread and that cities emerged. So, for at least 99% of human existence, the ancestors of all of us were gatherers and hunters.

CULTURE

It is useful to make a distinction between the social structural aspects and the contents of a culture. Social structure refers to the relatively stable ways that the members of a culture are organized to carry out the functions of their society, e.g., marrying, selecting political leaders, getting food. The social structure of a society gives it a basic character that distinguishes it from other societies, and that shapes the lives of its members. Industrial societies such as ours are very complex and have a variety of social structures dealing with the same function, e.g., food-related activities. Moreover, some of these structures are in the process of undergoing rapid change—e.g., the duration of marriages in the United States—so we shouldn't think of social structure as being permanent.

Social Structure

In an excellent book, Berry (1976) has discussed the interrelationship between the physical environment a society inhabits and its culture. One of the most interesting findings of this work is that the food-related activities of a society have a tremendous impact on other aspects of its social structure. Two structures of interest are social complexity (number of social roles) and social stratification (extent of status differences).

Regarding social complexity, e.g., number of occupational choices, Berry summarizes a number of studies in which the following pattern emerges. Societies that are semi-nomadic or nomadic, store little or no food, and live in small groups, e.g., gatherer-hunters, have very little role differentiation within the group. The roles one will have in these societies are quite limited and predictable from childhood on. Societies that are somewhat more sedentary, live in larger social groups, and rely to a moderate extent on food storage, e.g., horticulturists, have more role differentiation. These societies typically utilize two or more major ways of obtaining food, e.g., hunting and cultivation. Finally, societies that are sedentary, have high levels of food accumulation, and live in relatively large groups, e.g., the agricultural and industrialized peoples, have substantial role differentiation.

Let's now look at status differences (social stratification) within these societies. There are at least three fundamental ways that members in a group may attain different statuses: heredity, e.g., being born into the aristocracy or a low caste; wealth or material goods; and particular differences in ability valued by the society, e.g., political skills. As with role differentiation, a clear pattern emerges. The most important structural component in determining the extent of social stratification is the extent to which the society relies on food accumulation. Agricultural peoples, industrialized peoples, and herding societies rely on accumulation and have large status differences. The second most important component is permanency of the settlement. More permanent settlements are associated with large status differences. Thus herders are low on this factor, but some fishing societies, and all agricultural and industrial societies, are high on it. For the herders, status is primarily based on the size of the herd, but for the more sedentary societies, status can be based on hereditary class, wealth, or ability. Hunting and gathering societies typically have few status differences among the adult members.

Our discussion of a third social structure, family composition, is based on the research of Blumberg and Winch (1973). These authors make a distinction between societies in which 80% or more of all households consist of a nuclear family, i.e., mother, father (if still married) and their children (if they're still unmarried), and those societies in which at least 20% of households consist of more complicated family types, e.g., polygamous (multiple wives or husbands), two or more married brothers, parents and one or more married children. For convenience, we refer to the two types as "nuclear" and "non-nuclear." The basic findings are as follows: gathering, hunting, and urban-industrial societies are primarily nuclear; herding, fishing, gardening, cereal cultivation, and intensive agricultural societies are primarily non-nuclear. One partial explanation of these results is that if the economic activities of a family require the long-term commitment, cooperation, and involvement of several adults, then families will tend to be non-nuclear. On the other hand, if the husband and wife can support themselves and their children by their own work, without continuous involvement of the same group of adults, then families will tend to be nuclear. The latter are the typical conditions of hunter, gatherer, and industrial societies, and the former are the typical conditions of most of the remaining societies.

Contents

We now turn to contents. The contents of a culture are the long-term results of the social structures of that culture. Contents can be defined as the shared products of human learning which consist of "standards for deciding what is, standards for deciding what can be, standards for deciding how one feels about it, standards for deciding what to do about it, and standards for deciding how to go about doing it" (Goodenough, 1963, p. 259).

Let's follow Goodenough (1970) in elaborating this definition, taking one "standard" at a time. The first standard, "for deciding what is," means that the experiences each of us has of our world—our concepts and perceptions—are shaped or formed by our culture. The essence of these processes is the use of categories for making sense out of our experiences. We usually acquire these categories slowly through interactions with other members of our community. Early in development one's parents and siblings are the most influential "teachers" of these categories, and this teaching often has life-long effects. The most obvious basis for forming categories, and certainly one of the most powerful, is the language we speak. Gesture and other nonlinguistic behaviors are also important, but not as readily analyzable. For example, in most Western cultures we don't make linguistic distinctions between "older brother" and "younger brother," but do between "sibling" and "cousin." In some Pacific island cultures, just the reverse holds. Thus, our standards for determining what we see and how we "understand" what we see are in large part culturally determined.

"Standards for deciding what can be" refers to the propositions and beliefs by which we explain our experiences. Here, Goodenough is emphasizing that we organize our world as involving cause and effect relationships. We learn to see that events occur in and are defined by particular spatial, temporal, and symbolic contexts. We learn to see that events, objects, or people are included in, or excluded from, certain categories, e.g., friend or foe, family or nonfamily, edible or inedible.

We also learn that certain propositions are true, irrespective of their logic or illogic, and at times, even in the face of contradictory evidence. There are many in our culture who believe that vaccinations are consistently harmful, that snake bites are generally beneficial, that sparing the rod spoils the child (the U.S. Supreme Court seems to have upheld this principle in the schools), that Jews, or blacks, or Catholics (pick your group) are the cause of our national problems.

"Standards for deciding how one feels about it" refers to our values. By values, Goodenough (1970) means "the ways people associate things with their inner feeling states and with the gratification of their needs and wants" (p. 28). Values guide our actions. Obviously, some of our wants and needs depend on our evolutionary heritage, but most result from experiences we have in particular families, communites, and societies. The more similar these experiences are between different individuals, the more similar will be their values. Often our private values conflict with public values, and we have to accommodate to this regularly occurring stress. The more competent we are in this accommodation, the more likely we will be able to ultimately satisfy our wants and needs.

It is the nature of society that there will be inequalities between people in their needs and in their opportunities to gratify their wants and needs. Every system of values relates rights, duties, and privileges to certain social categories, such as age, sex, legal status, and generation, e.g., drinking and driving ages, employability as a function of sex. Moreover, the extent to which we have acquired skills, wisdom, and experience will have an appreciable effect on our abilities to satisfy our wants and needs. All these differences produce marked differences in the power or control people have in attaining that which they value. One consequence is that those with less power are often less committed to upholding societal values than those with more power. We might expect that pushes for change within families and other social groups will come from the most powerless.

In our attempts to accomplish our purposes, to achieve our goals, we often are involved with other people who are similary engaged in pursuing their purposes. Hence, we need "standards for deciding how to go about doing it." In order to be effective in our personal pursuits; (1) we must be effective in making sense out of the behavior of others; and (2) we must have the knowledge of the culturally approved behaviors for accomplishing regularly occurring objectives. Goodenough (1970) suggests that in all cultures, as a person develops he learns a "grammar" of the actions of others. This grammar is analogous to that involved with speaking and understanding spoken language (which we discuss in Chapter 6). Through our repeated interactions with other people we come to observe patterns in their behavior and in our own, e.g, those involved with "play" fighting and "real" fighting. Hence, we come to formulate conscious or unconscious rules (the grammar) for understanding behavior. We're also helped in this process by being able to be empathic (which we discuss in Chapter 5), and by knowing cultural conceptions, beliefs, and values.

In the above discussion, we've written about the contents of a culture as shared standards that are acquired during our lifetimes through our experiences in a given society. Since no two people in any culture have the same lifetime experiences, does it follow that the standards they've learned are somwhat different? Yes. Goodenough (1963) distinguishes between the *"private" culture* of individuals, their *"operating" culture*, and the *"public" culture*. Private culture refers to all the standards that a person has acquired in his lifetime, which he shares with at least some people in some community or some social class. For example, in discussing the game of marbles, Piaget (1932) encounters children who describe the different rules for the same game as it is played in different towns. Some children know two sets of rules (standards) and others know only one. As another example, some educators have argued that we ought to teach black "dialect" and white "dialect" in certain schools, thus respecting the different cultures or social classes of people in the same society.

There are aspects of our private culture that we may never or rarely use. In our day-to-day activities we consciously or unconsciously choose certain of our sets of standards to guide our behavior. When we're at work, or at home with our families, or out with our friends, we choose different cultures appropriate to those situations. These are our operating cultures.

Public culture is what most people think of when they think of the "culture" of a society. These are the standards that nearly all members of a society are aware of and follow, especially when others are watching. Nearly everybody follows the same language rules, driving rules (if they have cars), legal rules, and so on. Clearly, the more complex the culture, the less contact people in different communities or different social classes have with one another. The more that people from other cultures immigrate to or influence the society, the smaller will be the public culture. Another important factor is the pressures from within a society for change. The women's movement in our culture is having a profound effect on changing the public culture. Is a woman's place in the home? Yes puts you in one culture, No in another.

Social Class (SES) As Culture

As implied in the above discussion, cultural differences exist within complex societies such as ours. These differences may be based on religion, e.g., the Hasidic Jewish communities in New York; race, such as black urban communities; national origin, e.g., Scandinavian communities in the Dakotas; geography, such as small town Midwest; occupation, e.g., sailors, farmers; or any combination of them. These cultures often provide the settings for novels and plays. One of the most useful ways in which cultural differences in Western industrialized societies has been examined is by social class or socio-economic status (SES). SES has been measured in a number of ways (Gecas, 1979), nearly all concerned with education and occupation of the male head of the household.

The terms used most frequently to distinguish social class differences from higher to lower are *upper class, middle class, working class* and *lower class*. Sometimes the lower class is divided into the poor and the non-poor, based upon whether family income is above a specified minimum level. The middle and upper classes are also occasionally combined and referred to collectively as "white collar"; the working and lower classes are often referred to collectively as "blue collar." Basically, the more extensive a person's education, and the more prestigious his occupation, the higher the SES is. In Western industrialized societies, a very small percentage of people fall into the upper class; the majority fall into the middle and working classes, and a substantial minority fall into the lower class.

Membership in a particular social class has multiple effects on the ways in which parents train their children. Gecas (1979), drawing heavily on the work of Bronfenbrenner (1958) and Kohn (1977), summarized much of this literature. The present discussion is restricted to comparisons between the lower, working, and middle SESs, the social classes that most of the research has emphasized.

Gecas divides his paper into two major sections dealing with (a) empirical generalizations and (b) theoretical explanations. The topic of empirical generalizations is subdivided into five categories concerned with the following questions:

1. How do parents attempt to control their children? Gecas makes four generalizations relating to this question.
   (a) Parents of higher relative to lower[1] SESs tend to use reasoning and shame and guilt as disciplinary techniques.
   (b) Parents of lower relative to higher SESs are more likely to discipline by using physical punishment.
   (c) Higher relative to lower SES parents tend to take into account their children's motives and intentions before punishing them.
   (d) Parents of lower relative to higher SESs are more likely to punish their children based on what they did, and not why they did it.

In general, then, parents of higher relative to lower SESs are more psychologically oriented in attempts to control their children.

2. How are conflicts between parents and children resolved? Gecas makes two general observations about this issue:
   (a) Parents and children of higher relative to lower SESs have more democratic, equalitarian relationships.
   (b) Lower relative to higher SES parents have more autocratic or authoritarian relationships with their children.
3. How much affection is shown, and how actively are parents involved with their children? Two observations are made about this issue:
   (a) Higher relative to lower SES parents tend to be more affectionate and to spend more time interacting with their children.

---

[1]"Higher relative to lower" refers to differences in SES, e.g., working versus lower, middle versus working, and not to upper-class versus lower-class families.

    (b) Fathers of higher relative to lower SESs are more involved with their children.

4. To what extent do parents encourage independence and achievement in their children?

    (a) Higher relative to lower SES parents emphasize independent problem solving and academic achievement in their children.

5. How do parents talk to their children? Gecas makes three statements about this issue:

    (a) Lower relative to higher SES parents, when talking to their children, emphasize that they conform to social roles such as age and sex.

    (b) Lower relative to higher SES parents use coercive language such as commands and imperatives with their children.

    (c) Higher relative to lower SES parents, when talking to their children, emphasize their children's individuality.

Gecas points out that none of these findings are very strong. Therefore, there is considerable overlap in parents' behaviors across SES levels. Overall, however, child-rearing practices do form distinctive patterns in the different social classes. Parents at the higher SES levels emphasize their children's individuality, responsibility, motivation, and thinking. They encourage emotional expression and signs of affection. Parents at the lower SESs emphasize conformity, obedience, and respect for power. They are more interested in their children's behavior than in the motivations behind this behavior.

Gecas graphically portrays his explanation of these patterns in Fig. 2.7. In the figure, three causal chains linking SES differences to differences in parent-child interactions are emphasized. Gecas believes that there is strong empirical support for the causal explanation depicted in the boxes numbered 1, 2, 3, and 4. The key elements in this chain are the occupations and educations of the parents. Lower SES parents have jobs in which conformity is emphasized; whereas in the work of middle-class adults self-direction is stressed. Similarly, the more education adults have obtained, the more likely they have been encouraged to think and plan for themselves. One's values in life generally, and in parenting specifically, follow from these experiences—the higher SES parents value self-direction, the lower SES parents, conformity. Values of self-direction lead a person to being concerned with reasons and motivations; conformity leads to concerns about external behavior. Parent-child interactions in

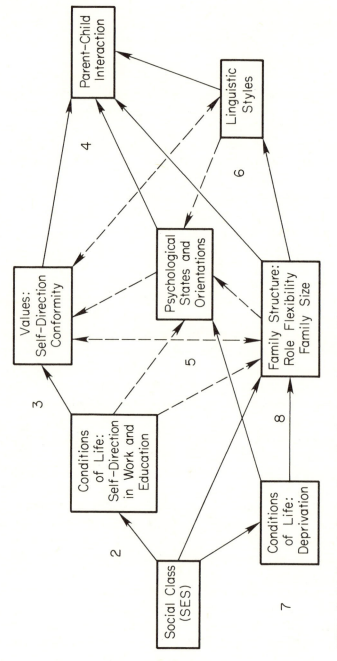

KEY: Solid lines indicate theoretically based propositions.
Hash lines indicate bridging propositions.

FIG. 2.7 Theoretical Model of Social Class and Socialization. (Source: Gegas, V. The influence of social class on socialization. In W. R. Burr, R. Hill, F. I. Nye, & I. L. Reiss (Eds.), *Contemporary theories about the family.* Vol. 1. New York: Free Press, 1979.)

higher SES families are thus oriented more toward achievement, independence, and psychological matters. The interactions in lower SES families are oriented more toward conformity and obedience.

Gecas believes that the empirical support is not quite as strong for the causal links between SES, structure, linguistic styles, and parent-child interactions (Box numbers 1, 8, 6 and 4). The key explanatory elements in this chain involve family size and interdependence between members of extended families. Gecas contends that the larger the nuclear family, and the greater the interdependence of the extended family, the more specialized a person's family role will be. Each person has to be "few things to many people," e.g., the nurturer, or the breadwinner, or the conflict resolver. Smaller nuclear and extended families, in which relationships between family members are not highly interdependent, lead to considerable role flexibility among family members. Each person has to be "many things to a few people." For example, a member has to be a nurturer, conflict resolver, and breadwinner. Generally, lower SES nuclear and extended families are larger and more interdependent than higher SES families. The decreased role flexibility of lower SES family members, Gecas argues, leads to the parents' using coercive language, which emphasizes their children's conformity to narrow social roles. The increased role flexibility of higher SES family members on the other hand, leads to the parents' emphasizing their children's individuality.

Gecas believes that the empirical evidence in support of the last causal link—SES, conditions of life, psychological states, and parent-child interactions (Box numbers 1, 7, 5, and 4)—is at best suggestive. The key explanatory element here is the extent of control families have over their own lives. He argues that lower SES families are more deprived than higher SES families, and hence feel more powerless to influence the course of their lives. This increased feeling of powerlessness of these SES families also leads to an orientation towards "fatalism" or a sense, on their part, of being controlled by external events. Finally, the greater a family's orientation towards fatalism, the more likely it is that parents will emphasize physical punishment and obedience, and focus on their children's external behavior.

This concludes the discussion on culture. However, in the next section—Socialization—we continue to emphasize the close relationship between culture and socialization.

SOCIALIZATION: THE INDIVIDUAL AND THE GROUP

Conflict in Groups

We've argued that man's basic evolutionary design is that of a member of a family that is in turn part of a subsistence group. As cultural evolution became added to genetic evolution the functions of the subsistence group in many cultures came to be distributed across several different groups. For example, in our culture, separate groups exist for education, work, and religion. Our recreational partners often live at some distance from us. Some of us as adults see our families of origin infrequently. With urbanization and industrialization, we have moved from a situation in which almost all of our individual needs were met within a single small group to one in which we are required to seek out and join many different groups. We've even created groups in which we're not members, that we do not control and may not even like, which carry out our individual and collective needs, e.g., police, courts, garbage collectors, politicians. In India the caste system has made membership in some of these groups an inherited characteristic. The "untouchables" care for garbage and handle dead bodies and other "unclean" specimens.

Life is, and always has been, lived in groups. This is not to imply that group living is easy. Tension, sometimes intolerable, is one outcome of group involvement. Lee and DeVore (1968) point out that even among gatherer-hunters, tension often becomes so strong that the subsistence group splits up and some families join other groups. Some of these splits may be permanent. This "fission" is not restricted to gatherer-hunter societies. Family feuds in our own culture can result in family members moving away and not speaking with one another. And we've all read about family members shooting and sometimes killing one another.

It is relatively safe to assume that conflict between individuals is central to group tensions. There are at least three kinds of conflicts between individuals in a group. The first kind occurs between any two people who have somewhat different values, beliefs, goals, preferred routes for achieving those goals. I like spaghetti, you like chop suey; I like Cincinnati, you like New Haven; I want to marry, you want to stay single. Maybe we'll compromise, perhaps not. These conflicts may produce a great deal of tension and may even lead to mutual avoidance by the two disputants. The personal desires of two of its members are at stake here, not the life of the group.

The second kind of conflict goes to the heart of the group. It deals with differences among the members concerning either how the group is organized or how it functions. Although there is no universally agreed-upon definition of a group, the following seem to be characteristics shared by most groups (e.g., Fisher, 1980). (1) It is an *entity* independent of any one of its members; e.g., your family of origin existed before you were born and probably continued to exist after you left home. (2) The members are *interdependent*. The tasks the group performs require the cooperation of its members; e.g., in a classroom the professor can teach only if the students will learn. (3) The members *share common goals;* e.g., the members of a soccer team want to win games, improve their skills, and have a good time. (4) The group has *norms* for its members, i.e., expectations concerning what is appropriate behavior. Nearly all professional athletic teams have a curfew the night before a game. (5) Finally, a group requires *leadership* in order to carry out its tasks. In families, the leaders are nearly always the parents, but in peer groups, leadership may change from task to task.

Conflict between individual members may emerge concerning any of those characteristics. Up to a point this conflict is beneficial to the group and tends to strengthen commitment (Fisher, 1980). But if the conflict is not resolved, the life of the group is at risk, and not just the interpersonal relations of some of its members. Divorce, the break-up of small business partnerships, and the dissolution of peer groups are just a few examples.

The third kind of conflict is related to the second, and is of special interest to us. This is the conflict that arises when the needs of the individual are incompatible with the needs of the group. In order to sustain membership in a group, each individual must set aside some of her personal needs, values, or beliefs, and conform to those of the group. Deviancy is tolerated, but only within limits. When the limits are exceeded, members are expelled or leave by their own choice. Those of us who read the sports section frequently read about players who are traded because of their failure to conform to some of the team norms. People often voluntarily leave groups because they can't tolerate the leadership, e.g., some of Nixon's people during Watergate. All of us are painfully aware of the large number of teenagers whose values are markedly different from those of their parents and who become runaways (Stierlin, 1974).

Even when one is in conflict with a group, "conform or get out" is rarely the only choice. Groups are always in flux. What you couldn't tolerate today may be changed tomorrow. Further, in the process of group decision making, each of us helps shape the goals, norms, and leadership of our groups. The individual often must accommodate (adjust, modify) his mode of satisfying his needs in order to remain in the group, and to a lesser extent the group must modify its mode of functioning in order to sustain its members. When the accommodation is not mutual, we see the splintering described above.

Interpersonal Needs

We've mentioned the "needs of the individual," without describing which ones are of particular interest. Most psychologists are familiar with Maslow's (1954) hierarchy of motives and Murray's list of needs (1938). Psychoanalytic conceptions of dependent, destructive, and sexual needs have been incorporated into Western civilization. But when we ask the question, "What is the individual within the context of the group attempting to accomplish?" we find that a modification of William Schutz's (1960) very simple description of interpersonal behavior is most suitable for this task.

Schutz describes three social needs that allow for a relatively complete understanding of interpersonal behavior: *inclusion*, *control*, and *affection*. For each of these needs, Schutz considers three relations: self to others, others to self, and self to self. The need for inclusion is the need to belong to and be a part of a group. People want to initiate contacts with others (self to others), to have others initiate contacts with them (others to self), and to feel that they themselves are significant (self to self). People also desire to exert some control over others, to have others treat them with respect, and to feel that they themselves are responsible. Finally, people wish to show love and affection to others, to have others show love to them, and to feel that they themselves are lovable. While you are pursuing these needs in relation to your group, others are pursuing them in relation to you. You can simultaneously satisfy these needs through mutuality; e.g., you try to control some, but not all, of your group behavior and cooperate with others when they attempt to exert control.

Our modification of this theory is slight but significant. Schutz includes "self-to-self" relations as part of the three basic needs. We believe it more useful to consider this relation separately—the *need to maintain self-esteem*. When we look at what people of all ages are attempting to accomplish (consciously or unconsciously), it is clear that maintaining self-esteem or self-worth is in the foreground. This need is so basic to human interactions that if we had to choose, we would give this one the nod as *the* most basic. Robert White (1960) has written elegantly of a major component of this need as the striving for competence.

Let's illustrate these needs by imagining a family sitting at breakfast. The family consists of father, his 5-year-old daughter, Sue, and her step-mother of 6 months. Sue is picking at her food and the following dialogue occurs.

Stepmother: Eat your cereal, Sue, it's good for you.
(Kindly tone)

Sue: You can't tell me what to do, you're not my mother.
(unkindly tone)

The stepmother has a need to be included in this new family unit, to develop an affectionate relationship with Sue and maintain her affection-ate relationship with Sue's father, to exercise authority (power, control) around parenting issues, and to feel competent in her relatively new role as parent (maintain self-esteem). The statement to Sue is the stepmoth-er's assertion that she is part of the family. The content of the statement attempts to put her in a one-up (control) position relative to Sue, and its tone is intended to please both Sue and her husband. Since it is often the job of competent mothers to make sure that their daughters (or step-daughters) eat a nourishing breakfast, the stepmother attempts to act competently and maintain her self-esteem by making this request of Sue.

Sue is also pursuing the four basic needs in this interaction. She wants to be included in her now non-existent original family and is unprepared at this time to shift any allegiance to this new and possibly temporary family. Sue also needs to be in control of her situation. She had no control over her parents' divorce or her father's remarriage, but she does over her body, at least what goes into it. So she in effect says to her step-mother "You're not my *boss*, I am." Sue now remembers that her own mother was often kindly and made few demands on her. Sue would like to be with her mother and re-experience some of the warm feelings she used to have. So when Sue says "You're not my mother," she's also saying "I want my mother." Finally, divorce is nearly always a dramatic assault on the self-esteem of children. Many young children feel somewhat responsi-ble for the divorce and may feel guilty about the fantasy of pushing the other parent out. One way to reduce the guilt and feeling of responsibility and thus increase her self-esteem is to be the perfect daughter. Hence, her statement can also be read as "My real mother *can* tell me what to do; I'm a good girl for her."

FAMILY, PEERS, AND SCHOOLS

Now that you have considered some basic ideas about individuals and groups, we can begin to describe the long process of socialization. Human socialization refers to all the influences people have on one another. Thus, socialization occurs in every known interaction. Most of these influences are short term and of little consequence, e.g., smiling at a stranger on an elevator; some are long term and of great consequence, e.g., learning your native tongue; and many fall in the middle, e.g., reading a long novel or biography. It will be difficult for you to think of any behavior, feeling, or thought that has not been socialized, including the ways you stand, sit, walk, eat, and throw or catch an object. Socialization is a life-long process—we can't ever escape influencing and being influenced by others, even in our dreams.

Most students of socialization are primarily interested in long-term, powerful, interpersonal influences. Brief, face-to-face encounters can be interesting and important. In fact, some exciting research has been done on just those brief interactions (e.g., Goffman, 1974). But to understand short-term interactions, we have to see them in the context of the broad sweep of the life course and understand first the persistent, enduring shapers of our development. These shapers are members of the significant groups in which we live or develop.

There are five major groups. Most people are members of them at some period in their lives and all have profound influences. These groups are (1) the family in which we are children (family of origin); (2) the family in which we are spouses and parents (family of procreation); (3) our peers; (4) the schools we attend; and (5) our places of work. Sheppard Kellam (1983) indicates two other groups that have a substantial influence on us; the schools our children attend, and the families our children form. Strictly speaking, we are not members of those groups, and unfortunately from a research perspective, we have little data on their influences. Other shapers are mass media (Achenbach, 1978), economic swings of inflation and depression, war, and the cohort with which one moves through life. In the remainder of this section we discuss some of the characteristics of the three major groups that influence children's development.

Cross-Cultural Comparisons of the Family: Sex Roles and Marriage Patterns

If we consider the twentieth century North American family in the context of family structures around the world, we discover that North American family organization is not typical. For example, when we talked about the different family groups that influence our development, we distinguished between the family of origin, the family of procreation, and the family of our children. This distinction is culturally bound. For males born in traditional China, there may be one family that includes all four generations, e.g., one's parents, one's self, one's children, one's grandchildren, and continues across time. For Chinese females, there are two families, the family they are born into and the family they marry into.

Chinese children traditionally lived in a house that included their parents, their father's parents, their unmarried brothers and sisters, and the wives of their brothers. When a boy reached a marriageable age, a wife was brought in for him (this was the "major" form of marriage). He and his wife were primarily responsible for raising their children, but all other adults in the household also had a voice. And when their sons reached a marriageable age, they brought in wives for them. The cycle continued. When a Chinese girl reached marriageable age, her parents tried to find a suitable husband for her. If they did, she moved to her husband's home and became part of his family for the rest of her life. Her children became part of her husband's family and not of her family of origin. One obvious consequence of the differential treatment of males and females was that males continued to be socialized in the home of their mothers and fathers, but females at adulthood become socialized in the home of their in-laws.

Let's consider a nonobvious consequence of this sex differentiation, in three-generation families. The oldest male in the family was the head of the household. His wife gained her influence in family matters through his seniority. In many Chinese households there was a period of time in which both grandparents and one or more of their sons' families were living together. This situation was frequently followed by a period after grandfather died while grandmother lived and the headship had passed on to their oldest son. Socialization effects on grandmother, daughter-in-law (mother), and grandchildren should have been different in these two periods. Olsen (1976) found this to be the case. When grandfather was alive, his daughter-in-law had to be odedient to grandmother, share grandmother's values, and model grandmother's behavior. Moreover,

daughter-in-law tended to raise her children in accordance with grandmother's values and behavior. After grandfather died, grandmother lost
her authority. The daughter-in-law acted much more independently in
household matters, values, and in child-rearing practices.

Family structure, marriage roles, friendship, residency rules for newly
married couples and inheritance rules are intimately related in all societies. And all can have a marked bearing on socialization throughout our
lifetimes. Kasden (1965) has examined several of these features and has
shown how they can have dramatic effects on whether or not a man will
marry, what occupation he will choose, and whether he will migrate from
his native country (Kasden does not deal with these issues for women).
The cultures he studied are close to the American experience: the rural
Spanish Basques, rural Norwegians, and rural Irish. In all three cultures,
the families of interest are those who live on small, self-sufficient farms
that are too small for any subdivision. Moreover, these farms are owned
by one person – the heir to the land.

The three cultures differ in the system of inheritance and mating patterns. For the Basques, the farm is nearly always inherited by the
firstborn son, but in some cases by the firstborn daughter. The firstborn
may marry before he or she inherits the farm, and live there with parents. Thus, from the day of birth, second- and later-born children know
they will be landless, and are reared as such. These non-heirs have several courses of action on reaching adulthood: they may emigrate to the
New World, stay there and marry, or return and marry a Basque; they
may join a religious order and stay unmarried; or they may stay on the
farm, but if they do so, they must remain unmarried.

For the Irish, the farm is also inherited by only one son, but it is not
necessarily the firstborn. The father chooses the heir, and usually waits
until he is well along in years before doing so. Those sons who want the
farm must continue to work on the farm until their father makes his
choice. None may marry during this waiting period. If one wishes to
marry, he must leave the farm, but of course, he'll have to find his own
way to support a wife. The son chosen as heir may marry and live on the
farm with his wife and children. Thus, each child has several choices open
to him prior to his father's decision: he may leave the farm and try to find
work in Ireland; he may emigrate to the New World; he may stay on the
farm, in a dependent relationship with his parents, work hard, and hope
to be the chosen heir; or he may join a religious order and be supported
by the church. The only ones who are likely to marry are those who emi-

grate and those who inherit the farm. And the latter will marry late in life.

The Norwegian system is similar to the Irish in that the heir is chosen and the farm is not split up; but there are three important differences. Unlike the Irish farm culture that encourages childhood dependency, the Norwegians encourage independence and initiative. They have a long tradition of their young men either going to sea or homesteading. And there is no tradition of joining the Church. Thus, many sons leave the farm before an heir is chosen, after which they either homestead, emigrate to the New World, or go to sea. All these sons may marry. The father chooses an heir based in large part on two criteria: the son's ability to manage the farm, and his ability to produce a family to help him run the farm. How is the latter accomplished? Since the only son who may marry and live on the farm is the chosen heir, the Norwegians have developed a system of "understandings." In the understandings, the sons mate with daughters of other farmers and have children. The children stay with their mother until such time as their father can marry their mother. If her mate is the chosen heir, they marry and mother and children move to the farm. If he is not chosen, then he has a number of options open to him, including not marrying his mate.

In the various family types we've touched on, "family of origin," "family of procreation," and "family of our children" mean very different things. The socialization experiences of family members were different in each culture. Nevertheless, there were some common elements. In nearly all cases married women left their family of origin and became part of the husband's family. Moving into adulthood appeared to be the major transition period. All cultures showed marked sex differentiation concerning potential developmental pathways. Finally, the inheritance patterns had a dramatic effect on the developmental choices, or lack thereof, of all children.

Cross-Cultural Comparisons of the Family: Family Life Cycles

Morioka (1967) analyzes family life cycles for Japan, China, and the United States. The *ideal* family system differs in these societies; for the Japanese, it is the *"stem"* family, which is essentially the same as that of the rural Basque, Irish, and Norwegians; for the Chinese, it is the *"joint"* family, as described above; and for the Americans it is the *"nuclear"* family, in which each married couple sets up its own independent household. What are the major stages of family developmet and what are the implications for socialization?

Morioka identifies three major stages for the stem family: Stage I, in which grandfather and grandmother live with their married son, his wife, and their children, grandfather is head of the household; Stage II, in which grandfather has either died or retired, and his married son is now head of the household; Stage III in which grandmother has died, and the new heir is unmarried. Thus, in this stage, the family structure is nuclear. When the heir marries, the family shifts to Stage I.

In Stage I, there are two major socialization issues. The first is the mutual accommodation of all family members to include the heir's wife in the family. The second is the mutual accommodation of all family members to the births of heir's children. In Stage II, the major socialization issues revolve around the changed power relations among the grandparent and parent generations. The son is now head of the household and is responsible for the care of his mother and retired father. When the grandfather dies, the power positions of the daughter-in-law and grandmother are somewhat reversed, with daughter-in-law being responsible for managing the household. If the accommodations in Stage I were shaky, then Stage II will prove to be difficult for all the survivors. In Stage III, the major socialization issues resemble those of the later stages of the American nuclear family, to which we now turn.

The end points in life cycle for the ideal American family are well defined. Stage I starts with marriage and setting up of an independent household by a young couple. The last stage ends with their deaths. The number of identifiable intervening stages is debatable. We'll present an approach based on Morioka's work and that of Minuchin (1974) and Haley (1973). In Stage I the major socialization issues involve the mutual accommodations between husband and wife and their parents concerning the independence of this unit. Minuchin refers to these issues as boundary marking between the families of origin and family of procreation. In Stage II–the birth of the first child–the major socialization issues involve new responsibilities of parenthood and marked changes in availability of husband and wife to each other. Stages III and IV emerge as a function of spacing between children, if there is a second child at all. In Stage III–the birth of second and subsequent children–the major socialization issues revolve around the ways both parents, but especially mother, distribute their time and affection to their children. It is highly likely that the firstborn will be intensely jealous of the younger sibling at some point in his development. For some firstborns, unresolved jealousy becomes a lifelong obsession.

In Stage IV – the firstborn's entry into school – the family is confronted with conflicts in values, attitudes, and behaviors between home and school. Socialization issues revolve around dealing with those conflicts. In Stage V – the children's deep involvement with peer groups – the family may be confronted with intense conflicts between peers and parents. Moreover, the children form strong allegiances with their friends, which the parents may experience as rejection.

In Stage VI the children leave the parental home to venture out on their own, to set up their own households, and to marry (this is the traditional ideal). Many parents experience this stage with elation, others with depression. The family group diminishes in size, which requires new accommodations among all family members, and the end of this stage results in a post-parental home. After 20 or more years of parenting, husband and wife must find a new basis to sustain their relationship. In Stage VII, either husband or wife, or both, are still employed outside the home. They are likely to be intensely involved in outside activities and outside groups. They must negotiate whether and how to continue their relationship. As long as they have their work, they can delay this decision. In Stage VIII, both are retired and must accommodate to all the changes retirement brings about. Not the least of these changes is the sheer amount of time they spend together. Some families experience retirement as the peak of family existence, others as the valley.

In the traditional Chinese family, all the sons share equally the inherited property of their dead father. Ideally, all should continue to live in the joint parental household with their wives and eventually bring in wives for their sons. The reality is that in almost all cases, after the father and mother die, the sons divide the property equally and each sets up an independent nuclear family. Eventually each forms a joint family, and the cycle repeats itself. Morioka identifies four stages in this family cycle. Stage I is that of the nuclear family in which the socialization issues parallel those of the American nuclear family at a comparable developmental period. Stage II is that of a stem family in which only one son has thus far brought a wife into the household. The socialization issues parallel those of the Japanese stem family in a comparable developmental period. Stage III is that of a joint family with two married sons and one or both parents living. The socialization issues revolve around conflicts and jealousies among daughters-in-law concerning rights, duties, and privileges; among sons concerning their leadership of and contribution to the well-being of the family; and among the two senior generations concerning family leadership and decision making. Stage IV, the period following the death of both parents, is usually brief. The unresolved conflicts in Stage III become magnified–the parents are no longer around to be peacemakers–and the family splits up, forming separate nuclear families.

Can we make some general statements about the family life cycle in these three societies? First, family complexity increases as one moves from a nuclear to a joint or stem family structure. This implies that both the number of social roles a person has to learn, and the complexity of the accommodations a person has to make, increase across the three structures. Second, the stem and joint family structures, but not the nuclear structure, provide support and care for the oldest generation. In cultures with the nuclear family ideal, other social institutions (e.g., Social Security) have to be developed to care for the aged. Third, the issue of *generational boundaries* is a critical one in all three family structures. By this term we mean the clarity of expectations, obligations, and behaviors of the members of each generation, e.g., grandparent, parent, grandchild. If the boundaries are firm within a family, then each person can carry out his tasks competently and with few intrusions from other family members. When the boundaries are not firm, role confusion may result. A parent may expect her child to act like a parent to her and not like a child. It is likely that generational boundaries will be put under pressure whenever several generations reside in the same household and there are no clear cultural norms concerning their behavior.

Finally, to understand the family life cycle and its impact on individuals, we must consider the culture of the family, the particular stage in the life cycle of the family, and the developmental history of each family member. In Stage III of the American family, for example, the firstborn has different socialization experiences than her younger sister. And in Stage IV of the same family, the socialization experiences of the mother will be different depending upon whether she works outside the home. We should also keep in mind that the above discussion has dealt with culturally "ideal" family types. We all know from daily experience that these ideals are not always met. We didn't discuss such important events as divorce, early parental death, or remarriage. Nor did we consider the potential effects of chronic illness, job loss, or frequent job-related moving. In subsequent chapters we deal with some of these issues.

Peers and Age Grouping: Evolutionary Considerations

From the perspective of the last quarter of a million years of human evolution (which is a relatively short time span) the emergence of child and adolescent peer groups is probably a recent innovation. Recall that the human design is that of a member in a gatherer-hunter subsistence group. These groups typically consist of about 25 men, women, and children—about four or five families—and until about 10,000 years ago nearly all our ancestors lived in this way (Lee & DeVore, 1968). It is safe to assume that about half of the group members were adults of various ages and the other half were infants, children, and adolescents. If the pre-adults were about evenly divided into males and females, i.e., if female infanticide was not widely practiced, then each group had about 5–9 boys and 5–9 girls between the ages of 0–17 years. It can be inferred, then, that few pre-adults had many same-sex, same-age peers living in their group.

Konner (1976) has written about peer groups from an evolutionary and cross-species perspective. He concluded that in all the apes and nearly all the monkeys, same-sex, same-age, pre-adult peer groups are absent. As with the gatherer-hunters, primate infants, juveniles, and adolescents are reared with and are involved with group members of both sexes and a wide range of ages. Typically, they spend their time in play and observation, usually preferring to be with those of the same sex. Konner argues that from the viewpoints of protecting the young, learning traditions and skills, and integrating members into the social group, pre-adult multi-age, heterosexual "play" groups are superior to same-age peer groups.

Adult gatherer-hunters distribute their time among family related activities, work, community, and peer involvement (Fishbein, 1976). Adult peers are typically different ages, but usually the peer group is either all male or all female. In these small groups the male and female peers are often *all* the males or *all* the females in the group.

When we compare modern urban societies with gatherer-hunter societies, we note both differences and similarities. Our pre-adults almost always form same-sex, same-age peer groups, no doubt encouraged by the structure of our schools. Our adult peer groups resemble those of the hunter-gatherers. Of course, our peer groups don't include all the males and all the females in our communities. In urban settings there are many more people to choose from, thus making it possible to form same-age, same-sex peer groups. It can be hypothesized that given a choice, pre-adults will form peer groups with those who resemble them the most. If gatherer-hunters had such a choice, they might do the same.

Peers and Age-Grouping: Cross-Cultural Considerations

Although attractive, the above hypothesis is incomplete. The factors influencing the formation of peer groups are much more complicated, and relate to the structure of the society as a whole. S. N. Eisenstadt, in *From Generation to Generation* (1956), showed that in order for a society to continue successfully over time, it must have methods to transmit its norms, values, and traditions over time. The basic fact of individual life is that it has a finite duration – everybody eventually dies. We transmit our genetic information through sexual reproduction. If our offspring survive, then we have been successful in continuing our species. We transmit our culutre to the younger members of our society. There are many methods for doing this; all involve forms of teaching and/or learning.

Central to Eisenstadt's thinking, is the distribution of *"social roles."* A social role is a general recipe or prescription for how to interact with other people in certain social contexts. Some common social roles are mother, son, teacher, pupil, political leader, judge, and religious leader. When parents are the school teachers of their children, for example, they must interact with each other differently when they are in the school context than when in the home context. Social roles are learned, and it is essential for society that these roles be filled. The way they are distributed among its members is a crucial concern for each society. One easy way to visualize this concern is to think about the ways Americans go about filling the social role of president.

For all known societies, age is a major basis for the distribution of social roles. No matter how democratic the society, certain social roles are restricted to certain 'age grades,"; e.g., the Constitution of the United States places an age minimum of 35 for president, 30 for senator, and 25 for congressman. Children must be at least 5 years old to be students in kindergarten, and in most states adolescents must be at least 16 years old to obtain a driver's license, i.e., to be a "driver," and at least 18 years to legally buy a beer, i.e., to be a "drinker." There are more subtle examples of age-graded social roles. Appropriate behavior from a 4-year-old might strike us as immature in a 6-year-old. A 16-year-old farm boy who mowed a field in an hour might be seen as lazy, whereas his 12-year-old brother doing the same would be considered a hard worker.

One basis for the existence of age grading is that social life requires a fitting between available social roles and individual capacities and interests. Most of us become keen observers of others and rapidly acquire this social knowledge. We don't expect old men to play soccer, but we might expect them to coach it. We don't expect old women to be mothers, but we do expect them to be helpful grandmothers. The psychological sophistication of people, however, is only part of the explanation of age grading of social roles. Some societies have many age grades, and others, only a few. These differences relate to the different social structures of different societies.

In essentially all societies, the most important social role is that of "full *social maturity*" or social adulthood. Eisenstadt makes a distinction here between physiological maturity and social maturity. Our evolutionary heritage and nutrition determine when the former will occur, but society determines the latter. In all societies, age is one factor determining social adulthood, but it is usually not the only factor. For example, in certain farming regions of Ireland it is not uncommon to refer to certain 40- and 50-year-old men as "boys." These are unmarried men who don't yet own a farm and are excluded from participating in the village councils. Their social role is that of a "boy" and not an "adult." This example highlights the fact that many of the major rights, privileges, and responsibilities of a society come with the attainment of social adulthood. Typically, social adults are married, have children, are economically productive, and have a political voice in their community. They may attain high political and social office as well. Thus, given the centrality of social adulthood in every society, it is crucial that the pathways for attaining this social role be clearly marked.

What do these considerations have to do with the formation of peer groups (age groups)? Eisenstadt has examined the social structure of a large number of societies, from Ancient Sparta to the Plains Indians, African chiefdoms, modern urban and rural societies. He has noted that in some societies, same-age peer groups (age-groups) are widespread and important socializing agents, whereas in others they are uncommon and unimportant. In these latter societies there are opportunities to form long-standing peer groups, and yet they don't occur. How is this explained?

His explanation is relevant to understanding our own culture. A society maintains continuity by preparing its members for all the necessary social roles and distributing these social roles among its members. Eisenstadt found that peer groups are relatively unimportant in those societies in which the family and *kin group* (e.g., aunts, uncles, cousins, grandparents) adequately prepare its members for social adulthood, and moreover, ensure that they reach this stage at a reasonable age. These are societies in which the distribution of roles and rewards is primarily based upon membership in a kin group, and not very much on the particular skills, knowledge, or abilities that a person has. Also in these societies the family and/or kin group is usually the basic economic unit; e.g., they own farms or cattle.

A child born into one of these societies, which Eisenstadt refers to as "familistic," can accurately predict his life course, barring accidents and illness. It is known approximately when he will marry, whom he will marry, how he will make a living, if and when he'll hold political office, what kind of political office it will be, where he'll live and die, and so on. During his life span most of his close associations and friendships will be with different-aged members of his family and kin group. He will learn traditions and skills from the older members and teach them to the younger ones. This will help ensure the continuity of the family, kin groups, and society as a whole.

Eisenstadt's second major finding is that age-groups are very important in those familistic societies that have an *authoritian family structure*. This means that the senior family members control the resources necessary for social adulthood and actively block or interfere with the younger members' attempts to attain that social role. We've previously given examples of this blocking in our discussions of Irish, Basque, and Norwegian farming communities. Recall that social adulthood comes with marriage and owning a farm, and that the parents typically hold off as long as possible before choosing an heir. If the young stay in the community they remain as "boys" or "girls" until they marry and become landowners. Some never reach social adulthood.

So far we've described mainly male age-and-peer groups. Baxter and Almagor (1978) point out that in societies in which age-groups are formally created, they are exclusively masculine. This exclusiveness occurs despite the fact that age plays an important part in the social lives of girls and women, and in some of these societies there are formal female initiation ceremonies. One possible explanation for this sex difference is that the girls are always intimately involved with domestic activities and typically marry near the onset of puberty. Thus they reach full social maturity at an earlier age than males and are very readily integrated into their adult social roles.

Eisenstadt's third major finding, and the one on which he places greatest emphasis, is that age-groups are widespread and important for social continuity in "nonkinship" societies. Nonkinship societies have the following three defining characteristics. One, many social roles exist independent of any particular family or kinship relationships, e.g., policeman, teacher, referee. People in these roles are expected to deal with others by different rules than those governing family relationships. That is a cultural ideal, and we all know exceptions to it, e.g., the football coach who unjustly favors his son as quarterback. Our resentment of this favoritism is caused by the fact that we expect people to act differently in their broader social roles than in their family roles.

Two, in nonkinship societies many important political tasks and roles are achieved, rather than given by membership in a particular family or kin group. Such membership may help, e.g., being a Taft, Roosevelt, or Kennedy in America, but it won't guarantee success. Three, in these societies the family or kin group is typically economically dependent on or interdependent with nonrelatives. Jobs are not completely controlled by the family or kin group. In some of these societies, some families can function more or less independently of others, but this independence is not the societal norm.

Fourth, and perhaps most central in Eisenstadt's analysis, is the observation that differences in status between members of nonkinship societies are based on such factors as wealth, occupation, political power, and individual talents and not on membership in a particular family. Underlying these status differences is the social value that the individual's personal abilities and achievements are important. We all resent the person who achieves high status based on "who he knows" instead of "what he does." This resentment is based on nonkinship principles. In familistic societies we'd expect status to be based on family ties and might resent the high-achieving "nobody."

We can see from the above that in order to reach social adulthood, attain status and rewards, and participate fully in society, one has to acquire roles regulated by and determined by the broader social system. Since the family in nonkinship societies can only inadequately prepare its younger members for social adulthood, other means must be devised to do so. All nonkinship societies have arrived at approximately the same solution—create age-groups that are regulated by the social adults. Some societies have a large number of these groups, others a few, but all have at least three, and in all of them, the groups form a status hierarchy. The three groups are, broadly speaking, "boys," "adolescents and young men," and "elders." (These categories include non-Western agrarian and modern societies.) In the Maasi, for example, the boys are not allowed to carry spears or to have sexual relations, and they are not circumcised. The adolescents and young men are circumcised, carry spears, are warriors, and are permitted to have sexual relations with unmarried girls, but they are not allowed to marry. The elders who have full adult status are allowed to marry, to become heads of a family, and to determine the ritual and political affairs of the community (LaFontaine, 1978).

Age-groups in modern societies differ in at least two ways from those in non-Western agrarian societies: There are age-groups for females, and the age-groups are not organized in the same formal ways with common initiation rites and traditions. Most modern societies contain three main kinds of age-groups: those of the schools; those of adult-sponsored agencies such as the Girl Scouts, YMCA, and Little League; and those that are spontaneously organized by individuals based on common needs and interests. The latter pre-adult groups are often not under direct adult supervision (indirectly they are in the sense that they must be law-abiding).

Eisenstadt (1956) summarizes the impact of age-groups on the individual member as follows:

> In all societies age groups are formed at the transitional stage between adolescence and adulthood, and are oriented towards the attainment and acknowledgement of the full status of their members. Through participation in the group its members develop their identity and self-evaluation, and it is terms of such evaluation that the common identification and solidarity (cohesiveness) of the group is evolved and maintained. This strong emphasis on common experience is found in every type of age group, and serves as the essential driving power for its individual members. (pp. 183–184)

Schools in the Community Context

In 1880 approximately 90% of American children between the ages of 6 and 13 were enrolled in private and public schools. Only 6% of adolescents between the ages of 14 and 17 were enrolled, and less than 2% of young adults between 18 and 21 were in college. In that same year, the high school graduating class represented only 2% of this country's population of 17-year-olds. Not only were there proportionately fewer children and adolescents enrolled in primary and secondary schools in 1880 than at the present time, but they attended class only about half as many days as do students today (Bane, 1977; Trow, 1961).

From 1880 until 1970 there was a large progressive increase in the proportion of adolescents and young adults enrolled in secondary and post-secondary programs. In 1920, about 30% of 14–17-year-olds were in high school, and 5% of the 18–21-year-olds were in college. In 1940, these percentages were 75% and 15%, respectively; and in 1970, about 95% of the 14–17-year-olds and about 45% of the 18–21-year-olds were in school.

Modell, Furstenburg, and Hershberg (1977) examined the ways that the transition to adulthood in America has differed for the years 1880 to 1970. They looked at five major events for these two periods: age of leaving school; age of entering the work force; age of leaving one's family of origin; age of marriage; and age of establishing one's own household. Consider leaving school as the start of the transition to full social adulthood, and establishing a household as the end of the transition. Adolescents in 1970 started the process about 4½ years later than those in 1880, but ended the process about 6 years earlier. Hence, the increased time that Americans spend in school today, relative to 1880, has not slowed down the transition to adulthood. We can't say it sped up the process, but most young people today do become full social adults at a younger age than did our nineteenth-century ancestors. In the transition from childhood to full social adulthood, schools have dramatically grown in importance as agencies of socialization over the last century.

Given the centrality of schools of the lives of our children, adolescents, and young adults, we should look closely at the functions they perform. It is clear that schools do much more than teach reading, writing, and arithmetic, or prepare people for careers. Norman Denzin (1977) lists a number of other functions. Schools teach political values, typically those held by their white middle-class teachers, principals, and school board members. Schools have important babysitting and caretaking functions. These functions are especially noticeable when there is a teachers' strike, and parents frantically try to find some place for their children to stay until the strike ends. Schools teach proper social etiquette, especially ways to show respect for authority. Schools teach culturally bound sex roles—certain activities are identified as appropriate for boys and others for girls. Have you ever seen male cheerleaders at female sporting events? Schools, through their typically rigid system of age grouping teach culturally bound age roles. Similarly, the choice of books and other materials also teach racial roles. The preferred role models are typically white, Protestant, and financially, politically, or militarily successful.

John Ogbu (1975) adds another major function. Schools prepare people to become taxpayers. Ogbu and others see this as having been one of the principal driving forces for the growth of schools in this country, as well as a current emphasis for upgrading the poor. If schools are successful, welfare roles will decline and profits will rise. Finally, schools teach us particular social identities—who we are, how valuable we are, how successful we're likely to be.

In order for schools to carry out their academic and nonacademic functions, community support is essential. This support must be economic, political, and moral. Let's look at the economic aspects. The voters of the Cincinnati School district during the 1970s, for example, voted down seven straight new tax levies in 10 years. They finally passed the eighth after the schools closed for lack of funds. Passage of the eighth permitted the schools to meet *minimum* state standards. Over that period of 10 years, class size increased, services decreased, and certain "fringe" programs such as art, music, and athletics were cut back. During that time span there was one teacher's strike and several threats of additional strikes. Most of the teachers in the public schools became demoralized, and many of them left the public schools to teach elsewhere or not teach at all. Then, coincidental with passage of the eighth tax levy, inflation rose substantially. Salaries that had previously been barely adequate for one person, let alone to support a family, now became clearly inadequate for either. The teachers and administrators felt unsupported by the community, and many reported that their teaching suffered. Unfortunately, the Cincinnati school story is a common one in America of the 1970s and 1980s. The details vary from district to district, and there are exceptions, but the message from the community at large to the students, teachers, and administrators is the same—"We'd rather spend our money elsewhere." Cincinnati chose to build a large, expensive new jail.

Schools are among our most vulnerable social institutions. They are public and yet not publicly owned, at least the way corporations are publicly owned. Thus, even those with a vital interest in the schools have little control over the way they operate. Many in the community have only a limited interest in their schools. The true authority structure of a school system is unclear. The teachers apparently have authority over their classrooms, but certain regulations are handed down by the principal, and course content is partially determined by the central administration. The principal is somewhat controlled by the higher administrators, who in turn are accountable to the school board. The latter are rarely academics and are usually elected by the voting adults in the community. Frequently their election is based on a single issue, such as holding down costs or circumventing social integration. It is our impression that an election is rarely based on issues dealing with educational philosophy. The net result of these circumstances is a great deal of uncertainty in responsibility for decision making and formulation of educational goals.

Lack of community moral support is most evident in relation to racial desegregation. The issue has been active since 1954 and promises to be with us for many years. In 1954 the United Stated Supreme Court ruled that racial segregation of schools inherently produces unequal educational opportunities for blacks and whites. A large number of school districts have been at least partially desegregated. And a consequence of that, some have argued, is that large numbers of white middle-class families moved to virtually all-white suburban school districts where segregation could more easily be legally justified.

The initial impact of desegration was often chaotic. Buses carrying black students into all white neighborhoods were occasionally attacked (this still existed in 1980). Once in the schools, the imported students, black or white, were sometimes shunned, threatened, or beaten. Desegregation produced a mixing of the races, and also often a mixing of social classes. Upper middle and middle SES black or white families have very different values and expectations about schools than do lower SES black or white families. Their children share these values and expectations and act upon them. In the desegregated school system John Ogbu studied, for example, many of the lower SES black families knew many black college graduates who were unable to secure jobs consistent with their education. Thus, the children often saw school as largely irrelevant to their futures, and were at best indifferent to the education offered. If a substantial portion of students are indifferent or hostile to the school, this discourages the students with more positive attitudes as well as their teachers.

The punch line is that the socialization influences of schools on students are heavily dependent upon their social context. Wealthy school districts socialize differently than poor ones. School districts in which the educational hierarchy is clear and in which the goals are consistent with those of the community are likely to be academically successful. Racially and socially integrated schools are vastly different for the students than are racially and socially segregated ones.

SUMMARY

This chapter places human development into three related contexts: evolution, culture, and socialization. Genetic evolution and learning are the two major processes by which members of a species become adapted to their environment. These processes are interrelated in two important ways. First, the evolution of a species determines the learning abilities of the members of that species. Second, the greater the learning abilities of a species, the greater the likelihood that the species can adapt to unexpected variations in the environment without undergoing genetic change. Flexibility in adaptation is greatest among the human species.

It is useful to view evolution as "designing" a species for life in particular environments. Natural selection, a weeding-out process measured by Darwinian fitness, is the primary mechanism for accomplishing this design. Evolutionary designs are generally very conservative, operating on the principle, "Keep it if you can, change it if you must." It is likely that canalization processes—a "collusion of genes"—form the basis for this conservatism. Canalization involes complex buffering mechanisms that protect developing individuals from genetic and environmental abnormalities. This ensures that all members of a species will develop on more or less the same pathways.

The effects of canalization processes can be seen in both prenatal and postnatal physical development. Presumably, teratogens have their most powerful impact on those anatomical structures entering critical periods of development. Some structures such as the arms, legs, and teeth have relatively short critical periods; whereas others, such as the central nervous system, eyes, and ears, have relaively long ones. Postnatally, there is good evidence that if abnormal external or internal environments (e.g., hormones) are not too severe or proloned, canalization processes will move development back to its normal trajectory.

Three broad classes of canalization are involved in the human design: mammalian, primate, and hominid. The most important mammalian behavior characteristic is mother-infant bonding. The most important primate characteristic is the subsistence group. In primate groups, mothers and their pre-adolescent offspring form the core of the group. Group membership is highly cohesive, and socialization occurs primarily by play and observation. The major hominid characteristic is the family. This involves food gathering by females, sharing, extensive adult cooperation, paternal hunting and involvement in their offspring, and grandparenthood.

In the discussion of culture, a distinction was made between social structure and content. Social structure refers to the ways members of a society organize themselves to accomplish important social functions such as marriage, food getting, "housing," and political leadership. Many aspects of social structures are related to the food-getting activities of a society. Two examples involved social complexity and social stratification. (1) Societies that are nomadic, don't store food, and live in small groups tend to have little role differentiation. (2) Societies that store food and live in permanent settlements tend to have many social status differences. Finally, societies in which families must engage in the long-term commitment, cooperation, and involvement of several adults for economic survival tend to have non-nuclear families

The contents of a society were defined (Goodenough, 1963) as the shared products of human learning which consist of "standards for deciding what is, standards for deciding what can be, standards for deciding how one feels about it, standards for deciding what to do about it, and standards for deciding how to go about doing it" (p. 259).

Within this framework, distinctions were made between the "private" culture of individuals, their "operating" cultures, and their "public" culture. Private culture refers to all the standards that a person has acquired in her lifetime, which she shares with at least some other people. The operating culture involves the different sets of standards we daily use in different settings, such as work, family, and play. The public culture involves those standards that nearly all members of a society are aware of and follow, especially when others are watching.

The cultural concepts were extended to include social class (SES) differences within a society. We briefly summarized Gecas' review (1979), which showed that there are substantial and persistent differences in the ways white-collar and blue-collar parents rear their children. The former emphasize individual motivation and responsibility, whereas the latter emphasize conformity and obedience.

Three aspects of socialization were discussed: family, peers, and schools. The common link among all of them is the context of social groups. In groups, individuals pursue four social needs – to be included, to exert some power or control over others, to give and receive affection, and to maintain a sense of self-esteem.

In discussing the American family, distinctions between "family of origin," "family of procreation," and family of our children" are made. That is, we are reared in one family, form another when we reproduce our own children, and our children in turn start their own family when they marry and perhaps have children. Chinese males spend life in only one family, living with grandparents and parents, brothers, and offspring. Chinese females have two families, the one they're born into, and the one they marry into. In Japan, the eldest male stays in one family his entire life; his youngest brothers have two families, the one they're born into and one they create when they marry; and females have two families, the one they're born into and the one they marry into. Most non-Western cultures have family types similar to those of either China or Japan. The ways families socialize us are profoundly influenced by the cultures we're born into.

Peers and families are two of the most important groups for transmitting the norms, values, and traditions of a culture over time. For gatherer-hunter groups and most nonhuman primate groups, peer groups rarely consist of same-sex, same-age individuals. In most urban societies peer groups have uniform age and sex membership. However, peer groups do not play a major socialization role in all societies. S. N. Eisenstadt (1956) has analyzed the latter issues and has divided societies into either "familistic" or "non-familistic" types. In familistic societies the social roles a person will acquire are determined mainly by the family and kin group. Those familistic societies that are further characterized by an authoritarian family structure (e.g., father makes all the major decisions), do have significant peer groups. In nonfamilistic societies individuals acquire social roles based on their own abilities and interests. In these societies peer groups are major socializing influences.

In the United States the proportion of adolescents enrolled in school has increased from 6% in 1880 to more than 95% in 1970. The socializing functions of schools have increased in importance. Norman Denzin (1977) points out that typically schools teach the political values of their white middle-class teachers, principals, and school board members. They teach particular ways to respect authority and particular culturally bound sex roles and racial roles. Wealthy school districts socialize children differently than poor ones. Segregated and integrated schools also socialized differently.

3 Personality Development

This chapter considers three related topics: Attachment; Development of personal identity; and Self-esteem. In the second chapter of this book we wrote about the individual's four basic social needs: to be included in significant groups, to have control over important resources, (including self and others), to be affectionate toward others, and to maintain self-esteem. The development of attachment with family members appears to be at the core of meeting these needs. The growing infant learns that he or she is closely connected with two or more adults in a stable family group, gives to and receives affection from them, exerts some control—for example, either by crying to bring them near, or by moving toward them to accomplish the same goal—and starts to develop a personal identity or sense of self that forms the basis of maintaining self-esteem.

What is personality (or the self)? First, it is an integrated collection of conscious and unconscious characteristics that the individual "knows" about him or her "self." Erikson (1963) describes these characteristics as being comprised of three dimensions; ways of consciously experiencing, of behaving, and unconscious inner states. Second, these characteristics influence the kinds of activities or interactions in which the individual will engage. For example, a child *confident in her athletic abilities* (a characteristic of the self) will likely participate in sports. Third, the self is constantly developing, more rapidly earlier than later in life, but never without change. Fourth, the sense of self primarily develops through interactions with other people. That is, the characteristics that we identify as being part of our "selves" are primarily those characteristics that get highlighted in our dealings with others. For example, if others treat us as competent in our self-initiated undertakings, we come to attribute "competence" as a characteristic of ourselves.

From both evolutionary and cultural views, the natural starting point for understanding personality development is infants' attachments to their caretakers. The major social outcome of caretaking man is the integration of the infant in the group. In humans the group consists of the immediate family as well as friends and relatives. In nonhuman primates, it is the subsistence group. Integration into the group means the learning of age, sex, and role-appropriate interdependence among members. These are all aspects of the self-concept. No one stands alone or is independent; rather we are constantly influencing and being influenced by the other members. For groups to function effectively and nourish their members, each person must know the rules of successful interaction. Individuals who have difficulty here are often shunned by their peers and may develop low self-esteem as a consequence.

In some cultures the infant may have two or more primary caretakers, e.g., mother and father. Group integration is almost always a two-stage process. First the infant and primary caretakers become mutually attached and stay in close proximity; second, they start to disengage, and the infant is encouraged to form attachments with other group members. The ways in which the first stage (caretaker-infant attachment) is accomplished appear to have important effects on how the second stage develops. Thus, successful integration into the group depends upon the nature of the infant's first attachments.

ATTACHMENT

Two of the pioneers in the study of attachment behavior are Harry Harlow, with monkeys, and John Bowlby, with humans. In large part Harlow started his research with monkeys because they have close behavioral similarity to humans, but he had freedom to perform experiments that were legally and morally impossible to carry out with humans. In his early research infant monkeys were either reared alone in cages or with "surrogate" inanimate mothers for periods varying from 3 months to a year. Experiments showed that infants raised with both a wire mother who "gave" milk and a cloth one who did not spent almost all their non-nursing time on or near the cloth mother. Other research found (1) that these infants became depressed when their cloth mother was removed; (2) that "her" presence gave them the courage to explore strange environments; and (3) that infants received comfort from their cloth mothers when frightened (Harlow & Mears, 1979).

These three characteristics – an intense emotional tie with caretakers, the use of caretakers as a secure base for exploration, and the comfort received from them when frightened – are also the defining characteristics of human attachment in infancy and early childhood. As the child matures and develops a partially independent social life, the caretakers are not needed as a secure base for exploration. As children and adolescents develop intense peer relationships, they typically turn toward peers rather than parents for comfort from fear. However, middle-aged men and women still turn to their parents in times of crises, e.g., illness of a child, divorce, loss of a job. The intense emotional ties we had with our caretakers during infancy usually stay with us during our lifetimes, even after those caretakers have died.

John Bowlby's work (1952, 1969) drew heavily from Harlow, the research of other primate investigators, and his studies with infants in orphanages and hospitals. He attempted to integrate evolutionary and psychoanalytic frameworks. One of the outcomes of the Bowlby-Harlow efforts has been the systematic study of nonhuman primate attachments with natural mothers in group-living situations and that of nonhospitalized, nonorphaned human infants and children in the home and in the laboratory. Following the lead of Harlow and Bowlby, we believe that the study of nonhuman primates enriches our knowledge of human attachment.

Attachment Between Monkey Infants and Mothers

In this section we focus on the research of R. A. Hinde (1977) and L. A. Rosenblum (1971). Both sets of research deal with mother-infant relations for monkeys living in laboratory settings in groups consisting of a single adult male, two or more adult females, and their offspring. Hinde worked with rhesus monkeys, the same species studied by Harlow, and Rosenblum worked with pigtail and bonnet monkeys.

The infant monkey at birth is not quite so helpless as its human counterpart, but nevertheless needs some help during the first weeks of life from its mother to cling to her chest and to find the nipple to nurse. After this short period, the infant is able to hold on without assistance, to readily find the nipple, and to start walking on all fours.

During the first 2 weeks of life, rhesus infants are always in contact with their mother. From 2 weeks until about 3 months of age the proportion of time the infant is off its mother dramatically increases and stabilizes at about 70%. Hinde says that even when infants are 1 year old, they spend about 30% of their time on their mother. During the period 2 weeks to 3 months of age, the infant spends increasing amounts of time out of its mother's reach.

What produces these changes? During the first 2 months of life, the mother rarely rejects her infant's attempts at physical contact, is largely responsible for maintaining contact, and seeks contact about as frequently as the infant seeks contact with her. Thus during the first 2 months of life, infants initiate the increasing distance from their mothers. From about age 2 to 7 months however, the mother increasingly rejects her infant's attempts to seek and maintain contact. Thus, the mother is pushing infant away, and her infant is trying to stay close. During this period of increasing maternal rejection, the mother-infant relationship becomes tense and the infant frequently has tantrums.

Hinde next turned his attention to the effects of social context on the separation of infants from their mothers. In these experiments four separation procedures were compared, all separations lasting 13 days: (1) The mother was removed from the group and isolated while the infant stayed with the group; (2) the infant was removed and isolated while the mother remained with the group; (3) both the infant and mother were removed and isolated from each other; and (4) both the infant and mother were removed from the group, but were not separated from each other. During the separation phase of the experiment the behavior of the infants in the different groups was dramatically different. Infants who remained with their mothers, but separated from their group, were little affected by the change. Infants who remained with the group, but their mothers separated, were very agitated on the first day of the separation, became depressed shortly thereafter, and stayed depressed for the remainder of the separation period. Infants in the remaining two conditions oscillated between extreme agitation and depression throughout the entire separation period. Thus, for rhesus infants, separation from their mother is not compensated for by remaining in the group. In fact, group life without mother has a very depressing effect.

On being reunited with their group, infants who had remained with mother were quickly reintegrated. During the first several weeks after reunion they spent a tremendous amount of time playing with their peers, and showed little agitation and no depression. The infants who remained with the group but whose mothers were removed stayed depressed and agitated for several weeks following the return of their mothers, who spent most of their time at reunion trying to reintegrate themselves into the group. The preoccupation of these mothers with their peers led to frequent rejections of infants' attempts for contact with them. The behavior of these mothers is very different from those mothers who remained with the group, but whose infants were separated. On reunion, the "stay-at-home" mothers were even more attentive than during the immediate pre-separation period, and as a consequence, their infants were rapidly reintegrated into the group and showed little agitation and depression. The infants from the experimental condition in which infants and mothers were removed from the group and isolated from each other showed a fair amount of agitation at reunion, but no depression. This was the case despite the fact that their mothers were preoccupied with reestablishing contact with other adults, and frequently rejected their infants' attempts for contact. The fact that these infants did not get depressed seems to be related to the observation that on reunion they spent a great deal of time reestablishing contact with their peers.

What can we conclude from the Hinde experiments about the effects of a brief separation on the infants' behavior? First, brief separations from the social group have little impact provided that the infant and mother stay together. Second, when infants are separated from their mothers, the speed of their recovery from distress depends upon the mothers' behavior. If the mothers accept the infants' attempts for contact, recovery is rapid: if the mothers reject attempts, recovery will be slow. Third, peers of the previously separated infants may help speed recovery, depending upon whether the infant had been separated or remained with them during the period it was separated from mother.

Rosenblum's work with pigtail and bonnet monkeys (who produce very different social systems) nicely complements Hinde's. These studies show that both mother-infant relations and the social organization of the group have a profound influence on the development of attachment and the effects of separation. Pigtail infants, who are raised by a highly protective, punishing mother who restricts their contacts with other adults, become strongly attached to her. During brief separations, they are profoundly distressed by mother's absence and do not seek contact with other adults. Infants raised by the more permissive, less rejecting bonnet mother who permits, and perhaps encourages contacts with other adults, will become less strongly attached to their mothers. During brief separations, they will be mildly distressed by mother's absence, and will seek and maintain contact with other adults.

The child-rearing practices of pigtail monkey mothers are consistent with a group social structure that permits physical and social contacts primarily along family lines. The single, adult, mother-headed family is the basic subunit of these groups; hence, when the mother is absent, the subunit tends to fall apart and infants are stranded. The bonnet monkey child-rearing practices are consistent with their group social structure. The group as a whole tends to be the subunit, especially after the infants are older than 2 months. Thus, no single adult female is necessary to hold the group together, and infants will form attachments with several adults.

In considering the Hinde and Rosenblum research together, it is important to understand that the effects of maternal child-rearing practices are influenced by both the mother and the social context in which child rearing occurs. The group influences the mother-infant pair, and the pair influences the group. We must keep this in mind when we study human parental child attachments.

Methodology in the Study of Human Attachment

Ainsworth, Blehar, Waters, and Wall (1978) have devised a procedure, called "The Strange Situation Procedure," which has been widely used by others to measure the strength of attachment between the infant and its caretakers. This procedure involves a fixed sequence of eight episodes in which the behavior of mother and infant can be assessed. Table 3-1 summarizes it. As can be seen, the eight episodes involve comings and goings of mother (or caretaker) and the stranger from the experimental setting for periods of about 3 minutes.

During all this time, one or more trained observers are watching from behind one-way mirrors, keeping records of the behavior of the infant. After the experimental session ends, these records are given to other experimenters who score them for type of attachment.

Types of Attachment

Ainsworth et al. (1978) examined the records of a large number of white, middle-class 1-year-olds and identified three major types of infant attachment to mother. The identification of these patterns was no small task. There are eight episodes in the Strange Situation, and each episode involves up to 24 separate scores. Other researchers have found the attachment types to be reliable and useful, and thus, the employment of these types in describing attachment research is widespread.

The first type Ainsworth calls Group A; their behavior in the Strange Situation is characterized by avoidance and anxiety. About 15% of the

TABLE 3.1
Summary of Episodes of the Strange Situation

Number of Episode	Persons Present	Duration	Brief Description of Action
1	Mother, baby & observer	30 secs.	Observer introduces mother and baby to experimental room, then leaves.
2	Mother & baby	3 min.	Mother is nonparticipant while baby explores; if necessary, play is stimulated after 2 minutes.
3	Stranger, mother, & baby	3 min.	Stranger enters. First minute: Stranger silent. Second minute: Stranger converses with mother. Third minute: Stranger approaches baby. After 3 minutes mother leaves unobtrusively.
4	Stranger & baby	3 min. or less[a]	First separation episode. Stranger's behavior is geared to that of baby.
5	Mother & & baby	3 min. or more[b]	First reunion episode. Mother greets and/or comforts baby, then tries to settle him again in play. Mother then leaves, saying "bye-bye."
6	Baby alone	3 min. or less[a]	Second separation episode.
7	Stranger & baby	3 min. or less[a]	Continuation of second separation. Stranger enters and gears her behavior to that of baby.
8	Mother & baby	3 min.	Second reunion episode. Mother enters, greets baby, then picks him up. Meanwhile stranger leaves unobtrusively.

[a]Episode is curtailed if the baby is unduly distressed.

[b]Episode is prolonged if more time is required for the baby to become re-involved in play.

(Source: Ainsworth, M., Blehar, M., Waters, E., & Wall, S. *Patterns of attachment.* Hillsdale, N.J.: Erlbaum, 1978.)

Ainsworth sample were typed as "anxious-avoidant," approximately evenly divided among males and females. What are the behaviors most characteristic of these infants? When the mother returns to the room in the reunion episodes, the baby avoids closeness to and interactions with her. Typically these babies either ignore the return of their mothers or casually greet her. When mother leaves the room during the separation episodes, they show little or no distress. Most show no distress when the stranger is present. Thus, any distress they show comes from being alone, and not by being left by mother. These babies generally don't seek closeness or contact with their mothers. When mothers initiate contact, they don't resist it, nor do they attempt to maintain it. Play behavior is little affected by the presence or absence of mother or the stranger, except when the infant is left completely alone. In general, the baby reacts to the stranger and mother in very similar ways.

About 70% of the sample was typed as Group B, "securely attached." These babies treat the stranger and mother very differently. They generally attempt either to have contact with their mothers or to be close to them. When mother returns, they give her more than a casual greeting, and either move toward her or cry and smile. When with mother, they rarely avoid or resist contact with her; and when they are in contact, they try to maintain it by either resisting being put down or protesting when put down. These babies may or may not have friendly interactions with the stranger, but when mother leaves, they are distressed by her absence, and not only by being alone. The stranger can provide some comfort, but not nearly as much as mother.

About 15% of the sample was typed as Group C or "anxious-resistant." Of the three types these babies cry the most frequently and explore the least. They are called "resistant" because relative to other infants they most actively resist the efforts of the stranger to make contact in the pre-separation and separation episodes, and often resist contact with and interaction with mother at reunion. Their behavior is puzzling because they also show strong tendencies to seek contact and proximity with mother and to maintain this contact. Sometimes resistance to contact and contact seeking are shown at the same time, as when following reunion, the infant approaches mother, is picked up and then struggles to get down. These babies are described as being either angrier than those of the other groups, or as being more passive.

We've already noted that this classification system is a reliable assessment of a 1-year-old's attachment to mother; different experimental

researchers agree on classifications of infant behavior. An equally important issue deals with the stability of an infant's attachment over time. The
notion of stability is a tricky one to evaluate, as discussed in Chapter 1.

Three recent studies have a bearing on this question. Two of them, by
Connell (1976) and Waters (1978), tested white middle-class infants from
stable families in the Strange Situation at 12 and 18 months. Both
researchers focused on babies' interactions with mothers and strangers in
order to classify them into attachment types. When overall *patterns* of
interactions were looked at, Connell found that 81% of the infants and
Waters found that 96% of them were classified into the same attachment
types at 12 and 18 months. Thus, despite changes in the specific ways
infants sustain their attachment – they often substitute one behavior for
another – the nature of their interactions with mother changes little in
this time period. These results clearly indicate that in stable environments, mother-infant attachment is a stable characteristic.

What happens in unstable environments? Vaughn, Egeland, Sroufe,
and Waters (1979) evaluated the stability of attachment type at 12 and 18
months for a large number of mother-infant pairs who were living in pov-
erty and changed residences frequently. In addition, all mothers were
single parents. Thus, these infants were raised in stressful, unstable
circumstances.

At 12 months of age, 55% of the babies were categorized as securely
attached, and the remainder evenly distributed between anxious-
avoidant and anxious-resistant. At 18 months, 66% were classed as
securely attached, and the remainder unevenly distributed between the
anxious types. Thus, the overall trend was for these babies to become
more securely attached as they matured. However, 38% of the infants
were classified differently on the two occasions, a much larger percentage
than in the Connell and Waters studies.

At the time of the second testing, mothers were asked to fill out a questionnaire that assessed frequency of stressful events during the previous
6 months. It was found that (1) babies who were securely attached at both
time periods had mothers who had experienced the least amount of
stress; (2) infants who had been securely attached at 12 months but
became anxiously attached by 18 months had the most stressed mothers;
and (3) babies who shifted from anxious to secure or were anxious at both
sessions had mothers who experienced an intermediate amount of stress.

We can conclude from the above three studies that an infant's pattern
of attachment is highly stable between the ages of 1 and 1½ years, pro-

vided that the infant has been reared in a relatively stable environment. Attachment, however, involves interactions with mother, and if she is under stress, the nature of the attachment may change.

Maternal Behavior and Infant Attachment

The present section deals with the relationship between mother's behaviors at home and infant's attachment behavior in the Strange Situation. There are two major studies bearing on this question, by Ainsworth et al. (1978), and Clarke-Stewart (1973). Ainsworth et al. discuss observations of mother during the first 3 months after the birth related to infant's behavior in the Strange Situation at 12 months. There were four major categories of mother's behavior: (1) *responsiveness to infant crying*, which includes how frequently mother ignores infant's crying; (2) *behavior relevant to close bodily contact*, which includes how long, affectionately, and carefully mothers hold infants, as well as how pleasant holding is for both; (3) *behavior relevant to face-to-face interaction*, whether mother is silent and unsmiling, in a "matter-of-fact" way, and gauges her responses to infant's behavior; and (4) *behavior relevant to feeding*, mother's sensitivity to baby's food preferences, pacing intake, knowledge of, and amount of feeding.

There were dramatic differences between mothers of securely attached and anxiously attached (resistant and avoidant) babies in all four categories. The former group of mothers soothe their crying babies more quickly, hold them longer, more affectionately, tenderly, and competently. They and their infants enjoy the holding experience more than mothers of anxiously attached babies. In face-to-face interactions, mothers of securely attached babies are less routine and more sensitive to their infants' behavior. Finally, in all measures dealing with feeding, these mothers are more knowledgeable of and sensitive to their babies.

Clark-Stewart (1973) studied the relationship between three categories of maternal behaviors assessed when the babies were 11 months old and their attachment behavior in the Strange Situation when they were 12 months old. Clark-Stewart labels the three maternal categories as *Expression of positive emotion, Contingent responsiveness*, and *Social stimulation*. There is no one-to-one correspondence between these categories and those of Ainsworth et al., although there is substantial overlap. The category of positive emotion includes affectionate holding, smiling, touching, and praising her infant. The category of responsiveness consists of responsiveness to crying, gauging face-to-face interaction, and being sensitive to the infant's needs. Social stimulation includes mother's holding and talking to the infant as well as playing with toys. Clark-Stewart found that mothers of securely attached infants were more responsive, socially stimulating, and affectionate than were those of anxiously attached infants.

The Ainsworth et al. and Clark-Stewart studies provide a very consistent picture of the kinds of maternal behavior that are associated with securely and anxiously attached infants. Mothers who enjoy interacting, are affectionate and responsive to their babies' needs and desires, have securely attached babies. Mothers who tend to be rejecting, emotionally indifferent, and insensitive to their babies' needs have anxiously attached infants. Mothers who are physically and emotionally available when they are needed have securely attached babies. Anxiously attached babies have mothers who are not so available physically or emotionally.

The Effects of Day Care on Attachment

Increasing numbers of women are working full time outside of the home and leaving their infants in the care of others. We have seen that the ways mothers interact with infants profoundly affects the nature of the infants' attachments to them, and we will see that the nature of infants' attachment to mothers can have marked effects on their subsequent social and cognitive competence. In light of these findings, it is important to determine what the effects are of day care.

Before continuing, an evolutionary framework is noted. Previously we stated that for 99% of human existence, we lived as hunters and gatherers in closely knit subsistence groups. Child rearing was a responsibility of family and nonfamily group members. Until they were about 3 years old, infants were nearly always with their mothers but not isolated with her. There were many caretakers. Socialization by the group and the continual presence of the mother are patterns shared by most primate species.

The North American (and Western industrialized) patterns of child rearing are generally quite different from the hunter-gatherer pattern. Infants with mothers who are not employed outside the home are nearly always at home with them, though not necessarily in the same room. It is relatively rare for these infants to be consistently involved with the same group of nonfamily adults and children. Infants with mothers working outside the home may spend a great deal of time with the same group of nonfamily members, but rarely in the presence of either their mother or father. Further, these infants spend far less time with their mothers than do infants of homemaker mothers. Thus, the typical homemaker mother-infant pattern conforms to some aspects of the hunter-gatherer pattern and the outside-of-home working mother-infant pattern conforms to other aspects. If the hunter-gatherer pattern is the species ideal, then neither pattern fits.

Returning more directly to the research bearing on day-care effects, two cautions must be noted. First, there are no published studies dealing with long-term effects of day care. Nearly all compare groups of infants/children at a particular point in time with no follow-up. So, if there were dramatic short-term effects, we would not know how long-lasting they were. Second, nearly all the studies involve very small numbers of children, typically 10–20 per group. If we were dealing with a very simple question, this small group size wouldn't be a problem. But with complex questions, and small groups, only part of the question can be addressed in any one study.

Three recent experiments compared home-reared and day-care infants under 25 months of age in the Strange Situation. Brookhart and Hock (1976) and Blanchard and Main (1979) tested infants from two-parent middle-class families. Vaughn, Gove, and Egeland (1980) tested infants from economically disadvantaged, predominantly single-parent families. Taken together, these studies indicate that there are no persistent or systematic negative effects on infants' attachment behavior. Vaughn et al. (1980) indicate that infants placed before their first birthday are more avoidant, but Blanchard and Main's results indicate that this avoidance stems partially from the short period of time they had been in out-of-home care. It takes about 6 months to adapt to life away from mother, and until that adjustment is completed, infants may suffer in their social-emotional development. Finally, the infants in the Vaughn et al. study were not placed in high quality day-care centers. Indeed, there is some suggestion from recent research by Rubenstein and Howes (1979) that infants placed in high quality day-care are more socially adept with peers than comparable home-reared infants.

Three recent studies compare the effects of day-care on attachment of older children, between 30 and 42 months of age. Moskowitz, Schwarz, and Corsini (1977) compared children of varying economic backgrounds and family structures. Portnoy and Simmons (1978) and Rogozin (1980) compared children from middle-class, two parent families.

It seems clear from these studies that attachment behavior to mother, as measured by the Strange Situation, is little affected by enrollment in day care. When negative effects have been found, it is reasonable to assume that they were attributable to temporary stresses produced during the transition into day care. Some studies show that day care experience is associated with a lack of interest in the stranger. It is not clear what accounts for this tendency, which might indicate anxiety or adaptation to strangers.

Attachment and the Development of Social Competence

At least five recently published studies deal with the relationship between attachment in the Strange Situation and subsequent social behavior with peers or adults. On the surface, it seems that we are looking at the consequences of early attachment to mother. But surface appearances may be misleading because an infant's early attachment is highly related to later attachment, which is probably related to lots of other mother-infant interactions. Affectionate, responsive, socially stimulating mothers of 12-month-old infants probably remain that way when their infants are older. So, despite the fact that we will discuss consequences of early attachment, keep in mind the likelihood that the bases of the early attachment are still in operation later on between the mother and infant.

The studies by Louderville and Main (1981), Matas, Arend, and Sroufe (1978), and Pastor (1981) measured attachment behavior in infants from lower- or middle-class families when they were between 12 and 18 months old. Between 6 and 9 months later, their social behavior with adults and peers, as well as motor skills, verbal development, and problem-solving-skills were measured. In all three studies infants who had been scored as securely attached performed in more socially and intellectually mature ways than those previously scored as anxiously attached. For example, the securely attached interact with their mothers and other adults in more obedient, cooperative, socially appropriate ways. Their play is more imaginative, and their problem solving more enthusiastic and task-oriented. They show more self-control. In two of these studies, verbal and motor skills were also better developed in the securely attached infants than in the anxiously attached ones. Thus, the short-term effects of a secure attachment to mother (attachment to father wasn't measured) appear to be very positive.

Two studies examine the relationship between attachment behavior at 15-18 months and social competence at 3½-5 years. Waters, Wippman, and Sroufe (1979) compared white middle-class infants classified as either securely or anxiously attached at 15 months of age on their rated peer competence and "ego strength" in a preschool classroom at age 3½ years. The attachment classifications were based on a situation similar to the Strange Situation. The classroom ratings were made by two independent raters, based on 5 weeks of observation.

There were 12 items concerned with peer competence. They included such characteristics as social withdrawal, suggestion of activities, and sympathy with peers' distress, and generally how much skill, initiative, and engagement children have in interactions. There were also 12 items concerned with *ego strength*: i.e., how self-directed, curious, confident, goal-directed, and persevering a child is. These were somewhat independent of peer interactions. The results were dramatic. On 11 of the 12 peer items the securely attached were rated as more competent than children classified as anxiously attached. On 5 of the 12 ego strength items, the securely attached scored higher than the anxiously attached. Thus, after a 27-month gap, and in markedly different situations, children who had earlier been assessed as securely attached were much more competent with peers and had greater ego strength than anxiously attached infants.

Arend, Gove, and Sroufe (1979) studied nursery school and kindergarten behavior of half the children from the Matas et al. (1978) experiment. In this study, the children were 5½ years old. Three kinds of measures were made of the children's behavior: ego resiliency, ego control, and curiosity. Ego resiliency is "the ability to respond flexibly, persistently, and resourcefully especially in problem situations." Ego control refers to the ability to be spontaneous, to delay gratification, and to act with a balance between impulse and overcontrol. Ego control and ego resiliency were assessed by teachers' ratings and performance on laboratory tasks. Curiosity was assessed with a laboratory task that measured time a child played with a novel toy, number of objects manipulated, and how frequently they were manipulated.

On both the teacher ratings and laboratory tasks, the children previously classified as securely attached were more ego resilient than the anxiously attached children. There were no substantial differences between the two groups on the ego control measures, although teachers tended to rate the securely attached as having more appropriate ego control than those children previously classified as anxiously attached. On all measures of curiosity, the securely attached scored higher than the anxiously attached children. Thus, after 4 years and in very different contexts, children previously classed as securely attached were found to be more curious and resilient in problem-solving situations than the anxiously attached.

The concluding statement by Arend et al. (1979) is a suitable summary of this section:

> At 18 months, the competent infant has established an affectively positive relationship with its caregiver, being active and effective in finding comfort when needed and using the caregiver as a secure base for exploring and mastering the world of objects. At 24 months, the competent toddler still maintains the positively-toned reciprocal relationship with its caregiver; confronts problems enthusiastically and persistently; finds pleasure in mastery; and, while in general functioning much more independently, willingly responds to and can secure caregiver resources when needed. The competent preschooler is enthusiastically involved with school tasks and peers; is (affectively) expressive in situationally appropriate ways; and is organized, persistent, and flexible when encountering problems and stress. (p. 958)

Attachment to the Father

In this section we are concerned with the growth of attachment to father and mother for the age range 6 to 30 months. Several issues concerning method are noted. First are the effects of testing in the home versus in the laboratory. As noted previously, one has to be cautious when generalizing about laboratory findings. Bowlby (1969) and Ainsworth et al. (1978) believe that attachment behaviors are triggered in times of stress. Since the home is less stressful for an infant than the laboratory, different patterns of results may emerge in these two situations. Another issue deals with the distinction between attachment and affiliative behaviors (Lamb, 1976a). Affiliation social behaviors occur at a distance: e.g., smiling, looking, talking, showing, or pointing. They are independent of physical contact. Attachment is social behavior that occurs close up – approaching within arm's reach, touching, reaching to be picked up, clinging, or holding on. Attachment, but not affiliative behaviors, is assumed to reduce stress. If the two are different, as Lamb argues, then different response patterns may be observed under different levels of stress. Ainsworth et al. (1978), on the other hand, view these two classes of behavior as reflecting different qualities of attachment, and not as distinctive kinds of social behavior.

The largest of the laboratory experiments was carried out by Kotelchuck (1976) with different groups of infants aged 6 to 21 months. The infants were exposed to 13 different episodes of father, mother, or stranger alone and in combinations in a modified Strange Situation procedure. Kotelchuck focused on the effects of the departure of an adult on the infant's play, crying, searching, and touching.

For all measures there were essentially no differences in the infant's behavior at 6 months and 9 months as a function of who left the room, which implies that in this situation they showed no attachment preferences to mother, father, or stranger. A clear pattern emerged at 12 months; infants showed most distress when their mother left, next for father, and relief when the stranger left. For example, play increased, but crying decreased when the stranger left, with the opposite holding when mother or father left. All the attachment measures were at a maximum at either 15 or 18 months, and all showed a decline thereafter. Nevertheless, at 21 months there were still clear differences in attachment toward each of the three adults.

The study by Cohen and Campos (1974) with 10-, 13-, and 16-month-old infants of white middle-class families attained results consistent with Kotelchuck's. Feldman and Ingham (1975) extended them by testing 1- and 2½-year-old infants from white middle-class families. For the 1-year-olds, greater attachment was shown toward the mother than toward the father, but for the 2½-year-olds the two were equivalent.

From these laboratory studies it can be concluded that in the age range 6 to 9 months, infants show no attachment preferences for parents or stranger. By 10 months they prefer mothers to fathers, and fathers to strangers. These differences reach a maximum between 15 and 18 months and decline thereafter. By the time infants are 2 years old, their attachment behaviors toward parents are essentially the same, both being preferred to strangers. It should be noted that these conclusions are based on group averages, and that in every experiment, some 10-month-old infants prefer their fathers to their mothers.

Is there a difference between affiliation and attachment? Lamb's research concerns the development of affiliative and attachment behaviors (Lamb 1976a, 1976b, 1977a, 1977b). He compared 12-, 18-, and 24-month-old infants in the laboratory in different modifications of the Strange Situation, and 7- to 24-month-olds at home with a visiting stranger. The infants were white and from lower- and middle-class homes. Let's consider the laboratory contest first. Lamb used the following conditions: parents and child, mother or father and child, a parent, child and stranger. The last should be the most stressing for the infant because of the presence of a stranger. If, as Lamb asserts, affiliative and attachment behaviors typically occur under different levels of stress, and if infants are differentially attached to their parents, then distinctive behavior patterns should be seen in these experimental situations.

What are the results? For affiliation, with the stranger absent, 12- and 18-month-olds prefer their father to their mother, but 24-month-olds show no preference. With the stranger present, 12-, 18-, and 24-month-olds show no preference for either parent. For attachment, with the stranger absent, 12-, 18-, and 24-moth-olds show no preference for either parent. With the stranger present, 12- and 18-month-olds prefer their mother to their father, but 24-month-olds show no preference.

Lamb's (1977a, 1977b) studies involve a very passive male observer and an active female "visitor" who freely interacted with the mother, father, and infant in their home for 1½ hours. The pattern of results was different from those seen in the laboratory. For affiliation, 7- and 12-month-olds prefer father to both mother and visitor, and visitor to mother. For 15- to 24-month-olds, father and visitor are preferred to mother, and visitor tends to be preferred to father. For attachment in 7- and 12-month-olds parents are equally preferred, both more than the visitor. For 15- to 24-month-olds, father is preferred to mother and visitor, and mother is preferred to visitor.

The above set of results from the home and the laboratory supports Lamb's assertion that affiliative and attachment behaviors reflect different psychological processes. In the home, and in the laboratory with the stranger absent, which are nonstressful situations, infants affiliate more with fathers than with mothers; and this difference is found over the entire age range studied. One possible explanation for these findings is that fathers are safe, relatively novel figures and hence, very interesting to their infants. Two important age-related changes occur during this developmental period. Infants get progressively attached to their fathers and they get progressively interested in strangers and visitors. In the laboratory, which is moderately stressful with the stranger present, infants show equivalent affiliation behaviors to their parents, both greater than to the stranger.

The changes we've discussed in the infant's affiliation with their parents and attachment to them are not inevitable. We've noted that in all studies, some infants do not follow the pattern typical for their age-group. Although the nature of parent-infant interactions that leads to attachment is not completely understood, it is clear that the interaction is crucial. Kotelchuck (1976) reports data that clearly indicate that the greater the involvement of the father with the infant, the greater will be the infant's attachment to him. It is likely that were fathers to carry out the traditional maternal role, and mothers the traditional paternal role, the above patterns of results would be reversed.

Some Cross-Cultural Comparisons

Apart from being interested in the study of different cultures for their own sake, there are at least two related reasons why a psychologist would find cross-cultural data to be valuable. The first is to answer the question whether the findings obtained in any given culture are specific to it, or are general across cultures. This concern is analogous to the comparison of findings between the home and the laboratory. Each has its unique aspects that may produce unique psychological findings, and yet there are enough commalities that general findings may be obtained. For example, infants do show attachment in the home and the laboratory (general finding), but the ages at which attachment is displayed and the extent to which strangers are threatening or interesting vary between the two settings (unique findings).

The second reason for studying other cultures is that occasionally certain questions can only or can most easily be answered in particular cultures. For example, Bowlby (1969) believes that each infant initially forms a strong attachment to one individual before forming attachments to others. However, in the United States and Great Britain, the two cultures where most research has been carried out, infants are typically reared in nuclear families and taken care of primarily by a single person, the mother. There are other cultures where child care is in the hands of two or more individuals, such as the Israeli kibbutz. Will infants reared in a kibbutz show the same kind of attachment behavior as they show when reared in nuclear families?

We have located several studies dealing with infants in different cultures, which will allow us to start to generalize the attachment findings. Ideally, one would utilize the same procedures with the same-aged infants in a variety of cultures in order to be confident in making generalizations. Fortunately, this was done in two of the studies. In the third study, that of Mary Ainsworth (1963), observations were made in a naturalistic setting, somewhat analogous to Lamb's home visits. However, unlike Lamb, Ainsworth had little control over either the identity or the number of persons present when she made her observations. Thus, attachment behavior was studied within the normal ebb and flow of the lives of these infants and mothers.

Ainsworth's research occurred over a 9-month period in Uganda during 1954–1955, with members of the Ganda tribe. Her particular subjects lived in six adjacent villages about 15 miles from a large town. In the families she studied, several of the mothers were unmarried, others were part of a polygamous unit, and the majority were monogamous. All of the mothers spent mornings tending gardens in order to provide vegetables and fruits for their families. Afternoons were typically spent visiting with friends at their homes. It was at visiting time that Ainsworth made her observations and, with the aid of an interpreter, interviewed the mothers. On the average, families were visited every 2 weeks for approximately 2 hours each time. There were 26 families in all, with two sets of twins, for a total of 28 infants.

All of the infants Aisworth observed who were under 6 months old at the beginning of the study, and those who eventually showed clear attachment to their mothers, did so by 6 months of age. Twenty-three of the infants did become attached, 16 securely and 7 anxiously. Five of the infants never became attached, though one was only 3½ months old at the end of the study. The remaining 4 were between 8 and 12 months old. The proportion of securely attached infants fits very well with that typically found in the North American and British research.

Ainsworth asked the question, What factors are related to strength and security of infant attacment? Three were found. Infants who received the most care from their mothers were generally securely attached, and infants who received the least care were nonattached. Second was the extent to which mothers consistently enjoyed breast feeding as contrasted with seeing it as a duty. Third was mother's excellence as an observer of her infant. Mothers who knew their babies thoroughly and could supply lots of details tended to have securely attached infants, whereas those who could provide few details tended to have nonattached babies.

These three factors are consistent with the maternal factors Ainsworth et al. (1978) found to be related to security of attachment in North American infants. Mothers who enjoy breast feeding are likely to enjoy other kinds of interactions with baby. Further, they spend a lot of time with their infants; hence it is likely that both spend many hours a day in enjoyable interactions. Finally, mothers who know their infants well, relative to those who don't, are probably much more responsive to them. The picture we get, then, of the Ganda study is highly consistent with the picture we get of the development or attachment from white middle-class North Americans.

Lester, Kotelchuck, Spelka, Sellers, and Klein (1974) studied attachment behavior to mothers and fathers from families of the Ladino culture of Guatamala. Ladinos are Spanish-speaking people who came from Indian-European stock. The families in this experiment lived in a small city and were of low socioeconomic status. The infants were 9, 12, 18, or 24 months old. The experimental procedure was modeled after that of Kotelchuck (1976), which we have previously described. Basically the infants' play behavior, crying, closeness, and searching were observed following the comings and goings of any adult.

The results of this experiment were remarkably similar to the work of Kotelchuck (1976). Infants of all ages played more with either parent present than when alone with the stranger. Crying increased when parents departed and decreased when the stranger left. Infants stayed much closer to parents than to the stranger, and searched for departed parents, but not for the stranger. Further, as with the American data, there were few attacment differences at 24 months to the three adults, but marked differences at 18 months. There were two major discrepancies, however, between the Ladino and American data. First, in the Ladino data, unlike the American, attachment behavior to mother and father was seen with the 9-month-old infants. Lester et al. (1974) suggest that this difference stems from the fact that Ladino infants are much less frequently separated from their mothers than are American infants. The second difference was that Ladino infants were not as strongly attached to their fathers as were the American infants. Lester et al. explain this finding by noting that Ladino fathers spend much less time with their infants than do American fathers.

Fox (1977) also used a modification of the Kotelchuck procedure to study attachment behavior to mother and metapelet (caretaker) of kibbutz-reared infants. The infants were either 8–10, 12–15, or 21–24 months old. All of them had been cared for by their metapelet for at least 4 months prior to testing. In the kibbutzim, infants are brought to an "infant house" 4 days after birth, where they are placed in the care of a metapelet. Mothers may spend as much time as they desire with their infants for the next 6 weeks, but then they gradually return to work at the kibbutz. As mother spends less time with her infant, the metapelet spends more time. When they are 3–4 months old, groups of about four infants are placed under the care of another metapelet, until they enter preschool at about age 3 years. During this interval, with the exception of a daily 3-hour visiting with both parents at their home, infants are completely cared for by their metapelet. Owing to job training and maternity leave, there is a high turnover rate of the metapelets. Hence, there was some variability in the amount of time the infants had been cared for by the particular metapelet they were tested with.

This situation allows us to study attachment to adults other than parents. Attachment behavior to mother and metapelet (relative to the stranger) varied with age, as Kotelchuck had observed for mother and father. That is, there were few differences toward the three adults for 21–24-month-old infants, marked differences for the 12–15-month-olds, and small differences for the 8–10-month-olds. Fox separately analyzed infants' behavior during the separation episodes (one of the two adults departed) and during reunion. During separation, infants displayed equivalent levels of attachment to mother and metapelet, both substantially greater than toward the stranger. During reunion, however, infants showed greater attachment to their mothers than toward the metapelet, both greater than toward the stranger. It can be concluded from this study that the development of attachment in kibbutz-reared children strongly parallels that observed for American, Ladino, and Ganda infants.

We can conclude from these studies that for infants reared in environments normal for a particular culture, attachment behavior to the primary caretaker(s) will develop in very similar ways. The extent to which an infant becomes attached to any caretaker seems to be related to how enjoyable and extensive are the interactions, and how responsive the caretaker is to the infant. Who feeds and diapers the infant plays a part only to the extent that the caretaker is responsive to the infant's immediate needs. Mothers of kibbutz-reared infants spend about 3 hours a day with their infants. The metapelets distribute their time among about four infants. In addition, the infants while in the nursery spend a great deal of time with their peers. Thus, it is not surprising that kibbutz-reared infants show attachment patterns to their mother similar to those of American, Ganda, and Ladino infants.

DEVELOPMENT OF PERSONAL IDENTITY

It should be clear from the above discussion that as children become attached to parents, they are meeting important social needs and developing a sense of personal identity. In that the development of attachment and personal identity involves interpersonal interactions, we might suspect that there would be parallels between them. Our suspicion is well founded. Recall that securely attached infants have mothers who are affectionate, socially stimulating, and responsive. Anxiously attached infants have mothers lacking in these attributes. Erikson (1963) writes the following about the development of basic trust versus basic mistrust as the earliest major characteristic of a sense of identity.

> The amount of trust derived from earliest infantile experience does not seem to depend on absolute quantities of food or demonstrations of love, but rather on the quality of the maternal relationship. Mothers create a sense of trust in their children by that kind of administration which in its quality combines sensitive care of the baby's individual needs and a firm sense of personal trustworthiness within the trusted framework of their culture's life style. This forms the basis in the child for a sense of identity which will later combine a sense of being "all right," of being oneself, and of becoming what other people trust one will become. Parents must not only have certain ways of guiding by prohibition and permission; they must also be able to represent to the child a deep, and almost somatic conviction that there is meaning to what they are doing. (p. 249)

As can be seen, the maternal behaviors that lead to basic trust as a characteristic of identity are essentially the same behaviors that lead to secure attachment. The securely attached infant has parents who provide a safe refuge for exploring the world and those infants have the personal security that they can trust themselves and others in their encounters with the world.

Self-Recognition in Nonhuman Primates

In the search for evolutionary continuities of any human characteristic, it makes most sense to examine the nonhuman primates. Is there evidence of a sense of identity in any of these species? And what would be the nature of this evidence? Gallup (1977, 1979) proposed an intriguing answer to these questions. Since nonhuman primates cannot be expected to verbally tell who they are, other techniques must be employed. The most basic aspect of identity involves the distinction between one's body and the bodies of others. Each of us has a certain appearance, smell, texture, and makes certain kinds of sounds. We are able to recognize ourselves in a variety of ways. For example, when you look in the mirror, you see that it is you whom you are looking at. Mirror reflections are a great source of enjoyment and information. Gallup reasoned that an animal that can recognize itself in a mirror is one with self-awareness—at a minimum, an awareness of its own body.

What happens when a mirror is placed in front of an animal? Most species treat the mirror reflection as if it were a strange member of the same species. That is, they socially respond to the reflection in the same ways that they respond to strangers. It is very easy for trained observers to notice this. In Gallup's initial research, he took a group of wild-born preadolescent chimpanzees and put them in a cage in an empty room for 10 days. In front of the cage was a full-length mirror. Each day Gallup measured the total amount of time the animals looked at their reflection, and the relative frequency of social and self-directed responses. Self-directed responses are behaviors that use the mirror to examine and/or experiment with parts of oneself previously inaccessible through vision, e.g., making faces, blowing bubbles, grooming previously "hidden" parts of the body.

For the first 2 days the chimpanzees spent a large percentage of their time looking at themselves, producing about 10 times as many social as self-directed responses. On the third day, looking time increased somewhat, but they now gave about 2½ times more self-directed than social responses. From the fourth day onward, looking time decreased markedly, but the rate of self-directed to social responses increased further. It would appear from these data that on the third day the chimpanzees recognized themselves in the mirror, and thus demonstrated a sense of self-awareness.

At this point Gallup did something even more imaginative. He anesthetized the animals and while they were unconscious painted one eyebrow ridge and the opposite ear with a bright red, nonirritating, odorless dye. Before they awoke, he removed the mirror, so that they could not see the red spots. After they awoke, Gallup counted the frequency with which they touched the marked eyebrow and ear. He then returned the mirror and counted touches on the red spots. The chimpanzees touched these critical areas 25 times more frequently while looking at their mirror reflection than when the mirror was absent. They would frequently touch the red spots and then taste and smell their fingers. It can clearly be concluded that the animals were recognizing themselves in the mirror, and noticing changes in their appearance.

To further strengthen this conclusion, Gallup took another group of chimpanzees with no experience with mirrors and performed the red dye marking procedure. When the mirror was first presented to them their behavior was essentially the same as that of the unmarked chimpanzees on the first day of the experiment. They exhibited no behaviors that indicated knowledge that they were marked with red spots, but rather treated the mirror reflection as if it were a strange chimpanzee.

Thus far, the mirror and dye procedures have been used with at least 12 different species of New World and Old World monkeys, two species of gibbons (lesser apes), and one group or orangutans (one of the three great apes). Only the orangutans have evidenced self-recognition, and hence a sense of self. Gallup reports that he exposed one monkey to a mirror for 2400 hours over a period of 5 months, and the monkey showed no signs of self-recognition. Other researchers have placed a polished metal mirror in a monkey's cage for one year, and the animal showed no signs of self-recognition.

It can be concluded from the experiment that the sense of a body self emerges with the evolution of the great apes. It is not clear what function this ability serves in the nonhuman species, but this "higher" capacity is consistent with other capacities they have demonstrated, e.g, tool use and nonverbal language abilities. From a developmental perspective, the chimpanzee and orangutan research does not tell us the ages at which the body self-concept emerges. With humans, however, there is a great deal of work bearing on this issue.

Self-Recognition in Human Infants

The most extensive work to date on the development of self-recognition in humans has been carried out by Lewis and Brooks-Gunn (1979). Their work with mirror reflections is based on previous work by Gallup with nonhuman primates, and by Amsterdam (1972) with human infants. In addition they have introduced other procedures to study this important issue. Lewis and Brooks-Gunn detail a large number of experiments performed with infants and children between the ages of 9 and 36 months. We will highlight three of them.

The first two experiments, entitled "Mirror Representation of Self," tested children between the ages of 9 and 24 months. The procedures involved four conditions: (1) infants are placed in front of a mirror without rouge on their noses; (2) mother places rouge on her infant's nose, pretending to wipe some dirt off his or her face and places infant in front of mirror; (3) mother places rouge on her nose while infant is not looking; and (4) infants are placed in front of the mirror provided that they had looked at mother in the third condition. A number of measures were taken of the infant's behavior during all conditions. Among the most important were (a) smiling, (b) touching the mirror, (c) touching own face or body, (d) pointing to the mirror, and (e) touching or wiping own nose.

In general, the 9- and 12-month-olds performed similarly, as did the 15- and 18-month-olds, and 21- and 24-month-olds. In the rouge-on-infant conditions, nearly all the infants at all ages smiled and touched the mirror. Approximately half the infants touched their bodies or faces. Few, however, of the 9–12 and 15–18-month-olds pointed to the mirror, whereas about half of the 21–24-month-olds did so. None of the 9–12-month-olds, about 20% of the 15–18-month-olds, and 75% of the 21–24-month-olds touched or wiped their noses. Although most of the infants recognized the rouge on their mothers' nose, this had no effect on their own nose-related behavior. Finally, comparing the initial "no rouge" condition with the "rouge" condition, infants touched their faces or bodies more in the latter condition.

Lewis and Brooks-Gunn suggest that these data support the idea that the development of self-recognition can first be detected in 9–12-month-olds. In the period between 12 and 24 months, self-recognition improves substantially, which is indicated by the high level of behavior directed at the rouge on their own noses.

In the next experiment, 9- to 36-month-old infants were each exposed to three conditions. In the first, the infant sat in front of a TV screen that showed the infant his or her own behavior as it was occurring. A girl entered the room while the infant was looking at the screen, and could be seen in the screen approaching from behind. This is called the "self-contingent" condition because what the infant saw on the screen was contingent upon what it was doing at the time. In the second condition, the infant was shown a videotape of itself made 2 weeks previously, also showing a girl approaching from behind. This is called the "self-noncontingent" condition. In the third condition, the infant was shown a videotape of another infant of the same sex and age. Again, a girl was shown entering from behind. This is called the "other-noncontingent" condition.

Two comparisons are of interest here. If infants can tell the difference between themselves and others, which implies at least a minimal self-concept, then their behavior should be different in the self-noncontingent and other-noncontingent conditions. If infants can tell their behavior happening in the present from behavior that happened in the past, this implies the notion of contingency in the self-concept. If infants have this level of self-concept, then their behavior should be different in the self-contingent and self-noncontingent conditions. A curious pattern of results is seen. The 9–12-month-olds turned toward the girl much more frequently in the self-contingent than in the self-noncontingent conditions and more frequently in the latter than in other-noncontingent conditions. The 15–18-month-olds showed a similar, but weaker response tendency. For the older groups, there was essentially no difference in behavior between the three conditions. These results indicate that the dimensions of "contingency" and self-other in an infant's self-concept emerge by 12 months of age. From 12 to 24 months, these dimensions get refined and apparently stabilize.

Lewis and Brooks-Gunn interpret their results as supporting the idea that development of self-recognition is a continuous as opposed to a stage-like process. As the infant develops, he or she "adds-on" new capabilities, which build upon the old. They see the process beginning with understanding the contingency between self-initiated behavior and television "reflections" of self, continuing with the use of "reflections" to discover aspects of self, and incorporating language in conceiving of the physical self.

Gender Identity

Sigmund Freud said that "anatomy is destiny." By this he meant that the psychosexual development of individuals and their sexual identity were largely determined by sexual anatomy. He believed that males and females felt, thought, behaved, and perceived differently, primarily because of their anatomical and physiological differences, and much less so because of their socialization experiences. It is clear from Freud's writings that he acknowledged the potent effects of culture, and especially of child-rearing experiences. In fact, one of his major clinical and scholarly concerns involved sexual deviancies. He typically argued that these deviancies were produced by abnormalities in child rearing as contrasted with genetic/anatomical abnormalities.

There is no easy way to disentangle the relative contributions of anatomy and socialization to the development of gender identity and behavior. Males and females have different chromosomes and some anatomical and physiological differences. We know, also, from a great deal of research, that when physiology is changed, for instance, through hormone injections, psychology changes too. When adults undergo sex change operations not only are their extenal genitals changed, but they are given hormone injections, which enhance the psychological direction of the sex change.

The sex change operation does give us a lead towards disentangling the "anatomy" versus socialization issues for gender identity. Money and Ehrhardt (1972) have reviewed a number of cases involving infants and children in which the external genitals were changed and sex identity was reassigned. One case deals with a normal pair of genetically male twins, with normal male genitals. At 7 months of age each of the boys was circumcised using an electrical technique. For one of them, the current was too high and his penis was burned off. A plastic surgeon recommended to the parents that the boy be reassigned as a girl and received appropriate surgical treatment. When the infant was 17 months old, the parents gave him a girl's name and started dressing and rearing him like a girl. At 21 months, the first surgical step was taken to change the external genitals from male to female. At the time of publication, Money and Ehrhardt had been in contact with the family for 6 post-surgery years. During this period, the child received no hormone injections, but was treated by her family, school and neighbors as a girl. It is clear from the parents' report that the twins have very different gender identities, behaviors, and interests, both normal for their respective sexes.

All of the other cases discussed by Money and Ehrhardt involved reassignment of genitally malformed children, who had both male and female characteristics. Typically, these are children who are genetically male, but owing to hormonal problems during pregnancy developed into hermaphrodites. It is clear from their discussion that the development of gender identity is relatively independent of the child's genetic make-up, and of prenatal hormonal and early postnatal hormonal influences. If a child has male external genitals and is treated by everyone as a boy, he will grow up to be a boy with a masculine identity. Similarly, a child with female external genitals, socialized as a girl, will become a girl. There are limits to this flexibility, however. Money and Ehrhardt suggest that gender identity can readily be changed if the surgery and changes in socialization occur before the child is about 18 months old. With increasing age, it becomes more difficult to make a successful gender change.

Is anatomy destiny? Only insofar as anatomy determines how one will be socialized. There is initially a great deal of flexiblity in gender psychology. As children mature their gender identity and behavior get increasingly locked in by all the socializing influences brought to bear. By school age, it is the rare child who does not have a clear sense of gender identity, thus making successful reassignment extremely unlikely.

In the remainder of this section we discuss three aspects of the development of gender identity, as well as research dealing with its origins.

Labeling, Stability, and Constancy of Gender Identity

In this subsection, research dealing with the developent of *gender label* (e..g, "Are you a boy or a girl?"), *gender stability* (e.g., "When you were a little baby were you a little boy or a little girl?" and *gender constancy* (e.g., to a boy, "If you played with girls and girls' toys, what would you be?"). Thus, gender label refers to the child's current self-perception. Gender stability refers to the child's perceptions of previous and future gender status. Gender constancy refers to perceptions relating sex-typed behaviors, dress, and hair length to gender status.

Thompson (1975) tested white middle-class boys and girls whose average age was 2, 2½, or 3 years on gender label for self and gender label for others. On the "self" test, the children were asked whether they were boys or girls, and in addition were shown boy and girl paper cutout dolls and asked which one they were like. On the "others" test, they were shown pairs of pictures, one of a male and one of a female, and were asked to apply gender-typed labels, e.g., boy-girl, mommy-daddy, to the pictures. On the "self" test, the 2-year-olds responded at a chance level, but the 2½- year-olds and the 3-year-olds responded well above chance. On the "others" test, all age-groups responded well above the chance, with the older children scoring higher than the younger ones. Thus, it can be concluded that by 2½ years old, most white middle-class children correctly label their own gender and that of others.

Marcus and Overton (1978) studied the development of gender constancy of self and others for white middle-class children in kindergarten, first, and second grades. Four gender constancy questions were used. Kindergarteners responded at a chance level, second-graders performed with few errors, and first-graders were in the middle. Additionally, all age-groups tended to show more constancy under the self than other conditions. It can be concluded from these findings that gender constancy emerges in white middle-class children at about 6½ years of age, and rapidly improves during the next year of life.

Eaton and Von Bargen (1981) were interested in whether 2½ to 6-year-olds attain gender label, stability, and constancy for themselves before others and for same-sex before opposite-sex others. Their hypothesis was that children would see themselves as being more similar to same-sex than opposite-sex children and hence would show greater gender understanding for the former. Eaton and Von Bargan used procedures similar to those in the above studies with a group of predominantly middle-class children in day-care centers. Nearly all the children answered the gender label questions correctly, about half of them got the gender stability questions correct, and very few answered the gender constancy questions incorrectly. Within each class of questions (i.e., label, stability, and constancy) children performed better on questions concerning the self than those dealing with the same-sex other, and better on questions concerning the same-sex-other than those dealing with the opposite-sex-other. These results confirm the experimental hypothesis. Regarding gender constancy McConaghy (1979) has shown its attainment is based on the realization that gender differences are based on genital differences which don't change with development.

The above set of studies indicates that by age 2½ years, middle-class children correctly refer to themselves and others as "boys" and "girls." Within the next 2 years, they come to believe that they always have been and always will be boys and girls, but base this belief on the clothes they wear, their hair length, and their behavior. At about age 6½, they start to understand that gender differences are based on genital differences. Generally, children first gain gender understanding about themselves, next about same-sex peers, and last, about opposite-sex peers.

Sex Roles and Stereotypes and Influences on Them

While young children are learning to label themselves correctly and that their gender is stable and constant, they are also acquiring knowledge about the kinds of behavior boys and girls can and should have. Sex roles are cultural prescriptions for appropriate gender-related behavior; e.g., boys shouldn't wear dresses. Different cultures require different sex roles. Sex stereotypes are generalizations about gender-related behavior, whether appropriate or not; e.g., girls are poor mathematics students. The two concepts are closely connected, and in the research to be discussed can't be easily disentangled. Theoretically, though, we may have some stereotypes about males and females that are inconsistent with their sex roles.

Children develop an understanding of sex roles and stereotypes from parents, peers, neighbors, and television. All of these sources don't always give the same message. Further, sex roles and stereotypes are not completely agreed upon in a given culture or even in the same family. So, we might expect a fair amount of variability among children on these concepts.

In the research to be discussed, several interesting findings emerge dealing with age changes, relationships with gender stability, and the effects of having a mother working outside the home.

Kuhn, Nash, and Brucken (1978) tested a group of middle-class 2½- and 3½-year-old nursery school children on "sex role stereotypes" (we'll use this phrase from here on instead of "sex roles" and "sex stereotypes"). The children were shown paper dolls of a boy and a girl and were read statements that adults and older children had judged to be sexually stereotyped, e.g., likes to play ball, likes to play with dolls, and so on. The children pointed to the paper doll that best fit the statement. When this procedure was completed, the children were tested for gender stability.

On the average, children agreed with the adult stereotypes about two thirds of the time, which is well above chance. There were no differences in amount of stereotyping as a function of children's age or sex. However, boys and girls did not always agree about the statements that they stereotyped. For example, boys and girls believed that girls like to help their mother, but only the boys believed that girls are slow and cry sometimes. In examining the pattern of disagreement, it appeared to Kuhn et al. (1978) that girls generally believe positive things about themselves and negative things about boys, with the reverse pattern holding for the boys. It is as if, in the process of finding out who you are, you have to devalue who you are not. The final result of interest to us was the finding that there was a strong positive correlation between gender stability and amount of sex role stereotyping. Children who had a clear sense of their own gender had clear stereotypes about both genders.

Edelbrock and Sugawara (1978) studied sex role stereotypes in 3½- and 5-year-old middle-class children enrolled in nursery school. The children were shown pictures of sex-stereotyped objects, e.g., boxing gloves, needle/thread, and asked who would be more likely to use the objects, boys or girls? The major results were found to be the following: older children scored higher on stereotyping than the younger ones; children of both ages scored higher on same-sex than on opposite-sex stereotypes; and girls had more knowledge of masculine stereotypes than boys did of feminine ones. Thus, unlike the above findings, age differences in knowledge of sex role stereotypes occurs between 3½ and 5 years. Not surprisingly, and consistent with the research on gender labeling, stability, and constancy, children learn first about same-sex role stereotypes before learning about those of the other sex.

The study by Ruble, Balaban, and Cooper (1981) in part deals with an important theme raised by Kuhn, et al. (1978)–the relationship between gender stability and sex role stereotypes. The children in the present study ranged from 3½ to 6½ years. They were shown a Bugs Bunny cartoon divided by a commercial. The commercial showed either two boys or two girls playing with a Fisher-Price Movie Viewer. Following the cartoon the children were allowed to play with the viewer and a stacking toy for 5 minutes. At the end of this period the experimenter asked the children whether the viewer was most appropriate for boys or for girls. Finally, the children were given a standard test for gender labeling, stability, and constancy.

The children were divided into high and low gender stability groups based upon their performance on the stability questions. The high stability children played with the viewer much more-often when the commercial showed two same-sex children playing with it than when it showed two other-sex children playing with it. A similar pattern was found when the experimenter asked them which sex the toy was most appropriate for. For the low gender stability children, there were no differences in playing time or in their verbal judgments about the toy as a function of which children were in the commercial. Thus, the Ruble et al. experiment importantly shows that sex role-stereotyped behavior and judgments in children are markedly influenced by self-perceptions of gender stability.

The final set of studies we'll discuss deals with the effects of maternal employment oustide of the home with regard to the development of sex role stereotypes. The central hypothesis of these studies is that children whose mothers work outside the home should be less sex role stereotyped than children whose mothers are primarily homemakers. Four recently published experiments bear on this issue: Marantz and Mansfield (1977) studied middle-class girls between the ages of 5 and 11; Gold and Andres (1978), working- and middle-class 10-year-old boys and girls; Cordua, McGraw, and Drabman (1979) studied 5- and 6-year-old middle-class boys and girls; and Meyer (1980) dealt with 6- to 12-year-old working-class girls.

A partially clear picture emerged from these studies. Middle-class children with externally employed mothers are less sex role stereotyped than those whose mothers are primarily housewives. One of the studies using working-class children showed a similar effect, but the other study found no differences in sex role stereotypes between children with employed and homemaker mothers. One possible explanation for the discrepancy between middle-class and some working-class children is that the middle-class mothers tended to be employed by choice and had jobs that satisfied them. Their children would be likely to perceive female employment outside the home, and other related traditionally male activities, as being acceptable for women. The working-class employed mothers had to work to help support their families. They may often have had jobs that were unsatisfying. Thus, their children would be likely to perceive employment for women as unacceptable, and as more appropriate for men.

The above research can be summarized as follows: sex role stereotypes emerge in children as young as 2½ years, generally become stronger over the next 6 years and level off well below adult levels. In the process of learning these stereotypes, children tend to overvalue the characteristics of their own sex and devalue those of the opposite sex. For preschool children there is a strong relationship between the development of gender stability and of sex role stereotypes. Thus age is not the crucial variable in stereotype development but rather the child's gender self-concept. Finally, for middle- and some working-class families, children with externally employed mothers develop less sex role-stereotyped attitudes than those whose mothers are primarily homemakers.

How is the development of sex role stereotypes influenced? From the research by Bloch (1973) and Hoffman (1977), we learn that there are at least four major values that shape the socialization of boys and girls in our culture; (1) girls are more vulnerable than boys; (2) boys should be encouraged to independently explore, (3) boys should receive pressure to achieve, and (4) boys should learn to control their emotions. From the research by Frisch (1977) and Smith and Daglish (1977), we learn that when strange adults interact with infants who have no sense of gender identity, the adults treat the infants in sex role-stereotyped ways. But when parents interact with their own infants, they do not do this, but rather respond to them as individuals. Studies by Noller (1978) and Tauber (1979) show that after the age when children have started to develop a gender identity, both mother and father treat them in sex-stereotyped roles. However, mothers are less consistent with boys in their sex role stereotyping than are fathers, although both are consistent with girls. Finally, studies by Langlois and Downs (1980) and Lamb, Easterbrooks, and Holden (1980) in nursery school and kindergarten settings show that peers are effective in their sex role stereotyping with both themselves and with others of the same age.

Cross-Cultural Comparisons

We will briefly summarize two very important studies dealing with differences in the socialization of boys and girls across a variety of cultures.

The first, by Barry, Bacon, and Child (1957) examined anthropological field reports that included clear and consistent observations about child-rearing practices for 4- to 12-year-olds. They considered five aspects of these practices that in our culture appear to be sex role stereotyped. These are (1) obedience training; (2) responsibility training; (3) nurturance training, focused on care of younger siblings or other dependent people; (4) achievement training, focused on competition or meeting high standards of excellence; and (5) self-reliance training, focused on caring for oneself independent of help from others. The number of different cultures for which data were available for these practices ranged from 31 to 84, and included cultures from all over the world.

For each culture, and for each child-rearing practice, Barry et al. assessed whether boys and girls were clearly treated differently. The results are very straightforward. For nurturance more than 80% of the cultures placed more emphasis on girls than boys, and none placed more emphasis on boys. For responsibility, about 60% placed more emphasis on girls and about 10% placed more emphasis on boys. For obedience, the majority placed an equal emphasis on boys and girls, but of those who differed, emphasis was placed on girls. For achievement and self-reliance, more than 85% placed more emphasis on boys, and essentially none placed greater emphasis on girls.

Barry et al. next examined a large number of economic, residential and social factors that distinguished these cultures from one another. They formulated two social/economic principles to understand their findings. Where a culture places a high premium on males developing superior motor skills requiring strength—e.g., hunting large game—there will be large socialization differences between boys and girls; where a culture places a premium on highly cooperative large family groups—e.g., certain types of agriculture—there will be large socialization differences between boys and girls.

The two principles imply that despite nearly universal sex role stereotypes concerning nurturance, responsiblity, achievement, and self-reliance, societies will maximize or minimize these differences depending upon the ways their members make a living. In our society people can earn a decent income without superior motor skills and with rather flabby muscles. Nuclear families predominate, and there is relatively little difference in the socialization of boys and girls. In the Israeli kibbutz where the ideology is equality of the sexes, there is nevertheless a need for large-muscled, skilled workers and high cooperation between family groups. Not surprisingly, women are primarily assigned to traditional "women's work" and men to traditional "men's work."

The study by Whiting and Edwards (1973) is a more fine-grained analysis of sex role-stereotyped behavioral differences between boys and girls and the socialization pressures that lead to those differences. Their paper is part of Harvard's Six Culture study, which focused on the relationship between culture and psychological development. The six communities studied were located in Kenya, Okinawa, India, Philippines, Mexico, and New England (U.S.). With the exception of the North Americans nearly all the families studied ran small farms. The societies which these communities were part of varied in complexity, in average number of children per household, in the structure of the family system, and in the type of tasks assigned to children. Three of the societies have predominantly nuclear families, and three predominantly extended families in which either grandparents or married brothers or co-wives share a common household. In three of the societies, children live with their parents and are primarily reared by them. In the other three societies they are reared by close kin.

A small group of children between the ages of 3 and 11 were selected and their interactions were observed in natural settings over a half-year to one-year time period. Their behaviors were grouped into seven categories that reflect traditional sex role stereotypes. The analysis distinguished between young (3–6) and older (7–11) children. The first category, *Dependency*, includes seeking help, attention, and physical contact, and was assumed to be more characteristic of girls than of boys. It was found that in nearly all cultures young girls seek help more frequently than young boys, that younger and older girls seek physical contact more than boys, and that younger and older boys seek attention more frequently than girls. The second category, *Sociability*, includes seeking or offering friendly interactions and was assumed to be more characteristic of girls than boys. Girls tended to be more sociable than boys, but the differences were slight. The third category, *Passivity*, is complex, and includes withdrawal from aggression by peers, compliance with attempts to dominate, the absence of counteraggression with peers (e.g., hitting back), and the absence of taking the initiative in interactions. The only differences found were that older boys were more counteraggressive than older girls and that boys tended to take more initiative than girls. The latter observation is consistent with the Barry et al. findings of a difference in socialization for "self-reliance."

The fourth category, *Nurturance*, includes offering help and giving support to others. In all cultures the older girls were more nurturant than the younger boys. These differences are consistent with the Barry et al. findings. The fifth category, *Responsibility*, involves attempts to influence others to carry out socially approved behaviors that will benefit the group as a whole. Younger girls in all cultures were more responsible than younger boys, but there were no systematic differences for the older children. The differences for the younger children are consistent with the Barry et al. findings. The sixth category, *Dominance*, involves attempts to influence others to carry out behaviors that only benefit the individual attempting to dominate. In nearly all cultures younger and older boys are more dominating than younger and older girls. The seventh category, *Aggression*, includes playing rough-and-tumble, insulting peers, and initiating physical assault against others. In four of the cultures, excepting the North American and Kenyan, younger and older boys were more aggressive than younger and older girls. To the extent that dominance and aggression are one aspect of achievement socialization, these findings are consistent with those of Barry et al.

Whiting and Edwards attempt to understand this pattern of results on the basis of two factors: (1) Who do boys and girls most frequently interact with—infants, peers, or adults? and (2) What is the nature of the tasks that are typically assigned boys and girls? The two factors are obviously related. For example, if children are assigned household tasks, they will have frequent contact with adult females. In general, it was found that girls interact more frequently with adults and infants than do boys, but boys interact more frequently with peers than do girls. Regarding tasks, in four of the cultures, excepting the Kenyan and United States communities, girls were more likely than boys to be assigned child care and household tasks, and boys were more likely than girls to be assigned farm jobs.

When children interact with infants, they primarily do so in a nurturant fashion, and when they interact with adults they primarily do so in sociable and dependent ways. When children interact with peers, they primarily do so in sociable and aggressive ways. Thus, the differential nature of the tasks assigned and the differential age-groups that girls and boys interact with, lead to their being socialized in traditionally feminine or masculine ways. For example, younger boys are typically assigned no tasks. But older boys and girls are typically assigned an equal work load. Thus, it would be expected that younger girls would be more responsible than younger boys, with the difference minimized for the older children.

The Kenyan and United States findings support this analysis. In the Kenyan group, where women spend about half a day working in their gardens, boys and girls under age 10 are frequently assigned the same household and child-care tasks. In analyzing the pattern of results across the six cultures, the behavioral differences between Kenyan boys and girls were slight. In the United States culture, where boys and girls were assigned few tasks of any sort, including child caretaking responsibilities, and had nearly equal opportunities to interact with peers, there were few sex role-stereotyped behavioral differences between boys and girls, the lowest of any of the six cultures.

The above studies help us to understand the pattern of results concerning gender identity and socialization. In every culture, in order to maintain itself and to thrive, older members have to be constantly replaced by adequately trained younger ones. The training (socialization) of the younger in larger part is geared to the nature of the functions they will be expected to carry out as adults. In all societies, domestic work and child-care activities are typically carried out by women, and work requiring great stamina and strength, by men. In societies where the adult work roles are similar, there will be less pressure to differentially socialize boys and girls. However, tradition is often a heavy taskmaster, much to the discomfort, even anguish of many, and the old gender-related roles and identities are difficult to change.

The Verbal Self

In our introduction to the topic of the "self" we said that it consists of both conscious and unconscious characteristics. Probably the easiest way to learn about some of the conscious aspects is to ask people to describe themselves. These self-descriptions are called the "verbal self." Self-descriptions are not the same as consciousness of self; there are no doubt large numbers of conscious characteristics that we are unable to or don't want to put into words. This issue is especially important when we look at the development of the verbal self. Three- and 12-year-olds, for example, have very different verbal abilities, and as a consequence, different linkages between language and self-consciousness. Researchers therefore ask younger and older children different kinds of questions. The important point to remember is that whatever techniques are used, the results only partially reflect the development of the consciousness of self.

The study by Keller, Ford, and Meachan (1978) used a variety of procedures with 3- to 5-year-old white middle-class preschool children. Summing across all these, Keller et al. were able to place nearly all of the children's self-descriptions into nine categories. The most frequently used categories involved these: (1) activities they carried out; e.g., "I help Mommy", (2) references to their bodies; e.g., "I have bones all over me," (3) references to their possessions; e.g., "I like school." In general there were few age differences in the verbal self, with the activity category being the most popular. The one category that does distinguish among the different age groups is "possessions." Three-year-olds are more likely than 4- and 5-year-olds to include possessions as a characteristic of their verbal selves.

Livesley and Bromley (1973) tested English, white, working- and middle-class children. We'll focus on the five groups whose average ages were approximately 8 to 12. They were "asked to write an impression of themselves as a person, that is, to describe the sort of person they thought they were." The experimenters placed children's statements into 30 categories. On the average, each child wrote about 12 statements.

The following lists the seven most frequently used categories across all the children in the study. For example, 24% of the children state personal likes and dislikes in their self-descriptions.

Category	Percentage	Examples
Personal likes and dislikes	24%	I like school, ice cream
Personality traits and temperament	10%	Friendly, moody, bad temper
Specific behavioral consistencies	9%	Careless of appearance, can't take a joke
Interests and hobbies	5%	Collecting stamps, interest in ships
General information about the self	6%	Name, age, sex, religion
Self-evaluations	5%	Nice, rude, cheeky
Appearance	4%	Tall, pretty, nice clothes

Of particular interest is the question of developmental patterns. The most striking observation that can be made is that there were no consistent age trends across the above seven categories. For example, for "appearance" and "general information," 8- and 12-year-olds scored relatively high and the remaining age-groups relatively low. For "personality traits" and "behavioral consistencies," 8-year-olds scored the lowest,

11-year-olds the highest, and the remaining age-groups scored in the middle. And three different patterns were found for "personal likes," "interests and hobbies," and "self-evaluations." Despite this lack of consistency, it is clear from reading the children's statements that there are developmental differences. Below are four examples presented by Livesley and Bromley.

A boy age 7
"I am seven and I have hazel brown hair and my hobby is stamp collecting. I am good at football and I am quite good at sums and my favorite car is an Austin."

A girl age 7
"I am 7 years old. I have one sister. Next year I will be 8. I like colouring. The game I like is hide the thimble. I go riding every Wednesday. I have lots of toys. My flower is a rose, and a buttercup and a daisy. I like milk to drink and lemon. I like meat to eat and potatoes as well as meat. Sometimes I like jelly (gelatin dessert) and soup as well."

A boy age 9
"I am quite good tempered when I get going. I like other children. I like to play practical jokes on people and I am in the habit of forgetting things. I like rough games especially rugby. I am hurt easily and my brother always picks on me. I am a scouser (a person from Liverpool, England). I always try to make friends with other children. I dislike jokes that are meant to be funny but aren't."

A girl close to 13
"I have a fairly quick temper and doesn't take much to rouse me. I can be a little bit sympathetic to the people I like, but to the poor people I dislike my temper can be shown quite easily. I'm not thoroughly honest I can tell a white lie here and there when it's necessary, but I am trying my hardest to redeem myself, as after experience I have found it's not worth it. If I cannot get my way with various people I walk away and most likely never talk to that person again. I take an interest in other people and I like to hear about their problems as more than likely they can help me solve my own. My friends are used to me now and I don't really worry them. I worry a bit after I have just yelled somebody out and more than likely I am the first to apologise."

How can we understand these age differences? The study by Mohr (1978) offers a suggestion for bringing consistency to the above findings. Mohr's technique for finding out about children's verbal selves was to ask them how they might change under three conditions: (1) "What would you have to change about yourself for you to become your best friend?" (2) "What will (not) change about yourself when you grow up?" (3) "What has (not) changed about yourself since you were a baby?" The children tested were approximately 7, 9, and 11½ years old.

Instead of examining a large number of specific categories, Mohr scored their responses on the basis of three general categories: *external—* physical characteristics, possessions, and general information;

behavioral—specific behavioral constancies, personal likes and dislikes, interests and hobbies; and *internal*—personality traits and temperament, and self-evaluations. Mohr discovered that the same age trends occurred with all three questions. The 7-year-olds primarily used external characteristics, 9-year-olds external and behavioral characteristics about equally, and 11½-year-olds primarily behavioral and secondarily, internal characteristics. Thus, there was a developmental shift from external through behavioral to internal self-descriptions.

Using Mohr's three-category scoring procedure, we went back to the Keller et al. and Livesley and Bromley studies, and rescored their data. Since the studies used different procedures, it is not reasonable to directly compare the percentages of responses. Rather, as shown in Fig. 3.1, we present the relative strength of these categories by combining the results of the three studies. As can be seen in the figure, there are gradual changes between the ages of 3 and 8. Children primarily rely on exter-

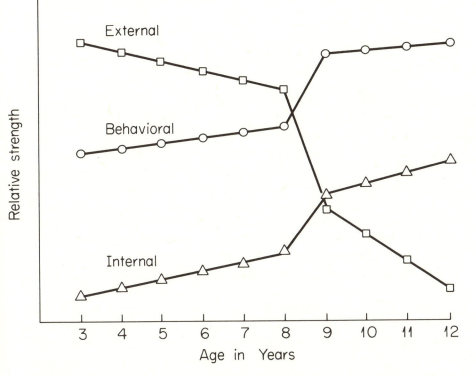

FIG. 3.1 The relative strength of external, behavioral, and internal self-descriptions with increasing age.

nal, then behavioral, and finally, internal descriptions. Between the ages of 8 and 9 dramatic changes occur in the use of all categories. At age 9, internal and external are approximately the same, both lower than behavioral descriptions. From age 10 on, gradual changes continue, with behavioral being the most common, followed by more internal than external descriptions.

Although our analyses form the basis of Fig. 3.1, we should be cautious about the specificity of the 8–9-year shift in the verbal self. It's likely that for some children the shift occurs earlier, for others, later, and for still others, the shift is more gradual. However, it is clear that somewhere in this age range, developmental shifts in the verbal self are often very rapid. Our analyses are consistent with observations made by Livesley and Bromley that children's descriptions of others undergo a rapid shift at about age 8. Further, Shantz (1975) in reviewing research on the development of social cognition also points out the importance of the age range 8–9 years. During this period children discover that in understanding self and others, appearances and labels are less important than behavior and values.

SELF-ESTEEM

Definitions, Measurement, and Stability

The present discussion is primarily influenced by the work of Stanley Coopersmith (1967), Susan Harter (1982), and Milton Rosenberg (1979). The topic of self-esteem is an old one by psychology standards, dating back to the writings of both William James at the end of the 19th century, and Sigmund Freud at the beginning of the 20th century. In the intervening years hundreds of professional articles and books have dealt with this topic. However, surprisingly little of this work has been concerned with studying the development of self-esteem in children.

There is a theoretical issue concerning self-esteem that is quite similar to that concerning intelligence. Basically, is self-esteem a broad general characteristic of a person independent of narrow self-esteems, is it a collection of narrow independent self-esteems, or is it a broad, general characteristic that depends on more narrow self-esteems? (For the field of intelligence, substitute the word "intelligence" for the words "self-esteems.") The alternative you choose will affect both how you define self-esteem and how you measure it. Most psychologists and sociologists choose the third alternative, although this choice seems to be based more on personal preference than on empirical data.

Coopersmith (1967) defines self-esteem thus:

> The evaluation which the individual makes and customarily maintains with regard to himself: it expresses an attitude of approval or disapproval, and indicates the extent to which the individual believes himself to be capable, significant, successful, and worthy. (p. 5)

According to this definition, self-esteem is the evaluation part of the self, which includes conscious and unconscious aspects. Self-esteem is usually measured by a questionnaire and so includes only the verbal self-attitudes a person holds.

Most writers make a distinction between self-esteem and self-confidence. Rosenberg (1979) puts the matter as follows:

> Self-confidence essentially refers to the anticipation of successfully mastering challenges or overcoming obstacles. . . .Self-esteem, on the other hand, implies self-acceptance, self-respect, feelings of self-worth. (p. 31)

Both Coopersmith and Rosenberg hold to the view that self-esteem is a broad general characterstic that depends on more narrow self-esteems. They chose two different techniques, however, in their attempts to measure it. Coopersmith reasoned that self-esteem would vary with the experiences an individual had and the situation being evaluated. A child might feel very worthy as a student, moderately worthy as a soccer player, and totally unworthy as an artist. The child's general self-esteem would be a function of his weighting of these different abilities.

Coopersmith constructed a 50-item questionnaire, called the Self-Esteem Inventory (SEI), covering four areas of a child's life – peers, parents, school, and personal interests. He administered the SEI to 1758 boys and girls between the ages of 10 and 12 years old, but intensively studied only 56 of the boys. For the latter group, Coppersmith found essentially no difference in SEI scores for the four areas. He concluded that the SEI for this age-group primarily measured general self-esteem. However, later research by Kokenes (1974) with 1500 boys and girls in each of grades 4–8 found evidence that the SEI was measuring at least eight different aspects of self-esteem and not only general self-esteem. Interestingly, Kokenes found that children's total SEI scores were most strongly related to either how inadequately they perceived themselves or how strongly they rejected themselves.

Rosenberg's (1979) technique for measuring general self-esteem was simpler and more direct than Coopersmith's. His complete questionnaire is shown below. It is a highly reliable test, which has been used with children and adolescents in grades 3–12. The asterisks represent low self-esteem responses.

TABLE 3.2
Rosenberg-Simmons Self-Esteem Scale (RSSE)

---

1. Everybody has some things about him which are good and some things about him which are bad. Are more of the things about you...Good, *Bad; or *Both about the same?

2. Another kid said, "I am no good." Do you ever feel like this? *Yes. No.

3. A kid told me: "There's a lot wrong with me." Do you ever feel like this? *Yes. No.

4. Another kid said: "I'm not much good at anything." Do you ever feel like this? *Yes. No.

5. Another kid said: "I think I am no good at all." Do you ever feel like this? *Yes. No.

6. How happy are you with the kind of person you are? Are you...Very happy with the kind of person you are; Pretty happy; *A little happy; or *Not at all happy.

(Source: Rosenberg, M. *Conceiving the self.* New York: Basic Books, 1979. Reprinted by permission of the publisher.)

Finally, Harter (1982) developed a 28-item questionnaire that assessed four different aspects (which she calls domains) of self-esteem. Three of the domains dealt with a child's perceived competence in the cognitive, social, and physical areas. The fourth domain, called "general self-worth," was independent of any particular competence area. Despite the fact that Harter assumes that individuals do possess a general self-esteem that depends on more narrow self-esteems, she did not construct her questionnaire to reflect that assumption. Rather, for children in grades 3–9, self-esteem scores in all four domains were highly independent of one another. For example, children could score high in general self-worth and low in the three competence domains, or vice-versa.

Boys and girls perform about the same on these three self-esteem questionnaires. Scores have also been found to be quite stable in the short run—over periods of 1 to 2 months. Thus far, only the Coopersmith SEI has been used with the same children for longer time spans. For the groups of children tested, the correlation between their initial and subsequent scores after a 3-year interval was .70, indicating remarkable stability.

Four Principles of Self-Esteem Formation

In this section, which closely follows Rosenberg's (1979) work, we discuss some general principles of how an individual's self-esteem is formed. Let's consider the following scenario. The Jones family consists of mother, father, 15- and 17-year-old sons, and two identical twin daughters who are 12. The girls look alike, have the same IQ, athletic ability, get along equally well with their parents, received the same grades in the same school, but are in different classrooms and have different sets of friends. Their "personalities" are similar, but not identical. One of the twins has high and the other low self-esteem. How is this possible?

It's clear that self-esteem must arise out of our experiences with other people in a variety of situations. We're not born with it, and if we never contacted other people, we would never develop a self-esteem (assuming we could survive a completely isolated life). All of us experience ourselves and others in different situations—no one who reaches childhood has always been in one situation. Somehow the twin girls have encountered and responded to these people and situations in sufficiently different ways which have led to their different levels of self-esteem.

Rosenberg helps us understand the Jones girls' dilemmas in the following way. Four general factors are simultaneously involved with the development of self-esteem: (1) Reflected appraisals, (2) Social comparisons, (3) Self-attribution, and (4) Psychological centrality. Two important components of reflected appraisals are called "direct reflections" and "perceived selves." Direct reflections means that our self-esteem is shaped by how others directly respond to us. If people tell us we're very worthy and esteemed we tend to feel worthy and esteemed. If told we're worthless, we tend to feel that way about ourselves. "Perceived selves" refers to how each of us thinks others perceive us. Obviously there is some connection between how others *really* perceive us, and how we *believe* they do, but the two are not the same. As an example, think of all the times you've avoided being truthful with someone because you didn't want to hurt that person's feelings.

In general, the way a person ranks herself, say in leadership ability, intelligence, physical attractiveness, is closely related to the way others rank her (direct reflections) on those characteristics. Importantly, the way a person ranks herself is even more closely related to the way she believes other people will rank her (perceived self). Thus, our identical twins may receive different direct reflections and perceived selves, owing to different friendships, classrooms, and relationships with their brothers.

Social comparisons refers to the observation that people learn about themselves through comparing themselves with other individuals and groups. In the process of making these comparisons, we often are led to evaluate ourselves negatively or positively. So, depending upon whom we compare ourselves to, we can see ourselves as smart or dumb, rich or poor, weak or strong. For example, one of the Jones girls may compare herself favorably with the average student in the class, whereas the other, unfavorably with the most outstanding student.

Self-attribution refers to the fact that people observe themselves in their daily activities and partially form their self-esteem upon these observations. The linkage between self-observation and what we attribute to ourselves is not perfect. Most of us know handsome boys or beautiful girls who feel they are unattractive, excellent athletes who feel they are only fair, fine students who say they are average. Most research relevant to self-esteem in children and self-attributions deals with actual academic achievement (school grades) and academic self-concept, i.e., being a "good student in school." In several studies the correlation between achievement and self-concept was about .50. This means that children link the two, but errors in self-attribution are often made. Given that the Jones twins are identical in so many ways, it's unlikely that this factor plays much of a role in producing self-esteem differences.

Psychological centrality refers to the observation that not all aspects of the self are equally weighted in forming a general self-esteem. Some of a person's narrow self-esteems count more (are more psychologically central) than others. For example, two excellent athletes who are poor students may have very different general self-esteem. One of the athletes may value academics highly and see herself as unworthy in that regard. The other athlete may be relatively indifferent to academics and base her general self-esteem primarily on her athletic abilities. This factor may account for much of the self-esteem differences in the Jones girls. One of the girls may highly value her strengths and be indifferent to her weaknesses, whereas the opposite may be true for the other.

Psychological centrality, perceived self, and self-esteem were examined in Rosenberg's Baltimore study. Psychological centrality was measured by asking children to indicate how concerned they were about others' opinions of them. Responses could vary from "cares very much" to "cares not at all." Seven "others" were chosen: Mother, father, teachers, kids in class, boys, girls, and siblings. Perceived self was measured by asking children to indicate whether each of the "others" was favorably or unfavorably impressed with them. Self-esteem was measured by Rosenberg's RSSE questionnaire. Several findings were of interest. For six of the seven "others" there was a relatively strong connection between psychological centrality, perceived self, and self-esteem. That is, if an "other," e.g., mother, was psychologically central (her opinion was cared about) and the child believed his mother had a favorable opinion of him (favorable perceived self), then his self-esteem tended to be high. If the child didn't care about the mother's opinion of him (mother wasn't psychologically central), then there was essentially no relation between perceived self and self-esteem.

Rosenberg's data clearly show how complicated is the foundation of self-esteem. Parents often ask, "How can my children be so different? They were raised alike in the same house." We know that no two people can ever be raised alike. But even if they were, and moreover were genetically identical, the fact that they are exposed to different people and situations will produce some psychological differences. More powerful still in self-esteem formation are the different ways individuals interpret their experiences. In a profound sense, each person constructs his or her self-esteem through choices made in the use of the four general factors of self-esteem development.

Peer Relationships, Achievement, and Motivation

This section deals with some linkages between self-esteem and three important aspects of the child's school-related behavior: interpersonal relationships, grades in school, and academic motivation. Coopersmith studied the relationship between self-esteem (SEI scores) and peer relationships for boys ages 10–12. He reports four measures bearing on this issue. One measure is based on peer ratings of popularity, two are derived from the child's own interview responses, and one is based on a laboratory experiment. The following generalizations can be made:

1. Popularity with one's classmates is unrelated to self-esteem.
2. Children with high and medium self-esteem report that it is easier to make friends than those with low self-esteem.
3. Children rated high are more likely to take leadership roles in group discussions than those with middle or low self-esteem.
4. High and middle-scoring children are less likely than those with low self-esteem to conform to group pressure.

All three writers report data on the relationship between academic achievement and self-esteem. Coopersmith and Rosenberg related their measures of general self-esteem to achievement, whereas Harter related her measure of perceived cognitive competence to academic achievement. The data in all cases are highly consistent – children rating high perform better academically than those with low self-esteem.

These findings raise an important theoretical question that has enormous practical consequences. That is, do children perform well academically because they have high self-esteem, or do they have high self-esteem because they perform well academically? If self-esteem precedes academic achievement, then it would be wise to use our resources to bolster the self-esteem of poorly performing students. Harter (1982) summarizes research dealing with this issue which provides a relatively clear answer. No studies demonstrate that high self-esteem precedes high academic achievement, whereas a number of studies show that high achievement precedes high self-esteem. These findings imply that high achievement at least partially produces high self-esteem. As a consequence, it would be the wise course to put our efforts into the academic realm rather than the self-esteem realm to help low achievers.

The final issue we'll deal with here is the relationship between perceived cognitive competence and academic motivation. In 1981, Harter reported a massive study dealing with the development of a questionnaire to assess "intrinsic versus extrinsic orientation in the classroom" (academic motivation) in children in grades 3–9. The questionnaire measured five "orientations," three of which are of interest here. They are (1) preference for challenge versus easy work, (2) curiosity/interest versus pleasing teacher/getting better grades, and (3) independent mastery versus dependence on teacher. An internal orientation – motivated to please one's self – involves preferring challenging tasks, working because of curiosity and interest, and trying to master problems and tasks on one's own. An external orientation means that one is motivated to please others. When these three measures were correlated with perceived cognitive competence, a strong relationship was found between intrinsic orientation and high perceived competence. Thus, children who are academically motivated to please themselves are highly likely to be the children who feel they are academically competent.

Taken together, research in the above three areas leads to the conclusion that high relative to low self-esteem children are internally rather than externally motivated, are academically successful, and take leadership roles in class. Although highs feel they have a relatively easy time making friends, they are not more popular with classmates than low self-esteem children.

Developmental Aspects of Self-Esteem

The most extensive study of age-related changes in self-esteem has been carried out by Rosenberg (1979). He examined the following six factors for children in grades 3–12 (aged 8–18): general self-esteem; stability of the self-concept; perceived self; depression; self-consciousness; and valued self-characteristics. *Self-consciousness* was measured by a questionnaire that asked children about their feelings concerning such activities as standing up and talking in front of class, going to parties at which they know few people. *Stability of the self-concept* was measured by a questionnaire that asked children about their consistency of feelings about themselves and others – e.g., "How often do you feel mixed-up about yourself, about what you are really like?" *Depression* dealt mainly with self-perceived happiness, cheerfulness, and joyfulness. *Valued self-characteristics* was measured by asking children whether they saw themselves favorably or unfavorably. *Perceived-self and general self-esteem* were measured as previously discussed. The results are summarized in Table 3.3.

For these analyses, Rosenberg formed three groups of children by age, roughly corresponding to elementary grades (ages 8–11), junior high school (12–14), and senior high school (15–18). He reported his results in percentages, but the patterns appear much clearer as presented in Table 3.3. "First," "Second," and "Third" indicate how the three age-groups were ranked on each measure. Thus, 12–14 and 15–18-year-olds were highest and tied for "high self-consciousness;" all three age-groups had approximately equal negative perceived selves by "opposite sex peers;" and for the self-characteristics of "well-behaved," "good-looking," and "work hard at school," 8–11-year-olds rated themselves most favorably and 15–18-year-olds, least favorably.

As can be seen there is a highly consistent pattern of results. Relatively speaking, 8–11-year-olds see their world through "rose-colored glasses," but from age 12 onwards, the glasses darken and become murky. On every measure the 8–11-year-olds view themselves either most positively or least negatively, including ties. The 12–14 and 15–18-year-olds, on the other hand, tend to experience themselves equally negatively, receiving tied rankings on most measures.

From these analyses we conclude that the major shifts in self-esteem development occur between the ages of 8 and 11 and 12 and 14.

TABLE 3.3
Six Factors in Self-Esteem Development

	8–11 years	12–14 years	15–18 years
High self-consciousness	Third	First	First
High instability of self-concept	Third	First	First
Low general self-esteem	Second	First	Second
Negative perceived-self by			
Parents	Third	First	First
Teachers	Third	First	First
Opposite sex-peers	Second	Second	Second
Same sex-peers	Third	Second	First
High feelings of depression	Third	First	First
Valued self-characteristics			
Smart, Truthful; Helpful	First	Second	Second
Well-behaved; good-looking; works hard at school	First	Second	Third
Good at: Sports; making jokes	Second	Second	Second

Rosenberg carried out a more fine-grained analysis on self-consciousness, instability, self-esteem, and depression by looking at year-to-year changes over the entire age span 8–18 years. He found in general that between the ages of 8 and 13 years, scores on all four measures changed. In this age range, children became increasingly emotionally disturbed along with decreases in self-esteem. From ages 14 to 18 self-consciousness and depression remained essentially unchanged, but self-images became more stable and self-esteem increased. The major exception to these patterns occurred for general self-esteem. On this measure, there was a tremendous decrease in self-esteem between the ages of 11 and 12, and a tremendous increase between the ages of 12 and 13.

Of particular interest is understanding the dramatic changes in self-esteem between the ages of 11 and 13. There are at least two possible explanations for these findings. The first is that these psychological changes are associated with entering junior high school at age 12, and then accommodating to the environmental changes by age 13. The second is that the changes are produced by the onset of puberty at age 12 and then by accommodating to these physiological changes by age 13. Rosenberg's data analyses support the environmental rather than physiological explanation. Among 12-year-old children, low self-esteem, high self-consciousness, and high self-concept instability are much greater if the child is in seventh rather than sixth grade. These three measures are essentially the same for 11- and 12-year-olds in sixth grade and for 12- and 13-year-olds in seventh grade. Thus, the transition to junior high school has a marked negative effect on the self-esteem of children.

From Rosenberg's analysis it appears that the elementary school years and the transition to junior high school have progressively negative effects on children's self-esteem. As they advance from third to sixth grade, increasing demands are placed on them by their teachers, and perhaps more is expected of them by their friends and by themselves. Reality hits them hard—they're not the greatest. The transition to junior high school is a further major insult to their self-esteem. Physically they are small relative to eighth and ninth graders, the academic environment is less protective, and their older peers appear much more competent in so many ways. As they progress through junior high school, these effects stabilize and self-esteem increases.

Antecedents of Self-Esteem

This section deals with some of the specific factors that are related to the development of high or low self-esteem. Surprisingly little research has emphasized this area. We saw in the last section that self-esteem is not a fixed characteristic of children, but changes a great deal between the ages of 8 and 14. These changes are not caused by aging as such, but by the different experiences children have at each age, and by the different ways they interpret these experiences.

In a theoretical paper dealing with age-related changes in self-esteem, Dickstein (1977) convincingly argues that each major developmental stage carries with it unique ways of influencing self-esteem. In infancy, where there is little self-consciousness, self-esteem is linked with how successfully the infant can independently operate in her environment. In early childhood, self-esteem largely depends on how successfully self-chosen activities are performed. Dickstein believes that children in this stage compare their successes with their attempts at success (infants don't do this) and base their self-esteem on the ratio of relative success. In later childhood through adolescence, the person is much more self-conscious than at younger ages, and self-esteem is largely based on discrepancies between their conscious ideal self and conscious perceived self.

One of the major implications of Dickstein's theory is that a child's self-esteem may change a great deal as she moves from stage to stage. Each stage seems somewhat independent of the previous ones, as constrasted with Freudian stages, for example, which build on one another. Each of Dickstein's stages gives one a fresh chance at developing high self-esteem.

Unfortunately, there are no empirical studies that prove or disprove Dickstein's theory. However, Rosenberg (1979) presents data consistent with it. Rosenberg found that between the ages of 5 and 18 there were continuous changes in children's "chief points of pride" and "chief points of shame." As one moves from younger to older ages, children report decreasing concerns about their physical characteristics, abilities, and activities. They show increasing concerns about their interpersonal characteristics and their self-control. Thus what is important for self-esteem at earlier ages becomes less important at older ages, and vice versa.

In contrast to Dickstein's approach, Coopersmith (1967) studied characteristics of mothers of 10–12-year-old boys and their child-rearing approaches as related to sons' self-esteem. In her review of similar studies, Harter (1983) states that Coopersmith's conclusions hold up relatively well. Based on extensive interview data, Coopersmith found that mothers of high self-esteem boys are likely to be emotionally stable, to feel capable of caring for their children, and to feel unburdened by motherhood. Low self-esteem boys have mothers without these characteristics. Regarding child-rearing practices, high relative to low self-esteem boys have mothers who (1) are emotionally accepting, (2) consistently enforce rules and demand that their children meet family standards, (3) firmly and consistently apply discipline, and (4) allow their children to participate in family decision making and to discuss family rules.

When we consider Dickstein's theory along with Coopersmith's research, and Rosenberg's four principles, the specific factors influencing a child's self-esteem are extremely complex. Accepting, competent parents no doubt can exert considerable positive influence; but peers, siblings, teachers, one's own competences, and one's developmental level all play important roles. Given this complexity, it is very unlikely that simple attempts to raise self-esteem will be successful.

SUMMARY

The recent study of the development of attachment in monkeys and humans has taken the form of examining the effects of mother-infant separation on the infant's behavior. Research with monkeys has shown that both the social organization of the group and specific ways mothers treat their infants strongly influence infants' reactions to separation and reunion. Infants who have active involvement with many adult group members are less distressed by the separation experience than are infants whose contact with adults is restricted to their mother. On reunion, infants recover rapidly if mothers readily accept their attempts for contact, but recover slowly if mothers are more rejecting.

Research on human attachment has generally utilized some form of Ainsworth's Strange Situation. Infants are classified into one of three patterns: Secure, Anxious Resistant, or Anxious Avoidant. These classifications are very stable between the ages of 12 and 18 months for infants reared in stable, middle-class homes, but not so for those raised in lower class, single-parent homes where mothers are under a great deal of stress. Securely attached infants have mothers who are affectionate, enjoy interacting with them, and are responsive to their needs and desires. Anxiously attached infants have mothers who lack these characteristics.

The effects of day care, early attachment to social competence, attachment to father, and cross-cultural comparisons were examined. A large number of studies have shown that any negative day-care effects seen on infant's attachment to mother are likely to be temporary. Typically, infants who have been in a day-care setting for more than 6 months show the same patterns of attachment as home-reared infants. Regarding social competence at 24 months, infants who were securely attached at 12–18 months relative to those anxiously attached are more compliant and cooperative with adults. Their play is more imaginative and their problem solving more enthusiastic and task-oriented. At 3½–5 years, infants who had been securely attached relative to those who had been anxiously attached are more competent with peers, have greater ego strength, greater curiosity, and more resiliency in problem-solving situations.

Infants typically show different patterns of attachment to their mothers and fathers. Using Lamb's distinction between affiliation and attachment behaviors, over the age range 7 to 24 months, infants affiliate more with their fathers than mothers in both the laboratory and at home. With a stranger present, however, infants affiliate equally with both parents. For attachment, a more complicated pattern of results is found, but basically infants get progressively attached to their fathers such that by 24 months, attachment to both parents is equivalent. The limited cross-cultural data indicate that attachment to mother develops in highly similar ways, whether mother spends only 3 hours daily with her infant, as in the Israeli kibbutz, or more than 12 hours daily, as in rural Uganda.

Self-recognition has been studied in monkeys, apes, and humans. Orangutans and chimpanzees show clear evidence of self-awareness, but monkeys do not. Using similar techniques with human infants, the development of body self-awareness starts to emerge at 9 months old, and substantially improves over the next year. The development of an understanding of "contingency" in self-initiated movements is clearly present by 12 months of age.

The research on gender identity makes a distinction between *labeling, stability,* and *constancy.* By 2½ years of age, children correctly refer to themselves and others as "boys" and "girls" (labeling). Within the next 2 years they come to believe that they always have been and always will be boys or girls (stability). By age 6½, they understand that gender differences are based on genital differences (constancy) and not on surface characteristics such as hair length or clothes. The development of sex role stereotypes also emerges at about 2½ years, but at age 11, this knowledge is well below adult levels. For preschool children there is a strong relationship between the development of gender stability and knowledge of sex role stereotypes.

The research on development of the verbal self distinguishes among three types of self-descriptions: *external,* e.g., physical characteristics, possessions; *behavioral,* e.g., personal likes and dislikes, hobbies; and *internal,* e.g., self-evaluations. Between the ages of 3 and 8, children primarily use external, then behavioral, then internal self-descriptions. Between the ages of 8 and 9, a dramatic shift occurs. At age 9, behavioral self-descriptions are most used, with internal and external equally used. From age 10 onwards, self-descriptions are primarily behavioral, then internal and least of all, external.

Cross-cultural studies show that there are widespread sex role stereotypes in the rearing of children between ages 4 and 12. In general, girls are trained to be more nurturant and responsible than boys, but boys are trained to be more self-reliant and achievement oriented than girls. Differences in sex role stereotypes are great in societies that either empha-size male development of superior motor skills and strength, or place great emphasis on highly cooperative large family groups.

The section concerned with the development of self-esteem in children relied primarily on the research of Coopersmith (1967), Harter (1983), and Rosenberg (1979). Self-esteem was distinguished from self-confidence and defined as involving self-acceptance, self-respect, and self-worth. Self-esteem scores measured with questionnaires are highly stable over 1–2 month periods. Scores on Coopersmith's questionnaires were found to be very stable over a 3-year period.

Rosenberg presented four general principles of how an individual's self-esteem was formed. They are Reflected appraisals (which include direct reflections and perceived selves), Social comparisons, Self-attribution, and Psychological centrality. Perceived selves and psychological central-ity are particularly influential.

Self-esteem has been related to three important aspects of the child's school-related behavior: interpersonal relations, grades in school, and academic motivations. Although high self-esteem boys are not more popular with classmates, they are more likely to take leadership roles in class. They achieve more academically, and are more intrinsically motiv-ated in school. Developmentally, self-esteem is high at age 8, decreases between the ages of 8 and 12, and then increases from 12 to 18. The greatest negative change occurs during the transition to junior high school. Finally, the specific influences on a child's self-esteem are highly complex and depend on developmental stage. One consistent influence is the positive effect of having an accepting, competent mother.

4 Social Development

Social development refers to the changing ways infants and children interact with other persons as they mature. In this chapter we have chosen topics which are highly significant for understanding social development, and for which there is a substantial literature. In order to gain some understanding of our evolutionary heritage, we first discuss play, aggression, and dominance in different monkey cultures. We then move on to a discussion of infant and children's play emphasizing Piaget's research and theory. We next take up sociodramatic play which makes extensive use of language and imagination, and has clear connections with dominance and other social relations. We round out this discussion with a cross-cultural view of games.

Children's play and games often involve aggression, dominance, altruism, cooperation and competition. In the next three sections we take up these themes individually and discuss children's development in each from early childhood to preadolescence. The section on cooperation and competition discusses some of the extensive cross-cultural literature in this area. In the last section of the chapter we emphasize how parental socialization practices influence children's social behavior with peers.

NONHUMAN PRIMATES

Development of Social Behavior in Social Context

With few exceptions, monkeys and apes are born into and reared in a social group made up of members of both genders and varied ages.

Although the amount of contact infants, juveniles, and preadolescents have with the different group members differs with primate species and living conditions, they do have contact with all categories of group members, e.g., peers and adults of both genders. The major "job" of pre-adult group members is to learn to fit into and contribute to the social group. In order to accomplish this job they have to develop both a set of social skills that are important to the group, and a stable set of social relationships with many, if not most, of the group members. For example, "grooming," which involves the careful inspection of the fur of another, is an important social skill. The pre-adult has to learn this, as well as which individuals can be groomed, and when. This is not very different from a young child learning to comb or brush her mother's hair. She shouldn't pull too hard when her hair is knotted, and she shouldn't attempt combing when her mother is busy or upset. She may also learn that father and older brother never like to be groomed, but older sister nearly always enjoys it.

The young group members learn the desired social skills and develop stable relationships primarily through (a) observing other group members; (b) imitating them; and perhaps most importantly, (c) interacting with them. Obviously, the three processes are related, and often come together in social interactions. It is during these interactions that social skills can be tested out and/or finely tuned, and also when relationships can start to stabilize. We would expect, based on our previous discussion of monkey attachment to mother, that it takes some time for any relationship to stabilize. For example, we saw tremendous changes in the nature of mother-infant interactions during the first year of an infant's life.

The following four questions are of interest to us. (1) What sorts of interactions are young monkeys involved in? (2) With whom do they have these interactions? (3) How do these interactions change with age? (4) How are peer interactions influenced by the presence of other group members? Two recent laboratory studies, by Suomi (1979) and Rosenblum and Plimpton (1979), go a long way toward answering them.

Suomi's research was carried out in the Wisconsin Primate Laboratory with rhesus monkeys. Four families of rhesus, each comprised of an adult male-adult female pair and their offspring lived in the "nuclear-family apparatus" during the entire duration of the experiment. The apparatus consisted of four medium-sized living cages surrounding the four sides of a large central play area. All the living cages, one family in each, were connected to the play area by a tunnel that was large enough for all the offspring to pass through, but too small for their parents to do so. Thus, each infant could come and go freely into every living cage and the play area, but all the adults were restricted to their own living cage. The cages were also constructed so that all the inhabitants could see and hear what was going on in the apparatus at all times.

There were 12 infants (0–4 months) and juveniles (21–24 months old) reared in the apparatus, 6 males and 6 females. Each one was observed 5 minutes a day, 4 days a week, for the first 2 years of its life. In Table 4.1 is a complete list of all the interactions that were scored during the observation periods. That is, at any moment in time, either the infant or juvenile was initiating one of these interactions or some other group member was directing one of them toward the infant or juvenile.

TABLE 4.1
Categories of Interactions

Contact: Any ventrally oriented contact or behavior that serves to maintain contact between any two animals. Motor patterns include nipple contacts, clinging, embracing, and cradling.

Protection: Movement toward the infant by the mother or the father (or vice versa) caused by some interference on the part of other animals or an extraneous source. Motor patterns include retrieval, running toward another while showing signs of fear, restraint.

Groom-exploration: Manipulatory inspection of the fur of another animal other than while in maternal contact.

Huddle-sit: Moving to and remaining within 6 inches of another animal. Motor patterns include dorsal or lateral surface contact, proximity with orientation toward another animal.

Play: Animated movements, gestures, facial expressions, and contacts of varying intensity and duration directed toward another subject. Motor patterns include low-intensity, mouth-open "threat" face, cuffing, "boxing," wrestling, chasing, running from, carom movements in response to, clasp-pulling, or nipping another animal.

Sex: Male or female sex patterns, movements, and postures directed at another animal. Motor patterns include hindquarter positioning, pelvic thrusting, hindquarter posturing, foot clasping.

Threat: Intense and protracted threatening, displays, or brief contactual assertions. Motor patterns include retracted threat face, "hard" cuffing, single bite or slap, cage shaking, barking.

Defense: Hostile or aggressive behaviors directed at the protagonist of an interaction involving a third subject.

(Source: Suomi, S. J. Differential development of various social relationships by Rhesus moneky infants. In M. Lewis & L. A. Rosenblum (Eds.), *The child and its family.* New York: Plenum, 1979.)

In general, about half of the interactions initiated by the infants and directed toward them were play. The majority of the remaining interactions were contact seeking and grooming-exploring. For juveniles, play comprised about three-fourths of their interactions with the remaining ones falling into the categories of groom-explore, huddle-sit, and sex.

Overall, infants directed about half their interactions toward their mothers, with the remaining half about equally distributed towards male and female peers. For male and female juveniles a different pattern was found. About half their initiatives were directed toward male peers, with the remaining initiations divided between female peers, then their mothers, then their fathers. Who directs interactions toward the infants and juveniles? Infants receive about equal interactions from male peers, female peers, and their mothers. Male and female juveniles receive about half their interactions from male peers, and about one third from female peers.

We see from the above that with increasing age pre-adults spend more time in play, more time involved with peers, and less time with their mothers and fathers. It is clear from Suomi's observations that the extent and type of interactions pre-adults have is different with different group members. Infants primarily initiate contact with their mothers, groom/exploration and play with their fathers, adult males, and adult females, and almost exclusively play with male and female peers. Juveniles primarily initiate huddling and play interactions with their mothers, and primarily play with all the other group members. Mothers primarily seek contact with their infants, fathers seek grooming, play, and defense about equally; adult males and adult females primarily threaten them; and male and female peers play with them. With juveniles, mothers shift their initiatives to grooming and defending; fathers shift to threatening, defending, and playing, and adult males shift to playing and threatening.

These observations provide answers to the first three questions voiced above for this particular primate species, for this particular social and physical environment—in short, for this particular *monkey culture*. The data highlight the following statements about socialization. First, that infants and juveniles are socialized differently by different group members. This allows them to learn the social skills and social relationships necessary to fit into the group. Second, the types of interactions pre-adults initiate with others, and vice versa, change with maturation. However, some relationships are more stable than others; e.g., those with peers are highly stable. Third, both infants and juveniles spend extraordinary amounts of time playing with their peers. In fact they do little else with each other. This implies that play is the major vehicle by which young primates socialize one another. Fourth, when infants and juveniles attempt to play with adult males and females, they are typically threatened by the adults. Hence, infants and juveniles have few interactions with them.

We now turn to the fourth question: How are peer interactions influenced by the presence of other group members? When Rosenblum and Plimpton (1979) discuss this issue they refer to William Golding's book *Lord of the Flies*. In that book a group of English schoolboys is stranded on an island without adults. They attempt to organize a life together so that they can survive, and in the process become very aggressive toward each other. This aggressiveness doesn't mimic that of adults, but rather seems to emerge because there are no adult restrictions or constraints on their behavior.

Rosenblum and Plimpton created three experimental groups of bonnet monkeys and housed them in pens that were approximately the same size as Suomi's play area. The first group—peers only—consisted of two male and two female 1-year-olds, previously unknown to each other. The second group—peers plus mothers—consisted of four 1-year-olds, plus their four mothers. The third group—peers plus adults—consisted of four 1-year-olds plus four unfamiliar adult females. Each infant was observed 14 minutes a day, 4 days a week, for 5 weeks, and their behavior scored in categories similar to those used by Suomi.

The behavior of the infants was quite different in the three conditions. The infants in the peers-plus-adults group were the most intimidated of the three groups, and those in the peers-only group the least intimidated. This was shown by the former group's high frequency of distress calls, their low activity levels, and their low levels of exercise play (solitary play) and social play. The opposite pattern was found for the peers-only group. Of especial interest were the measures of aggression shown by the infants. Males were more aggressive than the females in all conditions. However, much more aggression was shown in the peers-only condition than in the other two conditions. Thus, like Golding's English schoolboys, high amounts of aggression emerge in situations where adults are not present. At a still more general level, the patterns of findings indicate that infant social interactions are markedly influenced by social context. We know from Suomi's research, and Harlow's (1969) earlier work that peer play is crucial for normal development. If opportunities for this play are unusually restricted for long time periods it's likely that the infants will not be appropriately socialized.

Play and Dominance

One of the most important interactions involving group members is that of dominance. High dominant primates relative to low dominant ones get first choice over most of what's important in the social and physical environments, e.g., food, shelter, sleeping area, sexual partner, spatial location. For example, in Rosenblum and Plimpton's research, the top shelves in the pen were preferred to the bottom ones. In the peers-plus-adults group, the adults controlled the top shelves and the infants stayed on the bottom ones. This reminds us of the children's game "King of the Mountain," but it's not a game to the monkeys.

Generally, dominance relationships are stable for months or years in a primate group. These relationships provide a great deal of stability to the group, much the same way that hierarchies in human families stabilize those groups (Minuchin, 1974). Primate groups without stable hierarchies (dominance relationships) tend to be chaotic, with a great deal of direct aggression expressed between their members.

Dominance relationships in the group are maintained primarily by the threat of aggression, the fear of threat, and rarely by direct aggression. Low dominant primates typically avoid high dominant ones, withdraw when high dominant ones approach, or show deference to the high dominant ones by assuming a particular posture which means "I defer to you." The same kinds of interactions occur in stable human groups. For example, in family therapy, parents often complain that their children look at them in a "defiant" way (without deference). Their children's defiance sometimes leads to direct aggression, as it does in nonhuman primate groups.

Social play seems to be one of the major ways that monkeys and apes learn the skills required for stable dominance relationships. Nonhuman primates engage in basically two types of social play, called "rough-and-tumble" play and "chasing" play (Bruner, Jolly, & Sylva, 1976). There are large numbers of parallels to these play types in almost all human cultures (Schwartzman, 1978).

A play episode starts when one primate signals to another that it wants to play. The signal may be a particular facial expression, called the "play face," a particular body posture or walk, or some other unexpected movement or sound, e.g., reaching over and slapping the other. Frequently, the first physical contact of the primate initiating play is an aggressive one, e.g., slapping, biting, grabbing the tail, pulling the fur. Depending on the mood of the solicited primate, the social circumstances, the relationship of the two and the perceived intent of the initiator, a number of things can happen. A real fight can start, play can start, the initiative may be ignored, the solicited one may move away. Often in the latter two cases, the initiator will persist, leading to the same set of possible outcomes.

Play starts. Trained observers sometimes can't tell whether the two primates are playing or whether they're fighting. Often the play leads to aggression, as it does with human primates. One clear indicator of play, however, is the occurrence of either role reversal or "self-handicapping." Again the parallels to human play are striking. In role reversal, the dominant primate lets itself be chased or bullied by its less dominant play partner. In self-handicapping, the stronger or faster primate uses less than its full power, for example, by wrestling on its back, or running away at half-speed (Bertrand, 1976). The dominant and submissive roles rapidly shift in play, each player influencing the behavior of its partner. When the play gets too rough for one of the players, usually the younger, an adult or older sibling may step in to protect the roughed-up player.

Infants and juveniles play with many of their peers in the group. Typically they'll choose play partners who are close to them in age, and whose mothers have similar dominance ranks. They'll also play with siblings and occasionally with their mothers. (In wild-life conditions the fathers are typically unknown.) Through this wide range of play experience, they develop a sense of their own dominance status as well as that of their peers. They get to know whom they can beat, whom they can bluff, and whom they can team up with to dominate others.

Phyllis Dolhinow (1971) sums up the relation between play and dominance as follows:

> Rules of dominance are essentially based on strength and ability to use social signals, and if learning which animals are stronger involves some pain, the young monkey may learn the rules rapidly. For young juveniles, especially males, the opportunity to play dominant, as well as subordinate, roles may be a part of the attractiveness of play. From a broader view, the total experience of play makes ranking possible and seemingly inevitable.

> Social cues and complex communication patterns are developed in the relative safety of play. It does not do any good to be the strongest and largest in the group if at the same time most other adults can bluff their way past to a desired object. A monkey must know not only the form and context of each social gesture, it must also be able to execute each with style and finesse. Timing must be perfect, and since most fights are avoided by complex gestures of threat and submission, the monkey that bluffs best probably goes furthest in the long run. (p. 316)

PLAY IN INFANCY AND CHILDHOOD

Helen Schwartzman, in her book *Transformations* (1979), captures in the following quote much of what we consider essential in understanding human play.

> Children at play learn how to be sensitive to the effects of context and the importance of relationships; they develop the capacity to adopt an "as if" set towards objects, actions, persons, and situations; and they continually explore the possibilities of interpretation and reinterpretation, and with this the creation of new possibilities. These abilities are certainly all of great consequence to the individual and to society. (p. 328)

Play, then is a creative process, in which the infant and child attempt to gain new perspectives and understandings of their physical and social environments. By adopting an "as if" (pretend) attitude, they are free to test out in play different interpretations of the meaning of their environment. Each interpretation leads to a different possible course of action in the pretend environment. By comparing these possibilities with the nonplay environment, children deepen their understanding of their own and other's actions. For example, when boys and girls play house, they may take all the various roles at different times—mother, father, baby, child, and so forth—and play those roles in a variety of ways. They may be strict parents or soft, naughty children or nice, and explore different ways of interacting with each other in these different social contexts.

Piaget's Research and Theory

The type of play we've described above is called "symbolic" play (Piaget, 1962). Piaget describes three age-related categories of play: "practice" play, which characterizes that of infants between 0 and 18 months and nearly all nonhuman primate play; "symbolic" play, which is associated with infants and children between 18 months and 7 years, but declines between the ages of 4 and 7; and "games with rules," which characterize the play of children between 7 and 12 years.

Piaget argues that the three play types are associated with three distinct stages of intelligence, called sensory-motor (practice play), representational or preoperational (symbolic play), and concrete operational (games with rules). We discuss Piaget's stages of intelligence in Chapter 5 and focus here on play. One common element across these play categories is the notion of "mastery." Piaget views the infant and child as attempting to develop skills that will allow them to make sense out of their experiences and the world around them. These skills are seen by Piaget as intellectual tools called "schemas," which children gain mastery of through practice, repetition, and experimentation. An analogy would be your buying a calculator and playing with it repeatedly, testing out its various functions, until you have mastered it. The calculator is a tool, and by mastering it, you can use it to solve nonplay problems.

One of the elements that distinguishes the three play categories is the *objective* of the mastery—what it is to be mastered. In practice play, the infant attempts to master his own sensory-motor activities, e.g., reaching, grasping, pulling. Practice play, therefore, is focused on the self. In symbolic play, the child attempts to master her understanding and use of symbols, e.g., words, for the objects and events outside herself in the environment. In games with rules, children attempt to master their understanding of social relationships. Before we give examples of these categories, it's important to note that as children progress from one play category to the next, they include the old with the new. So, symbolic play often includes practice play, and games with rules often include the previous two.

Piaget states that practice play is not exclusively associated with the sensory-motor period, but occurs whenever a new skill is being learned. In the process of learning there is

> practice for the sake of practice, accompanied by the pleasure of "being the cause," or the feeling of power. The same thing often happens in the case of the adult. Having just acquired for the first time a wireless set or a car, it is difficult to resist the temptation to use them merely for the fun of using one's new powers. Even in a new academic post one tends to find a certain pleasure at first in the new gestures one works in public. (p. 114)

In his discussion of the development of symbolic play, Piaget divides the preoperational stage into two periods, from 1½ to 4 years and from 4 to 7 years. The first period involves the simple and often haphazard, but novel, use of language and nonverbal symbols with objects. The following are two examples. A child places a doll in a pan, covers it with a postcard and says, "Baby, blanket . . . cold." The pan is symbolic of a bed, and the postcard, of a blanket. In another, a little girl has been "feeding" her doll, talking to it the way her parents do when they encourage her to finish her meal and says, "A little drop more. To please Jacqueline, just eat this little bit" (p. 127).

The second period is distinguished from the first in three major ways. The symbolic combinations are more orderly; e.g., the child constructs a relatively long coherent scene with the actions of the characters following logically; the characters and the objects used in the play become more realistic, and collective symbolism appears; e.g., children play together using the same symbols, all taking on roles that complement each other, such as mother and father.

A recent study by Ungerer, Zelazo, Kearsley, and O'Leary (1981) tested two hypotheses dealing with the first period of Piaget's theory of the development of symbolic play. Following Piaget's logic, they reasoned that since symbolic play develops out of practice play, then the earlier phases of symbolic play should more closely resemble practice play than the later phases of it. They therefore hypothesized that younger children, relative to older ones (1) should treat objects in more concrete, less symbolic ways; and (2) should use objects more actively. Ungerer et al. individually tested North American white, middle-class children between the ages of 18 and 34 months in a situation in which an adult first played with toys in either a symbolic or nonsymbolic way. Then the children were given an opportunity to play with those and other toys.

The researchers scored the type of play into four categories, excluding direct imitations of the adult. The first category involved actively playing with an object in a concrete way such as a child picking up a teacup, saying "tea" and pretending to drink from the cup. The second category involved playing with an object in a concrete way but not following through with a symbolic action, e.g., didn't pretend to "drink" from the cup. The third category involved actively playing with an object in a symbolic way; e.g., the child picks up a block, says "tea" and proceeds to drink. The fourth category involved playing in a symbolic way without symbolic action.

Ungerer et al. found experimental support for both hypotheses. Older children were more likely than younger children to use objects in symbolic as opposed to concrete ways; and older children were more likely to use objects without symbolic action than were the younger children.

Piaget's major discussion of games with rules occurs in his book *The Moral Judgement of the Child* (1932). It is fair to say that this book forms the basis for the area of developmental psychology called "social cognition." We discuss here that aspect of the book dealing with the practice of rules of the game.

Piaget set out to engage children of different ages in the game of marbles. He would approach a child or group of children playing with marbles and ask them to teach him to play the game. While playing, he would question them about the history of the game and where they learned it, about exceptions to the rules and whether they could be changed, and about the fine details of the rules. His account is fascinating and has been described as a model of anthropological field work.

Piaget divides the practice of the rules into four stages. The first stage, which can be called that of *ritualized schemas*, describes the typical behavior of infants in the sensory-motor stage and children in the first period (1½ to 4 years) of the preoperational stage of development. In this stage there are no common rules as such. In fact, there is no game. Children may play alone or side by side and develop individual rituals of playing with the marbles. One child may drop them from a specific height over and over, while the other may bury them and dig them up repeatedly.

The second stage, which describes the typical behavior of children in the second period of the preoperational stage, is called *egocentrism*. In this stage children play together, state that they are playing by the rules (and even state some rules), but have no real sense of what the game is about. That is, they do not play with shared rules, do not play as if the rules were binding, and have no sense of winning or losing, even though they use those terms. For example, Piaget plays with a 6½-year-old named "Baum." Baum makes a square and places three marbles inside it and says "Sometimes you put 4, or 3, or 2." Piaget says, "Or 5?" Baum replies, "No, not 5, but sometimes 6 or 8." They play for a while and Piaget captures four marbles and Baum, two. Piaget asks Baum "Who has won?" Baum replies, "I have, and then you." In the next game Piaget captures none, and Baum, two. Piaget asks, "Who has won?" Baum replies, "I have." Piaget asks "And I?" Baum says, "You've lost."

The third stage, which Piaget calls *cooperation*, characterizes the play of children between 7 and 10 years of age. Children truly compete with each other and while doing so attempt to regulate their play with a binding set of rules. Both activities require true cooperation. Children at this stage, however, rarely agree upon a set of rules for more than one game. Moreover, they are unable to reason through problems that arise in interpreting the rules to settle disputes. In this sense they are still somewhat egocentric; i.e., they still tend to see things from their own viewpoint instead of from the perspective of the group as a whole.

In the fourth stage, *interest in rules for their own sake*, problems of the third stage, are solved. Children in this stage, typically 11 years or older, are aware that different sets of rules are available for any game, and discuss beforehand which rules will be followed. The main characteristic of this stage is that children seem more interested in the rules than they are in winning marbles. To state it another way, they're more interested in the process of the game than in the outcome.

Most of Piaget's research on the development of play and games was carried out with his own three children and with small groups of children from different communities in Switzerland. As a consequence, when he divides development into stages and places age range on these stages, it is clear to the student of Piaget's work that these age ranges should be taken as guidelines for when to expect psychological changes to occur. They should not be understood as rigid stone markers for development. Indeed, Piaget will often state that different environmental conditions may speed up or slow down normally expected development. Perhaps two of the most important aspects of Piaget's work are his description of the psychological processes that emerge at each stage of development, e.g., practice play, symbolic play, and his descriptions of the sequence in which these stages will occur. Other issues are important, but in our view, secondary.

Having said this, we note that Piaget frequently goes out on a limb on these secondary issues and makes statements for which he has limited data. In an extremely large-scale study in Israel, involving the observation of about 14,000 Jewish and Arab grade school children, Eifermann (1971) tested three such statements concerning the effects of children's age on the relative amount of practice play, collective symbolic play, and games with rules. First, Piaget asserted that after the sensory-motor period practice play should decline with age. Eifermann and her colleagues scored as practice play any unstructured play activities that did not obviously use either symbols or game rules, such as running, jumping, throwing or kicking objects, keeping balance. She found for both high and low SES schools that participation in practice play increased from Grades 5 and 6 to Grades 7 and 8, inconsistent with Piaget's assertion.

Second, he asserted that after the preoperational period, collective symbolic play should decline with age. Since the youngest children in Eifermann's study were 6 years old, it would be reasonable to assume that this type of play should be at its lowest level in the first or second grade. That is, there should be no differences between second-grade and eighth-grade children. For high SES schools, this is exactly what Eifermann found. For low SES schools, however, the amount of collective symbolic play continuously declined from Grades 1 and 2 to Grades 7 and 8. This suggests that high and low SES children leave the pre-operational stage at different times, which is consistent with Piaget's statements that environment influences development.

Finally, Piaget asserted that games with rules should increase with age throughout the grade school years. Eifermann's observations disconfirmed this assertion in all the schools studied. In the high SES schools, games with rules peaked as early as the second grade and declined thereafter. In one of the low SES schools, games with rules peaked as late as the sixth grade, and declined thereafter. The average peak for all schools was the fourth grade. Somewhat more consistent with Piaget's assertion was the finding that competitive game rules reached their maximum at a later age than noncompetitive games. But these games also showed a decline during the grade school years.

From these data we can conclude that environment, as reflected in SES, can influence the rate at which children enter and move through different developmental stages of play and games. This research also shows us that when children enter an advanced developmental stage, their play and games may often resemble an earlier development.

Sociodramatic Play

To a bystander, sociodramatic play, which Piaget calls collective symbolism, is a charming and rather harmless pastime. In the writings of Catherine Garvey (1974, 1979) and Helen Schwartzman (1978, 1979) the charm remains, but the power and meaning to the players are exposed. In sociodramatic play, children are interacting with one another, are using symbols to do so, and are pretending–setting up a drama. In Garvey's view, a major value of this sort of play is to allow the players to test out a variety of social roles they experience in their daily lives. By testing out these roles through interactions with others, children can increase the social controls they have at their disposal. For example, when they play the "stern" parent to someone else playing child, they elicit one kind of response. As "soft" parent they elicit another kind of response. By experiencing both effects, they learn to control their behavior in order to influence the behavior of others, including their parents.

Schwartzman emphasizes the role of paradox in this type of play. Paradoxical statements are self-contradictory. In sociodramatic play they have the form of saying "This is and is not what it seems to be." The little girl "playing" mother is saying she is (but not really) mother. The importance of paradox is that it allows the players to comment, in a relatively safe context, on their social relationships. These comments are expressed in the ways they enact the roles of the play drama.

Garvey (1979) set up a situation in a nursery school in which pairs of similar-aged 3–5-year-olds were left alone in a playroom for about 15 minutes. During that time they were observed and videotaped through one-way mirrors. Based on her observations, Garvey identified the following three abilities as underlying sociodramatic play. First, both children need to be able to make the near-simultaneous distinction between play and not-play, or play and reality. They often mark the state of play by asking their partner to "pretend," or by giving their partner an obvious pretend role; e.g., "You be the mommy and I'll be the daddy." They often end the play state by saying "I'm not playing any more." However, as with the monkeys and apes, the start and finish of a play state are frequently marked by nonverbal means.

Second, the children have to be able to follow essentially the same rules of the play procedure. Taking turns is the most basic of these rules. Children will often tell each other "It's your turn" or complain to each other that they went out of turn ("it's my turn"). Violations of this rule may lead to the play ending. Another important rule is that children must keep a consistent role. If a child is going to be daddy, he must remain as daddy for the entire "drama" and not shift to cowboy or uncle or doctor. Children correct each other when they shift roles. Related to role consistency is the rule that the role should be played in an appropriate (realistic) way. Cowboys wear cowboy hats, not fireman hats.

The third ability is the most complex. Both children have to simultaneously be able to maintain the play theme (dramatic theme) and spontaneously develop that theme in agreed-upon ways. This is an amazing ability. Consider the fact that neither child can read the other's mind, often neither knows where the drama should lead, and neither can completely control the way the other will develop the drama. Yet, each must accomodate to the improvisations of the other. Not surprisingly, sociodramatic play themes of young children typically last no longer than two minutes. It is difficult to follow the same theme, the roles of the play, and maintain the same play attitude for long time periods.

This relatively long scenario (about 90 seconds) illustrates the above three abilities (Garvey, 1979). The players are a verbal girl, 38 months old, and a less verbal boy, 35 months old. The two are together, looking at a teddy bear. The girl both directs the play—thus stepping out of character but controlling the development of the theme—and plays the part of the baby. The boy plays the part of daddy.

Girl: Say, "Go to sleep now" (Girl is director)
Boy: Go sleep now
Girl: Why? (whining)
Boy: Baby

Girl: Why?

Boy: Because

Girl: No, say "Because" (emphatically) (Girl is director)

Boy: Because (emphatically)

Girl: Why? Because why?

Boy: Not good. You bad.

Girl: Why?

Boy: Cause you spill your milk.

Girl: No, cause I bit somebody (Girl is director)

Boy: Yes, you did (Boy slips out of role)

Girl: And say, "Go to sleep, Put your head down." (sternly) (Girl is director)

Boy: Put your head down (sternly)

Girl: No

Boy: Yes

Girl: No

Boy: Yes, yes do ... Okay, I will spank you. Bad boy (spanks her)

Girl: My head's up (giggles)

Boy: (spanks her again)

Girl: I want my teddy bear (petulant voice)

Boy: No, your teddy bear go away (sternly)

Girl: Why?

Boy: Cause he does (walks off with teddy bear)

Girl: Are you going to pack your teddy bear? (Girl drops director and baby roles) (p. 113)

Schwartzman's study (1978) involved her being a "participant-observer" for 1½ years in a day-care center in a low SES community in Chicago. Her analyses are based on field notes, interviews, photographs, children's drawings, and other tools of the anthropologist's trade. The 23 children in the class were under 6 years old, and of several different ethnic/racial groups.

The following quotation is from her field notes one spring afternoon. The cast of characters consists of Thomas and Paul, who nearly always play together, with Thomas usually being dominant over Paul. Linda, who enters the play after it has started, is the most dominant child in the class—she can enter any play group without asking or being asked, and can usually redefine the theme of the drama without seeking permission to do so. Linda often plays with Paul and Thomas. Karen does not usually play with this trio, and in other play situations does not easily accept

Linda's leadership and dominance. Rather, Karen often tries to dominate the play groups she is part of. One of her typical strategies is to bring in a notoriously submissive person who will follow her lead. Sonia is such a person.

> Thomas, Paul, and Karen are playing in the block corner. Sonia enters the area and asks if she can play with Thomas and Paul. They emphatically say "No!" Karen says "Yes, she can. I know, you marry me (pointing to Thomas) and Sonia can marry Paul." Thomas and Paul respond again: "No!" Karen replies "OK, I'll marry her and you can marry each other." Again they reject this proposal, but then they respond reluctantly, "OK, she can play." Karen says to Sonia, "We'll be nurses, and you sleep in the tent." Karen explains to Sonia where the "boat," "tent," "water," "quicksand," and "alligators" are.

As the scenario opens, Karen seizes the opportunity to control the play by encouraging Sonia's admission to the group. Karen tries two different "tricks"–the two marriage proposals–which have the effect of coercing Thomas and Paul to either redefine the drama or accept Sonia. This sequence comments on Sonia's lowly position in the group and the shaky control Thomas and Paul have over the play drama. By allowing Sonia in, they pass some control over to Karen who instructs Sonia in the drama.

> Linda comes in from playing in the outside yard. She observes the play group briefly and then goes over to the block corner and falls in the designated "water" and "quicksand" area and screams: "Help! Something is biting my legs!" The group responds to Linda's action, and then Karen announces that "Captain Paul is dead!" At this point Thomas acts very upset and says forcefully (directing his statement to Paul, Karen, and Linda), "You guys never know what to do!" Karen leaves the group at this point and says, "I'm not playing anymore." (During this period, Sonia is busying herself in the "water" area, saying "Oh, I've found a small snail." "Look, a baby alligator, a baby raccoon, a baby parakeet, a baby bird." She becomes absorbed in this activity and the rest of the group ignore her.

In this sequence, Linda reaffirms her dominance in the group in a clever way. She joins in uninvited, but develops the drama along the lines initially set out by the others. Karen challenges Linda's dominance by saying "Captain Paul is dead," at the same time confirming Paul's less dominant position. After all, Karen doesn't kill off Thomas, the leader of the two boys. Thomas responds to Karen's challenge of his authority over Paul by saying "you guys never know what to do." Karen, whose attempts at control have been thwarted, now leaves. In the meantime, Sonia has faded out of the power struggle, and becomes a nonentity.

Thomas, Paul, and Linda shift their discussion to talk of "angels, wings, and heaven." At this point, Thomas, with very agitated body movements, falls to the ground, saying, "I'm dead." Linda responds to this by declaring that "Thomas is an angel." Paul now begins to fidget and act restless and states his desire to return to the original boat play theme. Linda responds by saying, "Well, I guess it was just a dream." The boat play theme is resumed. (pp. 240–241)

In this, the final scene, Linda, Paul, and Thomas are essentially playing alone. Thomas acknowledges the complete loss of his leadership to Linda by announcing "I'm dead." Linda needs followers in order to be a leader and cleverly incorporates Thomas's death into their immediately prior discussion of angels. "Thomas is an angel" also affirms to Thomas that he is being a good boy by following her leadership, and she has elevated herself to god-like status by conferring angel status on him. Paul has now lost his source of strength in the group—the now angelic Thomas—and wants to return to the boat with an alive Thomas. Linda, who wants to remain dominant, and part of the group, accepts Paul's request, renounces Thomas's death as a dream, and allows the group to return to the boat.

In closing the discussion of her research, Schwartzman notes that much of children's play is modeled after the large number of hierarchical relationships they experience. They have less power than their parents and older siblings at home, and less power than their teachers and many older classmates in nursery school. The drama of play allows them opportunities to comment on, interpret, and perhaps test out new ways of dealing with hierarchies. Through role reversal children may learn new ways of fitting into existing hierarchies and perhaps challenging them.

A Cross-Cultural View of Games

Borman and Lippincott (1982) have recently discussed the functions of games from a cross-cultural perspective and asked two questions. How do games influence the ways individuals interact with peers in nonplay situations? How do they influence the future roles individuals will play in adult society? Thus, it is assumed that there is cultural purpose to games. We noted earlier that rough-housing and chase playing are nearly universal; but some forms of games are not. Games that emerge and survive in cultures do so because they have deep meaning for those cultures. Games that are out of step with particular cultural values and needs will not last very long. For example, in some tropical cultures, with very simple economic and political systems, and few social class distinctions, competitive games are not played. In industrialized cultures like ours, however, these games are the rule, extending well into adulthood.

What is it about cultures that determines the types of games played? The most extensive analysis of this question has been carried out in a series of studies by John Roberts and Brian Sutton-Smith and their colleagues. They divided competitive games into three major categories, called competitive games of physical skill, chance, and strategy (1970). In games of physical skill, winning and losing are determined by the sensory-motor skills of the players as in target shooting and darts. In games of chance, the outcomes are determined by guessing or by some external events such as the throw of a die. In games of strategy, the outcomes are determined by the rational choices of the players as in checkers, chess, and go. In our cultures there are games of these pure types, but many of the games we're familiar with are combinations of two or three of these categories, e.g., table tennis, pool, team sports. For the most part, Sutton-Smith and Roberts restricted their analyses to the three "pure" types.

As noted above, some cultures apparently don't have competitive games. In general these cultures downplay or discourage competition both among themselves and with neighboring cultures. There is also little pressure placed on children to achieve relative to their peers. Cultures that engage only in games requiring physical skill are very similar to those cultures without competitive games. The major differences between them are that the gaming cultures have greater sex role differentiation than nongaming ones as well as a greater percentage of nuclear as opposed to extended families. These differences suggest that adult competitiveness, especially for spouses, may be part of the basis for the existence of competitive games. That the games require physical skills, as opposed to strategy, seems to be related to the fact that self-reliance in hunting is a very important value.

Cultures that primarily engage in games of chance range from the very simple to the very complex. The theme that seems to run through these cultures is "uncertainty." Many of these peoples live in harsh environments where food production or hunting success is highly unpredictable. In many, individual survival and success are also unpredictable. For example, divorce rates are often high, and success in finding a desired mate is often low. Finally, the stability of the group and/or the social system are unpredictable. Life is "chancy" and people often use religious and nonreligious chance procedures to make decisions. Games of chance, then, seem to mirror people's perceptions and beliefs about the human condition.

Cultures that primarily engage in strategy games, on the average, are the most complex of these pure-type game cultures. They have higher technology, more complicated food-producing systems, greater occupational specialization, judicial systems, and several levels of a political hierarchy. There are a large number of organizations—economic, military, political, religious—in which strategy skills lead to success. Thus, the skills that children learn in games of strategy can readily be seen as useful in adult life. In these same cultures, folktales emphasizing the development and use of strategies are also widespread (Roberts, Sutton-Smith, & Kendon, 1963).

Cultures like ours, which engage in all three game types and their various combinations, are the most complex of all. All the industrialized societies fall into this group. Complex societies require very complex interpersonal skills. They also allow a great deal of differentiation in skill learning. Thus, pure strategists will find their place as will pure-chance types. The most successful game players in childhood may well become the most successful in adulthood.

Sutton-Smith and Roberts (1970) summarize their findings in the following quotation. This quote completes the circle by bringing us back to the issues we discussed in the nonhuman primate literature.

> Our work . . . has led us to the formulation that games are, among other things, models of power. Games are, we suggest, models of ways of succeeding over others, by magical power (as in games of chance), by force (as in physical skill games), or by cleverness (as in games of strategy). We have speculated that in games children learn all those necessary arts of trickery, deception, harassment, divination and foul play that their teachers won't teach them, but that are most important in successful human interrelationships in marriage, business and war. Further that boys played games of physical skill because this is the power form that they can most easily command; and that girls showed a preference for games of strategy and chance because these are the lesser power forms available to them. (p. 339)

DEVELOPMENT OF AGGRESSION

Aggression and Dominance

We saw in the discussion of nonhuman primates that fighting, or aggression more generally, plays an important role in their individual and group lives. In order for a monkey or ape at any age level to achieve some of its goals, it has to be more dominant than others, or be affiliated with some-one who is more dominant. With the nonhuman primates, dominance is closely related to successful aggression. If you can "beat him up," or if he thinks you can, you are able to have things your way.

The research dealing with the development of human aggression and dominance is quite interesting in that there are striking parallels with the other primates, as well as some important differences. One parallel observed is that aggression by nursery school children has positive payoffs for the aggressors—they typically get what they want through aggression. The intensive study by Patterson, Littman, and Bricker (1967) makes this point clear.

Patterson et al. observed two groups of white, middle-class nursery school children every day for an academic year. There were 18 boys and 18 girls in all, whose ages ranged from 2½ to 4½ years. The researchers recorded three categories of behavior for each aggressive encounter: *Aggressive behaviors*, which included bodily attacks, attacks with an object, and threats; *Target's response/consequences*, which either rewarded the attack, e.g., passivity, crying, defensive postures, verbal protests, or punished the attack, e.g., telling the teacher, recovering property, retaliating; *Teacher interventions*, which involved breaking up the dispute. These occurred infrequently.

Overall the number of aggressive behaviors in each classroom ranged from 12 to 40 per hour. The majority of these attacks were carried out by only 20% of the children, but nearly all children were aggressive on occasion. Importantly, on the average, at least three fourths of the attacks led to a successful outcome for the aggressor. Patterson et al. emphasize that it is the victim who does the rewarding for his or her attacker. Victims who tell the teacher, fight back, or recover their property are less likely to be attacked in the near future than those victims who do not punish their aggressor.

Patterson et al. identified three groups of victims: (1) those who were frequently attacked and successfully counterattacked; (2) those attacked frequently, but were unsuccessful in counterattacks; and (3) those attacked and counterattacked infrequently. Only the first group showed substantial increases over the years in the frequency with which they attacked others. In short, they learned in school by their successful coun-terattacks that aggression pays off.

Independent of the Patterson et al. research, Brown and Elliot (1965) investigated the teacher's role in maintaining aggression in nursery school classrooms. They reasoned that when teachers get involved with settling verbal and physical disputes, this extra attention serves to reward the disputants. If teachers were to reward by praise non-aggressive interactions between children and ignore aggressive ones, then aggressive encounters should be minimized. They asked their teachers to do just that, and it worked! Many parents have told us of similar observations. When they step in quickly to settle their own children's arguments, their children continue to have many arguments. But when they let their children "settle things between themselves" arguing decreases.

The research by Strayer and Strayer (1976) also nicely complements that of Patterson et al. The Strayers asked the question, How stable are dominance relations between nursery school children? They videotaped nursery school boys and girls during the last part of the academic year, so that the children were well-known to each other. Three types of initiated aggressive behaviors were noted: physical attacks; nonverbal threats; and struggles over objects or positions. Five types of responses to initiated aggressions were scored: seeking help; submitting; losing an object or position; no overt responding; and counterattacking.

There are two aspects of dominance relations, called "pairwise rigidity" and "group transitivity." Consider three children, Sue, Bob, and Joe. If Sue is nearly always successful in her dominance encounters with Bob, then pairwise, their dominance relation is rigid. If she is dominant only about three fourths of the time, then the relationship is not rigid. Dominance is transitive if Sue is dominant over Bob and Bob is dominant over Joe, then Sue is also dominant over Joe. If Sue were not dominant over Joe, then dominance in the group would not be transitive. For monkeys and apes, dominance is pairwise rigid and group transitive.

The Strayers measured dominance in three ways. In the first, they counted the number of times that one child either attacked or threatened to attack another, *and* the other child either submitted or lost an object or position. Dominance relations assessed in this manner were found to be both rigid and transitive—the nonhuman primate pattern. When the Strayers measured who attacked whom, dominance relations were neither rigid nor transitive. Low dominant on average attacked high dominant children about one fourth of the time; and some attacked the high dominants more than they were attacked. Finally, when the Strayers noted how frequently an attack resulted in either no response or a counterattack, there were essentially no behavioral differences between high and low dominant children.

One of the important conclusions we draw from the Strayers' research is that a distinction must be made between aggression (the second and third measure) and dominance (the first measure). Although high dominant children tend to initiate more attacks than low dominant ones, they do not counterattack more often. In their study, the most dominant child—the child who won in nearly all aggressive encounters—was a girl below the group average in initiating aggression.

Hartup (1974) has reviewed the research literature on the quantity and quality of aggression in early childhood and has presented original data for middle childhood. Three trends noted in the age-range between 2 and 6 years are (1) the amount of verbal aggression increases, e.g., threats, insults; (2) fighting or threatened fights over objects or positions ("instrumental" oriented aggression) decreases by about half; and (3) the frequency of attempts to hurt another as an end in itself ("person"—oriented aggression) increases appreciably.

In Hartup's own experiment, two separate age-groups of boys and girls (4–6 years and 6–8 years) were observed over a 10-week period in free-play situations. Overall, more verbal and physical aggression was seen in the younger than the older children. Thus, the decline in aggression starting at age 2 continues to at least age 8. However, the older children carried out more person-oriented aggression than the younger ones, again consistent with the earlier age trends. Hartup also examined in detail children's reactions to two types of aggressive attacks—blocking another child from an object or position, and insulting another child. The younger and older children were equally likely to respond to blocking by insulting the attacker. However, younger children were twice as likely as older ones to respond to insults by hitting. Thus, over time, we would expect that when younger children insult each other, soon one will retaliate by hitting. Older children, consistent with their increasing language abilities, will tend to continue the insults or withdraw from the scene.

Unfortunately, the research dealing with dominance in middle childhood has been based on interviews with children as opposed to observing their behavior in free-play situations. In the interviews children are shown either pictures or a list of names of their playmates and asked to pick out the "toughest" child, next "toughest," and so on. They are also asked to compare their own toughness with that of their peers. Omark, Omark, and Edelman (1975) used this technique with North American and Swiss children in kindergarten through the third grade with consistent results across the two cultures. In both cultures and all grade levels, boys were ranked highest, followed by a mixture of boys and girls, and girls were ranked lowest. Also in both cultures, with increasing grade level, children showed greater agreement with each other about the class toughness rankings. This implies a greater interpersonal awareness on the part of older children than younger children. Finally, in both cultures, boys and girls had greater agreement in ranking the class as a whole and the boys as a subgroup than they did in ranking the girls as a subgroup. This suggests that toughness plays a greater role in boys' relations with each other than in girls' relationships.

This last point gains additional meaning in light of the study by Weisfeld, Omark and Cronin (1980). Weisfeld et al. followed up some of the boys from the above American group when they were in ninth and tenth grade. They and their ninth-grade male classmates were asked to rank each other on the following dimensions: dominance, leadership, and popularity. These rankings were correlated with their "toughness" rankings from third grade. The correlations were moderately high in all cases. The boys who had been toughest in third grade were seen by their male peers as the most dominant, most popular, and strongest leaders. In addition, toughness rankings in second and third grade were correlated with their perceived "desirability as a date and as a party guest" by ninth- and tenth-grade girls. The correlations were moderate in both cases. Thus, the long-term consequences for being a dominant eight-year-old boy are positive and substantial.

The last study we discuss, by Savin-Williams (1979), concerns how dominance hierarchies are formed in 12–14-year-olds. The 40 children were enrolled in a 5-week overnight camp. Each of eight cabins housed 4–6 boys or girls and a same-sex college-age cabin counselor. The eight counselors who were trained by Savin-Williams systematically observed their cabin members for about 3 hours a day while specific activities were being carried out, e.g., meals, cabin cleanup, athletics. The counselors scored eight types of behaviors that have been used as measures of dominance. Some of these are successfully telling another what to do; teasing or putting down another; winning a physical fight; imitating, giving compliments, asking approval from another; verbally or physically threatening another. In addition, measures were made of a number of individual characteristics such as IQ, physical size, physical maturation, athletic ability.

The results are quite interesting. For boys and girls in each cabin, the dominance ranks were highly similar for all eight measures of dominance. If a girl was dominant over a cabin mate in teasing, she was usually dominant in telling her what to do. For both sexes, the most typical dominance encounter involved teasing or putting down another, and the least typical involved taking an object or position from another. However, boys were three times more likely than girls to use physical means in dominating another, and girls were four times more likely than boys to show lesser dominance by imitating, giving compliments, and asking favors.

Unlike the nursery school data, dominance pairwise rankings were not rigid. Children close to each other in dominance rank showed reversals about one third of the time, and children further apart, about one fifth of the time. Like the nursery school data, the dominance ranks in the group were transitive. Children were also asked to rank the dominance order of their cabin, including themselves (this is analogous to the "toughness" measure). Sex differences emerged. In all four boys' cabins there was agreement in these rankings, and moreover, they corresponded well to the behavioral observations. In only two of the four girls' cabins was there agreement among themselves and correspondence with the behavioral observations. These findings support the view that dominance in older children is more important to males than females.

Finally, behavioral dominance rank for boys and girls was strongly correlated with athletic ability, physical maturation, and leadership. Additionally, physical fitness was strongly correlated with dominance for boys, and peer popularity, for girls. Number of dominance encounters, intelligence, physical size, age, and language creativity were unrelated to dominance rank.

The research described above presents a relatively clear picture of the developmental course of aggression and dominance for North American children. At all age levels and for both sexes, there are large positive payoffs for being dominant over one's peers. For children between 2 and 4 years of age, dominance is gained through successful physical aggression. From ages 4 to 8, children increasingly use verbal methods to assert their dominance, at the expense of physical methods. Overall, aggressive encounters decrease. This implies that during middle childhood, children are learning to quickly evaluate dominance relationships and to not challenge them often. During the latter part of this age range and into early adolescence, boys and girls start to place different values on same-sex dominance ranks. In late preadolescence and early adolescence, encounters are overwhelmingly verbal, with fights being rare. Increasing flexibility in pairwise dominance occurs during this age range, which is uncharacteristic of apes, monkeys, and young children. "Toughness" in boys seems to underlie their dominance rank throughout the entire age range discussed. No parallel characteristic appears to underlie dominance rank for girls.

Cross-Cultural Comparisons

This section highlights William Lambert's discussion (1978) of the Six Culture study, which we briefly discussed in the previous chapter. The six cultures were a New England Baptist community, a Philippine barrio, a North Indian caste group, an Okinawan village, a Mexican Indian village, and a Kenyan rural community. In each culture the researchers scored the children's social behavior into 12 categories such as "seeks help," "seeks attention," "offers help," "physically assaults," "insults." They then computed a percentage for each category for each child; e.g., 15% of Joe's social behavior was seeking help.

Through the use of a statistical technique called *factor analysis* (see Chapter 1), these twelve categories were found to be grouped into four broader categories – nurturant behavior versus demanding behavior, and hostility versus intimacy. Children in the two most complex cultures (United States and North Indian) tended to be demanding and those in the three simplest (Kenyan, Mexican, Okinawan) tended to be nurturant. The other two categories were related to typical family complexity. The United States community, which emphasizes nuclear families, had children who tended to be intimate, and the Kenyan and North Indian communities, which emphasize more extended families, had children who tended to be hostile.

Over all six cultures, about 10% of children's observed social behavior was scored as aggressive, which breaks down into 1.5 aggressive acts for each 10 minutes observed. About half of the aggressive acts were retaliations of some sort, and half were attacks for no apparent (to the observer) reason. There were no systematic age differences for any of these observations (3–6-year-olds versus 7–10-year-olds) but there were some cultural differences. The United States and Mexican children were least likely to make unprovoked attacks and the Okinawan children most likely.

Instrumental versus personal aggressions were also scored. Across all six cultures, about 80% of aggressions were instrumental and about 3% were personal, with little cultural variation, for either type. No personal aggression whatsoever was recorded for the Kenyan group, and the highest percentage (6½%) was recorded for the Okinawans. The only reliable developmental difference across cultures was the decrease with age in physical assaults, which we noted in the previous section.

Returning to retaliations, approximately 30% of the time a child was "picked on" he or she retaliated aggressively. There were no age differences in this percentage, and only small cultural differences. Mexican children retaliated the least and North Americans the most. Also, girls retaliated slightly less frequently than boys.

Probably the greatest age difference found in all cultures concerns where aggression occurs and whom it is directed toward. Older children were much more likely than younger ones to restrict their aggression to play situations. Young children didn't make clear discriminations between play and nonplay contexts. Another major age change is that older children were much more likely than younger ones to initiate aggression against nonsiblings. This finding is probably related to the observation that older children attacked others more frequently when an adult was absent than when one was present. The reverse pattern held for younger children. It appears, then, that adults place strong socialization pressures on 7–10-year-olds not to hit or insult. Since at home where adults are present, the easiest target is a younger sibling, the older children controlled their aggression. There was an exception, though. When either parent was present, older children contained their aggression. However, when only grandmother was present, they did not. Finally, aggression was lowest for boys and girls when either was alone with a child of the opposite sex; but it was high for boys and highest for girls in mixed-sex groups. So, a single opposite-sex child inhibits aggression, but a group of boys and girls exaggerates it.

The most striking aspect of Lambert's analyses is the great cultural similarity in children's expression of aggression. This similarity, in part, comes about because children were observed in comparable settings. In the previous section we saw that North American nursery school children frequently batter each other. We don't know what children of other cultures would do in that setting, but we expect they would behave similarly.

Sex Differences in Aggression

There is a fair amount of disagreement among psychologists concerning whether the observed difference in aggression between human men and women is biologically based. In a recent issue of the journal *Child Devel-*

opment (1980), Todd Tieger took the position that the differences were produced by socialization, and Eleanor Maccoby and Carol Jacklin, that the differences were produced by biology and socialization. This argument is particularly interesting because at the time the papers were written all the authors were located at the same university, had access to the same information, and yet reached different conclusions.

There are four points that the authors debate about: (1) the extent to which sex-linked hormones differentially produce aggressive behavior; (2) the extent to which there are sex differences in aggression in young nonhuman primates; (3) the extent to which there are aggression differences in cross-cultural studies of boys and girls; (4) the extent to which different socialization practices could produce sex differences in aggression in very young boys and girls. In order to strongly support the biological argument, all four of these points would have to be answered in the male direction; e.g., male sex-linked hormones produce greater aggression than female sex-linked hormones. The most crucial of the four points, however, are the last two. And unfortunately, we have the least amount of reliable data about them.

The issue of sex-linked hormones and aggression deals with the hypothesized mechanism underlying sex differences. A large number of researchers have assumed that androgen, the male hormone, and estrogen, the female hormone, are the biochemicals involved in aggression. These hormones can operate in either or both of two ways: differentially organizing the brain from conception to about 3 months of age—a period when males and females have different levels of these hormones; differentially activating aggressive behavior in children.

There is some evidence with nonhuman animals and with adolescent and adult humans that large amounts of androgen are associated with high aggression, and large amounts of estrogen, with low aggression (although Tieger notes a reversal of this with chimpanzee females). However, androgen and estrogen levels in boys and girls are essentially the same between age 3 months and the onset of puberty, making the differential levels argument irrelevant for children. The data dealing with brain organization comes from children with genetic errors. Infrequently it happens that genetic males and females receive an excess amount of androgens during prenatal development. They can be identified at birth and some have been studied during childhood and adolescence. These children of both sexes have greater activity levels than prenatal normals, but not greater aggression levels. Animal studies, however, do show links between prenatal androgen levels and later aggressive behavior. In summary, the evidence for a biochemical mechanism for aggression differences between boys and girls is weak.

The issue of sex differences in nonhuman primate aggression relates to our evolutionary heritage. Tieger raises two problems with this literature. We are more closely related to the apes than to the monkeys and baboons, and yet it is the baboons that show the greatest sex differences in aggression. Second, aggression is not a single entity, and females show more aggression in defending offspring, but males more aggression in mating situations. Both Tieger and Maccoby and Jacklin agree that chimpanzees are the closest relatives from an evolutionary view, but reach very different conclusions concerning sex differences in that species. Maccoby and Jacklin present some data, and Tieger, only the opinions of others. Overwhelmingly in three separate field studies male chimpanzees were observed as being more aggressive than females, supporting the biological position.

The issue of cross-cultural sex differences in childhood aggression indirectly deals with the biology question. If boys are everywhere more aggressive on average than girls, it is difficult to argue that different patterns of socialization produce the aggression differences. Each culture has unique ways of socializing children, and if boys are found to be more aggressive, support is gained for a biological basis. Tieger and Maccoby and Jacklin differ on their analyses of the published data. There seems to be little argument that in studies of North American, Swiss, and English children age 6 or younger, on average boys have been found to be more aggressive than girls. The problem comes from the Six-Cultures data, where the number of 3–6-year-old children observed was very small. Basically, in the five non-North American cultures boys tended to initiate more aggression than girls, but not to retaliate more aggressively. None of the cultures showed sex differences in rough-and-tumble play. Both Tieger and Maccoby and Jacklin believe that there are insufficient cross-cultural data to draw firm conclusions, but they interpret the Six-Culture results in opposite ways. We believe that the cross-cultural question is still open to debate, but tend to side with Maccoby and Jacklin that boys have been shown to be more aggressive.

The final issue concerning different socialization patterns for boys and girls is the muddiest issue of all. Given the fact that North American and English boys are on average more aggressive than girls, can their different social experiences explain this? Tieger says yes, and Maccoby and Jacklin say no. Tieger argues that boys' greater activity levels, their tendency to play at greater distances from adults, and their lesser ability to use language to control their social behavior provides a set of conditions that could lead to learning greater aggression. Further, both parents and television maintain strong sex role stereotypes regarding the expression of aggression, which likely influence boys' and girls' aggressive behaviors. Maccoby and Jacklin point to the observational studies that show that preschool boys and girls are equally likely to be rewarded and punished for aggression by peers, parents, and teachers; to studies that show that boys are more likely than girls to imitate others' aggression; and most importantly, to studies that indicate that children below age 6 do not modify their behavior on the basis of sex role knowledge. Thus, even if young boys and girls "knew" that boys are supposed to show aggression, and girls, inhibit it, this knowledge would not affect their behavior.

Our conclusion to this argument is similar to that of Maccoby and Jacklin. It is likely that there is a biological basis for sex differences in aggression. In early childhood there is great overlap between boys and girls in the expression of aggression, but the most aggressive children are typically boys. As children mature, different socialization pressures operate on them that reinforce and exaggerate these biological tendencies. Thus, in adolescence, where hormonal differences start to occur and in adulthood, males are substantially more aggressive, on average, than females.

DEVELOPMENT OF ALTRUISM

Nearly in direct opposition to aggression is altruism—the act of helping another at some cost to one's self. Altruistic acts can tremendously differ both in the amount of help given and in the cost to the giver. Picking up a book that someone has dropped involves both mild "helps" and "costs"; whereas throwing yourself on a live hand grenade to save another's life is the ultimate sacrifice. Most altruistic acts seem to be more along the mild side, but nevertheless they are very important socially—offering John a piece of gum while at the same time ignoring Jim makes a big difference to everyone concerned.

What has impressed psychologists and biologists is the cost aspect of altruism. On the surface it doesn't seem to make much sense that people or animals will choose to do something that is detrimental to themselves. In their analysis of this problem, some biologists have concluded that species that behave altruistically have genes for that behavior (e.g., Wilson,

1980). The biological argument is somewhat technical, but the punch line is that over the long haul of many generations, individuals with "altruistic" genes are more likely to have surviving relatives than those without these genes. Thus, what in the short run is a cost turns out in the long run to be a benefit. Fortunately, we don't have to decide whether humans are endowed with altruistic genes in order to study the development of altruistic behavior.

We restrict our discussion to altruism among peers. Three basic procedures have been used to study this issue: (1) in a laboratory setting, allowing children to act altruistically toward a child who is not present, e.g., donating candy to the "poor children"; (2) in a laboratory setting, allowing children to act altruistically to another child who is present, e.g., the winner sharing candy with the loser in a guessing game; (3) in naturalistic settings, observing the spontaneous altruistic behavior of children toward each other, e.g., helping another child pick up some blocks. These procedures are dramatically different from one another, but there are not enough data to tell whether they lead to different developmental conclusions.

Each of the procedures has certain advantages. In the first one, since no other child is present, it is impossible for an altruistic act to be rewarded by the child who directly benefited. Where reward is possible, you can argue that the act wasn't really altruistic, but was done to return a previous favor or to get a favor in return. In the second procedure, another child is present and the experimenter has good control over the situation, including the history of the children in that situation. Moreover, face-to-face situations are probably the most common occasions for altruism—the anonymous donor, in our experience, is rare. The third procedure offers the greatest opportunity for generalizing results. Most developmental psychologists are interested in the everyday lives of people, and not so much their laboratory behavior. Of the above procedures this has been the least frequently used.

Three recent studies by Eisenberg-Berg and her colleagues shed a good deal of light on the altruistic behaviors of 4–5-year-olds in naturalistic preschool settings. The first study (Eisenberg, Cameron, Tryon, & Dodez, 1981) parallels the Patterson et al. experiment (1967) by examining the consequences of altruistic acts (which they refer to as "prosocial" behavior). Eisenberg et al. distinguished between two kinds of altruistic behavior, "spontaneous" and "asked-for." With spontaneous acts, the altruist initiates the behavior without being asked to do so. In asked-for acts, the altruist responds to the verbal or nonverbal request of a peer.

Eisenberg et al. raise several questions about what happens when children behave altruistically, two of which are of particular interest. First, what is the relationship between altruistic children and peer and teacher reactions to them? It might be argued that children are altruistic because others reward them for it. For spontaneous acts, there was no relation between how often a child was altruistic and the amount of positive or negative reactions received from children or teachers. For asked-for acts, a striking observation was made. Children who usually refused to help another child when asked to do so would be responded to positively on the few occasions when they didn't refuse. But children who almost always said yes when asked for help would generally be responded to negatively by the child who asked for and received the help. Teachers, on the other hand, rewarded positively children who frequently carried out asked-for acts. However, teachers responded to altruistic acts less than 5% of the time, ignoring or being unaware of the rest. From these data it is clear that the frequency of altruism is unrelated to the positive responses children receive.

The second question is, What are the behavioral differences between the children who usually comply with asked-for altruism (high compliers) and those who don't? The high compliers, relative to the latter, are asked to help or share more, are more likely to ask teachers for help, are less likely to respond positively to the help they receive from peers, and are less likely to defend themselves from impingements. From these findings, it may be concluded that the high compliers are less socially adept and more submissive than their peers. These and the above findings strongly suggest that asked-for altruism is not altruism at all, but rather is a vehicle for maintaining dominance relations.

The study by Eisenberg-Berg and Hand (1979) deals with the relationship between children's reasoning in moral judgement stories and altruism. The assumption the authors make is that altruism is a form of moral behavior, and as a consequence, might be related to children's moral reasoning. The stories presented social dilemmas in which the needs of the central character were placed in conflict with others' needs; e.g., a child on the way to a birthday party is asked to help another child who just broke her leg. If the central character helps the injured child, she will miss the cake and ice cream.

Two major types of naturally occurring altruistic behavior were observed in the school setting, sharing toys in one's possession, and helping, e.g., bringing another a block that is not being used by anyone. The altruistic behaviors were scored by placing their answers into one of seven categories. The two most relevant ones for us were "hedonism" in which self-gain of the central character determines that character's response, and "needs-oriented" in which the needs of the other person are considered by the central character. Needs-oriented reasoning should be associated with altruism, whereas hedonism should not.

For spontaneous sharing, the more frequently children used needs-oriented reasoning, the more frequently they shared; and the more frequently they used hedonistic reasoning, the less frequently they shared. Asked-for sharing, and spontaneous and asked-for helping, were unrelated to moral reasoning. Eisenberg-Berg and Hand point out the different behavioral consequences of helping and sharing. When children help another, they give up no material object, and moreover frequently join in play the one they help. Thus helping often appears to be means for personal gain. When children share, however, they give up a toy and don't usually join the other in play. Sharing, then, usually leads to a greater cost than helping.

The study by Eisenberg-Berg and Neal (1979) nicely complements the above. The experimenters observed the children in the classroom and playground, looking for spontaneous acts of sharing or helping. When such an incident occurred the experimenter approached the altruist and said something like "Why did you give that to Mary?" If the child's answer was vague, the experimenter persisted, but was not always successful. Children's answers were placed into reasoning categories nearly identical with those used by Eisenberg-Berg and Hand. The results strongly suggest that the motivation for children's altruistic behaviors is rarely for exclusive personal gain. Rather, on most occasions they spontaneously help and share with others because of a caring for them.

The experiment by Bar-Tal, Raviv, and Leiser (1980) deals with the motives for sharing with a peer in a laboratory setting. This is a very clever and complicated study, but well worth our time. Bar-Tal et al. tested groups of 5-, 7-, and 9-year-old urban Israeli children. The children came to the laboratory in same-age, same-sex pairs and participated in a guessing game. The experimenter chose a number from 0 to 10 and each child tried to guess it. Five games were played and the experimenter rigged it so that one child won two games and the other three. The three-game winner received seven pieces of candy and was told that he could do with it as he pleased. The loser received nothing.

Bar-Tal et al. manipulated the motives for sharing by setting up a sequence of five conditions that tapped different motivations for the winner to share. The first condition is called "altruism" in which the experimenter left the room, returned, and noticed whether the winner had shared. If not, the second condition, "normative," involved the experimenter reading a story about good children sharing candy with other children who don't have any. The experimenter left the room, returned, and noticed whether the candy was shared. If not, "internal initiative and concrete reward" was initiated.

In this condition, the experimenter told the two children that their teacher had just said that a child who shared candy would get an important role in a class play the teacher was preparing. The experimenter then went to another part of the room and busied herself with work. If the child had not shared, the fourth condition, "compliance," was started. In this condition, the experimenter told the winner to share with the loser, and went to another part of the room. If the winner still did not share, the fifth condition, "compliance and concrete-defined reinforcement," began. In this condition, the experimenter told the child to share and promised the winner a big prize if he did so. No one refused to share at this point. After a child shared, he was asked his reasons for sharing. These reasons were placed in categories that roughly corresponded to the motives associated with the five conditions.

The results are relatively straightforward. As children get older they are more likely to share under the altruistic and normative conditions and less likely in the big prize condition. Only 2% of the 9-year-olds, but 24% of the 5-year-olds shared under the latter condition. Consistent with these findings, older children gave more altruistic and normative reasons for sharing than did the younger ones. However, children in all age-groups tended to give higher level reasons for sharing than the actual condition. Thus, a child who shared under the compliance condition may have given an altruistic reason for doing so. Bar-Tal et al. conclude that moral development underlies altruistic behavior, noting that the reasons children give do not necessarily correspond to their behavior. It is as if we have two somewhat related and independent systems developing; verbal moral judgements and altruistic/normative behaviors. As children mature, both systems develop, and partially influence each other.

Two recent books by Mussen and Eisenberg-Berg (1977) and Staub (1979) and articles by Rushton (1976) and Underwood and Moore (1982) have reviewed nearly all the published research dealing with the development and socialization of altruism. In the remainder of this section we summarize some of this material.

There is fairly complete agreement about the following conclusions: (1) older children are more altruistic than younger ones; (2) there are no consistent sex differences in altruism; and (3) there is some, but not a great deal of generality of altruism across situations. Children who are altruistic in one setting only tend to be so in other settings.

The above writers are chiefly concerned with identifying the psychological factors that lead to altruism. In that altruism increases with age, and children differ from one another in how frequently they behave altruistically, it is assumed that an underlying psychology explains these phenomena. Underwood and Moore's analysis provides a useful and clear integration of the issue.

These authors argue that the development of altruism is related to at least four different forms of perspective taking, called perceptual, social, moral, and empathic. Perspective taking is the ability of a person to take the viewpoint or position of another. Perceptual perspective taking, the ability to predict what another person experiences in the sensory realm (sight, sounds, etc.), is thought of by some writers to form the base on which other perspective abilities are built. Social perspective taking refers to the ability to predict another person's thoughts, motives, intentions, or interpersonal behavior.

Underwood and Moore view moral judgements and empathy as special cases of perspective taking, built on the development of the above two. In order to make a moral judgment you have to be able to predict another person's social perspective in a situation, and then make a decision based on it. For example, a child may know that if she gives a playmate one of the blocks she's playing with, the playmate will be able to complete a project (social perspective taking). The child's decision to give the block to the playmate is a moral judgement. Empathic perspective taking is the ability to predict the feelings of another *and* to experience those feelings to some extent. If a child knows that his friend will feel sad if the friend loses a quarter (perspective taking) the child may experience his friend's sadness (empathy).

Given that a child has acquired the relevant perspective-taking abilities for altruism, the question of motivation remains. There is no agreement on this question, and perhaps the easiest way to deal with it is to side with the biological view – altruism is a built-in psychological characteristic created by evolutionary forces. It follows a developmental course and takes different forms in different situations. In principle, the development of altruism is no different from that of any other psychological characteristic.

Underwood and Moore review the literature concerning the relation between each type of perspective-taking ability and altruistic behavior.

The following conclusions are made: (1) In general, the greater children's perceptual perspective-taking ability, the greater their altruism; (2) in general, the greater children's social perspective-taking ability, the greater their altruism. In both cases, the effects of perspective-taking ability were over and above those of age. However, these relationships were not strong. Thus, knowing a child's perspective-taking ability would not allow you to accurately predict her altruistic behavior.

There are a number of studies relating moral judgement to altruism using very different measures of morality. Some of these measures score moral judgments on a developmental scale from low to high. Others, such as used by Eisenberg-Berg and Hand, score specific categories of moral thought. Pooling all these together, Underwood and Moore conclude that there is a strong relation between moral judgment and altruism. Note here that the authors place the Eisenberg-Berg studies under morality and not empathy. Finally, the authors suggest that for children there is no consistent relation between empathy and altruism, but for adolescents and adults there does seem to be a positive relation between the two. This suggests that the links between empathy and altruism develop later.

COOPERATION AND COMPETITION IN CROSS-CULTURAL PERSPECTIVE

Games are reflections of cultural values, but also serve the purpose of instilling those values in the players. We earlier noted that in urban-industrial societies such as ours, competitive games are the norm, but in simpler societies, they may be totally absent. What would happen if a novel game, which could be played in either a cooperative or competitive manner, were presented to children of different cultures? Our guess is that they would play it along the lines of their cultural values. The research we'll now describe provides some answers to this question. These answers are somewhat disturbing, but like a magnifying glass or microscope, the games allow us to see more clearly what may have only been hinted at.

Millard Madsen of the United States invented two games, shown in Fig. 4.1, for the purpose of studying children in different cultures and different settings (rural versus urban) within any culture. The cooperation board is described by Madsen and Shapira (1970) as follows:

> The cooperation board was 18 inches square with an eyelet fastened to each corner. Strings strung through these eyelets were connected to an object

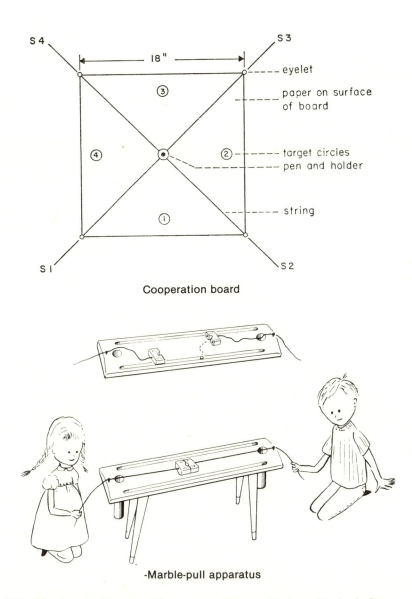

Cooperation board

-Marble-pull apparatus

FIG. 4.1   Cooperative-competition games. (Sources: Madsen, M. C. & Connor, C. Cooperative and competitive behavior of retarded and nonretarded at two ages. *Child Development*, 1973, *44*, 175–178. © The Society for Research in Child Development, Inc. Madsen, M. C. & Shapira, A. Cooperative and competitive behavior of urban Afro-American, Mexican-American, and Mexican village children. *Developmental Psychology*, 1970, *3*, 16–20.)

which served to hold a downward pointing ballpoint pen. A sheet of white paper was placed on the board prior to each trial. When the subjects, who were seated at each of the far corners of the board, pulled the strings, responses were automatically recorded by the pen. Because of the eyelets, individual subjects were only able to pull the pen toward themselves. It was therefore necessary for the subjects to cooperate in order to draw a line over designated points which were not in a direct path from the starting point in the center of the board to any of the corners. (p. 17)

The marble-pull apparatus is described by Madsen and Conner (1973) as follows:

The marble pull consists of a rectangular table with an eyelet screwed into each end. Strings strung through the eyelets connect to a Plexiglas marble holder that is initially placed in the center of the table. When the marble holder is pulled to either end of the table, the marble drops into a cup, thus being delivered to one of the two subjects seated at opposite ends of the table. A simple tug-of-war situation is precluded by the fact that the marble holder is held together by magnetic inserts. When subjects pull against each other the marble holder breaks apart, and the marble rolls into a groove along the edge of the table. The table top declines slightly from the center to the slides for that purpose. (p. 176)

These games have been used with children between the ages of 4 and 14 in an extraordinary number of cultures including Blackfoot Indians of Canada, Columbians, Mexicans, Israelis, Australian Aborigines, Maoris, Polynesians, South Koreans, Hungarians, former headhunters from Papua New Guinea, and North Americans. In almost all of thse studies either rural children were compared with urban children, or within an urban setting recent immigrants from rural areas were compared with children from more established families.

When the cooperation board was used, the four children usually first received "group reward" instructions. They were told that in order to receive a reward (money, candy, or toys) a line would have to be drawn through all the target circles. All children in all cultures quickly learned to cooperate and received rewards. Following a number of one-minute trials, a new set of instructions, called "individual reward," was given. The experimenter wrote each child's name across one of the circles and told the children that they only received a reward when a line was drawn through this circle. In some experiments the circles were placed in a direct path from the center of the board to the corner, and in other experiments the circles remained as shown in Fig. 4.1.

Logically, in order to receive rewards, the children merely had to continue doing what they had been doing all along—cooperate. Psychologically, for children in some cultures, all hell broke loose. These children, which included nearly all those living in cities, started pulling frantically at their strings, preventing anyone from receiving a reward. Often the experimenter had to hold the board down to stop it from flying across the room. In most cases cotton strings had to be replaced with nylon because in their illogical competition the cotton strings frequently broke. Children from rural areas nearly always behaved in a logical way, continuing to cooperate, and received rewards. Performance with the marble-pull apparatus was highly similar to that with the cooperation board—rural children cooperated by alternating marble wins from trial to trial, and urban children competed, winning essentially no rewards.

Two of the fascinating findings are that wherever 4-year-olds were subjects, whether in urban or rural settings, they cooperated as much or more than all the older children, e.g., Shapira (1976) for Israeli city- and kibbutz-reared boys and girls. Second, Madsen and Connor (1973) tested with the marble-pull apparatus 6–7 and 11–12-year-old mentally retarded and normal IQ children attending the same United States urban school. Initially the age 6–7 mentally retarded children cooperated 75% of the time, the age 11–12 mentally retarded, 30% of the time, and the two normal groups, less than 3% of the time. After the experimenters demonstrated to the children how each could win a marble on alternative trials (cooperating), the mentally retarded children cooperated between 75% and 80% of the time and the normals cooperated between 15% and 30% of the time. Why do 4-year-olds and mentally retarded children behave more cooperatively (and seemingly more logically) than older normal children? We return to this question after first discussing the rural/urban cross-cultural findings.

It's obvious that living in a rural setting does not *make you* cooperative and living in an urban setting, competitive. Rather, it's your socialization experiences and the cultural values you are taught that predispose you to act one way or another in Madsen's games. In most rural settings, in most cultures, families are engaged in agriculture or agriculture-related work. Typically, family members must work together in highly cooperative ways to accomplish at least a minimal standard of living. Competition either among family members or between families is actively discouraged in that it can be destructive. When someone wins, someone else loses, and that loss may prevent food from reaching the table. The clearest examples of socialization for cooperation are found in communal living cultures such as gatherer-hunters and Israeli kibbutzim.

Urban settings are frequently quite different in many respects. It is rare that groups of families work together toward common subsistence goals or that the members of a single family work together. Exceptions are small family-owned businesses such as grocery or confectionery stores, where the children pitch in after school and Mom and Pop stay all day. In the cities competition and personal gain are the norm, even if they are at some cost to others. "If I win, you lose, and that's the name of the game." Nearly everyone likes winners, and losers are a sorry lot.

There are other important differences between socialization in the city and in the country. Stanley Milgram (1970) summarizes some differences related to social responsibility. In the cities people stand by while their neighbors are in obvious trouble, even if they are being attacked with a deadly weapon. They don't even call the police. People in cities are generally unwilling to trust or assist strangers. Cities are potentially dangerous places and a first principle is "protect yourself." People in cities are discourteous, often bumping into each other without an apology. Milgram points out that in cities people sometimes make excuses for being courteous as if afraid others will think them weird. People in cities often have to compete for scarce facilities such as parking places or seats on the bus. The anonymity of the city contributes to all of this.

If being raised in cities socializes for competition and being raised in the country socializes for cooperation, what happens when country folks move to the city? Three recent studies answer this question. Knight and Kagan (1977) using a different task than the two shown in Fig. 4.1, with children in grades 4, 5, and 6, studied the behavior of Anglo-Americans, second generation urban Mexican-Americans, and third generation urban Mexican-Americans. All children attended the same school. Knight and Kagan found the Anglos to be the most competitive, followed by the third generation, then second generation Mexican-Americans. The fact that the children differed in competition implies that the family was more important than peers in socializing competition. The fact that there were differences between the second and third generation Mexican-Americans implies that over time, the cultural values of families shift to accomodate their new environment.

Miller (1973) using the cooperation board with 8-year-olds compared Blackfoot Indians attending a rural nonintegrated school, Blackfeet attending a more urban integrated school, white Canadians attending the same school, and white Canadians attending a more urban nonintegrated school. The most cooperative were the nonintegrated Blackfeet, the least cooperative, the nonintegrated whites, with the other two groups falling in between. The differences between the nonintegrated Blackfeet and nonintegrated whites are as expected. The similarity in performance between the other groups implies that each group has been socialized by the other. The Blackfeet became more competitive, but the whites became more cooperative.

Sommerlad and Bellingham (1972) compared three groups of 12-14-year-olds on the cooperation board: (1) white Australians in an academic track; (2) aborigines in a nonacademic track; (3) aborigines in an academic track. Those in the nonacademic track were being prepared for traditional jobs in their community. Those in the academic track were being prepared for white-collar careers in the predominantly white urban society. The most competitive were the whites and the least competitive, the aborigines in the nonacademic track. Thus, the aborigines maintained some of their cooperative cultural values but those children intending to leave their culture were being socialized to be more competitive.

These three studies show that *acculturation*–the acquisition of values and behaviors from a different culture–occurs in the socialization of competition, but it is not immediate. Cultural values transmitted through the family can persist through at least three generations in a new culture. Finally, it appears that the values of cooperation and competition are more heavily influenced by a child's family than by his or her peers.

The studies by Madsen and Lancy (1981) and Kagan, Knight, Martinez and Santana (1981) shed additional light on the rural/urban differences. Kagan et al. interviewed three groups of Mexican children between the ages of 4 and 12. One group lived in a large city, one group lived in a small commercial town, and one group in a small noncommercial rural town. The children were asked "what they would do if another child their age (1) took away one of their toys and (2) hit them." Responses were classed in one of three ways: (a) nonconflict; e.g., "I would do nothing"; (b) mediated conflict; e.g., "I'd tell a teacher"; and (c) direct conflict; e.g., "I would hit his head in with a stone." Children from the commercial town had more direct conflict and fewer nonconflict responses than the other two groups, who responded similarly to each other. In that competition puts someone in conflict with another, these results remind us that the specific socialization experiences a child receives influences his cooperative or competitive behavior, and not just the size of the community or its rural versus urban setting.

The Madsen and Lancy study used both the cooperation board and the marble-pull apparatus with 12 different cultural groups of children from Papua New Guinea in grades 4, 5, and 6. The groups varied in a number of dimensions including rural versus urban, recency of urban living, and type and amount of contact with urban centers. Some of the groups were cooperative on every trial, and others were virtually never cooperative. Generally, children in urban settings were more competitive than those in rural settings, but there were reversals. Madsen and Lancy interpret their findings, including the reversals, on the basis of two factors: how much the particular culture emphasizes strong ties and commitments to members of that culture; and how much urban living has weakened these ties and commitments. Thus, children who live in the city who still have strong ties to members of their culture are cooperative with them in the Madsen games. Children who live in rural settings may be fairly competitive with children of their culture either because the culture itself doesn't emphasize strong ties and commitments, or because urban influences have weakened the ties.

Let's now return to the highly cooperative 4-year-olds and mentally retarded children. Are they really more logical than older normals? We think not. Several other explanations are possible. Kagan and Madsen (1971), discussing differences between younger and older normals, suggest that the younger children may not sharply distinguish between their own goals versus group goals. The young child may be interested in someone winning, and it makes little difference who that person is. As children mature, the "I" or "we" become stronger, and in competitive societies, they want to win. Madsen and Conner (1973), discussing differences between the mentally retarded and normals, suggest that the former group have developed personality styles that avoid competition. This personality development stems from their past history of failure and frustration in competitive situations.

A third possibility, and the one we prefer, stems from Fishbein's (1976) discussion of the development of the norm of reciprocity. Fishbein makes a distinction between a universal norm of "taking turns," which children in nearly all cultures learn at an early age, and a norm of reciprocity. The latter starts to emerge at about age 6 and continues to develop thereafter. This norm emphasizes paying back punishments with punishments and rewards with rewards, conditional on the motivation you perceive in the other person. It takes a certain level of cognitive development to be able to figure out the motivation of a fellow game player, and 6–7-year-old mentally retarded children don't have it. Neither do 4-year-old normals. These children operate at the level of "taking turns" and thus everyone wins. With the emergence of the norm of reciprocity, children in competitive cultures are unwilling to "give" without first "getting." This leads to the apparently irrational behavior of everybody losing because once someone has prevented you from winning, you in turn prevent that person from winning.

As a final note, distinctions should be made between cooperation and altruism, and between aggression and competition. When two children cooperate on the Madsen games they are acting out of self-interest. Each child helps the other, at no cost to himself, and in fact, gains by the interaction. Everybody wins when everybody cooperates. When children play the Madsen games in a competitive fashion, they often get angry and do inflict damage by preventing each other from winning. Inflicting damage on another is aggressive behavior, but in this situation it is more than aggression because the act of aggressing causes you to lose. We can talk about competition in this situation as "mutual retaliation," but again, when you retaliate, you lose. Unfortuately, in the Madsen games, it only takes one person to force the game into a competitive mode—three cooperating and one competing leads to everyone losing.

PARENTAL INFLUENCES ON CHILDREN'S PEER AND SCHOOL BEHAVIOR

In this section we'll discuss results from two research programs that have examined parent-child interactions as related to children's behavior in either a preschool or primary school setting. The first involves a long-term study of white two-parent middle-class families with very bright children, and the second involves a comparison of white, middle-class, divorced and two-parent families.

The Baumrind Studies

Diane Baumrind has written about child-care practices as related to children's behavior since the middle 1960s. Originally she published several studies dealing with 4-year-old nursery school children, and in recent years she has followed up on these same children at 8 to 9 years of age. Her publications are among the most widely discussed in this research area.

In Baumrind's earlier reports the children studied had an average IQ of 125, which is approximately the top 5% of the population, and their parents were highly educated. Their social behavior was observed in school over a 3-month period, and parent-child behavior was recorded during two home visits. Although seventy-two categories of nursery school behavior were scored, through the use of factor analysis, seven clusters emerged that nearly completely describe the children's social interactions with peers and teachers. These are listed in Table 4.2 with examples from each end of the cluster. In general, boys relative to girls were more hostile to peers, resistive to adults, and domineering; and less achievement-oriented. On the remaining three clusters, their scores were similar.

Baumrind suggests that these seven clusters can be further thought of as falling on two separate dimensions of social-psychological functioning. The first dimension she refers to as "socially-responsible versus irresponsible" and includes the hostile-friendly, resistive-cooperative, and achievement-oriented behavior clusters. The second dimension is referred to as "independent versus suggestible" behavior and includes the remaining four clusters.

Table 4.2

Children's Preschool Behavior Clusters

1. Hostile-Friendly with Peers
   Bullies other children (Hostile)
   Nurtures or sympathetic towards other children (Friendly)

2. Resistive-Cooperative with Teachers
   Tries to evade adult authority (Resistive)
   Obedient (Cooperative)

3. Domineering-Tractable with Peers and Teachers
   Manipulates other children to get what he or she wants (Domineering)
   Timid with other children (Tractable)

4. Dominant-Submissive with Peers
   Peer leader (Dominant)
   Suggestible (Submissive)

5. Purposive-Aimless with Peers
   Self-starting and self-propelled (Purposive)
   Spectator (Aimless)

6. Achievement-Oriented-Not Achievement-Oriented with Peers, Teachers and Tasks
   Likes to learn new skill (Achievement-Oriented)
   Does not persevere when he encounters frustration (Not Achievement-Oriented)

7. Independent-Suggestible with Peers, Teachers, and Tasks
   Individualistic (Independent)
   Does not question adult authority (Suggestible)

(Source: Baumrind, D. Current patterns of parental authority. *Developmental Psychology Monographs*, 1971, *4*, No. 1, Pt. 2.)

The behavior of the parents in relation to their child was scored along 15 dimensions, which included expecting participation in household chores, enriching the child's environment, firmly enforcing rules, demanding obedience, encouraging independence, and promoting respect for authority. With the aid of factor analysis, four major patterns of parenting behavior were identified. These patterns involve unique combinations of the 15 dimensions. The underlying assumption of this approach is that combinations rather than isolated practices should be examined in order to understand how children develop.

Authoritarian parents place great emphasis on demanding obedience from their children and promoting respect for authority. They often use physical punishment both to attain this obedience and respect, as well as to discourage their independent action and discussion of family rules. Authoritarian parents are rigid and traditional.

Authoritative parents are also actively involved with structuring their children's behavior, but do so with flexibility. They encourage independence in children, but at the same time firmly and clearly enforce family rules. These parents are interested in the expansion of their children's knowledge and activities and place emphasis on enriching their environment.

Permissive parents are the least involved in actively structuring their children's lives. They are very accepting of their children, but seem to do so by the absence of demands. They do *not* firmly enforce family rules, expect obedience, promote respect for authority or discourage infantile behavior. As might be predicted, these parents don't often express anger.

Nonconforming parents share some similarities with both permissive and authoritative ones. They place great emphasis on enriching their child's environment, are flexible and clear about family rules, and willingly discuss these rules with their children. They are self-confident as parents and encourage their children's independence. They do not demand obedience or emphasize respect for authority.

The relationships between patterns of parenting and children's social interactions in school are seen in Table 4.3. We constructed the table by examining the average scores Baumrind (1971) reported for each group of children for each behavior cluster and noting which groups scored highest and lowest. In two cases, for Hostile and Achievement-Oriented in boys, two groups had very similar high scores. The following are examples of how to read the table. For Hostile, girls of authoritarian parents were the least hostile and girls of authoritative parents, the most hostile. For Dom-

TABLE 4.3

Children's Preschool Behavior Clusters Related to Patterns of Parents' Behavior

	Hostile*	Resistive*	Domineering**	Dominant**	Purposive**	Achievement-Oriented*	Independent**
Girls							
Authoritarian	Low					Low	Low
Authoritative	High	High	High	High	High	High	High
Permissive							
Nonconforming		Low	Low	Low	Low		
Boys							
Authoritarian	High						
Authoritative	Low	Low	Low		High	High	
Permissive	High	High	High	Low	Low	Low	Low
Nonconforming				High		High	High

*Clusters comprising social responsibility
**Clusters comprising independence

inant, boys of nonconforming parents were the most dominant and boys of permissive parents, the least dominant.

In looking at this table from the point of view of rearing children to be socially responsible and independent, we can draw several conclusions. First, girls of authoritative parents are, on average, the most independent, but the least socially responsible of the four groups. Girls of nonconforming parents tend to be the least independent. There is no strong pattern for high social responsibility. Second, boys of authoritative parents are the most, and boys of permissive parents, the least socially responsible. Boys of permissive parents are also the least independent, while those with authoritative and nonconforming parents tend to be equally independent.

Finally, highly similar patterns of parenting generally lead to different levels of social responsibility and independence in boys and girls. For example, boys and girls of both authoritative and authoritarian parents, relative to their same-sex peers, scored in opposite ways in several of the behavior clusters. This is perhaps the most interesting and puzzling finding of all. We don't know whether these effects are caused by an interaction of biology and culture, or whether the total set of effects is restricted to cultures of very bright children of highly educated bright parents.

In the follow-up study when they were 8 to 9 years old, Baumrind (1982) discussed a different set of both social interaction behaviors in the school and current parental child-rearing practices. Three child social dimensions were identified: *social assertiveness, cognitive competence,* and *social responsibility.* Children's scores on social assertiveness were primarily based upon how self-assured, open, successfully competitive, aggressive, and resistant to peer coercion they were. Their scores on cognitive competence were based on how achievement-oriented, creative, and intellectually mature they were and how able they were to negotiate with adults. Social responsibility scores were measured by how friendly, cooperative, and socially mature they were with peers and adults. Overall, boys were higher in social assertiveness, girls were higher in social responsibility, and the two genders were approximately the same in cognitive competence.

Four dimensions of parental behaviors were assessed. *Demanding* was primarily measured by how firmly they exerted controls over their children, how extensively they required participation in household help, and how much they demanded age-appropriate behavior. *Restrictive* was scored by how closely the child's activities were monitored, how intrusive and overprotective parents were, and how conventional and traditional were the values imposed on the children. *Responsive* was measured by how supportive, warm, open, and accessible they were, and secondarily by how readily they expressed anger. *Psychological differentiation* refers to how much autonomy parents encouraged, primarily measured by how much intellectual stimulation they provided, and how clear and self-confident parents were of their own values and expectations for the children.

The relationships between the four child-rearing dimensions and the three social interaction dimensions are shown in Table 4.4. Following are two examples of how to read the table. Boys whose parents were demanding tended to score high on both cognitive competence and social responsibility. No systematic relationship was found with social assertiveness, which is left blank. Girls whose parents were high on restrictive scored low on social responsibility. One aspect of restrictive was positively related to cognitive competence and another was negatively related to the dimension, hence, "mixed."

As can be seen, parents who are demanding, responsive and/or psychologically differentiated tend to produce children who interact with peers and other adults in socially assertive, responsible, and cognitively assertive ways. The responsive and differentiated dimensions, however, have stronger effects with boys than with girls. Restrictive parents tend to have negative effects on their children's social interactions. From this table, and Baumrind's later report, it's not clear how restrictiveness interacts with the other child-rearing practices. For example, we don't

TABLE 4.4
Child-Rearing Practices and 8–9-Year-Olds' Social Interactions

| | Parental Practices | | | |
	Demanding	Restrictive	Responsive	Differentiation
Girls				
Social Assertiveness	Positive			Positive
Cognitive Competence	Positive	Mixed		Positive
Social Responsibility		Negative	Positive	
Boys				
Social Assertiveness		Negative	Positive	Positive
Cognitive Competence	Positive		Positive	Positive
Social Responsibility	Positive	Negative	Positive	Positive

know whether parents who are demanding and restrictive will produce socially responsible or irresponsible boys.

In that Baumrind's later report is very incomplete, and moreover that the parent and child measures from the report and the preschool data are not directly comparable, it is difficult to draw general conclusions about her findings. In both sets of data, highly similar child-rearing practices had different effects on boys and girls. For the 8–9-year-olds, however, these differences were not dramatic. Restrictive child-rearing practices, which are most closely associated with the authoritarian pattern, tended to have negative effects on children's social behavior at both age levels. Demanding child-rearing practices, which are most closely associated with the authoritative pattern, tended to have positive effects at both age levels. Finally, psychological differentiation, which is most closely associated with the authoritative and nonconforming patterns, tended to have positive effects at both age levels.

Children of Divorced and Intact Families

In 1978 only 63% of American children under age 18 were living with their natural parents for whom this was their first marriage. Approximately 10% were living with one natural parent and a stepparent, 17% were living with their mother, and 1.5% with their father. It is estimated that the number of children who will experience the divorce of their parents will reach at least 40% by 1990. (Glick, 1979).

Despite the high frequency of divorce in this country, we know surprisingly little about its effects on children. Probably the best study to date has been carried out by Hetherington, Cox, and Cox (1979a, 1979b), and that study dealt with only 48 mother-headed divorced families and 48 intact families. The parents in both groups of families were, on average, highly educated and between 27 and 30 years old. The boys and girls were about 4 years old at the start of the study, all enrolled in nursery school. The children of divorce and their parents were observed and tested 2 months, 1 year, and 2 years following the divorce. The "intact" children and parents were observed and tested at three comparable time periods. In addition to interviews with parents and observations of parent-child interactions in the laboratory and at home, children's social interactions at nursery school were also evaluated.

Divorce has a profoundly negative effect on parents, producing economic, emotional, and family stress. Divorced parents frequently suffer a loss in self-esteem, as well as guilt, depression, and anxiety. Mothers who now headed the household typically felt incompetent in managing those tasks that their husbands had been responsible for, such as house maintenance, taxes, and insurance. Most of these difficulties improved considerably by 2 years following the divorce, but relative to parents of intact families, problems lingered on. Obviously difficulties that parents experience will influence their children's behavior and development.

In general, divorced parents had a much more difficult time managing their children than married couples. The parent-child relations in broken families were much more strained. The greatest difficulty occurred for divorced mothers with their sons. For example, in the area of obedience to parental commands, boys who lived with fathers were most obedient, boys with "intact" mothers and divorced fathers were next, and boys with divorced mothers were least obedient. A similar pattern held for girls, but 4–6-year-old girls were more obedient than 4–6-year-old boys. By 2 years following the divorce, these patterns still held, but the differences between intact and divorced families narrowed.

Divorced parents, relative to couples, during the first year of the divorce, seemed to interact with their children along the lines of the permissive and restrictive parents described by Baumrind. This was especially the case for divorced mothers with their sons. They made fewer maturity demands, were less clear in communicating, less affectionate, less consistent in discipline, and yet paradoxically made more controlling demands, were more negative in doing so, and were less effective.

Children of divorced parents, especially boys, gave their mothers a very difficult time. Boys were negative, complaining, and aggressive, whereas girls were whining, complaining, but obedient. During the first post-divorce year, children acted immaturely and were inattentive and dependent. They had difficulty sustaining play, and as a consequence, nagged and made demands on their mothers. Great improvement occurred over the two-year period, such that there was little difference between girls of divorced and intact families. However, some of these negative behavior patterns were still observed in the boys of divorce.

How are these differences between intact and divorced families reflected in the preschool setting? Two months following the divorce, boys and girls played in a more immature, disrupted way than their peers from intact families. Their ability to sustain long, cooperative and imaginative play were all reduced relative to "intact" peers. Children from divorced families were more often seen in solitary play or as observers. One year following the divorce, the play of "divorced" children improved substantially, and by 2 years post-divorce, there were essentially no differences between "divorced" and "intact" girls. The problems with boys of divorce were still seen at 2 years. They were often ignored by their male peers, and as a consequence, frequently played with younger boys and same-age girls, both activities uncharacteristic of 6-year-old boys. One exception is that boys of divorce who shifted nursery schools between 1 and 2 years after the divorce were perceived and responded to by peers and teachers in more positive ways than boys who stayed at the same preschool. Hetherington et al. (1976) comment about this as follows:

> This finding runs counter to the notion that stability in a child's environment following divorce facilitates adjustment. When a child has been labeled by peers or teachers in a negative fashion, the value of a move and a fresh start in a new environment may far outweigh the deleterious aspects of coping with a new school situation. (pp. 43–44)

In comparing children's behavior between school and home, Hetherington et al. conclude that the patterns for children of divorce, including disobedience, demandingness, dependency, and aggression were highly consistent during the first year post-divorce. Teacher and parent evaluations of the children were highly similar and consistent during the first year post-divorce. During the second year post-divorce, however, there was much less consistency between behavior at home and behavior at school. Hetherington et al. suggest that as the trauma of divorce subsides, children are able to respond more appropriately to the situations they encounter and thus make greater distinctions between the school and home settings. Different rules and roles apply to both, and as their stress diminishes, behavior becomes more appropriate to the social setting.

SUMMARY

This chapter deals with several of the major ways children interact with their peers. Play is the starting point of peer involvement. It has obvious and powerful evolutionary roots, which are seen in studies of monkeys and apes. From Suomi's research of monkey families living in the nuclear family apparatus, we saw that infants and juveniles initiate different kinds of interactions with the various members of their "culture." Moreover, the interactions they have with mother, father, nonrelated adults, and male and female peers each produce different kinds of socialization experiences. From Rosenblum and Plimptom's research dealing with the influence of adults on peer interaction, it was found that the greatest amount of peer aggression occurred when no adults were present. This finding is especially interesting in light of the fact that the "peers only" living condition was the least stressful. From our general discussion of primate-play, we noted that it is one of the most important ways skills are acquired for the establishment of stable dominance relationships.

Human play is also a creative process in which the infant and child attempt to gain new perspectives and new understandings of their phsyical and social environment. Piaget maintains that there are three play types associated with three stages of intelligence: practice play, symbolic play, and games with rules. Each play type has as a focus a different objective to be mastered. In practice play, the infant attempts to master his own sensory-motor activities. In symbolic play, the child attempts to master her understanding and use of symbols. In games with rules, children attempt to master their understanding of social relationships. In evaluating research concerned with testing aspects of Piaget's theory of play we concluded that the sequence of development and not the ages of each stage is most important. Age should be used as a rough guideline for the emergence of certain psychological functions.

Sociodramatic play by nursery school children has been extensively studied by Garvey and Schwartzman. Garvey shows us this form of play allows children to test out a variety of social roles they experience in their daily lives. These experiences lead to their learning to better control their own social behavior as well as to influence the behavior of others. Schwartzman points out the importance of paradox – self-contradictory statements – in play. Paradox permits the players to comment on, interpret, and perhaps test out new ways of dealing with dominance hierarchies. These comments and interpretations get played out in the ways children enact the roles of their drama.

Games were discussed in a cross-cultural context. Games that emerge and survive in cultures do so because they have deep meaning. Life in cultures that primarily engage in games of chance is highly uncertain. The stability of the family group and/or social group is unpredictable. Life in cultures that primarily engage in phsyical skill games requires some competition for social success and also requires well-developed physical skills for survival. Cultures that primarily engage in strategy games are generally more complex than the above cultures. There is a great deal of occupational and political specialization in these cultures which involve sophisticated interpersonal skills. "Gaming" knowledge is important for success. Sutton-Smith and Roberts suggest that a valuable way to view games is that they are models of power—ways of succeeding over others in the culture.

As with monkeys and apes, aggression and dominance are closely related in young children. Nursery school boys and girls learn that aggression pays off—they get what they want from their victims. Victims of aggression who successfully counterattack subsequently become aggressors themselves. Like the nonhuman primates, dominance relations for preschool children are both rigid and transitive. By the time children are 12–14 years old, dominance relations are neither rigid nor transitive. In the interval from age 4 to 14 years verbal aggression increases, physical aggression decreases, but attempts to hurt another as a goal in itself increase. The bases for dominance relations shift during this period and come to be primarily determined by athletic ability, physical maturation, and leadership.

Lambert's discussion of aggression in the Six Culture study was summarized. The most striking finding was that 3- to 6-year-olds and 7- to 10-year-olds express aggression in highly similar ways despite dramatic cultural differences. As an example, in all six cultures the older children contain their aggression when either parent is present, but when grandmother is the only adult with them they freely attack others.

In the discussion of the biology of sex differences in aggression, evidence relevant to hormonal bases, nonhuman primate sex differences, cross-cultural differences, and differing socialization practices for boys and girls were evaluated. We reached a conclusion similar to Maccoby and Jacklin. There is probably a biological base, but socialization practices are very important, and there is great overlap between boys and girls in the expression of aggression.

The study of altruism in children has largely been restricted to the laboratory. However, naturalistic observations by Eisenberg and her colleagues indicate that the frequency with which preschoolers are altruistic is related to their moral reasoning. Eisenberg's research also shows that spontaneous sharing has very different psychological meanings than either sharing on request or helping others. In an extensive review of altruism research, Underwood and Moore show that the level of altruism in children is related to their perceptual, social, and moral perspective-taking abilities.

Cross-cultural research in cooperation and competition involving the use of the Madsen games revealed striking cultural differences. Generally children in rural areas cooperate much more than those from urban areas, and recent immigrants to cities cooperate more than second- and third-generation urban dwellers. Young children generally cooperate more than older ones from the same culture. Three factors seem to be at work in determining children's cooperation levels: how much the culture emphasizes competition; how much the culture emphasizes strong ties and commitments to members of the culture; and the extent to which urban living has weakened those ties.

From Baumrind's studies of parental influences on children's peer behavior, we saw that for 4-year-olds and 8- to 9-year-olds highly similar practices had different effects on boys and girls. For both sexes, and both age levels, however, authoritarian/restrictive parental practices tended to have negative effects, and demanding/authoritative practices tended to have positive effects. Parents who made psychological differentiations tended to have positive influences on their children.

Finally, from the Hetherington, Cox, and Cox studies of the effects of divorce on children's peer relations, we saw that boys living with their divorced mother had a slower and more difficult adjustment than girls. For parents and children, the first year post-divorce was the most stressful. Children's peer behavior in school closely paralleled their home behavior with mother. By 2 years post-divorce, essentially no negative effects were observed in the girls.

5 Cognitive Development and Social Cognition

This chapter deals with the development of children's perceptions, conceptions, and ways of learning about their physical and social worlds. The words "cognitive" and "cognition" refer to activities of the mind. Our interest is in how infants' and children's minds shape what is perceived and thought about, how they organize experiences and acquire different ways of making sense of their world. This search for meaning is a fundamental characteristic of all human beings. Writing from an evolutionary perspective, Fishbein (1976) notes:

> Evolutionary processes are fundamentally involved with the acquisition of information or knowledge about the environmental niche of the species. In general, the greater the knowledge that members of a species have about the environment in which they develop, the more effective will be their actions in that environment, and hence, the greater will be their chances of surviving and reproducing. (p. 861)

Implied in this quote is the idea that knowledge about the environment can be genetically passed on across generations. And it can. For example, we are attracted to sweet- and repelled by sour-tasting foods. The former foods in their natural state are nearly always beneficial (in moderation) and the latter harmful. This knowledge is built into our genetic makeup. A more subtle form of innate knowledge is in the workings of our minds; that is, our brains have been evolutionarily organized in such a fashion that human minds will operate along certain channels. We can't help but think in certain ways because that is how we're built. This point is elaborated when we compare the cognitive development of human, monkey, and gorilla infants.

There are parallels in the development of cognitive abilities in different species. These parallels have to do with the evolution and development of the brain. At birth, the brains of all Old World primates are immature, and thus, not fully functional. Monkeys reach brain maturity faster than apes, which are in turn faster than humans. At full maturity, however, cognitive abilities are greatest in humans, then apes, and finally, monkeys. It's important to point out that cognitive abilities don't emerge solely because of brain maturation. In order for any characteristic (psychological or nonpsychological) to develop fully, the developing individual must be reared in environments normal for the species. Non-normal experiences can lead to deviant development (See Chapter 2 for a discussion of abnormalities in embryological development).

In the study of cognitive development two broad research trends can be seen—Piagetian and non-Piagetian. Piaget started writing in the 1920s and continued to do so until his death in 1980. His studies became influential in English-speaking countries only since the 1960s. Prior to then research was performed without reference to Piaget's theory. At the present time, there is some connection between the two trends, but usually the methods used and research questions asked are independent. In the following sections, we'll discuss aspects of both research approaches.

PIAGET'S THEORY AND RESEARCH

Four concepts are central to nearly all of Piaget's work in cognitive development: *schema, assimilation, accommodation*, and *equilibration*. Although Piaget doesn't use this metaphor, he views individuals as builders. In order to successfully build a house you need materials, e.g., wood, nails, glass; tools for using the materials, e.g., hammers, wrenches, screwdrivers; and knowledge about how such tools are used. Knowledge is usually slowly acquired over time through use. The master builder has all three components at her disposal. The beginner may have the materials and tools, but lacks much of the knowledge required to use them.

Piaget's builders are concerned with constructing clear and accurate conceptions of the world. The materials used are the experiences we have in our daily lives. The tools we use are mental activities, which Piaget calls *schemas* (1963, 1970, 1971). Knowledge is what we acquire through applying our schemas to experiences. For example, the first schemas (tools) infants have are the innate reflexes such as sucking, swallowing, grasping, looking, and listening. When an infant experiences mother's breast, he uses his schemas to gain knowledge of it. It can be sucked, swallowed, felt but not grasped, looked at, but not listened to. Any subsequent experiences that involve the similar use of those schemas, will be "breast" experiences. That is, breasts are objects which when interacted with are suckable, swallowable, and so forth. More generally, an experience has meaning for us – can be understood – because we are successful in using our mental schemas with it.

Piaget uses two terms, based on biological processes, to describe how schemas are used to acquire knowledge – *assimilation* and *accommodation*. Assimilation involves a "taking-in" and accommodation, a "modifying of." When we use our reflex schemas with breasts, we take in our breast experiences with these schemas. But since no two experiences are ever the same, we modify these previously used schemas to fit them with our current experiences. For example, the infant's head will always be at a slightly different angle to the nipple each time he nurses. His schemas for sucking and swallowing will allow him to suck and swallow (assimilation), but because of his different position, he will do so a little differently than the last time (accommodation). To give another example, we have a number of schemas for reading the letter *a*. This letter can be printed or cursive, in lower case or capitals. When we see a strange cursive, lower case *a*, we apply our *a* schemas to interpreting it. Since the new cursive *a* is similar to previous ones we've seen, we will probably successfully assimilate it. Since it is different than every other *a* we've experienced before, however, we must first accommodate our *a* schemas before being able to assimilate it.

The fourth concept, *equilibration*, refers to the relationship between assimilation and accommodation. Individuals are always trying to make sense of their experiences. They do this by assimilating experience to their schemas. When they cannot do this, they are placed in conflict. The experience is occurring and it can't be interpreted. The conflict is resolved by accommodating the schemas. This is usually, but not always, possible. Most of us cannot understand someone speaking Greek, but we can usually understand "baby talk." Equilibration is the process whereby schemas are accommodated so that experiences can be interpreted and understood. One major implication of this process is that growth in knowledge comes from resolving conflicts. Where there is no conflict, we learn nothing new.

The study of Piaget's writings is a difficult but fascinating enterprise. Piaget took on the monumental task of trying to describe the growth of mind. He was not so much interested in describing *what* knowledge was acquired over a lifetime as he was in discovering the processes underlying *how* we construct reality. Piaget's stages of cognitive development, then, are primarily descriptions of knowledge acquisition. When we examine the above four concepts from this point of view, the conclusion emerges that the stages of cognitive development are descriptions of different types of schemas used in constructing reality. Of course, associated with these schemas are different interpretations of experience—different constructions of reality. The following is a useful analogy, equating schemas with tools. Very small objects can be seen with the naked eye (a tool). The invention of the microscope gave us new experiences and allowed us to interpret our old experiences in new ways. The later invention of the electron microscope deepened and elaborated these processes even more.

Piaget describes four stages of cognitive development, called *sensory-motor, preoperational, concrete operational*, and *formal operational*. In the sensory-motor stage, which typically covers the period from birth to 1½ years, the infant's schemas are sensory-motor, such as reflexes and habits. The infant knows as much of the world as he can outline by different patterns of sensory-motor activities. This stage comes to an end when he develops schemas that symbolically represent the world. Language, imagination, intuitive thought are all examples. Piaget emphasizes that these and all subsequent schemas are based on action—the earlier sensory-motor schemas. Symbols or representations extend the world of the child in that earlier experiences can be brought to mind without carrying out sensory-motor activities. The child can now perform experiments in his head, and can often anticipate how different actions will turn out. The second stage is called preoperational (1½–6 years old) because of the particular kinds of limits on mental activity—the child is unable to make logical inferences and deductions.

In the stage of concrete operations children approximately 6 to 11 years old can make logical deductions and inferences, but only about concrete objects and events in their experience. Space, time, and causality are understood as they relate to these experiences. The schemas that permit them to make their constructions of reality are called concrete operations. There are two major types of concrete operations, both of which deal with mentally reversing images or representations. Picture a balance scale. Place four ounces in each tray, which are located exactly 6 inches from the fulcrum. If one ounce is added to the left tray, the balance will drop to the left. The concrete operation of *inversion* will allow one to imagine removing the additional ounce in order to re-balance the scale. The concrete operation of *reciprocity* will allow one to imagine re-balancing the scale by either adding one ounce to the right side or moving the left tray closer to the fulcrum. Preoperational children cannot perform these mental activities.

Two types of schemas emerge in the stage of formal operations (age 12 onwards). The first permits inversion and reciprocity to be carried out at the same time, for example, balancing the scale after one ounce has been added and the tray has been moved 2 inches towards the fulcrum. The second allows operations to be performed on hypothetical situations of which the children have had no previous experience. For example, the formal operational but not concrete operational child can list all the possible ways four different objects can be placed on four chairs. Many adults have difficulty with some formal operational problems.

Before describing major experiments from the first three stages (formal operations are not extensively discussed), one final point will be made. Piaget (1971) asserts that these stages are canalized. As described in Chapter 2, this means that all infants and children reared in normal environments will pass through these stages in the same sequence. The ages at which the advanced schemas will first appear may differ considerably between children. Also, there is clear evidence that the same child may use advanced schemas for only some but not all tasks. These variations probably have to do with the particular kinds of experiences children have had and the nature of the tasks they're confronting. However, no convincing theory has been proposed that explains most, if not all, of these differences.

The Sensory-Motor Stage: Monkeys, Gorillas, and Humans

Bower (1982), a major researcher in sensory-motor development, has summarized recent studies dealing with the object concept in humans. Many authors, including Piaget, consider this development the most significant in infancy. The essence of this concept is that objects retain their identity independent of where they are located when last seen, and whether presently visible or covered. Piaget describes six stages infants go through in acquiring this concept. They are summarized in Table 5.1 from Bower's book.

TABLE 5.1
Stages of Development

Stage	Age (Months)*	Success	Fail
I	0–2	No particular behavior shown in response to hiding event	
II	2–4	Infant will track a moving object that goes behind a screen.	Infant continues to track a moving object after it has stopped.
		Infant can learn to track an object from place to place.	Infant will look for an object in its familiar place even when the infant sees the object moving to a new place.
III	4–6	Infant no longer makes tracking errors of Stage II.	Infant cannot recover an object that has been fully covered by a cloth.
		Infant recovers an object that has been partially covered by a cloth.	
IV	6–12	Infant can now recover an object that has been completely hidden under a cloth.	Infant searches for an object in the place where it was previously found, ignoring the place where it was seen to be hidden.
V	12–15	Infant no longer makes place error of Stage IV.	Infant cannot cope with invisible displacements of an object.
VI	15–18	Complete success— infant can find object no matter where or how it it hidden	

*These ages are approximate; there may be considerable individual differences.
(Source: Bower, T. G. R. *Development in infancy.* 2nd Edition. San Francisco: W. H. Freeman and Company, 1982.)

In the first stage infants make no particular response when objects (toys, balls) they are looking at are covered by a cloth or removed from sight. When an object is moved on a track in front of them, they don't follow it with their eyes. In the second stage, the infant will follow a moving object, and even continue following its path when it moves behind a screen. However, when the ball is stopped short of the screen, the infant continues following the object as if it were still moving behind the screen. Bower asserts that infants make this error because they fail to equate the moving object with the stopped one. In essence, infants were observing two objects, one moving and one stopped. In a clever experiment to prove this, Bower moved one object back and forth on a track from point A to point B. The infants learned to follow the movements with their eyes. What happened when Bower moved the object from B to another point, C? If infants were following the movments of a single object, they should follow it on the path to C. If the infants had learned to follow three objects—the stationary one at A, the moving one between A and B, and the stationary one at B, they should follow with their eyes the path from B to A. That is what they did.

In the third stage, infants are able to follow moving objects, including complex paths while hidden from sight. This means that they have learned that an object while stationary is the same one while moving. Further, if you take an object and partially cover it with a cloth, the infant will reach for and grasp it. However, if while the infant is watching, you completely cover the object, she will make no attempt to take it. This is very puzzling because these infants track moving objects that are hidden and are able to remove transparent cups covering objects. It is as if covering the object transforms it into something else. Bower suggests that Stage III infants haven't learned that two objects can be in the same place at the same time.

In the fourth stage infants will reach for and grasp a completely covered object. However, if a toy is hidden in the same place (A) several times while the child is watching, and he is allowed to find it, and then while watching, the toy is hidden in another place (B), the child will search for it at (A). This is an amazing result, but many researchers have successfully repeated it. The child's concept of an object at this stage seems to be limited by his failure to distinguish between the location of a hidden object and the object itself. To put it another way, it's as if a property of hidden objects is the location at which they were previously found.

In the fifth stage children accurately search for objects in the last place hidden independent of its hiding history. They do make another type of error concerning a hidden object. In the usual procedure, the child watches while a toy is hidden under one of two identical cloths on a table. While the child is still watching, the adult places one hand on each cloth and reverses their positions by moving them along the table. Thus, the toy was originally hidden at A, but after being moved, is now at B. This is called an invisible displacement of an object. The Stage V child looks for the hidden toy at A, its initial location. The reason for this error is that the child does not have a representation in his mind of the invisible toy that he can imagine moving from place to place.

The child in the sixth stage solves the above problem. This ability means that he has entered the stage of preoperational thought.

Wise, Wise, and Zimmermann (1974) studied the development of object permanence in two laboratory-raised infant rhesus monkeys, and Renshaw (1978) investigated it in four hand-reared infant gorillas and two human infants. Both studies used materials similar to those described above with two exceptions: screens were used instead of cloths to hide the toys; and two or more tasks were often used at each stage. In both experiments the subjects were initially presented with the simplest task, which was repeated several times each session. When the infant was successful, the next most difficult task was presented. Testing for the monkeys began when they were 10 days old, and continued daily until all tasks were successfully mastered. Testing for the gorillas and humans began when they were 2 weeks old and continued at 4-week intervals until all tasks were mastered.

The results can be seen in Fig. 5.1. The curves represent the average age in weeks at which each stage was mastered. Focusing on the human curve, it appears that the two infants moved through these stages more quickly than is typical. The two most interesting findings, however, are that monkeys, gorillas, and humans proceed through the stages in exactly the same sequence, and monkeys complete the sequence first, followed by gorillas, then humans. The latter finding can be explained by their different rates of brain maturation, so it should not be too surprising. That the three species proceed in the same sequence is extraordinary. These results indicate that the brains and minds of Old World primates follow highly similar patterns of cognitive development in infancy. That is, monkeys, gorillas, and humans construct the reality of objects during infancy in the same ways.

It is reasonable to ask whether the minds of these species develop the same way for other types of tasks. Renshaw presented data relevant to this question. In one experiment she studied the development of the use

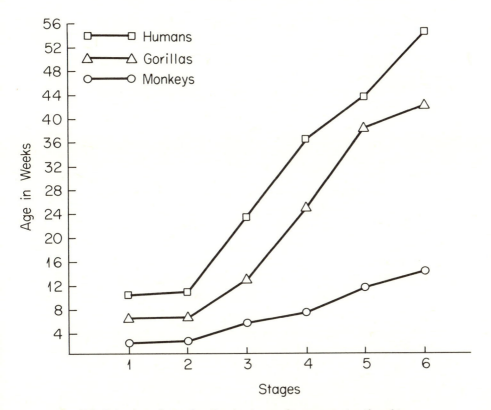

FIG. 5.1   Age of entering the six stages of sensory-motor thought.

of objects to obtain toys. For one task, the toy was on a cloth, in others, the toy was attached to a string, and in one, the toy was out of reach but could be retrieved by using a stick. The gorillas and humans proceeded through the tasks in different sequences. With the exception of the stick retrieval task, the gorillas succeeded at younger ages. For that task, the humans were successful at 56 weeks, whereas only one gorilla was successful by 26 months of age. In a similar vein, in another experiment, the humans built a tower of two blocks at 48 weeks, but none of the gorillas succeeded by 26 months.

These results cannot be explained by differing rates of brain maturity in gorillas and humans, but rather we must focus on differences in the ways their brains and minds are organized. For humans, developing an understanding of the use of objects in relation to each other is easily acquired. For gorillas this understanding is slowly if ever acquired. Fishbein (1976) argues that species' differences in tool use are based on their evolutionary history and design. For humans, extensive tool use was essential for survival but for gorillas and other nonhuman primates, tool use was relatively insignificant.

Cross-Cultural Comparisons of Preoperational and Concrete Operational Thought

There has been an explosion of cross-cultural Piagetian studies during the past decade. The overwhelming majority of them have dealt with the transition from preoperational to concrete operational thought, with a small proportion focused on sensory-motor and formal operations. The results of studies dealing with sensory-motor development have been summarized by Werner (1979). In that monkeys, gorillas, and English babies proceed through the substages of object permanence in the same order, it should not be surprising to learn from Werner that "the ordering of the substages of sensory-motor intelligence are identical in African, American, Asian, and European infants, from nomadic to rural to suburban to urban settings" (p. 215). Further, the ages at which infants proceed through these substages are nearly identical. Where differences occur, they mainly reflect various types of experiences cultures impose on their infants, and not genetic differences.

These close parallels in development are highlighted by the following striking observations. Dasen (1977) compared rural Baoule from the Ivory Coast with infants from day-care centers in suburban Paris. In one task, a plastic tube and a small chain of paper clips were presented to the infants while seated on their mothers' laps. No instructions were given. Dasen remarks as follows:

> Why should the infant wish to combine these two objects? He may just as well look through the tube, roll it on the table, put the chain around his fingers, or throw it at the experimenter. Yet, after stage 5A (13–15 months of age) almost every infant starts to search for some way of making the chain pass through the tube. When this tube is presented to a Baoule infant, it seems even more ludicrous, since the subject will never have seen a plastic tube or paper clips before. Yet he takes these two strange objects, and combines them exactly as the infants in the day care centre of Paris did; not only does he get the idea of combining them, but he does this following the same steps, with the same errors, and finding the same successively more and more adapted solutions. (p. 165)

The study of preoperational and concrete operational thought relies heavily on the use of language. The research literature published during the 1960s and early part of the 1970s typically reported marked differences – up to 7 years – favoring children in Westernized over developing countries in solving the same concrete operational problems.

Kamara (1971), in analyzing these studies, pointed out three serious defects that called their results into question. The first defect is that nearly all experimenters were relatively unsophisticated about either the culture or the language of their subjects. The Piagetian techniques call for the use of clinical interviewing methods, and the interviewer's deficiencies in either language or cultural knowledge would seriously interfere with children's performance. We'll present the results from a recent study by Nyiti (1982) that bears on this.

The second defect is that many experimenters attempted to overcome problems with clinical interviews by using standardized tests requiring little language use. Piaget has criticized this procedure because it doesn't gather enough information about children's thought processes. Another criticism is that in most developing countries, standardized tasks are unfamiliar, which handicaps the children taking them. The third defect is that the subjects' ages in developing countries were typically approximated, and these approximations could be in error by as much as 2 years. Kamara suggested techniques for attaining highly accurate birth dates in the absence of birth records.

Nyiti (1982) used three of Piaget's *conservation* tasks. Such tasks typically deal with understanding physical properties and involve a sequence of three steps. In Step 1, the experimenter asks the child if two objects equal in shape, size, and weight, e.g., balls of modeling clay, are equal in amount. If the child says yes, (which essentially all do) then in Step 2, the experimenter changes the shape or spatial configuration of one of the objects, e.g., rolls one of the clay balls into a "wiener," while the child is watching. In Step 3, the experimenter asks the child if the two objects are still equal in amount and to give reasons for his judgment. The general concern in conservation tasks is whether children can "conserve" the essence of some physical property despite changes in its physical appearance. Correct performance in these tasks requires reversibility in thought – concrete operations. For example, when the experimenter rolls a ball into the wiener, the concrete operational child, in her mind, can reshape it back into a ball. When she does this, it becomes clear that nothing was added or taken away during the rolling process, and the two balls are still equal. The preoperational child cannot reverse actions in thought, and thus gets stuck on perceptual differences. She might say that there is more clay in the wiener because it is longer than the ball.

As with much of Piaget's experimentation, the conservation tasks are remarkable in their effects. Parents who see their preoperational children "fail" one of these tasks are absolutely dumbfounded. One of the great problems with the conservation tasks, however, is that not all are solved at the same age. In fact, the easiest conservation task – number – is typically solved at the age of 6 by North American children, and the most difficult – volume – is typically solved at age 12. Clearly, there is more to conservation tasks than concrete operations.

The three conservation tasks Nyiti (1982) used were of *substance, weight,* and *volume.* These are the most widely used tasks in cross-cultural studies. The example we gave of the two balls of clay is the substance task, usually solved by age 9. For weights, typically solved by age 10, the two balls of clay were put on a balance scale so that the children could see they weighed the same. One was then flattened into a pancake shape and the child was asked if the two weights were equal. For volume, two equal balls of clay were dropped into two equal glasses of water. The child noted that the water levels of both glasses with the clay immersed were equal. The experimenter then took one of the clay balls, rolled it into a wiener shape, and asked the child whether the wiener would change the water level the same amount as the ball.

Nyiti compared two different cultural groups of 10- and 11-year-old Canadians: urban, white, English-speaking Canadians, and reservation Micmac Indians whose home language was Micmac but whose school language was English. All the white students and one half of the Micmacs were tested in their schools by an English-speaking adult. The other half of the Micmac children were tested in Micmac by a Micmac Indian adult. The results were dramatic. The performance of the white Canadians and Micmacs tested in their home language was virtually identical and comparable to that of United States, Canadian, and European children. The Micmacs tested in English were far behind both groups. At both age levels, approximately twice as many of the children tested in their home language solved each conservation task than did the Micmacs tested in English. These findings strongly call into question results of previous research that did not have interviewers of the same language and cultural background as the children.

In recent years, three other projects have met Kamara's criticisms in evaluating children of developing countries. Nyiti (1976) himself a Meru, tested Meru children of Tanzania; Kamara and Easley (1977) studied the Themne children of Sierra Leone, and Kiminyo (1977) tested the Kamba of Kenya. All used the same three conservation tasks as Nyiti (1982), with children approximately 7–12 years old. The results of these studies are very clear and consistent: the ages at which the three conservation tasks were correctly solved are highly comparable to those of United States,

Canadian, and European children. There is a tendency in some of the data that 11- to 12-year-olds who have never attended school have more difficulty than their schooled peers in solving the volume conservation task.

What do these results mean? Piaget (1970) describes four factors involved in the cognitive development of children: maturation, experience of the physical environment, experience of the social environment, and self-regulation. Maturation in itself doesn't produce cognitive development, but provides opportunities for this development to occur, and sets limits on it. Advanced cognition cannot occur with an immature brain, and a mature brain won't guarantee it.

The developing child must have experience in the physical world for cognitive growth to occur. Her contact with objects and events requires her to develop new schemas for understanding them. It is through these contacts that assimilation and accommodation processes will build up increasingly more adequate schemas to do so. But physical experiences frequently occur in a social context, be it with family, peers, or school. People are "objects" who have to be understood in their own right, and moreover, people use symbols, e.g., language, in their interactions with each other. The nature of these symbols can influence the rate with which cognitive development will occur. For example, in the above studies there is the suggestion that schooling speeds up age of success in volume conservation. Finally, the individual's own self-regulation processes put the above three factors together to ensure that development occurs in an integrated fashion. Self-regulation is a property of all living things, and plays an active role in all aspects of their functioning.

In looking at the cross-cultural data, it is impossible to use any one of these factors as *the* explanation for the consistencies obtained. Rather, all four factors must have been at work in approximately the same ways. This means that despite the differences in physical and social experiences the children had, all were nevertheless appropriate for cognitive development to proceed through the stage of concrete operations. Although these findings don't "prove" Piaget's theory, they certainly indicate that he has identified important and perhaps universal aspects of cognitive development.

DEVELOPMENT OF ATTENTION AND MEMORY

This section closely follows and updates Fishbein's (1976) treatment of the same topics. We stated earlier that the greater the knowledge an individual has learned about her environment, the greater are her chances for survival and reproduction. Attention and memory processes go to the heart of acquiring this knowledge: there is essentially no learning without attention, and memory is a major component of learning. In the actual study of these two processes, especially with infants, the distinction between them is often not clear.

Attentional processes function to bring sensory information into sharper focus. Fishbein defined these processes as "those which underlie how we orient our sensory receptors to the environment, how we identify information, how we explore the environment, and how we select information for additional processing" (p. 208). Memory processes operate on information that individuals have already received. These processes influence which information we keep, how we organize it, or how we bring it into consciousness.

Attention and memory processes are closely interdependent in most situations. In order to decide which environmental information to bring into sharper focus, e.g., pay closer attention to, we compare it with previous information (memory) we have received. For example, in studying for a psychology examination you were highly selective in which information you explored further. You based this selection partly on your memory of what the professor emphasized in lectures. The information that you paid close attention to was probably remembered better than that to which you paid little attention. One way some people emphasize attention to textbook information is to underline it in yellow. You may notice after taking the test that you in fact remembered better the underlined than nonunderlined material. You may also notice unfortunately, that you often emphasized the wrong material. That is not a problem of either attention or memory.

Attention and memory processes dramatically change during infancy and childhood. With increasing maturity not only does capacity for both increase, but also there are changes in the ways people attend to the environment and remember. In general, with increasing age, children are able to make finer discriminations and integrate information.

Attention and Memory from Birth to Age Three

All the studies discussed in this section deal with attention to and memory of visual stimulation. Perhaps the most obvious way to study attention in infants is to examine how long they look at some stimulus. The longer they look, the more they are attending to that stimulus. Measuring looking time is very simple to do—think how easy it is to tell whether another person is looking into your eyes.

How to study memory in infants is not so obvious. The measures that have been developed are indirect, one set based on the concept of "habituation" (Sokolov, 1960), and the other on "discrimination learning." Habituation is an internal process with two components: (1) building up a memory of external stimulation, and (2) building up inhibition that depends on memory and suppresses responses to that stimulation. When you are repeatedly shown a drawing of a human face, for example, you look at the drawing for progressively shorter periods of time. When a novel drawing of a face is presented, you look at it much longer. Thus, there are two measures of habituation—decreases in looking time to the same stimulus, and differences in looking time between the old and novel stimuli. The latter measure bears some similarity to discrimination learning.

In the discrimination learning procedure (Brody, 1981) the infant is trained to respond differently to two stimuli, for example, a lit and unlit screen. When the infant touches the lit screen, he receives a reward, but not when he touches the unlit screen. Memory for which screen was lit can be tested by delaying the time interval between when the light is turned off and the infant has a chance to respond (you hold the infant's hands for the desired delay period).

The major findings are as follows: between birth and about 2 months of age, infants are "captured" by stimuli. They do not show a preference for novel stimuli over previously seen stimuli, nor does their looking time decrease when old stimuli are repeatedly presented. They look far longer at moving stimuli than stationary ones and at stimuli high rather than low in black-white contrast, e.g., bold black and white stripes versus greys. If a simple drawing of a face is shown, they look at only a small portion rather than explore most or all of it.

From about 2 to 6 months of age a number of changes occur. Infants start to show habituation to old stimuli and preferences for novel ones, indicating development of memory. They attend more to patterned than to unpatterned stimuli and more to faces than to other patterns. By 6 months of age they are able to recognize drawings of unique faces. During this age range they also attend to and remember different dimensions, say color and form. For example, infants make distinctions among red and green triangles and red and green circles. By the age of 6 months, they attend to and remember the orientations of familiar objects, e.g., whether a face is shown upright or at an angle. Moreover, they can remember 2 weeks later a face they had seen for only a 2-minute exposure, (Cohen, 1979).

Between the ages of about 3 months to 1 year, infants progressively improve at identifying and exploring stimuli. Their looking times decrease with no cost to memory. This suggests that they are developing abilities for classifying and organizing information (Kagan, 1970; Lewis, 1969). Using the discrimination learning techniques, Brody (1981) found that short-term memory dramatically increases during this period. Eight-month-old infants forget the location of a lit screen in less than a second, but 1-year-olds remember it after a 9-second delay.

Between the ages of 1 and 3 years, children increasingly use symbolic activities in both attention and memory. Kagan (1970) in the area of attention refers to these as "hypotheses." Hypotheses are essentially interpretations of new experiences based on previously used "schemas." Kagan assumes that (1) the more hypotheses activated in a situation, the longer will be attention time; (2) older children have more hypotheses available than younger ones; and (3) moderately unusual stimuli will elicit more hypotheses than both highly familiar and unfamiliar ones. Finley, Kagan, and Layne (1972) tested these ideas with urban, white, middle-class North American children and rural Mayan Indian children from Mexico with average ages of 1, 2, and 3 years. They presented the children the face and man pictures shown in Fig. 5.2. They assumed that the abstract figures would be too unfamiliar and the blank face and trunk too familiar for activating many hypotheses. In that the older children were more cognitively advanced than the younger, they assumed there would be age-related differences in looking time for the scrambled and normal faces and figures. In general, the results supported Kagan's assumptions. Older children looked at the stimuli longer than younger ones (more hypotheses). Three-year-olds looked at the scrambled figures longer than at the remaining ones; 1-year-olds looked at the normal figures the longest; and 2-year-olds peformed in between. There were no cultural differences at any age level.

Short-term memory ability continues to increase between the ages of 1 and 3. Kagan (1981) summarizes research carried out with North American and Fiji children, using tasks similar to Brody's. While the child was watching, a food reward was placed under one of two to eight different-looking cups. Immediately afterwards the cups were visually blocked by a screen for up to 10 seconds. The best performance by 1-year-old children was to remember the location of the food for a 1-second delay with four cups. One-and-a-half-year-olds could remember the location for up to 5 seconds. By 2 years of age children remembered location for 10 seconds with eight cups. Improvements in memory were found between the ages

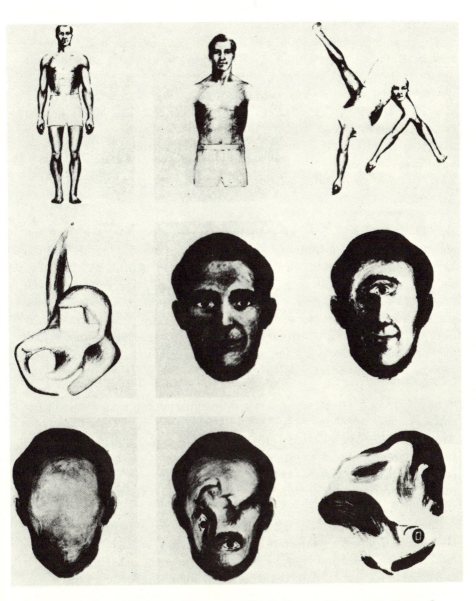

FIG. 5.2 Cambridge man and face series stimuli. (Source: Finely, G. F., Kagan, J., & Layne, O. Jr. Development of young children's attention to normal and distorted stimuli: A cross-cultural study. *Developmental Psychology*, 1972, *6*, 288–292.)

of 1 and 3 when identical-looking cups were used. There were essentially no cultural differences.

The results described in this section are highly consistent with Piaget's theory. Children show tremendous increases in attention and memory abilities during the first 3 years of life. They proceed from being reactive to stimuli with essentially no memory, to being highly selective with substantial memory, and guided by symbolic thought. The highly similar cross-cultural findings regarding the timing of development strongly suggest that these behaviors and processes are canalized.

Development of Attention from Age Three to Adolescence

In this discussion we'll make a distinction between the exploratory and selective aspects of attention. When you show a child an object and tell him to look at it carefully because you're going to test his memory, you set the stage for measuring how he explores it. Television courtroom drama often hinges on such exploration—"Tell the jury, Mr. Forbes, how you're so sure that you've seen this revolver before." In selective attention, you tell the child which aspects of the object are central for a future memory test, and determine whether he remembers these central aspects better than the incidental ones.

Exploration.   There are at least four experiments that assessed the ways children explored stimuli for future memory. Two of them, by Abravanel (1968) and Lehman (1972) dealt with exploration by touch; and two, by Zinchenko, Chzhi-tsin, and Tarakanov (1963), and Vurpillot (1968), with vision. Despite major procedural differences in these experiments, all reached highly similar conclusions. For the sake of brevity, we'll summarize only the vision studies.

Zinchenko et al. presented 3- to 6-year-old Soviet children with irregularly shaped objects projected on screens. They were told to become familiar with them in order to remember their shapes. Children's eye movements were recorded during both the familiarization and the recognition phases of the study. Figure 5.3 shows a typical example of the behavior of 3- and 6-year-olds during these two phases. As can be seen, during the familiarization phase, the 3-year-olds made relatively few eye movements, most of them focusing near the center of the figure. The 6-year-olds, on the other hand, made many eye movements, most of them confined to the figure outline, which gives maximum shape information.

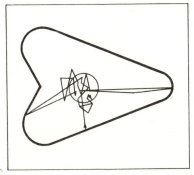

Trajectory of eye movements of three-year-old in familiarization with figure (20 seconds).

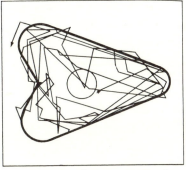

Trajectory of eye movements of six-year-old in familiarization with figure (20 seconds).

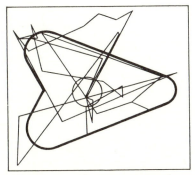

Trajectory of eye movements of three-year-old in recognition of figure (9 seconds).

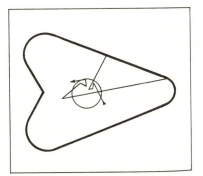

Trajectory of eye movements of six-year-old in recognition of figure (4 seconds).

FIG. 5.3   Eye movements of a three year old and a six year old. (Source: Zinchenko, V. P., Chzhi-tsin, V., & Tarakanov, V. V. The formation and development of perceptual activity. *Soviet Psychology and Psychiatry*, 1962, *2*, 3–12. Armonk, NY: M. E. Sharpe.)

The 4- and 5-year-olds behaved similarly to the 3-year-olds, except that they made more eye movements and tended to explore in detail one part of the figure.

On the recognition task, the 3s made 50% errors, the 4s 30% errors, and the 5- and 6-year-olds made none. As can be seen from Fig. 5.3, the 3-year-olds made more eye movements, explored more of the figure, and for a longer time, than the 6-year-olds. The 4- and 5-year-olds behaved midway between the other two groups.

Zinchenko et al. drew several conclusions from their findings. First, with increasing age there is a gradual improvement in the ability to explore and isolate the relevant aspects of an object. Second, there is a gradual improvement in the ability to differentiate the two tasks. Famliarization and recognition should involve different psychological functions, which was clearly reflected in the behavior of the oldest, but not the youngest children. Finally, with increasing age, children became more economical or efficient in their exploratory behavior. The oldest children explored only what they had to, but the youngest explored too much or too little.

In Vurpillot's study, the 3- to 10-year-old children were given a task in which they had to determine whether a pair of pictured houses was the same or different. Two examples are shown in Fig. 5.4. The houses shown were either identical, or differed by one, three, or five corresponding windows. While the children explored the pictures, their eye movements were recorded.

Overall, accuracy of performance increased with age, the oldest children making essentially no errors. Accuracy was best when the houses were identical, next when five of the windows were different, then three, and then one. Why should this be? Vurpillot measured two aspects of children's exploration: the number of windows looked at, and of corresponding pairs noted, i.e., looking in sequence at two windows located in the same relative place.

The exploratory behavior of the 3- to 5-year-olds was uneconomical and the same for identical and different houses. That of the 8- to 10-year-olds was highly efficient and varied with the stimuli. The 6- and 7-year-olds were in the middle. Specifically, when the houses were identical, a child would have to look at all 12 windows in order to be certain of her judgment. Further, the most efficient way to do so would be to look at corresponding pairs. The oldest, but not the youngest, children did this. For houses that were different, a child could stop looking as soon as one corresponding pair was found to be different. To continue looking at windows after finding a difference would be uneconomical. The number of corresponding pairs, and number of windows looked at by the oldest children, increased with the similarity of the two houses. The 3- to 5-year-olds, on the other hand, showed no behavior changes as a function of house similarity.

Fishbein (1976) summarizes these studies as follows:

> In the age range from three to about five, children explore limited aspects of objects in ways which make it unlikely that they will identify those objects at some future time. . . . During the age range from about five to seven exploratory mode . . . becomes more extensive, economical, complete

FIG. 5.4   The top pair of houses have differences in three corresponding windows. The bottom pair of houses are identical. (Source: Vurpillot, E. The development of scanning strategies and their relation to visual differentiation. *Journal of Experimental Child Psychology*, 1968, *6*, 622–650.)

and task-relevant. . . . From age seven onwards, exploratory mode starts to stabilize, but children from eight to twelve do show progressively more economical exploration with increasing age. . . . It is noteworthy that the age range seven to twelve is the approximate period during which concrete operations become fully organized. (p. 222–223)

Selective Attention.   In the usual incidental learning procedure, children are shown pictures with two familiar objects belonging to two different categories, as shown in the first row of Fig. 5.5. The children are asked to remember the location of one category of objects, in this case either the animals or household items. Usually no mention is made of the other category. After they have been shown the pairs a small number of times, they are tested for location memory of both the central and incidental categories. The extent to which they remember the location of the central object relative to the incidental object is assumed to indicate their selective attention ability. If they show good memory of the central cate-

FIG. 5.5   Stimuli of the five tasks in the study. From top to bottom rows, the tasks are: pictures and colored shapes, used in Experiments I and II; colored background, shape-color separated and animal-color separated, used in Experiment II. (Source: Hale, G. A. & Piper, R. A. Developmental trends in children's incidental learning. *Developmental Psychology*, 1973, *8*, 327–335.)

gory and not the incidental, it is assumed that they are able to exclude irrelevant information. If they show equal memory for both, it is assumed that they are unable to exclude irrelevant information.

Hagen and Hale (1973) have summarized the results of a large number of experiments. In general, with increasing age from 5 to 12 central memory increases while incidental memory remains constant. However, some studies find a decrease in incidental memory for 11- to 12-year-olds relative to the younger children. Further, for younger children there is a positive correlation between incidental and central memory performance, whereas for the older children there is a negative correlation. In discussing these and more recent confirming findings, Lane (1980) suggests two alternative explanations. First, with increasing age children are better able to focus their attention on relevant information as indicated by the negative correlation between central and incidental memory. Second, the results may only indicate that with increasing age children's overall attention capacity increases. Lane mathematically shows that both explanations are consistent with the data. It's possible that both are correct— older children develop a greater attentional capacity and a greater selective ability.

Two experiments by Hale and his colleagues relate to this issue. Hale and Piper (1973) reasoned that selective attention involves mental activities concerned with choosing information for further processing over and above exploration of stimuli. Exploration determines which environmental information you receive, whereas selective attention determines what you do with it once you have it. In nearly all incidental memory studies, the central and incidental stimuli were physically separated, as shown in the top row of Fig. 5.5. It's possible that age improvements in selective attention are produced through increases in exploration and not selective attention abilities. That is, the older children may have been better able than younger children to restrict their exploration to the central category. Further, Wheeler and Dusek (1973) showed that as the physical distance between central and incidental stimuli was increased, amount of incidental memory decreased. If the central and individual categories were made part of the same stimuli, however, then exploration abilities could be ruled out in explaining age-related differences.

Hale and Piper tested out these ideas using the stimuli shown in Fig. 5.5 with 8- and 12-year-olds. The children were always instructed to remember the shape location. In the second row each geometrical shape was a different color. In the third row, the shapes were all the same color and each background was a different color. In the fourth and fifth rows, each oval was a different color and the geometrical shapes and animals were the same color. The crucial stimuli are in the second row where the central and incidental categories are bound up in the same figure. How can you identify a triangle without also identifying its color?

Their results were quite interesting. When they used the stimuli in Rows 1, 3, 4, and 5, 12-year-olds showed greater central and equal or lower incidental memory than the 8-year-olds. These results are consistent with previous studies. When they used the Row 2 stimuli, they found both central and incidental memory to be greater in the older children. These are novel results and are consistent with the explanation that the apparently superior selective attention abilities of older children are related to their superior attentional *capacity* and not superior *selectivity*.

The study by Hale, Taweel, Green, and Flaugher (1978) deals with selectivity. They investigated this by asking whether there are age differences in children's ability to shift attention on command. If 5-, 8-, 9-, and 12-year-old children are instructed to attend to one of the categories (color versus shape) of the Row 2 stimuli in Fig. 5.5, then central versus incidental memory scores should reflect differences in selective attention abilities. Different patterns of results were found for the 5-year-olds, on the one hand, and all the older children, on the other. The 5-year-olds showed some selective attention abilities, but these were limited to modifying attention to nondominant color stimuli. For the older children, location memory for color and shape depended upon instructions. Thus, older children can shift attention to both dominant and nondominant categories.

The results of these experiments, using visual stimuli, indicate that 5-year-olds have a smaller overall attention capacity and are less able than older children to shift attention. In the usual experiments where children are instructed to attend to dominant visual categories, the superior central to incidental memory performance of older children is probably produced either by their greater attentional or exploration capacities. Selecting out information already received is probably a mentally effortful process, and children will carry out this selectivity only when instructed to do so or when there is some gain. Parents and teachers are familiar with this problem.

Development of Memory from Three to Adolescence

A father gives his daughter Diane some money and asks her to go to the store and buy one package of yeast, one stick of butter, and two oranges.

Diane agrees to do this, gets her bike, and starts to ride to the store, repeating to herself "one package of yeast, one stick of butter, and two oranges." Along the way she meets some friends, stops to talk, then play, and "forgets" about her job. After a short time passes, Diane happens to put her hand in her pocket, feels the money, and "remembers" that she had to buy something at the store, but she can't remember what. Diane goes to the store, hoping that she'll see what she has to buy, passes the bread rack, and "remembers" that her father wanted yeast and butter, probably in order to make bread. When she passes the the fruit section, she notices the oranges, and remembers to buy them also.

Although this story has little literary merit, it is interesting from the point of view of memory processes. There are three types of processes that we'll be discussing: those dealing with (1) *acquiring* information, i.e., putting information into memory storage; (2) *organizing* stored information; and (3) *retrieving* it from storage to consciousness. When Diane repeated the yeast, butter, oranges message she was attempting to acquire information. Repetition is one strategy people use for this purpose. Elaboration—going beyond the information given—is another strategy. When Diane saw the bread and remembered the yeast and butter, we must assume that she stored this elaboration of her father's request. We don't know exactly how Diane organized the information, but based on the way she retrieved it, we can say that she made at least three distinctions: store, butter and yeast, and oranges. Finally, she had considerable difficulty retrieving the stored information. It was not until she perceived some external cues that she was able to retrieve it. When she saw the bread, she *recalled* the yeast and butter, and when she saw the oranges, she *recognized* two oranges.

We know from research on memory development that in the age range three to adolescence, older children recall and recognize stored information better than younger ones. We know from the most recent research whether this ability is produced by superior acquisition, organization, and/or retrieval processes.

Acquisition Strategies and Memory-Monitoring

Acquisition strategies are any intentional activities used by individuals to improve their memory. Table 5.2 is Flavell's (1977) summary of the typical developmental course of their use, which includes rehearsal (repetition), elaboration, and organization. In the first column, "Strategy Not Available," children don't have the ability to use the strategy, and as a

TABLE 5.2
Typical Course of Development of a Memory Strategy

	Major Periods in Strategy Development		
	Strategy Not Available	Production Deficiency	Mature Strategy Use
Basic Ability to Execute Strategy	Absent to Poor	Fair to Good	Good to Excellent
Spontaneous Strategy Use	Absent	Absent	Present
Attempts to Elicit Strategy Use	Ineffective	Effective	Unnecessary
Effects of Strategy Use on Retrieval	———	Positive	Positive

(Source: Flavell, J. H. *Cognitive Development*. Englewood Cliffs, N.J.: Prentice-Hall, 1977. Reprinted by permission of the publisher.)

consequence, attempts to get them to do it are ineffective. Pressley (1982) summarizes research concerning elaboration strategies. One type of elaboration involves presenting children with pairs of objects or words asking them to remember the pairs by visually imagining the members of the pairs interacting with each other. For example, if the pair were the words "horse" and "apple," the child might imagine the horse eating the apple. Four-year-olds are unable to use this strategy with words, but can do so if they are instructed to show the interaction by playing with toys.

The second column "Production Deficiency" means that the child has the ability to use the strategy, doesn't do so spontaneously, but can if asked and reap benefits from it. The pair of experiments by Flavell, Beach, and Chinsky (1966) and Keeney, Cannizzo, and Flavell (1967) nicely demonstrate this. In the Flavell et al. study, kindergarten, second, and fifth-grade children were shown seven pictures spread out before them. The experimenter pointed to three in a particular order, rearranged them, and after a 15-second delay, asked the children to point to (recall) the three pictures in order. During the 15-second delay the experimenter read the lips of the children to see if they were overtly rehearsing. Older children rehearsed and recalled more accurately than the younger ones.

These results strongly suggest that overt rehearsal aids memory. The Keeney et al. experiment tested this out using two groups of first graders in a similar task. One group never or rarely overtly rehearsed (nonrehearsers) and one group almost always rehearsed (rehearsers).

Both groups were presented with 10 trials and asked to overtly rehearse. This was followed by 3 trials in which they had the option of rehearsing. On the first 10 trials both groups rehearsed and their performance was equally accurate. On the final 3 trials, the majority of nonrehearsers stopped rehearsing and their performance fell off. The rehearsers continued to rehearse, and kept their high performance level. The finding that the nonrehearsers dropped the rehearsal strategy is puzzling–why tamper with success? One possible reason is that they have some lack in memory monitoring, a topic we'll discuss after completing our discussion of Table 5.2.

The third column "Mature Strategy Use" means that the child has the ability to use the strategy and does it spontaneously and effectively. The study by Niemark, Slotnick, and Ulrich (1971) demonstrates this in dealing with the strategy of organization. Children from grades 1, 3, 4, 5, 6 and college students were shown 24 pictures. The pictures could be grouped into four categories of six each: animals, transportation vehicles, furniture, and articles of clothing. The children and adults were given 3 minutes to study them and told that they could move the pictures around if they wished. At the end of 3 minutes the pictures were removed and recall was tested. What did the subjects do during the 3-minute study period? Virtually none of the first and third-graders organized the pictures into the four categories: many of the fifth and sixth graders did, but incompletely; whereas nearly all the college students organized the pictures into the four categories. The correlation between amount of organization and recall was high. Thus, high organization as an acquisition strategy led to good recall, with only the college students demonstrating "Mature Strategy Use."

Let's return to the puzzle of the nonrehearsers who stopped using the successful strategy of rehearsal. Memory monitoring is the ability to predict one's capacity and to evaluate whether to-be-remembered information can in fact be recalled. Actors are one group who have to be quite accurate in their memory-monitoring abilities. Perhaps children in the "Production Deficiency" column are inaccurate in this ability, and as a consequence can't tell whether they benefit from strategies.

Kail (1979) summarizes research bearing on this issue. In a typical experiment children are shown a group of pictures and asked to study them for future recall. Before the recall, they are asked to predict how successful they will be. They are then given the recall test and afterwards permitted to choose some, but not all, of the pictures for further study. They are asked to predict their success again, and given another recall test. In general, there are tremendous differences in memory-monitoring ability between children under 7, who show very limited and inaccurate abilities, and those over 7, who show substantial capabilities, which improve with age. In the above example, children below 7 are inaccurate in predicting how successful their recall will be and furthermore are as likely to choose for additional study pictures they've just remembered as those they've forgotten.

In summary, children as young as 4 years can successfully use memory strategies when asked to do so. Between the ages of 4 and 7, children's spontaneous use of simple strategies such as rehearsal increases, but it is not until after age 7 that nearly all children spontaneously use a strategy. Between the ages of 7 and adolescence, mature use increases for many but not all strategies. One of the key elements in spontaneous strategy use is a child's memory-monitoring ability. This ability appears to strongly emerge at about age 7, and improve thereafter.

Development of memory organization. As noted, the way information is organized in memory storage cannot be determined directly. The two indirect ways organization has been studied are (1) to present information organized in different ways and note whether these differences show up in children's recall or recognition, and (2) to not preorganize the information and note whether children recall or recognize the information in organized ways. In the opening story, father didn't preorganize the information for Diane, yet her recall and recognition showed that she had organized it into three distinct categories.

The research dealing with this issue can be divided into the above two categories. Conrad (1971) presented two different types of pictures (the first procedure) to children between the ages of 3 and 11, who were asked to remember their order. In one type, the names of the pictures all sounded alike, e.g., rat, bat, cat, hat, and so on, and in the other type, they all sounded differently. If children organize their memory of the pictures by name and appearance, then like adults, they should perform more poorly on the alike than different-sounding pictures. Conrad found that children between 3 and 5 had equal difficulty with both types, but older children found the alike sets more difficult to recall than those with different sounding names. Thus, children under 5 apparently don't organize their memory of pictures by their names.

The experiment by McCarver (1972) tested kindergarten, first-grade, fourth-grade, and college students for memory of picture location. For half the subjects the pictures were presented one at a time at the same rate, and laid face down in an evenly spaced horizontal row. For the other half, the subjects were asked to remember the location of pictures in sets of two. The pictures were presented at different rates, in pairs, and laid face down in pairs, in a horizontal row. Overall performance accuracy was better for older than younger subjects. Importantly, the kindergarten and first-grade children performed essentially the same under the paired and unpaired conditions, whereas the two older groups were more accurate under the paired conditions. Since the younger children did not benefit from the spatial and temporal organization of the pictures, it can be concluded that they did not use these categories to organize picture information in memory.

Finally, Mandler and Robinson (1978) used two different picture organizations with children in grades 1, 3, and 5. Half the children were shown complex picture scenes of objects organized in a meaningful way. For example, a desk might be shown with a chair and wastebasket next to it, and a lamp on top. The other half saw scenes of the same objects, but placed in random positions. Children were then shown a set containing both previously seen and new pictures, and asked to recognize the old ones. When the old set involved random scenes, there were essentially no age differences in performance. When the old set involved organized scenes, performance improved with age. Thus, children beyond first grade show increasing evidence of organizing information in memory.

We'll conclude this section by summarizing two experiments that did not vary information organization. Lehman and Goodnow (1972) asked kindergarten, second-, fourth-, and sixth-grade children to reproduce, on different trials, three patterns of tapping: (.. ..), (. .. .), and (.. ...). As expected, older children performed more accurately than younger ones. Children were asked how they remembered the sounds. About half of the kindergartners merely counted the number of taps, but none reported using numbers to remember the pattern. More than 85% of the older children used numbers, and at all three age levels the numbers were frequently used in patterns. For example, the sound pattern (.. ...) was often remembered by "1,2,1,2,3" or "2,3." These results strongly suggest that a marked change occurs in organizing memory information through langauge use between ages 6 and 8.

The study by Liben and Posnansky (1977) reaches similar conclusions with very different tasks. Kindergarten, first- and third-grade children were asked to memorize sentences contained in short stories, and then tested for recognition. On the recognition test, the old sentences and several types of new ones were presented. The kindergarten and first graders were likely to incorrectly recognize a new sentence if it had the same noun order and relational terms, (e.g., taller-shorter, earlier-later) as the old ones. The third-graders were most likely to err on new sentences with the same meaning as the old one. These findings imply that after age 7, children structure sentences in memory based on accuracy of meaning, whereas younger children organize sentences based on word order and particular terms used.

The groups of studies strongly imply that the period around age 7 is critical in memory organization. At about this age children start to employ a variety of memory organizations, and use language effectively to remember stored information. From age 7 on, these organization abilities show steady improvement.

Development of retrieval processes. Retrieving stored information is like fishing. If the fish are there, it takes the right bait or lure to bring them out. If the information is stored in memory, it takes the right retrieval cue to bring it out. Tulving (1974) talks about this as "cue-dependent forgetting." The essential idea is that during acquisition a set of cues is present that gives one access to this stored information. If for any reason the cues are no longer available to a person, then she loses access to these memories. In our shopping-for-father story, Diane lost the cues for her task once she started playing with friends. The money in her pocket provided cues for shopping, and the cues in the store gave her access to the remainder of the stored information.

Much of the research on the development of retrieval processes has been concerned with comparing retrieval with the acquisition and storage of information. In the typical experiment, children of different ages are presented words or pictures to memorize, followed by variations of the available cues during recall or recognition. If under the "best" retrieval conditions there are no age-related differences in recall, then it can be concluded that storage was essentially the same at those ages. Given that there are no differences in storage, then recall differences must be a function of retrieval. Where recall or recognition is different under all retrieval conditions, statistical techniques can sometimes be used to determine how much of the difference is determined by acquisition and storage and how much by retrieval. We'll briefly discuss three studies bearing on these issues.

Perlmutter and Myers (1979) compared 3- and 5-year-olds in the recall of nine toys, which belonged to three different conceptual categories, e.g., animals, clothes, furniture. During recall, either the children were asked to freely recall (no cues) the names of all the toys they had seen, or they were given the category names as cues. Under both conditions, the 5-year-olds performed better than the 3-year-olds, and for both age groups, performance was better under the cued than the free recall. Importantly, the amount of improvement shown by each group in going from free to cued recall was essentially the same. This implies that the age-related performance differences were produced by acquisition and storage differences and not retrieval. We can't be completely sure of this, because neither group achieved perfect performance in either condition.

In Kobasigawa's (1974) experiment, first, third, and sixth graders were asked to memorize 24 names of common objects, 3 from each of eight categories. The children were shown pictures of the objects and the category (cue) to which they belonged; e.g., a fruit stand was shown with each fruit. Recall occurred under one of three conditions: *free* recall, and *cue* recall, as in the above experiment; and *directive* recall in which the experimenter presented the cues one at a time and asked the children to recall all three objects that went with it. In general, recall was higher for the sixth than for the first and third graders. However, sixth graders performed better under cue recall than free recall, whereas there were no differences between these conditions for the first and third graders. This means that the sixth graders had easier retrieval access to storage than the younger children. Finally, under the directive recall condition, there were no performance differences as a function of age, all recalling about 85% of the names. These results imply that there were probably no age-related acquisition and storage differences with these materials and procedures. Rather, the poor recall seen for the younger children was produced by retrieval deficiencies.

In the experiment by Chechile, Richman, Topinka, and Ehrensbeck (1981), first graders, sixth graders, and college students were asked to remember the location of five pictures of objects, presented one at a time, and turned face down in a row. After a short interval in which they performed another unrelated task, three tests were given: free recall and two cued recognition tests. By comparing relative performance across age under free recall with the two recognition procedures, inferences can be made about the development of acquisition and storage processes, and retrieval. The acquisition and storage measures showed improvements between first and sixth grade, but none between sixth grade and college. The retrieval measures showed improvements between each grade level. Thus, acquisition and storage processes develop more quickly than retrieval.

Overall, the three experiments indicate that retrieval processes progressively develop from ages 3 to 20. Acquisition and storage appear to stabilize at about age 12; however, for some tasks, there may be no differences in the age range 7 to 12. These experiments also suggest that where "forgetting" occurs by children, it is highly likely that the source of the forgetting was in retrieval deficiencies. Younger children seem to need more retrieval cues than do older ones.

SOCIAL COGNITION

Social cognition refers to the understanding individuals have of situations involving the interactions of two or more people. Theoretically, then, social cognition can range from understanding one's self in social situations to studying whole societies of people interacting with each other. Social cognition includes aspects of virtually all the social sciences, including economics, political science, and history, as well as law and religion. Obviously, we'll have to limit our discussion.

There are two broad traditions in the psychological study of social cognition (Shantz, 1975). One stems from Piaget's work in cognitive development, but especially that concerned with moral judgments (Piaget, 1932). The other is social psychologists studying adults' social judgments, e.g., the motives one person perceives as underlying another's behavior. The developmental research over the past 20 years has been greatly influenced by Piaget's work, but several interesting recent papers have bridged both traditions.

Even restricting ourselves to the psychological study of the development of social cognition, the field is still too extensive to summarize in this chapter. An evolutionary approach will help narrow the field and bring cohesion to our discussion. The evolutionist Simpson (1949) wrote the following:

> Man is much the most knowing or thinking animal, as our predecessors rightly recognized in bestowing on him the distinctive qualification of *sapiens*. Man is also the responsible animal. This is more basic than his knowledge, although dependent on it, for some other animals surely know and think in a way not completely inhuman, but no other animal can truly be said to be responsible in anything like the same sense in which man is responsible. (p. 310)

What is the unique sense in which humans are responsible? Fishbein (1976), building on Piaget, argued that it is reciprocity. In evolution, "the key to understanding the form human group life took . . . is the idea of 'reciprocal obligations' " (p. 135). Gatherer-hunter groups are comprised of interrelated sets of reciprocal obligations, each member being responsible to several others because of what he or she has done for them. For example, men and women become obligated to each other and their relatives through marriage by carrying out reciprocities such as food sharing, child care, and the care and protection of parents and in-laws.

Fishbein emphasized that reciprocal acts are "obligations" and as such, become like moral rules. When group members don't reciprocate, they are often punished, and unlike nonhuman primates, the punishment may occur long after the rules were broken. For example, food sharing among gatherer-hunters often involves very elaborate procedures that must be closely followed in order to prevent considerable conflict. Reciprocal obligations play a very important role in modern Western societies as well. Failure to reciprocate in friendship strains that relationship. Exchanging money for goods and services is the modern way to share; and think how hurt and angry you become when you've been cheated.

Piaget (1932) also strongly emphasizes the link between reciprocal obligations and morality. For example, he maintains that children start to develop a mature moral understanding when they attempt to cooperate with peers and discover the importance of reciprocity.

When we step back from Piaget's book as a work on moral judgments, we see that he is basically writing about children's understanding of social relations. Given its close connection with an evolutionary view of human development, a central theme emerges for discussing social cognition— moral development. We'll presently show that this encompasses some of the most important and interestiing work in the development of social cognition.

Piaget's Research and Theory

Piaget (1932) starts his book by saying,

> Children's games constitute the most admirable social institutions. The game of marbles, for instance, as played by boys, contains an extremely complex system of rules, that is to say, a code of laws, a jurisprudence of its own. . . . All morality consists in a system of rules, and the essence of all morality is to be sought for in the respect which the individual acquires for these rules. (p. 13)

It is Piaget's task to understand the moral development of children. He reasons that morality is any system of rules governing the interaction of people. Thus, games of marbles and any other rule-governed behavior involve morality. The essential ingredient in these interactions is that individuals respect the rules. What is the nature of this respect? How do individuals acquire it? Does it change with age? Piaget assumes that by studying how moral knowledge is acquired in games, he is learning about how children generally develop moral knowldge. This seems like a questionable assumption. After all, is breaking a rule in marbles like lying or stealing? Surprisingly, yes, as we'll shortly see.

Piaget's basic technique in the study of marbles was to "hang out" with marbles players. Typically he would approach a group of players, marbles in hand, and ask if he could join them. If they agreed, he would ask what the rules were, and start shooting. During the course of the game he asked them a number of questions about the rules, such as where they came from, whether they could be changed, and who could change them. It is from this set of questions with different-aged children that he drew conclusions about the development of rule knowledge.

Piaget describes three stages in rule knowledge, which cover the same age range as the four stages of game playing discussed earlier. The first stage overlaps the stage of motor rituals, from about ages 1 to 3. Piaget had a good deal of difficulty in interviewing these children owing to their limited language abilities. He emphasized two aspects of rule knowledge: whether the rules of play are obligatory, and whether they are self-imposed or come about through social interactions. Piaget believes that in the motor stage, some of the rules are obligatory—the children feel they must follow them—and some are not. Further, where there are rules, they are self-imposed. Of the three stages, this is the only one where the rules have this latter characteristic, and as such are not really moral rules.

The second stage overlaps all of the egocentric and about half of the cooperative stage—until about age 10. This stage can be referred to as that of "unilateral respect and coercive rules." During this time children believe there are "real" rules that must be obeyed. They believe that the rules have existed for a very long time, have always been the same, and were established by adults. Children in this stage think it would be wrong to change the rules even if all the players agreed.

Piaget asks "Leh," 5½ years old, whether the younger players could be allowed to shoot closer to the circle than the older ones. "No," answers Leh, "that wouldn't be fair." "Why not?" "Because God would make the little boy's shot not reach the marbles and the big boy's shot would reach them" (p. 58). Piaget asks "Ben," age 10, whether it would be cheating if he invented a rule that everyone agreed to. He said it would be cheating "because I invented it; it isn't a rule! It's a wrong rule because it's outside the rules. A fair rule is one that is in the game" (p. 63). The psychological processes underlying this stage are that children have almost a mystical respect for adults and feel forced by them to obey the rules. If they obey the rules, they are therefore being obedient to their elders.

The third stage emerges at about age 10 and can be referred to as "mutual respect and rational rules." In this stage "the rule of a game appears to the child no longer as an external law, sacred insofar as it has been laid down by adults, but as the outcome of a free decision and worthy of respect in the measure that it has enlisted mutual consent" (p. 65). Thus in this stage, the unilateral respect for adults and their alleged rules is replaced by mutual respect for peers and mutually agreed-upon rules. All rules can be changed, and all changes are fair, provided that everyone agrees to them. These children don't believe that all the rules have existed for a long time, nor that they were established by adults. The two psychological factors underlying this stage are the children's growing awareness of their freedom from certain kinds of adult rules and their strong desire to cooperate with peers. When these factors emerge and children play games, they often come into conflict about the rules. They resolve the conflicts by mutually agreeing to some rules and not appealing to adults.

Piaget extends these ideas to the study of clumsiness, stealing, and lying, placing emphasis on the second and third stages. As with the research on games, this material is both charming and insightful. Piaget's basic procedure is to tell two brief stories about "wrongdoing" children, and ask the listener which child is naughtier and why. We have told some of these stories around the dinner table to children and they work as if by magic. The following (Piaget, 1932) is probably the most famous pair:

A. A little boy who is called John is in his room. He is called to dinner. He goes into the dining room, but behind the door there was a chair. On the chair was a tray with fifteen cups on it. John couldn't have known that there was all this behind the door. He goes in, the door knocks against the tray, bang go the fifteen cups and they all get broken!

B. Once there was a little boy whose name was Henry. One day when his mother was out he tried to get some jam out of the cupboard. He climbed up on to the chair and stretched out his arm, but the jam was too high and he couldn't reach it and have any. But while he was trying to get it, he knocked over a cup. The cup fell down and broke. (p. 122)

In the stories dealing with clumsiness and stealing, Piaget varies the intentions of the principal character and the amount of material damage done. In the above stories, John has good intentions in that he is coming to dinner when called, but by accident does a lot of damage. Henry has bad intentions by trying to take jam without mother's permission, and by accident does little damage. In some of the stories, children steal things with either good or bad intentions.

In the stories dealing with lying, one of the pair contains an exaggeration that no adult would believe, but was made with no ill intention. In the other, the child intentionally lies, and the lie is believable. Examples are seeing a dog as big as a cow, and receiving a good grade on a spelling test.

The results of these interviews were fairly consistent. Up to about age 10, children will often say that the child who did the most damage, independent of intent, was the naughtiest. Similarly in stories dealing with lying, they will often say that the child who told the least believable story, independent of intent, was the naughtiest. The following is part of Piaget's interview with "Fel," age 6, discussing the dog/cow-good grade pairs of stories.

P: Which of these two children is naughtiest?
F: The little girl who said she saw a dog as big as a cow.
P: Why is she the naughtiest?
F: Because it could never happen.
P: Did her mother believe her?
F: No, because they never are (dogs as big as cows).
P: Why did she say that?
F: To exaggerate.
P: And why did the other tell a lie?
F: Because she wanted to make people believe that she had a good report.
P: Did her mother believe her?
F: Yes.
P: Which would you punish most if you were the mother?
F: The one with the big dog because she told the worst lie and was the naughtiest.

After age 10, children nearly always base their judgments on the intentions of the actor and not on either amount of material damage or improbability of the lie.

The theme that ties these results together is referred to as "objective responsibility." When a child bases her moral judgments on this type of responsibility, she is only looking at external results, and not at intentions. The more damage done, and the more improbable the exaggeration (because it deviates most from reality), the naughtier is the child. Piaget argues that this type of moral thinking stems from the unilateral respect children have for adults. This unilateral respect leads to an unquestioning acceptance by the child of external authority and as a consequence, a concern about external results. When the child starts to look within herself as a somewhat independent person, and also to develop mutual respect with peers, the moral emphasis shifts from external to internal concerns. In order to cooperate with others, your intentions and theirs have to be made explicit and taken into account. This process naturally leads to a morality primarily based on intentions.

The last topic Piaget discusses is the idea of justice. In this section he presents children from ages 6 to 14 with six categories of stories and asks them to make judgments about the outcomes. The first category deals with the issue of whether people should be punished severely for breaking rules versus punishment matching the wrongdoing. The second category focuses on individual versus collective responsibilities when rules are broken. The third category deals with belief in an "imminent justice" – that punishment will follow wrongdoing even if no human knows about it. The fourth stresses "equality" of treatment versus "equity" – that everyone should be treated alike as opposed to taking special circumstances into account. The fifth category deals with conflicts between obeying authority and equal or equitable treatment. Martin Luther King's civil disobedience is an example of this. The sixth focuses on justice between children, independent of adult rules or interferences.

As can be seen this is very broad and extremely rich set of issues. Owing to space limitations, we'll give one example showing a flavor of the results. This story (Piaget, 1932) is from the sixth category, but also has implications for the fourth one.

> Two boys, a little one and a big one, once went for a long walk in the mountains. When lunchtime came they were very hungry and took their food out of their bags. They found there was not enough for both of them. What should have been done? Give all the food to the big boy or to the little one, or the same to both? (p. 310)

Here are examples of three different developmental levels of justice.

Fal (7½): The big boy should have the most.
      P: Why?
Fal (7½): Because he's the eldest. (p. 311)
Wal (7): Each must be given the same.

> P: Another time they had five bars of chocolate. The
>   little boy asked for three. Was it fair?
> Wal (7):   They ought to have had two and a half each. (p. 312)
> Schmo (10):   They should have given more to the little boy because
>   he was smaller.
> P: They both ate the same. Was it fair?
> Schmo (10):   Not quite so fair. (p. 312)

In the first example, Fal believes that favoring authority (the bigger boy) is more just than equal shares. Wal believes that equality is the most just distribution. In Schomo's responses we see equality as giving way to equity as the basis for justice. Piaget finds essentially the same two bases for children's ideas of justice as described above. Children who base justice on adult authority are in favor of severe punishments and individual as opposed to collective responsibility, believe in imminent justice, place obedience as the highest value, and give a higher priority to authority than to equality or equity. Children who have developed mutual respect for peers and have discovered reciprocity as the basis for fairness respond in advanced ways, e.g., favor punishments that fit the crime, collective responsibility, and don't believe in imminent justice.

To sum up, Piaget maintains that moral knowledge and judgments by children undergo a major transition at about age 10 (for Swiss children). This transition involves a shift from obeying adult authority and their alleged values to accepting one's self and peers as both authorities and rule-givers. We use the word "alleged" because adults usually base moral judgments on intentions and operate with flexible rules, at least among themselves. The act of attempting to cooperate with peers who are respected is the primary teacher of mature morality. Children discover that objective responsibility and inflexible rules are poor ways to do business with one another. They find that intentions are quite important, rules are designed to serve people, and that reciprocity is the essential basis for many social interactions.

Kohlberg's Theory and Research

Kohlberg's (1969, 1971) work in moral development is heavily based on Piaget's research in cognitive and moral development. Like Piaget, Kohlberg set out to describe the ways children and adults progressively understand moral issues. He did this by presenting dilemmas in story form to his subjects and asking them to resolve the central moral issues.

Unlike Piaget, Kohlberg did not give a general definition of morality. Rather, by analyzing the reasons given for moral choices, the stage-related definitions of morality emerge.

The following dilemma, taken from Rest (1968) is perhaps the best known of the ten typically used:

In Europe, a woman was near death from cancer. One drug might save her, a form of radium that a druggist in the same town had recently discovered. The druggist was charging $2,000, ten times what the drug cost him to make. The sick woman's husband, Heinz, went to everyone he knew to borrow the money, but he could only get together about half of what it cost. He told the druggist that his wife was dying and asked him to sell it cheaper or let him pay later. But the druggist said, "No." The husband got desperate and broke into the man's store to steal the drug for his wife. Should the husband have done that? Why?

The subject's responses are recorded word by word and analyzed on the basis of 25 "coded aspects of moral judgment." Some of these aspects follow:

1. How does the subject use punishment or negative reactions?
2. To what extent is conscience or self-condemnation discussed?
3. How are property rights or possessions discussed?
4. How is reciprocity dealt with as a motive for either conforming or deviating from social roles?

Thus, each response is examined to see if it relates to each aspect and then classified into a given stage of moral development. The stage assigned to a subject is the average of his scores on all aspects for all dilemmas.

Kohlberg identifies three age-related levels with two stages in each. The "Preconventional" level is characteristic of the moral reasoning of 4- to 10-year-olds. Moral acts are interpreted in terms of either their physical consequences, e.g., punishment, reward, exchange of favors, or whether the acts are consistent with the rules set up by those with superior physical power. In Stage 1, the children base moral judgments primarily on obedience and fear of punishment. In Stage 2, they base moral judgments primarily on whether one's needs are being met. The beginnings of an understanding of reciprocity are seen here.

The "Conventional" level of moral thinking emerges in the age range 10 to 20 years. Most adults in all cultures are classified at this level.

Kohlberg described conventional thinking as conformist in that individuals seek to support and maintain the social order as it is. The rules are seen as valuable in and of themselves, and moral behavior toward individuals is that which pleases others and meets their expectations. In Stage 3, the children and young adolescents base moral judgments primarily on whether the behavior intentionally pleased or helped others. In Stage 4, moral judgments are primarily based on whether one did his duty, showed respect for authority, and attempted to maintain the social order.

The "Postconventional" level of moral thinking is not characteristic of any age-group. If it emerges, it will be seen after age 18. Morality is thought of in terms of rules or principles that apply to essentially all societies and individuals. These principles stand on their own, in the sense that their "truth" does not depend on the particular individuals or groups who maintain them. In Stage 5, duty is defined in terms of a social contract that exists between all members of a society. In this contract each of us should avoid violating the rights of others, and attempt to uphold the welfare of the majority. In Stage 6, the "good" or "right action" is defined by universal principles based on logic, justice, reciprocity, and conscience. The highest principles involve the equality of human rights and the inherent dignity of all individuals.

Table 5.3 presents examples of the six stages relevant to the motivation aspects of moral thinking. These examples are responses to the Heinz/dying wife dilemma. In reading through this table pay special attention to the material in parentheses starting with Stage 2. This material briefly describes how each stage is differentiated from the immediately preceding one. Kohlberg asserts that moral development involves logically higher differentiations and integrations of the immediately preceding stages. Thus, at each higher stage, individuals can make finer moral distinctions than at lower ones (differentiation) and moreover, their reasoning will apply to a wider range of situations (integration).

Kohlberg (1969) summarizes three types of empirical research that tend to confirm the validity of his theory. First, he and his colleagues used these dilemmas with a group whose initial ages were 10 to 16 years. They periodically tested them for the next 12 years. In nearly all cases, stage of moral reasoning increased over the 12-year period. In no cases did it decrease, nor did anyone skip any stages in their progress; e.g., no one went from Stage 2 to Stage 4 directly. Second, urban 10- to 16-year-olds in Taiwan and Mexico, and rural youths in Turkey and Yucatan, showed age-related stage progressions highly similar to North Ameri-

TABLE 5.3
Motives for Engaging in Moral Action

Stage 1. Action is motivated by avoidance of punishment and conscience is irrational fear of punishment.

     Pro- If you let your wife die, you will get in trouble. You'll be blamed for not spending the money to save her and there'll be an investigation of you and the druggist for your wife's death.

     Con- You shouldn't steal the drug because you'll be caught and sent to jail if you do. If you do get away, your conscience would bother you thinking how the police would catch up with you at any minute.

Stage 2. Action motivated by desire for reward or benefit. Possible guilt reactions are ignored and punishment viewed in a pragmatic manner. (Differentiates own fear, pleasure, or pain from punishment-consequences.)

     Pro- If you do happen to get caught you could give the drug back and you wouldn't get much of a sentence. It wouldn't bother you much to serve a little jail term, if you have your wife when you get out.

     Con- He may not get much of a jail term if he steals the drug, but his wife will probably die before he gets out so it won't do him much good. If his wife dies, he shouldn't blame himself, it wasn't his fault she has cancer.

Stage 3. Action motivated by anticipation of disapproval of others, actual or imagined-hypothetical (e.g., guilt). (Differentiation of disapproval from punishment, fear, and pain.)

     Pro- No one will think you're bad if you steal the drug but your family will think you're an inhuman husband if you don't. If you let your wife die, you'll never be able to look anybody in the face again.

     Con- It isn't just the druggist who will think you're a criminal, everyone else will too. After you steal it, you'll feel bad thinking how you've brought dishonor on your family and yourself; you won't be able to face anyone again.

Stage 4. Action motivated by anticipation of dishonor, i.e, institutionalized blame for failure of duty, and by guilt over concrete harm done to others. (Differentiates formal dishonor from informal disapproval. Differentiates guilt for bad consequences from disapproval.)

     Pro- If you have any sense of honor, you won't let your wife die because you're afraid to do the only think that will save her. You'll always feel guilty that you caused her death if you don't do your duty to her.

     Con- You're desperate and you may not know you're doing wrong when you steal the drug. But you'll know you did wrong after you're punished and sent to jail. You'll always feel guilty for your dishonesty and lawbreaking.

Stage 5. Concern about maintaining respect of equals and of the community (assuming their respect is based on reason rather than emotions). Concern about own self-respect, i.e., to avoid judging self as irrational, inconsistent, nonpurposive. (Discriminates between institutionalized blame and community disrespect or self-disrespect.)

     Pro- You'd lose other people's respect, not gain it, if you don't steal. If you let your wife die, it would be out of fear, not out of reasoning it out. So you'd just lose self-respect and probably the respect of others too.

     Con- You would lose your standing and respect in the community and violate the law. You'd lose respect for yourself if you're carried away by emotion and forget the long-range point of view.

TABLE 5.3 *(continued)*

Stage 6.	Concern about self-condemnation for violating one's own principles. (Differentiates between community respect and self-respect. Differentiates between self-respect for general achieving rationality and self-respect for maintaining moral principles.)

Pro- If you don't steal the drug and let your wife die, you'd always condemn yourself for it afterward. You wouldn't be blamed and you would have lived up to the outside rule of the law but you wouldn't have lived up to your own standards of conscience.

Con- If you stole the drug, you wouldn't be blamed by other people but you'd condemn yourself because you wouldn't have lived up to your own conscience and standards of honesty.·

(Source: Rest, J. R. *Developmental hierarchy in preference and comprehension of moral judgment.* Unpublished doctoral dissertation. University of Chicago, 1968.)

cans. The rural youths, however, did not advance as high as the urban ones. Other more recent studies dealing with rural children and adolescents show that they move through the stage sequence at a slower rate than urban dwellers, e.g., White, Bushnell, and Regnemer (1978) for Bahamian school children. Third, when individuals are asked to paraphrase (put into their own words) the moral reasons given by others, they can do so for statements up to one stage above their own, but are unable to do so for statements two or more stages higher. This implies that the moral reasoning a person uses is approximately at the upper limit of his moral understanding.

There have been a number of criticisms of Kohlberg's work. Kurtines and Grief (1974) point out two problems with the clinical method of scoring moral reasoning. First, it appears that only people trained by Kohlberg can reliably use his scoring manual. Second, the scoring reliability of these people is far from perfect. The two problems are being overcome, however, by the development of objective and highly reliable measures of Kohlberg's theory, e.g., Rest (1979). A more serious set of criticisms is that the theory is biased in favor of Western men as opposed to women (Gilligan, 1977) or members of non-Western cultures (Simpson, 1974). A third criticism is that the Kohlberg dilemmas primarily deal with conflicts about prohibitions, e.g., breaking laws, being disobedient to authorities, and not with other kinds of moral issues such as altruism (Eisenberg, 1982).

Despite these problems, Kohlberg's theory and research provide us with a deep analysis of the development of moral thinking. It is clearly an advance over Piaget's work and will no doubt provide a solid ground for further advances in the field.

Morality Versus Social Convention

Elliot Turiel (1978, 1983) has seriously questioned Piaget's and Kohlberg's assumption that moral issues comprise a single category of social understanding that develops with age and experience. Rather, Turiel argues that there are at least two distinct categories of social rules—morality and social convention—that are concerned with different issues, develop in different ways, and moreover are distinguished by children at any early age. Social conventions are arbitrary and highly cultural-specific, such as driving on the right side of the road or saying "Thank you." They are consistent patterns of the ways North Americans or others do business with one another. Although they are arbitrary—we could by common consent agree to drive on the left and not say "Thank you,"—social conventions are very important for maintaining the social organization of a given culture. According to Turiel, many if not all sex roles are social conventions. When men or boys start acting like women or girls (and vice versa), people often become very upset. Think about how long it has taken to even minimaly sexually integrate Little League baseball. Social conventions, when broken, often lead to punishment, and as such are taken very seriously by the culture.

Morality, Turiel maintains, is neither arbitrary nor culture-specific. That is, by common consent a moral act cannot be changed into an immoral one, or vice versa. Moreover, what is moral in one culture, is moral in all cultures. Morality, which is defined as being concerned with justice, is thus narrower than social conventions. Actions towards another can be evaluated from a moral view on the basis of their consequences "such as harm inflicted on others, violation of rights, effects on the general welfare" (p. 80, 1978). Actions are judged as moral or immoral independent of any public rules or laws about them. Indeed, a law may be immoral in that it is unjust. Racial segregation of schools is an example of such a law because of its harmful consequences to both blacks and whites. Turiel is obviously aware of the fact that people will dispute both the meaning of justice and the morality of specific situations. Also, he is aware that in some cases it will be difficult to decide whether an action falls in the category of social convention or morality. Nevertheless, the concepts underlying these two categories are relatively clear, and we can evaluate for ourselves whether the distinction is useful.

Turiel suggests three ways of evaluating this distinction: (1) Do children react differently to moral and social convention transgressions (rulebreaking)? (2) Do children's concepts of the two categories differ? (3) Is development of social convention different than moral concepts?

At least three recent studies deal with the first question. Nucci and Turiel (1978) observed 3- to 5-year-olds interacting in their nursery school. Based on extensive observations, the experimenters classified all naturally occurring transgressions by children into either the social convention or the morality categories. Examples of social convention transgressions were playing with certain materials in either the wrong place or time; not joining a group activity; eating a snack while standing rather than sitting as was the school rule. Examples of moral transgressions were physically or psychologically harming someone; taking something that belonged to others. Following the observation of a transgression, it was noted how and whether teachers and children reacted to it. The experimenters also interviewed a child who had observed the transgression, but we'll discuss these data in dealing with the second question.

The results are very clear-cut. Teachers nearly always made some corrective reaction to social convention and slightly less so to moral transgressions. Children rarely made any response to social convention but did respond to a majority of the moral transgressions. Thus, at the level of "response versus no-response," children distinguish between the two categories.

Nucci and Nucci (1982a) observed second-, fifth-, and seventh-grade children in their classrooms and on the playground, scoring for social convention and moral transgressions. As in the above study, they noted how and whether teachers and children responded. They also interviewed children who observed the transgression. As in the above study teachers responded to social convention more frequently than to moral transgressions, with the reverse holding for children of all ages. Thus, the results of this study are consistent with the above, supporting the distinction between the two categories of transgressions. In addition, children showed different patterns of reactions to moral and social convention transgressions. Children at all grade levels were more likely for moral than social convention transgressions to complain about injury or loss, comment about the unfairess of the behavior, and ask the transgressor to consider the feelings of others. On the other hand, they were more likely for social convention than moral transgressions to complain that the behavior was disruptive and that there were rules against it, and to command the transgressor to stop. The patterns for teachers were similar. These results strongly support the view that children treat moral and social convention transgressions as distinct categories of behavior.

Nucci and Nucci (1982b) raised the question whether the above pattern of results would be found in playgrounds, where children were not under adult supervision. They observed children who were playing in groups of five or more, and estimated their ages to fall into two categories, 7 to 10 and 11 to 14. In this situation, the social convention transgressions were those that the children had created, such as sucking on grass, spitting, two boys on a sled, one lying on top of the other, and a boy and girl sitting too close together. For example, in the sled incident, another boy watching them yelled, "you faggots." The moral transgressions were similar to those occurring in school settings. In general, the results of this study are completely consistent with the Nucci and Nucci (1982a) observations, supporting the distinction between morality and social convention.

Let's turn to the second question: Do children's *concepts* of social conventions and morality differ? In the Nucci and Turiel study, observers of transgressions were asked if there was a rule in the school about the observed act, and whether the act would be all right if there were no rule against it. When the preschoolers said that the act (transgression) would be all right if there were no rule against it, the act was scored as a social convention. If they said the act would not be all right, it was scored as a moral transgression. Nucci and Turiel found that the categories based on children's judgments were in agreement with the experimenter's categories for 83% of the cases. In other words, preschoolers use rule arbitrariness as a basis for accurately distinguishing moral from social convention transgressions.

The Nucci and Nucci (1982a) study used the same criteria as above for scoring children's judgments as social convention or moral. In this case, agreement with the experimenter's categories ranged from 86% to 92%, which is essentially the same level of agreement between the experimenters themselves. It's of interest that children between the age of 3 and 13 make these distinctions in highly similar ways.

Finally, in the study by Weston and Turiel (1980), children between the ages of 5 and 10 were read stories dealing with four types of behaviors in school settings: undressing on a playground because it was hot; hitting another child; leaving toys on the schoolroom floor; and refusing to share a snack with another child. For each type of behavior, two schools were then described, one permitting it and one prohibiting it. In each case, the children were asked questions concerned with evaluating the behavior, the school policy dealing with it, and the teacher's probable reactions.

Generally, the children evaluated all four behaviors negatively, with hitting more so than the others. When they were told that the school permitted each behavior, then undressing, leaving toys, and refusing to share were evaluated positively, but hitting was still evaluated negatively. When children were asked to predict how the teacher would respond to each behavior in a school permitting it, they again distinguished between hitting and the other three behaviors. Thus, hitting was judged to be a moral transgression, and the others as social convention transgressions.

The three experiments taken together strongly support Turiel's argument that children have different conceptions of morality and social conventions. This distinction is inconsistent with both Piaget's and Kohlberg's theories of moral development.

We now turn to the last question concerning the relative development of morality and social convention concepts. Turiel (1978) read stories to children and adults (ages 6 to 25) which dealt with social convention issues. For example, in one story a child was raised by his parents to call people by their first names. In school he was expected to address teachers formally and thus came into conflict with them and the principal. How should he resolve this conflict? Turiel analyzed their responses and identified seven age-related levels of social convention concepts. We'll briefly describe the first four levels, which cover the age range 6 to 13.

At the first level (ages 6 and 7), children identify social conventions as behaviors that are nearly always associated with certain categories of people or activities; e.g., teachers should be called "Mr.," "Miss," or "Mrs."; people should eat with a knife and fork and not with their hands. These children don't express a concept of the social necessity of social conventions. Rather, what is, is as it should be. Hence, social conventions should be followed.

At the second level (ages 8 and 9), children identify social conventions as arbitrary, based on custom, but not necessity. That is, they see no necessary social reason for these behaviors to be maintained in the culture, even though nearly everybody carries them out. Unlike the Level 1 children, what is, is not necessarily as it should be. Hence, social conventions need not be followed.

At the third level (ages 10 and 11), children also identify social conventions as arbitrary, but believe that it is necessary to follow them. This belief is primarily based on the view that authorities (persons with power) must be obeyed, and secondarily on social needs, e.g., keeping order. These children are not clear, however, about a connection between following rules and social needs.

At the fourth level (ages 12 and 13), children also identify social conventions as arbitrary, but don't believe it is necessary to follow them. If the rule governing behavior is reasonable, then the behavior should be followed. Otherwise, it should not be. These children generally view conventions as social expectations, and not as rules that must be followed. The importance of conventions lies in helping people communicate with each other, and not so much with maintaining social order.

As can be seen, this sequence of four levels is quite different than the two major levels described by Piaget or the six stages of Kohlberg. One interesting pattern observed by Turiel, which has no parallel in Piaget or Kohlberg, is the alternation from one level to the next in obeying and not obeying social conventions. Turiel suggests that this pattern of "affirmation" and "negation" leads to increasingly elaborate understandings of social processes. By partially rejecting the old ways of thinking, new ways can readily be constructed.

In summary, the data support the idea that moral rules and social conventions are different concepts with unique developmental histories. Children react differently to moral and social convention transgressions, have different concepts of them, and develop these concepts in unique ways. Turiel's work is still in its infancy. Thus, many theoretically and practically important questions are unanswered. For example, what life experiences lead to the differentiation of the two concepts? Do social convention concepts have stage-like properties? How can schools and parents assist children in their development of these concepts? Is it possible that moral concepts are canalized and conventions are not? Fishbein's (1976) analysis suggests that this would be the case.

Intentions and Consequences in Making Moral Judgments

In evaluating wrongdoing Piaget (1932) reported that children between the ages of 6 and 10 oscillate in their use of two "strategies": (1) Children whose intentions are bad are judged naughtier than those with good intentions, irrespective of amount of damage; (2) children who produce the most damage are judged naughtier than those who do little damage, irrespective of intent. After age 10, Swiss children base moral judgments on intentions. Thus, children under that age are clearly aware of the importance of intentions, but owing to the unresolved conflict between unilateral respect for authority and mutual respect for peers, they do not consistently base their judgments on it.

Piaget's research in this area has been criticized by many, e.g., Shantz (1975), Keasey (1978), and Karniol (1978). Two major criticisms are that in Piaget's stories good intentions and high damage were contrasted *only with* bad intentions and low damage, and not other combinations. Second, in both cases the *damage occurred by accident*. The child attempting to take the forbidden jam didn't intend to break the cup. It's possible that even very young children, for example, would always judge a child who intentionally broke 1 cup to be naughtier than one who accidentally broke 15.

We believe that Piaget was aware of these and other possible criticisms, and chose to ignore them. In examining much of Piaget's research, we find that he generally ignores some obvious deficiencies in method. It's clear that this ignoring is deliberate and that he follows a particular research strategy: demonstrate the usefulness of concepts in as many situations as possible, rather than taking one research situation and making it as free from criticism as possible. The two concepts of interest for him were "unilateral respect" and "mutual respect." By showing the role they play in a huge variety of situations he tries to convince you of their usefulness, even though each situation is technically flawed.

Many researchers have decided that the issue of intentions in moral judgments is a very important problem in its own right, independent of Piaget's concerns about unilateral and mutual respect. As a consequence, they have corrected the technical flaws and have raised a number of new questions. For example, Berndt and Berndt (1975) makes us aware of the distinction between *intentions* and *motives*. Jean Valjean in *Les Miserables* intended to steal the bread (and did). His motive was to feed his starving children. Surely Valjean's act is different from that of a person who intends to steal the bread (and does) in order to sell it at a big profit. An example of another extension is by Leon (1982) who informs us that the responses people give after causing damage are important in moral evaluations. We judge the person who says, "I'm sorry, I shouldn't have done it" differently from the one who says "I don't care how much trouble I caused" (Leon, 1982).

Berndt and Berndt (1975) presented 5-, 8-, and 11-year-old children with four films showing two grade school boys interacting in a nursery school setting. They played out four scenarios: *Instrumental aggression*, in which one boy takes another's airplane and also pushes him into his tower of blocks; *Accidental,* in which the teacher is going to give one boy the airplane, and while the boy is running to get it, he knocks down the other boy's tower of blocks; *Altruism,* in which one boy offers another the use of the airplane, and while running to get it, he knocks down the second boy's tower of blocks; and *Displaced aggression,* in which the plane is taken from one boy, and in his anger, he pushes the other boy into his tower of blocks. Thus, the blocks were either knocked over intentionally or by accident and the actors had either positive or negative motives prior to knocking them down.

Children were asked to make a variety of judgments about the actors, which measured their understanding of intentions, motives, and moral evaluations. The results showed that at all ages children understood intentions and motives. However, the 5-year-olds considered motives but not intentions when making moral judgments, whereas the older children considered both. This pattern of results has been supported by Keasey's (1978) research. Keasey showed that children as young as age 3 consider a person's motives when making moral judgments. But it is not until about age 6 that children consider a person's intentions.

The issue about intentions and consequences is more interesting and more complicated. Both Karniol (1978) and Keasey (1978) have pointed out that when the stories or films depict good, accidental, or bad intentions, and little or substantial damage is done, younger and older children have different patterns of moral judgments. For all ages 6 or above, children consider bad intended acts to be morally worse than accidents, whether little or substantial damage is done. However, 6- and seven-year-olds, but not older children, base their moral judgments on amount of damage when the actor's intentions were good. These findings imply (1) that children learn about the importance of bad before good intentions; and (2) that for young children the consequences of the act determine its moral value when the actor's intentions were positive or accidental.

A similar pattern of results occurs when the consequences don't involve damage, but rather an adult's approval or disapproval. In the study by Constanzo, Coie, Grumet, and Farnill (1973), 6-, 8-, and 10-year-old children were read stories in which a boy emptied a box of toys on the floor either to properly arrange them (good motive/intention) or to make a mess (bad motive/intention). The boy's mother, not knowing of his motives/intentions came into the room and either approved or disapproved of the behavior. The children were asked to make moral judgments about the boy. When the mother approved of the behavior, children at all ages based their judgments on the boy's motives/

intentions. When the mother disapproved, the 6-year-olds, but not the older children, thought the boy was bad, independent of his motives/intentions.

How are these results explained? Karniol (1978) suggests that parents punish their children, in part, on the basis of how much damage was done. This has the effect of teaching them that amount of damage and amount of wrongdoing are connected. She says, "Additionally, parents tend to be more concerned with inhibiting undesirable behavior than with promoting commendable behavior and are therefore more likely to punish than reward. Since ill-intended acts are likely to lead to punishment, and well-intended acts are less likely to be rewarded, children will have greater experience with the social consequences of ill-intentional acts than with . . . well-intentional acts" (p. 83). Therefore, children will learn more quickly about the connection between moral evaluations and bad intentions than moral evaluations and good intentions.

The study by Leon (1982) extends this area of research by including the "rationale" story characters offer after they have behaved in particular ways. Leon presented stories to 6- and 7-year-olds which differed in three dimensions. The story character bumped into a ladder that a workman was using while painting a house. The character either accidentally bumped it, hit it on purpose because he had had a bad day at school, or hit it on purpose to mess up the workman (intention variations). Either nothing happened when the ladder was bumped, or a paint brush fell to the ground and got dirty, or the ladder fell and broke a window (damage variations). After this occurred, the character either apologized, saying he shouldn't have done it, admitted his guilt saying he was fooling around, or said he didn't care how much trouble he caused (rationale variations). The children were asked to decide how much punishment the character should receive.

The results were quite interesting. About half the children used all three dimensions in making a decision. That is, they considered accidents less serious than bumping on purpose, high damage more serious than low or no damage, and the character who didn't care, worse than the one who only admitted his guilt. He, in turn, was judged worse than the one who was apologetic. Moreover, the children made their decisions as if they had assigned numbers to each dimension and added them up! For example, consider three story characters who were alike in all ways except for the rationale they gave. If the one who apologized was given a punishment score of 7, then the one who admitted his guilt would be given a score of 8, and the one who didn't care would be given a score of 9.

This implies (1) that 6- and 7-year-old children make very fine distinctions in their moral judgments; and (2) that intention doesn't replace damage considerations, but the two are added together.

The remaining half of the children based their punishment decisions on two of the three dimensions. In nearly all cases, however, one of these dimensions was always rationale, and either damage or intent was ignored. These results strongly imply that in making moral judgments, rationale is more important than intentions or damage. This makes sense in light of the tremendous emphasis in our culture on requiring children to apologize and sometimes forgiving them when they spontaneously do so. On the other hand, the child who doesn't apologize and who shows no regret is often punished harshly. Our religions also emphasize these practices for adults. The truly repentant sinner is forgiven, and sinners are urged to ask for forgiveness.

When the above studies are considered together, the following pattern emerges. Children in our culture apparently first learn the importance of considering another's motives in making moral decisions. Shortly afterwards they also utilize the rationale a person gives. They next acquire the ability to consider negative intentions irrespective of damage variations. At this point in development, moral judgments following accidents or positive intentions are based on amount of damage. Finally, at approximately age 8, children consider positive intentions in their moral evaluations. By about age 6 children are able to simultaneously weigh damage, intentions, and rationale in making their judgments. The amount of damage done apparently continues to be a factor after this age in moral evaluations. This is not surprising in light of the fact that our laws also consider damage to be a factor in criminal prosecutions. The person who intends to steal but is unsuccessful is charged with a lesser crime than one who intends to do so and succeeds. Also those who steal a little are charged with a lesser crime than those who steal a lot.

Empathy and Role-Taking Development

Empathy, in the psychological literature has two meanings: having the same or a highly similar emotional response as another person; predicting the emotional or other psychological responses of another. When *E.T.* joins his friends and leaves earth feeling very sad, our own tears of sadness reflects empathy in the first way. When you predict that a friend will feel upset after failing a test he had studied hard for, but don't feel upset yourself, that is empathy in the second way. If you then see your unhappy friend and feel that unhappiness, that is empathy in the first way. Fishbein (1976) and Hoffman (1978) have argued that both forms of empathy have been essential characteristics of human evolution. Hoffman emphasizes the part empathy plays in altruistic behavior and Fishbein emphasizes its part in reciprocal obligations. Owing to the cognitive emphasis in this chapter, we focus on "predictive empathy" (which is also called "role taking").

Fishbein maintains that the two necessary psychological characteristics for establishing reciprocal obligations are self-awareness and role taking. Self-awareness, as we've already discussed, involves the ability to objectively look at and reflect upon one's self. At a minimum, this requires that a person be aware of her actions in a given situation and how these affect others. Role taking, in its most general sense, is the ability to take the other person's point of view (e.g., "I see where you're coming from"). Fishbein (1976) notes that "in order to be reciprocally obligated it is necessary to be aware of the potential effects your actions will have on others, and consequently to act in ways which would be satisyfing to yourself if you were in the other's place" (p. 17).

Sound familiar? In the Old Testament it is written "You shall love your neighbor as yourself." This simple statement was reinterpreted in the New Testament as "Do unto others as you would want them to do unto you," and by Rabbi Hillel as "What is hateful to you, do not do to others." In all three cases the goal was to provide a guide for moral interpersonal behavior. If you love your neighbor as you love yourself, you will probabaly not do what's hateful to her, and probably will do what pleases her. The underlying psychology involves self-awareness—knowing what you find pleasing and hateful—and role taking—predicting that others will respond the same way as you. As a rough guide this biblical advice is sound, but you may get into trouble if you serve Jewish or Muslim friends your favorite dish—pig's knuckles.

In the last 20 years, psychologists have written an enormous amount about the development of role-taking abilities. We briefly referred to some of this material in our discussion of altruism. "Perspective taking" and "role taking" are one and the same. Recall that in general, children who have greater perspective-taking abilities are also likely to be more altruistic. These children successfully predict that others would be pleased by their behavior and act on that prediction. In that discussion several types of role-taking abilities were described, and all were not equally related to altruistic behavior.

Why should this be? Ford (1979) reviewed the published research in which two or more types of role-taking abilities were measured with the same children. In nearly all cases he found low or zero correlations between these abilities. Children who scored high on predicting what others would see might score in the middle on predicting what others would feel, and low on what others would think. It is true that on all these tasks older children perform better than younger ones, but individual children are rarely consistently high, middle, or low in their performance. Ford concludes that unlike certain psychological characteristics, such as IQ, children do not possess a generalized role-taking ability.

The following discussion focuses on the typical developmental sequence for role taking the feelings and thoughts of others. Although the research dealing with perceptual empathy is large and the results clear, we believe that this form of empathy has little bearing on either interpersonal relations or moral understanding. A distinction is made between "simple" and "flexible" empathy. Simple empathy refers to the ability to predict another person's responses. "Flexible empathy refers to the ability to predict, keep distinct and yet simultaneously relate the different viewpoints of others to objectively the same external events" (p. 281, Fishbein, 1976). An example of flexible empathy is being able to understand how one child given a dog for her birthday might be joyful, while her best friend receiving the same breed of dog might be unhappy. Objectively, the external events were the same, and yet the two children responded differently. Two of the most common reasons for people's different responses to the same situation are that they have different histories; e.g., one girl was bitten by a dog; or that they have different privileged information; e.g., for one of the children, receiving a dog means not getting a cat. In the research dealing with flexible empathy, either the child tested is given privileged information, which he has to put aside in order to predict another's feelings or thoughts, or he has to figure out how others can respond differently to the same situation.

Borke (1971) studied simple empathy of feelings for children between the ages of 3 and 8. The children were told short stories about other children such as their eating a favorite snack or losing a toy, and then shown four "emotion" pictures. These pictures depicted "happy," "sad," "afraid," and "angry" faces. The subjects were asked to point to the pictures that indicated how the child in the story probably felt. If the child pointed to the "correct" face, i.e., the one adults pointed to, then she demonstrated simple empathy for that emotion. Children of all ages had the easiest time with stories calling for a happy face, and the most difficult time with sad stories. The 3-year-olds performed the poorest, but above a chance level, and from age 5 onwards there were few differences. Thus, 3-year-olds show some simple empthy for feelings, and by age 5 this ability starts to stabilize.

Brandt (1978) studied flexible empathy of feelings and thoughts in 4½-, 6½-, and 8½-year-olds. The children were told stories in which one of the characters had "privileged" information and one did not, and were asked to predict the responses of the latter. For example, in one story a boy was fingerpainting in the kitchen, and as his father was going outside he told him to keep the paints in the kitchen. While the boy was washing his hands, the family dog jumped on the table, got paint on his tail, and brushed his tail against the door, leaving paint on it. When the boy's father returned, he saw the paint on the door. Who did he think got the paint on it? The children were asked to tell this story from the point of view of the father, who did not have the privileged information about the dog, and to answer the above question. The results were clear: 4½-year-olds showed little flexible empathy, and consistently attributed their privileged information to the father. The 6½-year-olds showed substantial, and the 8½-year-olds the most, flexible empathy.

A study by Gove and Keating (1979) indicates another way that young children have difficulty with flexible empathy. Four- and five-year-olds were read stories calling for either simple or flexible empathy. The simple empathy stories were similar to Borke's, and the children were asked to describe how each story character felt and why. The flexible empathy stories described two children having the same objective experience, e.g., receiving a dog for a present, but with very different reactions. The stories did not contain reasons for these different reactions; rather, the subjects were asked to supply them. Their ability to do so was the measure of flexible empathy.

On the simple empathy tasks the 5-year-olds performed better than the 4-year-olds, both groups comparable to the children in Borke's experiment. On the flexible empathy tasks, the younger ones were able to give plausible reasons only about a quarter of the time, whereas the five-year-olds did so more than half the time. Of particular interest was the nature of the non-plausible reasons given. In order to understand these stories, the children erroneously changed them in one of two ways: they said that both characters felt the same way; or that the situations were objectively different for the two characters; e.g., one did and one did not receive a dog. Thus, these children seem to be operating on principles similar to the biblical rule: People treated alike will respond similarly, and people treated differently will respond differently. This rule must be overcome to develop flexible empathy.

The research and theorizing by Selman and his colleagues (Selman & Byrne, 1974; Selman & Jacquette, 1978) integrates much of the work in this area. Children and adolescents were tested and observed in a wide variety of situations. Based on these studies, four stages of the development of role-taking abilities are described. Children generally perform at a given stage, but there is some variation from situation to situation. The first stage, characteristic of 3- and 4-year-olds, is called *egocentric role taking*. Children assume that others have the same reaction as they do, which allows for simple empathy, but they are unable to distinguish other viewpoints. The second stage, for ages 5 to 7, is called *subjective role taking*. Children are aware of the different reactions of others, but they have some difficulty in keeping privileged information distinct, and in relating various viewpoints to each other. The third stage, characteristic of children between 8 and 12 years old, is called *self-reflecting role taking*. These children typically perform well on flexible empathy tasks. Not only can they relate various points of view and keep privleged information distinct, but they are also aware that other people see them differently than they see themselves. The fourth stage, in the teens, is called *mutual role taking*. Adolescents can maintain distance and view a situation from an outsider's or third-person perspective. The "mutual" part is the ability to see how we are simultaneously involved in a number of self-other relationships, influencing and being influenced by them.

In this section we've argued that role-taking abilities are essential for the development of reciprocal obligations and moral behavior. The research dealing with perspective taking and altruism supports this view. Another way to show these connections would be to look at the opposite—children who are antisocial. If role taking is really crucial for socially appropriate behavior then two conclusions should follow: (1) Antisocial children should have poor role-taking abilities and (2) if the role-taking abilities could be improved, then appropriate social behavior should increase. Michael Chandler and his colleagues set out to demonstrate these connections in two highly imaginative experiments.

Chandler (1973) studied two groups of 11- to 13-year-old boys: delinquents and nondelinquents as determined by court records. Additionally, none of the nondelinquents engaged in serious antisocial activities according to their teachers. All the children were given a test of flexible empathy similar to Brandt's, and the delinquents made three times as many errors as the nondelinquents, confirming the first conclusion above.

Following this testing, the delinquents were randomly divided into three groups. The *role-taking* group met for about a half a day a week for 10 weeks and made films emphasizing the awarenesss of different viewpoints and their interrelationships. The *placebo* group met on the same schedule, also made films, but the films had no bearing on role-taking abilities. The *control* group was left alone for 10 weeks. Flexible empathy tests were given after this 10-week period. The boys from the role-taking group showed substantial improvement, whereas those in the other two groups showed little or no improvement over their initial performance.

Finally, arrest records were examined for the 18 months preceding and following the experiment. There was a slight decline in the postexperimental period for the placebo and control groups, but the frequency of arrests for the role-taking group was cut in half. The results of this experiment show that delinquents have poorer role-taking abilities than nondelinquents and that following improvement of role-taking abilities, delinquency decreases. Thus, the connection between antisocial behavior and role-taking abilities is supported.

Chandler, Greenspan, and Barenboim (1974) carried out a similar study with institutionalized emotionally disturbed 9- to 14-year-old boys and girls. None of these children were diagnosed as either psychotic or mentally retarded; rather, the large majority were referred to the institution for antisocial behavior in the school and home. These children were given tests of flexible empathy and role-taking ability measuring communication skills. On both tests these children performed much worse than comparable normal children.

Chandler et al. selected the children with the poorest role-taking abilities and divided them into three groups. The *role-taking* group received essentially the same experiences as that in Chandler's (1973) experiment. The *communication* group met on the same schedule but carried out enjoyable tasks that emphasized improving communication skills. The *control* group received no special training. Flexible empathy and communication tests were given after this 10-week period. The role-taking and communication groups substantially improved their flexible empathy performance, whereas that of the control group stayed about the same. On the other hand, only the communication group showed improvements on the communication tests.

Finally, two senior staff members of the institution were asked to rate all the children in terms of positive and negative changes in "social and interpersonal behavior" for the 1-year period following the second testing. The role-taking group improved the most, followed by the communication, then the control groups. Thus, once again, the connection between antisocial behavior and role-taking abilities was supported.

The research reported in this section lends strong support to arguments that we should systematically arrange the interpersonal teaching that goes on in our schools. As was noted in Chapter 2, this informal teaching is powerful and often has negative effects on certain groups of students, e.g., the poor and black. Teachers could easily incorporate into their instruction readings and discussion of role-taking abilities. We have seen how improvements in this area can have positive social effects.

SUMMARY

The discussion in this chapter was strongly influenced by both Piagetian and evolutionary views. Piaget's lifetime of research and theory provide both the broadest and deepest framework for understanding cognitive development and social cognition. An evolutionary view helps us to understand "mind" as a product of evolution, which ultimately underlies our social adaptations and survival.

We discussed in detail two general aspects of Piaget's theory of cognitive development. First, there are four concepts central to his work: schema, assimilation, accommodation, and equilibration. Schemas are mental activities, based on actions, which are the tools we use for acquiring knowledge. Assimilation involves fitting our schemas to experience in order to make sense of it. In that no two experiences are alike, the schemas are modified (accommodated) each time they're used. Equilibration is the process whereby schemas are accommodated so that experiences can be interpreted and understood.

Second, Piaget describes four stages of cognitive development: sensory-motor, preoperational, concrete operational, and formal operations. In the sensory-motor stage, from birth to about 1½ years, the schemas are of actions, such as habits and reflexes. This stage ends when schemas emerge that symbolically represent the world. Development during this stage is highly similar for monkeys, gorillas, and humans. In the preoperational stage, from 1½ to about 6, the child uses symbols, e.g., language, and representations like imagination to extend his world and carry out experiments in his head. He has limited logical abilities, though, which are overcome in the concrete operational stage (6 to about 11). In this stage children can perform two new mental operations, inversion and reciprocity, both of which involve mentaly reversing an observed sequence of experiences. Cross-cultural research strongly confirms the universality of these three stages.

Formal operations in Westernized cultures emerges at about age 12. Childen can now carry out inversion and reciprocity at the same time and can do so on hypothetical situations.

In the discussion of attention and memory, it was pointed out that the two processes nearly always operate together, and in infancy are difficult to distinguish. From birth to age 3, infants show tremendous increases in attention and memory abilities. They proceed from being reactive to stimuli with essentially no memory, to being highly selective with substantial memory, and guided by symbolic thought. From age 3 to adolescence, attention appears to develop in three phases. From ages 3 to 5, children explore limited aspects of their environment, making it unlikely that they will remember what they've attended to. From ages 5 to 7, their exploration becomes more economical, more complete, and task-relevant. From ages 7 to 12, attentional abilities stabilize.

The discussion of memory from ages 3 to adolescence was divided into three topics. First, 4-year-olds can successfully use *memory strategies* when asked to do so. Between 4 and 7, their spontaneous use of these strategies increases substantially. From age 7 onwards, the mature use of strategies seems to be linked to their newly emerging ability to *monitor* their memory. Second, the period around age 7 is critical for *memory organization*, when children start to use a variety of organizations. From 7 onwards, their abilities show steady improvement. Third, *retrieval processes* progressively develop from ages 3 to 20, whereas acquisition and storage processes appear to stabilize at about age 12. Forgetting by children is most likely to be caused by retrieval deficiencies.

Social cognition refers to the understanding individuals have of situations involving the interactions of two or more people. Our discussion of this topic emphasized Piaget's work on moral development and the research and theorizing that followed it. Piaget defines morality as a system of rules whose essence is in the respect people acquire for them. He describes three age-related stages in the acquisition of rule knowledge: *motor rules* (ages 1 to 3), *unilateral respect and coercive rules* (ages 4 to

10), and *mutual respect and rational rules* (ages 10 onwards). In the motor rules stage the rules are self-imposed, and as such, are not moral rules. In the unilateral respect stage the children believe there are external rules handed down by their elders that must be obeyed. Obedience to the rules stems from the unilateral (one way) respect they have for authority. Wrongdoing is based upon objective consequences. In the mutual respect stage, this unilateral respect is replaced by mutual respect for peers and their agreed-upon rules. All rules can be changed, and all changes are fair, provided that everyone agrees to them. Wrongdoing is based on intentions rather than consequences.

Kohlberg's work in moral development is a highly elaborate extension of Piaget's using similar methods. Kohlberg assesses 25 aspects of the reasoning individuals use in resolving moral dilemmas. Kohlberg describes three levels (two stages in each) of moral reasoning, which cover the age span 4 through adulthood. In the Preconventional level (ages 4 to 10) moral acts are interpreted in terms of either their physical consequences or whether the acts were consistent with the rules set by authorities. In the Conventional level (ages 10 to 20), the rules are seen as valuable in and of themselves, and moral behavior toward individuals is that which pleases others and meets their expectations. In the Postconventional level (after age 18 for a small percentage of adults), morality is thought of in terms of universal principles, which apply to all societies. These principles stand on their own, independent of the individuals or groups who support them. Cross-cultural research shows that children move through the first two stages at about the same rate; that children and adolescents from urban cultures move through the third and fourth stages faster than those from rural cultures; and that essentially no adults from rural cultures reach the fifth and sixth stages.

Turiel has provided evidence that there are two separate systems of rules governing social interactions: moral rules and social conventions. Moral rules are nonarbitrary and universal, and are concerned with justice. Social conventions are arbitrary and highly cultural specific. Children learn about these two systems at a very early age and respond to moral and convention transgressions differently.

Recent research on intentions and consequences in moral judgments has greatly expanded Piaget's methods and conclusions. By 3 years of age children consider another's motives in making moral decisions, but it is not until about age 5 that they consider intentions. Negative intentions are evaluated at an earlier age than positive ones or accidents. From about age 6 onwards, they are able to simultaneously weigh damage, intentions, and rationale in making their moral judgments. The amount of damage done continues to be a factor after this age.

The last section dealt with empathy and role-taking development, which is important from both evolutionary and social interaction views. The golden rule of the Bible "Do unto others, etc." is closely related to simple empathy as a guide for moral action. This type of empathy is clearly seen in 3-year-olds and starts to stabilize at age 5. Flexible empathy, which involves simultaneously relating different viewpoints of others, starts to emerge after age 5 and continues to develop through about age 12. Research by Chandler indicates that juvenile delinquents and emotionally disturbed antisocial children and adolescents show positive social changes following training that improves their flexible empathy skills. It is suggested that schools integrate this training as part of their instructional programs.

6 Language, Intelligence, and Symbol Use

The brain is a crowning achievement of human evolution. Jerison (1973, 1982) measured the brain size relative to the body size of large numbers of living and extinct species and estimated the number of "extra neurons" (nerve cells) available for high-level information processing. This estimate started with the assumption that the number of neurons required by basic physiological processes such as eating, breathing, and sleeping depend on body size. Any number of neurons above that requirement can be used for higher level processing. Humans were found to have the largest number of extra neurons.

The major implication of this finding is that humans have far more information-processing capacity than other primates. Jerison believes that the evolutionary increase in human information-processing capacity was an adaptive response stemming from our increasing reliance, as time passed, on higher symbolic cognitive capacities, such as language, imagery, and self-consciousness. In short, we became a successful species by outthinking our competitors rather than by outrunning or overpowering them.

Intimately related to increased brain size was the further evolutionary development of intelligence and symbol use. For Jerison, intelligence is related to information-processing capacity, language, and the ability to construct reality. Other definitions have been offered, some of which will be discussed here. What most definitions share is the idea of the ability to understand and use symbols—e.g., words, drawings. In an evolutionary context, then, humans became more intelligent than other species because of our increased symboling capacities. Concerning the evolution of culture, the eminent anthropologist, Leslie White (1959), stated:

> In the course of the evolution of the primates, *man* appeared when the ability to symbol had been developed and become capable of expression. We thus define man in terms of the ability to symbol and the consequent ability to produce culture. (p. 3).

There is evidence to indicate the early ancestral use of human symbolic activity. Lieberman (1973) has shown that the vocal tracts of the Cro-Magnon race of 40,000 years ago were essentially the same as those of contemporary humans. Thus, there is reason to believe that their language use was equivalent to ours. Elegant cave paintings and drawings found in Spain and France also date back as far as 40,000 years ago (Leroi-Gourhan, 1968). The fossil evidence suggests, moreover, that the brain structures underlying these abilities emerged hundreds of thousands of years earlier, even, than this (Holloway, 1968). Therefore, high-level symboling capacities are probably very ancient in the evolution of our species.

Although the use of graphic symbols such as cave paintings dates back at least 40,000 years, two of the most important current uses—writing words and numbers—were invented only 5,000 years ago (Braidwood, 1967). Examination of this early writing suggests that keeping track of the numbers of things was a fundamental requirement of complex, usually urban, societies. The first writers were in all likelihood accountants. The Incas of South America solved the accounting problem by inventing a system involving strings of different lengths and colors. To the best of our knowledge they never used written words or numbers.

Owing to the recency of writing, and the few people initially involved in this activity, it is highly unlikely that writing ability was a characteristic that natural selection operated on. Rather, the capacity for symbol use and fine motor control evolved, and these abilities permitted the cultural development of writing. Writing emerged in answer to the need for keeping order in complex societies. Moreover, writing and reading became widespread only after the invention of the printing press about 500 years ago.

To summarize, one major characteristic of human evolution was the dramatic increase in intelligence. Central to most definitions of intelligence is the ability to use and understand symbols. Three of the main classes of contemporary human symbol use are spoken language, written words, and numbers. The latter two classes are relatively recent cultural inventions associated with the emergence of complex societies.

The above discussion serves as a framework for the rest of this chapter. We attempt to determine how intelligence, language, reading and mathematics are acquired by children. All are connected by our genetic heritage involving the use and comprehension of symbols. Because the human species has close evolutionary links with the apes, our understanding of human language and intellectual development will be enhanced by examining relevant nonhuman primate research. After examining this research, we discuss selected literature on human language development. The child's language abilities rapidly and markedly exceed those of the most advanced apes. We then describe the studies that have been done on intelligence. In this discussion, the effects of heredity and parental socialization on IQ development are examined. We end the chapter with extensive discussions of reading, reading disabilities, and mathematics understanding. Cross-cultural comparisons are emphasized in order to determine which aspects of the development of children's symbol use are universal and which reflect particular cultural influences.

INTELLIGENCE AND LANGUAGE OF APES

Premack's Research on Chimpanzee Intelligence

David Premack states in his 1976 book, *Intelligence in Ape and Man*, "Language is so deeply enmeshed in intelligence that a discussion of the psychological prerequisites for language is at the same time a discussion of some of the mechanisms of intelligence. . . . In acquiring language one acquires labels for existing concepts" (p. 336). In other words, you can't study language independent of intelligence. Although Premack does not present an all-encompassing definition of intelligence, he does list the following mechanisms of intelligence in chimpanzees: understanding cause and effect relationships; understanding intentions; being able to form representations of relationships (e.g., "red on green" as opposed to "green on red"); having a highly elaborated memory; and being able to form second-order relations (e.g., "name of?" means that the individual must supply the appropriate name of each different object).

Regarding language, he maintains that the two most basic properties are (1) the existence of arbitrary items that name or refer to objects, agents, actions, or properties of the environment; and (2) the capacity to understand and generate novel sentences comprised of these items—a grammar. Virtually all psychologists agree with Premack that these two characteristics are basic, but they add others when describing human language. Roger Brown (1973) includes *displacement* as one of the three basic properties: Displacement means that language is not only here-and-now, but also refers to objects, agents, and so on, that may occur in different places and different times. Paula Menyuk (1982) includes a number of other characteristics, the most important for our purposes being *phonology*. Human languages have words made up of phonemes—sounds that typically are meaningless in and of themselves.

Early studies of the intelligence of apes inferred the presence of concepts from elaborate behavioral routines. For example, Harlow (1949) asked whether nonlinguistic monkeys could acquire the concept of oddity. He presented three objects to them, two the same, and one different, and rewarded the animals with a tasty treat every time they touched the odd one. Once they were always correct with the original objects, a new set of three was used, and touching the odd one, rewarded. This procedure continued until either the animals were correct on the first presentation of a novel set of three objects, or they showed no improvements from one set to the next. As an alternative, one of the great advantages of using words to investigate intelligence is that you can "talk" to the apes directly.

The "words" Premack (1976) used were pieces of plastic differing in shape, size, color, and texture. Premack worked with four preadolescent chimpanzees, three females and one male, but his star pupil was Sarah, who started her language learning at age 5. Premack first taught them words for favorite objects, e.g., tasty foods, then certain verbs, e.g., "give," "insert," names of themselves and their trainer, and then additional verbs, names, and relationships, e.g., same-different. Word order (grammar) was taught at the same time as the first verbs, e.g., "Give apple," "Insert banana." In all, Sarah learned approximately 130 words, with the others learning far fewer.

Premack studied the chimpanzee's concept of causality in three ways: with plastic words, objects, and words and objects. He reasoned that at the heart of understanding causality is understanding the logical connectives "If-then." If you believe, for example, that kicking the ball *causes* it to move, then logically you are saying "*If* the ball is kicked, *then* it will move." If a chimpanzee can be taught to correctly use the "If-then" logical connective, this means that it understands that concept.

Premack's research assistant, Mary, taught Sarah to respond properly to plastic word sentences like "If Sarah take apple, then Mary gives Sarah chocolate." Whenever Sarah, who loved chocolate, took a piece of apple, Mary gave her a piece of chocolate. When Sarah was consistently interpreting these sentences correctly (and receiving chocolate), then a large number of novel sentences were presented such as "If Sarah no eat banana, then Mary give candy Sarah," and "If Sarah give red card Mary, then Mary give candy Sarah." Sarah's performance on these and other novel sentences was nearly errorless, thus demonstrating understanding of "If-then."

On the tests of understanding causality with objects, Premack examined three actions—cutting, wetting, and marking. The experimenter presented the chimpanzees with three "items" and three choices. For example, a whole apple, the plastic word for "question," and two halves of an apple were placed in a line, and below these, three choices—a knife, a bowl of water, and a marker (pencil or crayon). In essence, the experimenter is asking "What causes an apple to get this way?" If the chimpanzee consistently pointed to the appropriate implement, e.g., chose the knife in the above example, this implies that it knew that using a knife can cause an apple to be cut in half. The three female chimpanzees chose correctly about 80% of the time (chance being 33%). Following this test, the trials were repeated, except that the plastic words for the three choices were used. Thus, the chimpanzees were required to point to a word, not an implement. On these trials, Sarah and Peony were correct 90% of the time, and Elizabeth only 40%. Premack concludes that these results and those dealing with "If-then" provide strong evidence that these chimpanzees understood the concept of causality.

Using techniques similar to the above, Premack has shown the following. The name of a fruit (eight were learned) provides as much information about the characteristics of the fruit, e.g., color, type of seed, peel, stem, as the whole fruit itself. This implies that words for chimpanzees are highly elaborated in memory. The linguistic property of displacement was shown by the experimenter's writing statements like "brown color of chocolate" (chocolate not being present), followed by "take brown" and then presenting four colored discs, one of which was brown. The chimpanzees consistently made the correct choice, implying the use of language to refer to objects not present. Examples of second-order relations are the words "name of," "same," "different," "color of." When a chimpanzee successfully chooses the word for apple when shown an apple and the plastic word for "name of," and performs correctly when banana, marker, and other objects are shown, this means that "name of" stands for an entire set of relations.

Woodruff and Premack (1979) in a nonlinguistic study, showed that chimpanzees will intentionally deceive human trainers, or tell them the truth, depending on whether the human is competitive or cooperative. The procedure involved one trainer hiding food in a room adjoining the chimpanzee's cage, while it was watching. Another trainer (X) then entered and tried to discover the location of the food. When X was cooperative–gave the chimpanzee the food–the chimpanzee gave accurate nonverbal signals concerning food location. When X was competitive–kept the hidden food–the chimpanzee gave false signals.

As Premack (1976) notes, other species have demonstrated some of the acts of intelligence carried out by chimpanzees. Typically these are highly specific to a particular context, as when birds feign injury as predators approach their nest. It is the breadth shown by the chimpanzee (and by gorillas and orangutans in other research) that makes ape intelligence so impressive.

Teaching Language to Chimpanzees and Gorillas

Premack is one among many researchers who have studied ape language acquisition. The first major breakthrough came from Beatrice and Allan Gardner (1969) who taught American Sign Language (ASL) to Washoe, a young female chimpanzee. ASL is the primary language of approximately 500,000 deaf North Americans. It is a manual language comprised of both unique gestures for individual words, analogous to Premack's symbols, and parts of words analogous to phonemes. Washoe's training started when she was about 1 year old and continued for 4 years. It primarily consisted of "molding" her hands and arms, demonstrating signs to her for objects and events in the environment, prompting and observing humans signing. She was rewarded for good performance by verbal praise, hugs, and tasty foods. By the time Washoe was 5 years old, she had learned about 130 signs. The Gardners subsequently taught ASL to three other chimpanzees, and a former student of theirs, Roger Fouts, has taught six more (e.g., Fouts, 1977). Herbert Terrace and his associates (1980) spent four years using similar methods teaching ASL to the chimpanzee "Nim," who also learned about 130 signs. Finally, Francine Patterson (1980) has taught ASL to young gorillas. One of them, Koko, has learned at least 185 signs.

There is one other major longstanding research project concerned with chimpanzee language learning, that of Duane Rumbaugh (1977) and Sue Savage-Rumbaugh (1980). The first chimpanzee to participate in this program was Lana, who started her computer-assisted language training at about 2 years. In her cage was a computer console with keys marked by symbols, one different symbol for each word. Lana's trainer had a similar console, and above them was a screen that reproduced the symbols as the keys were pressed. Lana was first taught to associate each symbol with particular consequences, e.g., receiving an apple, and then taught to use short sequences of symbols, e.g., "Please, apple, period." Pressing the "period" symbol indicated the end of a statement of some sort. Two male chimpanzees have also been trained this way, starting when they were about 4 years old. Lana's vocabulary reached about 75 words, and the males about 50 words.

The above researchers, their critics, and supporters have generated hundreds of articles and books dealing with the question, "Have apes learned a language?" The answer to this question is not obvious in that it first depends upon how language is defined, and second, on the type of proof required to answer it. For example, nearly everyone agrees that one requirement is that apes be able to generate grammatical sentences. Terrace et al. (1980) clearly show that Nim's two-word statements followed a particular word order, which implies use of grammatical rules. Yet, Nim's three- and four-word statements did not. Terrace et al. conclude that Nim hasn't shown grammatical use. The Gardners (1975) take similar data as evidence that their chimpanzees do "speak" grammatically.

Ristau and Robbins (1982) have analyzed most of the available studies dealing with this question, which we'll briefly summarize. Three broad issues are involved: (1) Are the ape data adequate enough to answer the language question? (2) Do the apes understand "words" the way humans do, or are words used only as arbitrary responses that lead to rewards— are they analogous to rats' rewarded bar presses? (3) Do the apes understand and generate grammatical sentences?

Regarding adequacy of the data, critics correctly point out that the ASL studies rarely have records of the apes' behavior as it was occurring. The experimenters in these studies nearly always made data entries minutes or hours afterwards, and the data are thus subject to many human errors. The Gardners made a brief demonstration film of Washoe's language, and Terrace has about 4 hours of videotape of Nim's signing interactions. Patterson has many hours of videotape of Koko's language behavior, but little has been analyzed thus far. One of the primary requirements of any scientific endeavor is that the observations made be public and open to the scrutiny of others. Such availability is thus far sorely lacking.

These criticisms partially apply to Premack's and the Rumbaughs' data. In neither case have films or videotapes been made available of the training or testing sessions. Thus, the nonlinguistic ways in which experimenters interacted with the chimpanzees cannot be evaluated. It has been repeatedly shown that the expectations researchers have can markedly influence the experimental outcomes. (This concern is especially voiced for the ASL studies.) On the other hand, nearly all the linguistic interactions of the apes and their trainers were recorded by these researchers at the time of occurrence. However, the methods used in this research, unlike the ASL projects, are subject to another criticism. These methods prevented the apes from using the same word twice in the same sentence; e.g., Premack presented only one symbol of each word. This is an artificial limitation that restricts spontaneous language usage.

Ristau and Robbins indicate that these criticisms call into question the strength of the conclusions made by ape researchers. The researchers themselves are aware of these procedural deficits and have taken steps to overcome them. Nevertheless, the criticisms do not invalidate the research; rather they lead us to be cautious about the inferences drawn from the data.

Ristau and Robbins discuss several aspects of ape word meaning: labeling, novel word uses, errors in generalization, elaborateness of meaning, and words used as categories. All the apes learned to use particular ASL signs or symbols (labels) in conjunction with objects, persons, and actions. Many learned to use correctly the symbols "name of" and "not-name of." Nearly all the ape "speakers" used the labels in a way that demonstrated displacement. These behaviors strongly suggest that apes used words as labels. It is not clear from the research whether their label use is equivalent to that of human children with comparable vocabularies.

There is some evidence that several of the ASL signing chimpanzees and Koko used words in novel metaphorical ways. Washoe used the word "open" to ask for help or permission, as well as to open various doors and containers. Most of these uses were her invention. When Roger Fouts denied a request of Washoe's, she insulted him by signing, "Dirty Roger." When Patterson told Koko, "I think Mike (Koko's gorilla playmate) is smart, is he smarter than you?" Koko, who often acted jealous of Mike, signed, "Think ... Koko know Mike toilet." In more formal testing, Patterson found that Koko used words in a metaphorical sense similarly to young children.

When children learn new words they often overgeneralize their use, as when a cat is pointed to and the child says "dog." When Washoe was taught the sign for flower, the trainers presented her with flowers and took deep breaths to smell them. Washoe took a major meaning of "flower" to be "odor" and used it to refer to pipe tobacco and kitchen smells. Koko learned the sign for straw by being shown a drinking straw. She subsequently labeled plastic tubing, clear plastic hose, a pen, an antenna, and cigarettes, as "straw."

We've already discussed Premack's research concerning elaborate word meaning in memory. None of the other researchers report comparable data. Ristau and Robbins note that Premack's analysis applies to only a small number of words. Thus, we know that Sarah is capable of highly elaborated word meaning, but we don't know how extensive this capacity is, nor what training techniques are required to produce it.

The Rumbaughs investigated the question of whether chimpanzees can place words into categories, specifically "tools" and "food." They tested three apes, Lana, Sherman, and Austin. Lana's training has already been described–it emphasizes associating specific symbols with specific objects. Sherman's and Austin's training also included using tools to gain access to inaccessible food. The Rumbaughs first trained all these apes to place three food items into one bin and three tools into another. They then taught the apes the words for "tools" and "food," two distinct categories, using the same three foods and tools. When different foods and tools were presented, Austin and Sherman correctly categorized them nearly 100% of the time, whereas Lana made many errors. As a final test, the two males were presented with the names of different foods and tools, and Austin and Sherman categorized them essentially without error.

The above results concerning word meaning strongly support the view that apes acquire very rich concepts involving word symbols. There is very little support for the position that their use of words is restricted to that of merely being "rewarded stimulus-response" connections analogous to bar presses or maze turns by lower animals.

Do Apes Use Grammar?

The final issue, apes' understanding and use of grammar, is the most hotly debated and least settled. There is a good deal of agreement that apes understand grammatical sentences–word order makes a big difference in their behavior. The dispute is whether they generate grammatical sentences. Among the ape language researchers, Terrace (1980) is the most dubious about this. He has carefully analyzed the videotapes of Nim and made the following observations. (1) A very large percentage of

Nim's statements were either complete or partial imitations of the previous sentence made by his trainer. (2) Unlike children who imitate parental language less frequently as they get older, the reverse was true for Nim. (3) Nim, unlike children, showed no evidence of taking conversational turns. He interrupted his trainer's speech as often as not. (4) Unlike children, when Nim's statement length increased, he rarely added new information, but rather repeated the old, e.g., "Eat drink, eat drink." (5) Unlike children, Nim's statement length did not increase appreciably with vocabulary increases. (6) There was no evidence of consistent word order (grammar) in Nim's three- and four-word statements.

It is clear from Terrace's analysis that Nim's language use is quite different from that of young children. Nim and the other apes do seem to use language primarily as a vehicle for getting rewards—indeed they were trained to do so, which is quite different from the ways children are taught language. Given the differences in language training that apes and children receive, we should expect differences in their language use. To state the issue another way, there is no a priori reason for viewing children's grammatical use as the only standard by which to judge ape grammar. Ristau and Robbins (1982) take the issue one step further and question whether young children's speech is grammatical: "Indeed, we would probably find it difficult to describe young children's productions as linguistic, if we did not know that these children will almost invariably grow up into language-using adults" (p. 247). Our conclusion, then, is that trained apes use at least a rudimentary grammar that is different from that of children.

We began this section with a question about what studying ape language can tell us about the nature of human language development. We can state several tentative conclusions. First, language development and the development of intelligence are closely tied together. Apes (and children) are capable of the meaningful use of words to the extent that they understand the underlying concepts. Piaget (1966) talks about this issue in terms of "thought preceding language." Second, the way language is taught has a powerful effect on the way it is used. Not only do children from different cultures use different words, they employ different grammars, and have somewhat different understandings of the world. Third, the central nervous system places severe limits on language-learning ability. Apes and humans have different brains, with humans capable of much more mental complexity than apes. Humans with Down's syndrome, for example, are also more intellectually limited than normals, and their language development reflects these limitations. Finally, to a large extent language learning is a problem-solving process in apes and humans. For humans, owing to our evolutionary history, this process is easy, natural, and enjoyable. For apes, just the opposite seems to be true. Stated another way, humans are motivated to learn language for its own sake, whereas apes are externally motivated to do so.

HUMAN LANGUAGE DEVELOPMENT

This has been one of the fastest growing research areas in psychology. During the 1960s and early 1970s, work was largely guided by a framework that focused on describing the unfolding of a universal innate grammar (Chomsky, 1968). Meaning of words and sentences, and communication between persons, were lesser concerns. As results from studies emerged, psychologists and linguists saw that grammar (syntax) acquisition played a secondary role in early language development. Further, the great variation in language learning among children from the same social class called into question the unfolding of an innate grammar (Bloom, 1975; Clark, 1982; Nelson, 1981). During the past 10 years, research has been guided by a cognitive development framework that includes concerns about the social context of language and interpersonal communication. Early language development is now seen as strongly paralleling the cognitive achievements of sensory-motor and preoperational thought (Sinclair-deZwart, 1973).

Ruth Clark (1982) has recently pointed out a number of "simplifications" stemming from the earlier theory and research, which have now been corrected. Some of these are as follows. When the child's speech was limited to one-word "sentences," many believed that she had some knowledge of grammar, which obviously was not able to be expressed. When she then started speaking two- and three-word sentences, often grammatically correct, this was taken as proof of the previously learned grammar. Clark summarizes research that shows that children's early two- and three-word sentences are often ungrammatical. Moreover, there is no evidence that shows that children put grammatical rules to the same use as more competent adult speakers.

Analogous to the above, many believed that children in the one-word "sentence" stage and more fluent speakers assigned highly similar meanings to those words. For example, when the child says "break" while watching mother cooking, and mother says "Mommy breaks the eggs," researchers assumed that the mother's sentence is essentially what the child meant. Virtually all researchers have noticed that parents' expansions of their children's one-word sentences seem correct. Clark points out that many expansions of one-word sentences are plausible, often with opposite meanings, e.g., "I want to break the eggs," "Don't break the eggs," "Did the eggs break?" "Break the glass," and so on. It really is highly unlikely that children with 10- to 50-word vocabularies mean the same things by those words as do their parents and other adults.

A third simplification is that children can always understand aspects of language before they can produce them. This view is analogous to Flavell's work on memory strategies. Most of us have had the experience of making a request to a one-word "sentence" child, e.g., "Please bring me the book from the sofa," and have it correctly carried out. We forget the times that such requests are carried out incorrectly. Clark also makes the important point that sometimes children use sentences they don't understand in order to gain understanding of them. (This is not necessarily a conscious effort.) The child may hit a block against a bowl and say "break" and be corrected by mother.

In the remaining sections, five aspects of language development are considered. Based on an evolutionary perspective, the issue of language canalization is evaluated. This evaluation primarily hinges on comparisons of motor and language development in Down's syndrome and normal children. Then we focus on the precursors to speech, and the child's first 50 words. In this section the interplay between biology, culture, and cognitive development is emphasized. The following section deals with the next "stage" of language development—preschool children's first sentences and sentence combinations. This discussion reflects the current research emphasis on meaning as opposed to grammar, as well as the role of individual differences. In the next section, we describe the development of grammatical understanding in school children. This discussion reflects the relatively older research emphasis on grammar, but is nevertheless important and valid. We conclude the discussion of language development by examining how children use language in their interactions with others. This section reflects recent cognitive and social research emphases.

Canalization of Language Acquisition

Canalized behavior is learned behavior. But it is behavior that is nearly always learned by all members of a species in a particular sequence. This sequence is probably linked with maturation of the central nervous system and the various muscular and neuromuscular systems of the body.

Canalized behavior is protected from minor environmental and genetic abnormalities, but children with severe genetic abnormalities and those reared in severely abnormal environments, e.g., children raised by wolves, will not be protected, and will not develop the canalized behavior.

Eric Lenneberg (1966, 1967) has provided the best evidence that certain aspects of language development are canalized. He studied the relationship between motor and language development in normal children and those with Down's syndrome (formerly called "mongolism"). Down's syndrome is caused by an extra chromosome and produces a variety of anatomical and behavioral symptoms, including reduced intelligence and slower language and motor development. It is assumed that motor development is a canalized process. The basic argument is that if motor and language development occur in nearly a lock-step fashion for both normal and Down's syndrome children, then language development is also canalized.

Table 6.1 summarizes some of the major developmental milestones of language and motor development in normal children. Several comments should be made about this table. First, the lock-step appearance of language and motor development should not be taken to mean that one causes the other. Both unfold under a maturational schedule, and there have been many documented cases with abnormal children in which one schedule has unfolded at a much slower rate than the other, e.g., children who start speaking at age 3 or 4. Second, the table contains average ages, with some children moving along faster and others slower than the designated age-related milestones. Lenneberg asserts, however, that when development is slowed down or speeded up within the normal range, the language and motor milestones still covary. When children learn to run, they have also acquired the ability to use two-word phrases. Finally, the language environment to which the child is exposed apparently has little effect on the relationship between these two classes of milestones. For instance, children from "primitive" societies and hearing children of deaf parents seem to show the same developmental patterns depicted in this table (Lenneberg 1967).

There is no available table similar to this for Down's syndrome children. Over a 3-year period Lenneberg and his colleagues studied 61 Down's syndrome children who were living at home and being raised by their normal parents. The children were seen two or three times a year, and at each visit they were given a battery of tests. A close positive relationship was found between IQ and language development, with some children never progressing beyond the stage in which only single words and two-word phrases were used. All the children below age 14 made

TABLE 6.1
Milestones in Language and Motor Development

Age	Motor Development	Language Development
12 weeks	supports head when in prone position	smiles when talked to and makes cooing sounds
16 weeks	plays with rattle when placed in hands	turns head in response to human sounds
20 weeks	sits with props	makes vowellike and consonantlike sounds
6 months	reaches, grasps	cooing changes to babbling which resembles one-syllable sounds
8 months	stands holding on: picks up pellet with thumb and finger	increasing repetitions of some syllables
10 months	creeps; pulls self to standing position; takes side steps while holding on	appears to distinguish between different adult words by differential responding
12 months	walks when held by one hand; seats self on floor	understands some words; says mama, dada
18 months	can grasp, hold, and return objects quite well; creeps downstairs backward	has repertoire of betweeen 3 and 50 spoken words, said singly
24 months	runs, walks up and down stairs	has repertoire of more than 50 words; uses two-word phrases
30 months	stands on one foot for about two seconds; takes a few steps on tiptoe	tremendous increase in spoken vocabulary; many phrases containing 3 to 5 words
3 years	tiptoes three yards; can operate a tricycle	vocabulary of about 1000 words; pronunciation clear
4 years	jumps over rope, hops on one foot	language apparently well established

(Source: Lenneberg, E. H. *Biological foundations of language*, 1967. By permission of John Wiley & Sons.)

some progress on their motor and language development during the period of study. If motor and language development are canalized, and Down's syndrome both slows down and places an upper limit on behavior, then the following three findings should occur for such children:

1. the sequence of motor and language milestones should remain unchanged;

2. the various milestones should occur later in development relative to normals;
3. the time intervals between the various milestones should be proportionately longer.

This is exactly what was observed. For example, in normals, the time interval between sitting and putting words together is about 13 months, and language is well-established about 20 months later. In the Down's syndrome children, if the interval between sitting and putting words together was about 24 months, then language was not well established until an additional 60 months had elapsed. This pattern of results along with those shown in Table 6.1 is consistent with the view that many aspects of language development are canalized.

From Listening to the First 50 Words

As Table 6.1 shows, when children's vocabularies reach about 50 words, they start to form two-word sentences. Even before infants start to babble, e.g., "dadadada," at about 6 months, let alone say words, they show both an intense involvement with language and a knowledge of word-like sounds. Menyuk (1982) has summarized some of these observations. During the first month of life, infants prefer listening to people speaking than music playing. By about age 2 months, they can discriminate very similar sounding syllables such as "ga" and "ba." The basic research procedure is to habituate the infant to a single syllable, e.g., "ga" as shown by stable heart rate or sucking rate, and then to present another syllable, e.g., "ba." Discrimination is shown by a change in heart or sucking rate. Even more interesting is the finding that infants (like adults) don't often discriminate between different pronunciations of the same syllable. However, Eimas and Tartter (1979) have shown that some of this discrimination ability disappears if the syllables are not part of their language environment.

The sound-making abilities of infants change in the same regular ways in all cultures studied. From birth to 2 months of age, babies' sounds are essentially reflections of their physiological state, mainly crying and discomfort. *Cooing* emerges then, and involves the tongue and lips shaping the sounds produced by the vocal tract. Cooing gives way to *babbling*, in part because of increased control and coordination of the speech apparatus. Babbling by Japanese infants is initially virtually indistinguishable from that of Americans despite some dramatic differences in their language environments. However, by 1 year of age babbling babies start to sound more like their parents. Deaf babies babble, too. However, their range is not as broad as that of hearing babies, and before they're 1 year old, babbling virtually stops.

The above patterns of results are highly consistent with the canalization model. Listening and sound-making abilities follow definite sequences that can be disrupted by abnormal environments, e.g., the lack of hearing by deaf children. The canalized behaviors are not rigidly fixed, like that of insects, but vary to some extent as a function of experience. Thus, Japanese and Americans during the first year of life start to hear differently and to use the different sounds from their language environments.

Between the ages of 1 and 2 years, nearly all normal children acquire at least a 50-word vocabulary. Table 6.2 presents some results from Katherine Nelson's study (1973) of white, middle-class North American children's early vocabulary. This vocabulary can be divided into six categories: *Specific Names*, e.g., Daddy, Dizzy; *General Names*, e.g., ball, doggie; *Action Words*, e.g., go, up, out; *Modifiers*, e.g., big, pretty, allgone; *Personal-Social*, e.g., please, want, no; and *Function Words*, e.g., where, is, to. As can be seen from the table the percentage of the first 10 words falling into each of these categories is not very different from that of words 40–50. The percentage of Specific Names drops off, and that of General Names increases, which makes good sense— "Mommy" and "Daddy" comprise 20% of the first 10 words.

Nelson (1974) summarizes the literature dealing with children's early vocabulary as follows:

1. There is a small set of words that are learned at the outset by a large number of children. These consist largely of names for food, people, animals, and things that move or change in some way. The one outstanding characteristic of the early words is their reference to objects and events that are perceived in dynamic relationships; that is, actions, sounds, transformations—in short, variation of all kinds.

2. In addition, it has been widely observed by students of child language that when a word that expresses his meaning is not available, the young child from the very beginning of language acquisition will frequently invent one. Such productions must reflect the child's preexisting conceptual organization which does not always quite match that of the language community.

3. Once acquired, a word is usually generalized to other "similar" things. Similarity may be based on many different dimensions, of which the static perceptual dimension of shape or form is only one; others include function, action, or affect. ... Furthermore, the child's meanings may also be underextended or simply "different from" adult meanings." (p. 269)

TABLE 6.2
Percentage of Words in Each Grammatical Category

	Word Acquisition Order					
	1–10	11–20	21–30	31–40	41–50	Overall
Specific Names	24	12	14	12	9	14
General Names	41	45	46	60	62	51
Action Words	16	15	14	12	9	13
Modifiers	8	10	8	8	12	9
Personal-Social	5	13	11	4	4	8
Function Words	6	4	7	3	3	4

(Source: Nelson, K. Structure and Strategy in Learning to Talk. *Monographs of the Society for Research in Child Development*, 1973, *38*, Ser. no. 149.)

The Sentences of Pre-School Children

In all languages studied, when children acquire approximately a 50-word vocabulary, they start using two-word sentences (Slobin, 1971). Braine (1963) studied in detail the language development of three children and found a phenomenal increase in the number of different two-word sentences spoken over a 7-month period—14, 24, 54, 89, 350, 1400, and 2500+. At about the time that the majority of a child's speech consists of two-word sentences, he starts to speak three- or more-word sentences.

These are substantial individual differences in the nature and development of these sentences (Bloom, 1975; Braine, 1976; Nelson, 1981). In Nelson's analysis of the research, she identified two broad patterns. In the first, called *referential*, children rarely use two- or more-word sentences before vocabulary size reaches 50, a large proportion of their rapidly increasing vocabulary is object names, words are pronounced clearly, and combinations emphasize nouns and verbs. In the second, called *expressive*, poorly pronounced sentences are used before the 50-word boundary; e.g., "I'll get it," usually without pauses, pronouns rather than nouns are emphasized, vocabulary size grows slowly, and combinations emphasize pronouns and relational terms, e.g., "allgone."

Nelson strongly suggests that these two patterns may exist in the same child, who uses them in different social contexts, e.g., playing with other children versus "reading" a book with father. Moreover, as the referential children use more pronouns and the expressive ones acquire a larger vocabulary and improve their pronunciation, the speech patterns of the two groups start to merge.

As previously noted, theory and research have shifted toward semantics (meaning), away from grammar. Psychologists have concluded that where constant sentence word orders have been seen, they reflect the preschooler's growing knowledge of semantics, not grammar. Recall that Terrace argued that chimpanzees' sentences did not reflect grammatical knowledge. There is a fine line being drawn here. The basic grammatical sentence consists of a *subject* (S) followed by a *verb* (V) then an *object* (O). These are grammatical terms. "The boy hit the ball" is such a sentence. Semantically, the same sentence can be referred to as consisting of an *agent* (boy), an *action* (hit), and an *object* (ball).

Schlesinger (1971) argued that children have semantic intentions – they intend to convey certain meanings – and learn relatively simple semantic (not grammar) rules for doing this. He described a number of such rules for combining two words. For example, when children want to convey that a person (agent) is doing something (action), they form this sentence as agent + action, e.g., "Mama come," and not action + agent, e.g., "Come Mama." Another example involves the intention to convey some characteristic (modifier) of an object (head noun). The child says "big boat" or "more nut" and not the reverse. Schlesinger and others argue that the understanding of grammar, e.g., subject and verb, emerges from using these semantic rules. Brown (1973) and Bloom (1975) examining the same data suggest that grammar is either being acquired at the same time as the semantic rules or precedes them.

Braine (1976) has analyzed the early word combinations of children learning English, Samoan, Finnish, Hebrew, and Swedish. Several of his observations were (1) there were marked individual differences in both the kind of word patterns used, and the rate of acquiring them; (2) most children made substantial numbers of "errors," i.e., didn't follow the patterns; (3) for some a "groping pattern" was observed in which a varied order was used before a particular word order to express specific meanings. Braine concludes that children's early word combinations follow neither grammatical nor Schlesinger's broad semantic rules. Rather, children develop word order "formulas," which are used to convey narrow meanings, narrower than semantic rules.

There is general agreement that after about age 3 children develop grammar. They appropriately combine related two, into three-word sentences; e.g., "Adam hit," and "hit ball" into "Adam hit ball." Older children appropriately expand S-V-O sentences, e.g., "I go store" into "I am going to the store." And they develop the ability to grammatically transform S-V-O sentences into negations; e.g., "I am not going to the store"; questions, and demands; e.g., "Go to the store." By age 5, they have become full-fledged communicators, but their language learning is not yet complete.

Grammar Development in School Children

In this section research bearing on two grammatical issues is discussed: use of the passive tense; and ability to detect sentence ambiguity. The results of these studies are clear and highlight the fact that grammatical understanding continues to develop into adolescence. Menyuk (1982) describes a number of other knowledge gains in this age range.

The use of the passive tense, e.g., "the ball was hit by the boy," instead of the active tense, e.g., "the boy hit the ball," though common in written materials, is very infrequent in normal speech, occurring less than 5% of the time (Palermo & Molfese, 1972). Passive sentences are grammatically more complex than active, declarative ones, and in addition, they may be more difficult to understand due to semantic reasons, i.e., figuring out which noun is the subject and which is the object of the sentence. The latter problem is especially prominent when passive "reversible" as contrasted with passive "nonreversible" sentences are used. A reversible sentence is one that would be plausible if the action were reversed, e.g., "the girls were chased by the boys." The correct interpretation of this sentence is that the boys chased the girls, but it could be plausibly and incorrectly understood that it was the girls who were doing the chasing. In a nonreversible sentence, e.g., "the leaves were raked by the boys," it is not plausible to understand that the leaves were doing the raking. Active sentences may also be described as reversible or nonreversible, but it turns out that the semantic difficulty produced by reversibility is much smaller in active than in passive sentences (Slobin, 1966; Turner & Rommetveit, 1967).

In the Slobin (1966) study, the subjects were four groups of middle-class children with average ages of 6, 8, 10, and 12 years, and one group of 20-year-old college students. On each trial, either an active reversible, active nonreversible, passive reversible, or passive nonreversible sentence was read to them. Following this, a picture was shown and the subjects were to respond as quickly as possible by pushing either a "Right" or a "Wrong" button indicating whether the picture accurately depicted the meaning of the sentence. For all groups, speed of response to nonreversible was faster than to reversible sentences, but this was much more pronounced for the passive than active sentences. Also, for all groups, active reversible sentences were responded to more quickly than were passive reversible sentences.

The above pattern of results was confirmed by Turner and Rommetveit (1967), who used very different procedures. In their experiment, the subjects were five groups of middle-class children from 4 to 9 years old. Each child was tested on three different tasks utilizing the four sentence types described in Slobin's experiment. In the imitation task, the child was asked to merely repeat the sentence uttered by the experimenter. In the comprehension task, a picture was presented to the child and two sentences were read, one accurately describing the picture, and the other reversing the action, e.g., "The grandmother washes the dishes," "The dishes wash the grandmother." The child was asked to indicate whether each sentence was an accurate or inaccurate description of the picture. In the production task, procedures similar to the comprehension task were used, except that the child was asked to repeat the sentence that accurately described the picture.

In general, the nonreversible active sentences were the easiest, followed by the reversible active, then nonreversible passive, then reversible passive. By age 6, subjects were responding correctly at least 90% of the time to the active sentences, but it was not until age 9 that this occurred for the passive sentences. Finally, for the 8 and 9-year olds, performance with the passive nonreversible was nearly identical to that with the active sentences.

The detection of sentence ambiguity goes to the heart of communication and language functioning. The experiment that we will discuss was carried out by Schultz and Pilon (1973). The thrust of their research was to evaluate how well children of different ages could detect four different types of sentence ambiguity – phonological, lexical, surface-structure, and deep-structure. Phonological ambiguity is produced by different words having the same sounds; e.g., "The doctor is out of patience (patients)." When this sentence is heard, it is not clear whether the doctor is getting impatient, or whether his last patient has gone. The sentence can be made unambiguous by stating that the doctor has lost his temper. Lexical ambiguity is produced by the same word having more than one meaning; e.g., "He went lion hunting with a club." When this sentence is heard, it is not clear whether he intends to club the lion into submission, or whether he went with a group of fellow hunters. The sentence can be made unambiguous by stating "He went hunting with a group of friends." Surface structure ambiguity is grammatical unclarity produced by the existence of two or more ways of relating or grouping the words in a sentence;

e.g., "He sent her kids story books." When this sentence is heard, it is not clear whether the woman will receive kids' story books, or whether the woman's kids will receive story books. Deep-structure ambiguity is grammatical unclarity produced by different possible semantic intentions of the speaker. This leads to a sentence in which a single grouping of the words reflects these different meanings; e.g., "The duck is ready to eat." When this sentence is heard, it is not clear whether the duck will do the eating, or will himself be eaten. The sentence can be made unambiguous by stating that the duck is ready to eat the food.

The subjects in the experiment were four groups of middle-class children with average ages of 6, 9, 12, and 15. On each trial, they were read either one of the four types of ambiguous sentences, or an unambiguous but comparable sentence. The four ambiguous and unambiguous sentences just given as examples were used in the experiment, along with several other sentences of each type. After the child heard the sentence he was asked to tell the experimenter in his own words what it meant, i.e.; to paraphrase it. If only one interpretation was given, the experimenter asked the child if the sentence had another meaning. Then the experimenter presented two pictures to the child that illustrated the two different meanings of the ambiguous sentence, and asked the child to point to the picture(s) that depicted the meaning of the sentence. The child was also asked to justify his response.

All subjects correctly interpreted the unambiguous sentences all of the time. For the ambiguous sentences, phonological ambiguity was easiest to detect at all ages, ranging from about 20% correct detections at age 6, to 90% at age 15. Lexical ambiguity was next easiest to detect, about 10% correct detections at age 6, 80% at age 15. There was essentially no difference in detectability between surface- and deep-structure ambiguity, i.e., the two types of grammatical ambiguity. Virtually none of the 6- and 9-year-olds detected grammatical ambiguity; i.e., they could justify only one meaning for the "ambiguous" sentences, whereas the 12-year-olds had about 50% and the 15-year-olds 65% correct detections. These results indicate that grammatical development lags behind phonological and lexical development, and that children's acquisition of grammar is incomplete at age 15.

Speech Acts (Conversational Units)

Jeremy, age 8, wants a drink of his brother's pop. Aaron, age 5, loves pop, and is usually unwilling to share it with his older brother. How does

Jeremy solve this problem? Consider the following "speech acts" as possibilities:

1. Aaron, can I have a drink of your pop?
2. Aaron, if you give me a drink, I'll give you a nickel.
3. If you don't give me some pop, I won't play soccer with you.
4. Boy, does that pop look good!
5. Gee, am I thirsty.
6. Aaron, remember I gave you some of my pop yesterday?
7. Aaron, where'd you get that pop?

Jeremy would likely choose one or more of these speech acts until either he was given a drink, or he gave up his quest. The first three are the most *direct* and can be understood by anyone who is not familiar with the context. The last four vary in degree of *indirectness* and require some knowledge of the situation. Clearly, much more is required of the listener to make sense of the latter statements than the former.

Conversation is a complex problem-solving situation in which speakers and listeners are each attempting to accomplish some positive outcomes; eg., to get something, to keep friendships alive, and to avoid negative outcomes, such as antagonizing the listener by making unreasonable requests. When Jeremy says "Aaron, where'd you get that pop?" he's conveying an interest in the pop, which may place a subtle demand on Aaron to share with him. Yet, Jeremy protects himself both from rejection by not directly asking, and perhaps from some future request by Aaron to him. Aaron can respond to Jeremy's question in a variety of ways, depending upon which outcomes he's interested in at that moment. If he has had enough to drink he may say "You can have the rest." If he is still very thirsty, he can say "In the refrigerator" or "Mom gave it to me." If it was the last bottle in the house, this might further influence his speech acts.

Herbert and Eve Clark (1977) have summarized the recent research on children's use of speech acts. Following Searle's (1975) analysis, they divide these conversational units into five categories:

1. *Representatives.* In this category, speakers' statements assert or represent the truth (to varying degrees) of something; e.g., "That is the last bottle," or "Doggie all gone."
2. *Directives.* In this category speakers attempt to direct the listener to do something. They may do this through requests, orders, pleas,

commands, or questions; e.g., "Let's hug," or "Mommy, up" (Mommy, pick me up).

3. *Commissives.* In this category, speakers commit themselves to do something in the future; e.g., "I'll save some pop for you," or "I'll call you tonight." The typical commissive is a promise.

4. *Expressives.* In this category, speakers express their psychological state about something; e.g., "I'm sorry I hurt you," or "That makes me angry."

5. *Declarations.* In this category, speakers' statements declare a new state of affairs for people or objects; e.g., "You're fired," or "I pronounce you husband and wife." Declarations are usually associated with particular cultural roles such as minister, employer or judge. Children's games sometimes model these roles and use declarations.

In all cases, speech acts are intended to have some effect on listeners. Directives call for some action on their part. But in the other categories listeners, at a minimum, are required to acknowledge the statements made to them; e.g., "Uh, huh," "OK," "You promise?" For children and adults, representatives and directives are the most frequently used categories. Developmentally, they are the first two categories acquired. Between the ages of 5 and 7, children start to use commissives properly. Prior to then, for example, they frequently confuse the words "tell" (directive) and "promise" (commissive). Expressives and declarations are the last two categories of speech acts to be learned. Clark and Clark suggest that when young children use phrases like "I'm sorry," they are mimicking adult use, and not really trying to convey their psychological state. This interpretation is consistent with research on the verbal self, which shows that until age 10 internal states play a small role in self-descriptions.

Finally, and not surprisingly, the art of speech indirection is slowly acquired during childhood. Between the ages of 3 and 5, for example, the portion of indirect to direct speech acts increases dramatically. This portion continues to rise thereafter. The use of indirection is presumably related to cultural preferences for polite speech. Lakoff (1973) interprets this preference to mean (1) don't impose on others; and (2) give others response options. Thus, Jeremy imposes on and gives Aaron few options when he directly asks for a drink of his pop. But when Jeremy says he's thirsty, he doesn't impose and gives Aaron a number of options; e.g., "That's a shame," "Have some of mine," "Ask Mom." Using indirect relative to direct speech requires greater cognitive abilities, greater understanding of cultural values, and greater understanding of social contexts. As such, we would expect learning indirection to be a long-term process.

We began this topic by indicating that language acquisition is not merely the unfolding of a universal innate grammar. Language acquisition reflects, instead, the influence of social and cognitive development, as well as the constraints of canalization processes. Consistent with the latter, we saw from Lenneberg's research that language and motor developmental milestones for normal children and children with Down's syndrome are parallel. The early speech sounds of infants also appear to be strongly canalized.

There are two factors that help to determine an infant's first words: his cognitive development and social experiences. These influences continue throughout the rest of a child's acquisition of language. A child's development from late infancy onward is influenced by his attempts to construct, or make sense of, reality. Children differ in the nature of the early word combinations that they create. The reason for this is that they experience different social contexts. Moreover, the form of these sentences seems to be based on the meaning they intend to convey rather than syntax. For children 3 years old and older, syntax plays a progressively greater role in their speech. As a child grows into adolescence, his understanding and use of syntactical rules continue to develop. Obviously, one of the primary uses of language is conversing with others. The type of speech a child uses—e.g., direction versus indirection—is strongly influenced by his level of cognitive development and the social context he is confronted with.

DEVELOPMENT OF INTELLIGENCE

Issues About a Definition

There is no strong agreement among psychologists concerning the meaning or definition of intelligence. In exasperation some have said "Intelligence is what intelligence tests measure." Where is it written, however, that intelligence can be measured by tests?

Most people, young and old, have some ideas about the nature of intelligence. When we ask students about it—"In what ways are the people you know more (or less) intelligent than you?—they talk about such things as better memories, greater knowledge, planning and problem-solving abilities, and quick learning. These are just the kinds of things many psychologists talk about, at least when they want to measure "it." Rarely do people focus on emotional or artistic sensitivity, interpersonal awareness and skills, or mind-body integration.

Intelligence, in the minds of most North Americans and Europeans seems to be closely identified with those abilities related to academic success. This is a cultural bias, which historically received its impetus from the work of Alfred Binet at the turn of the century. At that time the French government asked Binet to develop some techniques for determining which children would succeed in public schools and which, owing to mental retardation, would not. With his colleague, T. Simon (whom Piaget later worked for), he developed the first "IQ" test to successfully predict academic success. Their test was subsequently modified for American use by Lewis Terman and his colleagues at Stanford University and is currently known as the Stanford-Binet (Terman & Merrill, 1937).

Why should intelligence be defined in terms of academic success? We noted in Chapter 2 that widespread public schooling is a recent cultural invention, so from the viewpoint of evolution this linkage makes little sense. Moreover, we know from recent work by Jencks et al. (1972) that intelligence, as measured by IQ tests, poorly predicts future occupational or financial success. Our guess is that this academic-intelligence linkage still exists because schooling is the one set of experiences that all children in an industrialized culture must undergo. No other situation comes close to school in allowing, indeed forcing, comparisons to be made. If all young people had to spend 5 hours a day for 12 years making clay products, intelligence might be defined quite differently, as it is in some non-Western societies.

There are at least three rational approaches to defining intelligence as a characteristic: (1) it is species-specific; (2) it is developmental within a species; (3) it differentiates one individual from another. When thinking about intelligence as a species characteristic, we try to identify those mental activities that distinguish one species from another. An evolutionary approach is useful, such as that taken by Harry Jerison (1973, 1982). Jerison (1973) suggested that intelligence relates to the ability to identify *invariances* in the environment. An invariancy, in Piaget's terms, is a *conservation*, an aspect of the environment that stays the same despite apparent change. Taking Jerison's view as a starting place, intelligence as a species characteristic could be defined in terms of the number and type of invariances that can be identified. We assume that humans would score higher than apes, who in turn would score higher than monkeys, and so on. Also, each species would identify relatively unique invariances, depending upon their evolutionary history.

When thinking about intelligence as a developmental characteristic, we try to identify those mental activities within a species that systematically change with maturation for normal members. Presumably intelligence grows, stabilizes, and decays, as do virtually all other psychobiological characteristics. The person who has elaborated this theoretical approach most profoundly is Piaget. In his book, *Psychology of Intelligence* (1966), Piaget defined intelligence as constituting "the state of equilibrium towards which tend all the successive adaptations of a sensori-motor and cognitive nature, as well as all assimilatory and accommodatory interactions between the organism and the environment" (p. 11). Thus our previous discussion of Piaget's work on cognitive development was from his perspective about the growth in intelligence.

When thinking about intelligence as a characteristic within a species, (individual differences) we try to identify those mental activities that distinguish one member from another. From an evolutionary point of view, the most important criterion in defining intelligence in this way is that the mental activities be related to genetic survival (Darwinian fitness). Presumably, in the evolution of our species those individuals who were most intelligent either reproduced more or helped their close relatives to do so. We stated in Chapter 2 that over 99% of our existence as a species was spent as gatherer-hunters. Thus, intelligence was selected for in that context.

If intelligence is an adaptive characteristic, then individual differences must be defined in terms of Darwinian fitness. There is no research bearing on this issue. We do know that some forms of mental retardation are associated with genetic sterility, and that generally, the mentally retarded reproduce less than the nonretarded. However, it's not clear that their lower rate of reproduction is related to their reduced intelligence—it could be reduced sex drive, for example. Some psychologists talk about intelligence as an adaptive characteristic, e.g., Charlesworth (1976), but when we look closely, the adaptation they're dealing with is academic, playground, or job success. We have no idea whether any of these is related to Darwinian fitness.

Where does all this lead? During the twentieth century definitions of intelligence were linked with individual differences in academic success. Tests—called IQ tests—largely dependent on language abilities were developed for this purpose. They have been remarkable in identifying mentally retarded, and have been moderately useful in predicting academic success. Although construction of most IQ tests was not based on any coherent theory of the development of intelligence, all note that performance is age related. No existent test is based on either species differences or evolutionary considerations.

Two Broad Approaches — Abilities Versus Processes

Is intelligence a single entity, a collection of independent characteristics, or some combination of the two? These questions reflect the "Abilities Approach" to the study of intelligence and the construction of intelligence tests. Binet's work falls into this category, which is also known as the Psychometric Approach (mental measurements). Intelligence is measured by how much of this ability a person has. The Processes Approach is heavily influenced by computer studies of artificial intelligence and information processing. Intelligence in this view is seen as the steps or processes that people go through in solving problems. One person may be more intelligent than another because she moves through the same steps more quickly, is more efficient, or knows the required problem-solving steps.

The abilities approach, which dominates the field of intelligence testing, received its major impetus from the work of Charles Spearman (e.g., 1927), who laid the groundwork for the statistical techniques of factor analysis (see Chapter 1). After thousands of people have been tested on large numbers of mental activities (e.g., memory, vocabulary, arithmetic), factor analysis allows one to determine how many broad underlying intellectual abilities (factors) exist. Spearman's research led him to conclude that intelligence consisted of one general factor "g" and a number of specific factors "s," which related to the particular tests used. One person was more intelligent than another because he had more "g."

Spearman's conclusions were challenged by L. L. Thurstone (e.g., 1947). Factor analysis is somewhat of an art form; researchers using the same data can reach different conclusions. Moreover, if different mental tests are used, then the same person can reach different conclusions. Thurstone was struck by the common observation that all mental tests don't correlate equally. Rather they appear to form distinct groupings. Thurstone concluded that there was not a single general factor underlying all mental abilities, but rather, seven primary ones: verbal comprehension, word fluency, number, space, reasoning, memory, and perceptual speed. Of course, each test carried with it specific abilities, "s's," but these counted for little, as with Spearman's theory.

Is intelligence a single trait or is it seven? Many researchers questioned Thurstone's conclusions. They noted that despite the existence of groupings of mental abilities, people who scored high on one also tended to score high on most of the others. In school, for example, when students do poorly in a single subject and well on the rest, clinicians become suspicious that either there is some emotional difficulty or there is a personality clash between student and teacher. Vernon (1950) noted test performance patterns and concluded that intelligence is neither a single general mental ability, nor a small number of less general independent ones, but both. General intelligence plays a part in all mental activities, joining with the more narrow abilities, e.g., space, number, to produce behavior. Of course, the specific abilities, "s's," still influence performance. From a psychometric perspective, this combined approach is the current viewpoint among psychologists.

Two of the most active researchers in the processes approach are Robert Sternberg (e.g., 1979) and Earl Hunt (e.g., 1983). Their points of view are similar in that they focus on (1) how information is internally represented; (2) the kinds of strategies people use in processing that information; (3) the nature of the components (e.g., memory, inference, comparison) used in carrying out any strategy; and (4) how decisions are made concerning which strategies to use. Analogous to Piaget's work, they are interested in developing a theory about universal intelligence. And like the mental abilities researchers, they want to describe individual differences in information processing. Intelligence, in this approach, is neither an "it," e.g., "g" or a "them," e.g., primary abilities, but everything the mind does in processing information. Some aspects, however, are strongly correlated with mental abilities as measured by intelligence tests. An example from Hunt and Sternberg will be clarifying.

A typical task assigned by Sternberg (1979) is an analogy. For example, subjects are asked to solve the problem "Lawyer is to Client as Doctor is to (a) Medicine (b) Patient?" (p. 225). Sternberg envisions one strategy to be as follows. The subject first *represents* in her mind the words "lawyer" and "client" and second, makes an *inference* concerning the relation between the two; e.g., the lawyer provides a service for the client. She next *represents* the word "doctor" and fourth *searches* for, in her mind, an ideal higher order relation linking "lawyer and client" with "doctor and X" (the solution term); e.g., doctors and lawyers are professionals who provide services. Fifth, she *compares* the ideal higher order relation with each of the possible solution terms—medicine and patient. Sixth, she *chooses* the best match to the ideal, and seventh makes an *overt response*—"patient!" Sternberg has been able to demonstrate that college students in fact use this strategy, by measuring the time each step in the strategy takes. He has also been able to help students improve their analogy performance by teaching them new strategies.

A typical task used by Hunt is called the "sentence verification" procedure. A student is presented with a simple sentence such as "Is the plus above the star?" and a picture of the plus and the star, one above the other. The student's decision time is measured. Hunt has found that decision time changes as a function of sentence complexity; e.g., "Plus not below star" is more complex than the above sentence. Student's speed of decision on these tasks is moderately correlated with tests of verbal ability. Hunt has also been able to demonstrate that some students internally represent the sentences by memorizing the words (verbalizers) and others make an internal picture of what the sentence depicts (visualizers). Speed of performance for verbalizers is moderately correlated with tests of verbal ability but not with tests of visualization, and the reverse is true for visualizers.

A promising study by Globerson (1983) has recently appeared, which starts to bridge the gap between Piaget's theory and the information-processing and psychometric approaches. Globerson tested an important concept of Pascuel-Leone (1970) derived from Piaget's theory, and consistent with an information-processer's approach. This concept is called "M-space" or "Central computing space" and refers to the number of schemas that individuals can attend to and manipulate within any time span. M-space is assumed to grow with maturation and to be relatively unaffected by specific learning, knowledge, or skills. M-space is pure cognitive capacity.

Globerson tested three age-groups of Israeli children, 8, 10, and 12, who were either from high or from low social class backgrounds. Four types of tasks were used, which varied in the extent to which previous learning was expected to influence performance. On all tasks, performance was predicted to improve with age—and hence, size of M-capacity. However, social class was predicted to have no effect on tasks measuring pure M-capacity, but a substantial effect on tasks where previous learning plays a major role, i.e., short-term memory, spatial-analytic ability, and Verbal IQ. Both sets of predictions were borne out by the results, lending strong support to Pascual-Leone's concept. Moreover, individual differences in performance were moderately correlated on all tasks, which is consistent with the psychometric approach.

Extrapolating from Globerson's results, the following merger of the two broad approaches is tentatively offered. Intelligence is viewed as consisting of both a general overall ability to process various kinds of information, and several more specialized processing abilities reflecting different content areas, e.g., word fluency, space, memory. The overall ability, usually referred to as "g" may be estimated by measures of M-space capacity. M-space capacity increases with age and differs among same-age individuals, as do various measures of "g." In general, the greater children's M-space, the more efficient will be their information-processing abilities. The development of the specialized processing abilities depends on M-space capacity, the nature of learning opportunities, e.g., social class membership, and genetically determined specialized capacities. Thus, children who have large M-space capacity will generally perform well on tasks calling for specialized abilities. However, those who have had limited learning opportunities and only a slight genetic predisposition in any given area may perform poorly.

Age Changes in IQ

Fig. 6.1 is a summary of results from the Berkeley Growth Study showing the correlations between IQ in adulthood with scores from infancy onwards. In this study (Bayley & Schaefer, 1964), the tests used at each

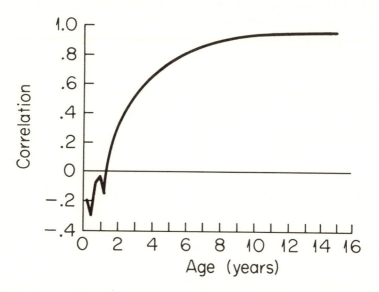

FIG. 6.1   Correlations of IQ at 18 years with mental test peformance at earlier ages. (Source: Bayley, N. & Schaefer, E. S. Correlations of maternal and child behaviors with the development of mental abilities: Data from the Berkeley Growth Study. *Monographs of the Society for Research in Child Development*, 1964, *29*, 1–50. © The Society for Research in Child Development, Inc.)

age dealt with the developmental accomplishments at that age. Prior to age 2 few of the test items required verbal responses, but after that age, progressively more did. Representative items were as follows: at 2 months, turning eyes to a light; at 10 months, putting a cube in a cup; at 16 months, making a tower of three cubes; at 26 months, understanding the word "big"; and at 33 months, naming seven pictures.

As can be seen from the figure, prior to age 2, there is virtually no correlation between IQ scores and those of adulthood. From 2 onwards, IQ becomes a progressively better predictor of adult IQ, such that by age 8, scores correlate about .8 or better with later performance. The fact that IQ prior to age 2 is such a poor predictor of later IQ strongly suggests that the early and later tests are measuring different kinds of intelligence. Shouldn't there exist some factor such as "g," which continues throughout development? We return to this question, shortly.

Fig. 6.2 summarizes some of the results from the Fels Longitudinal Study of Development (McCall, Appelbaum, & Hogarty, 1973). Large numbers of middle-class children were evaluated every 1 to 3 years on a battery of tests starting at 2½ and ending at age 17. The figure shows the IQ changes of those subjects who took a test every year. McCall et al. identified five patterns of age changes. The children who comprise the most stable group (the curve numbered "1") changed an average of about 10 points. Approximately half the children fell into this group. The average child in the study shifted 28 points, and one child in seven shifted 40 or more IQ points over the 15½-year period. Even if we restrict our gaze to changes after age 8, IQ can still change markedly afterwards. Doesn't this contradict the Bayley and Schaefer results? No. First, because in general children who initially scored above or below the group average continued to do so. Second, the average IQ of these children was about 118, the top 15% of the population. This restricted range of scores makes it a certainty that correlations over time will not be high.

What happens to IQ during adulthood? Schaie and Strother (1968) have summarized a number of studies that collectively allow us to infer what happens when the same people are tested from age 20 to 70. Most aspects of verbal intelligence either slightly increase or stay the same throughout the age range, e.g., vocabulary, verbal reasoning, educational aptitude. On the other hand, most nonverbal measures of intelligence start to decline at about age 40. The tests that showed the greatest decline were those requiring quick mental agility such as writing down as many words of a certain type within a short time interval. Quick thinking, like quick reflexes, appears to be an attribute of the relatively young.

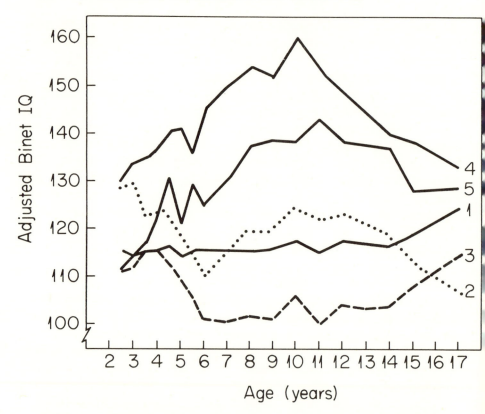

FIG. 6.2   Clusters of IQ changes from ages 2 to 17 years. (Source: McCall, R. B., Appelbaum, M. I., & Hogarty, P. S. Developmental changes in mental performance. *Monographs of the Society for Research in Child Development*, 1973, *38*, No. 150. © The Society for Research in Child Development, Inc.)

Let's return to the apparent lack of continuity between mental activities prior to age 2 with those in later childhood. Two recent studies, by Fagan and McGrath (1981) and Lewis and Brooks-Gunn (1981), have shown striking correlations between attentional capacities in infancy and IQ at 2, 4, and 7 years of age. In the Lewis and Brooks-Gunn study, 3-month-old infants were habituated (recall the section on attention and memory in infancy) to a repeated visual stimulus and then presented with a novel one. The amount of "recovery" was measured by comparing how much time they looked at the novel stimulus relative to the old one. These recovery scores were moderately correlated (about .5) with IQ measured at 2 years. In the Fagan and McGrath study, 4- and 7-month-old infants were shown pairs of face photographs, one familiar and one novel. Their recognition memory was scored by noting the relative amount of time they looked at the novel photograph. These scores were found to be moderately correlated (about .5) with verbal IQ measured at either 4 or 7 years.

The two studies provide strong evidence that childhood IQ can be predicted from attentional activities in infancy. Is there continuity of mental abilities from infancy through childhood? We believe that there is, given the assumption of a general "g." The linkage is then straightforward. In both studies individual differences in memory (habituation) were measured. Memory is a mental ability closely connected to "g." The intelligence tests given in childhood also reflect individual differences in "g." Thus, the two studies show continuity in "g" as assessed by different tests estimating general intellectual ability.

Heredity of IQ

This is one of the most heated areas of study in psychology. Richard Herrnstein, who has taken a strong heriditarian position, has recently documented the difficulties he has had with the American media in communicating accurate views on this subject (1982). In one sense, the question of the inheritance of IQ is the dumbest question possible. *Everything* is inherited, from our toes to our nose. We also know that *everything* is influenced by the sequence of environments in which we develop. The technical question that is not dumb concerns *heritability* – the extent to which individual differences in any characteristic (including IQ) are genetically controlled.

Performing heritability studies is often extremely simple to do. You vary both the genetic relatedness and the environments between individuals, measure the characteristic of interest, and then use well-known statistical methods to give you an answer. Heritability for such human characteristics as height, weight, and eye color is well worked out. Most behavioral geneticists also think this is the case for IQ, where the estimates of heritability range from .50 to .80 (Herrnstein, 1982). Thus, most active researchers in the area believe that between 50% and 80% of individual differences in IQ can be attributed to genetic differences. That leaves a lot of room for the environment to have an impact. In fact, we saw from the Fels study that the typical bright child experiences a 28-point IQ shift between the ages of 2½ and 17 years.

So, what's the problem? Table 6.3 shows average IQ correlations of most of the relevant information. If heritability is high, then, by definition the closer the genetic relationship, the higher should be the correla-

TABLE 6.3
Correlations of Intelligence Test Scores

Correlations Between	Median Value
Unrelated Persons	
Children reared apart	−.01
Children reared together	+.20
Adopted child with adoptive parents	+.40*
Collaterals	
Second cousins	+.16
First cousins	+.28
Uncle (or aunt) and nephew (or niece)	+.34
Siblings, reared apart	+.46
Siblings, reared together	+.52
Fraternal twins, different sex	+.49
Fraternal twins, same sex	+.56
Identical twins, reared apart	+.75
Identical twins, reared together	+.87
Direct Line	
Grandparent and grandchild	+.30
Parent (as adult) and child	+.50
Parent (as child) and child	+.56
Parent (as adult) and child adopted and raised by others	+.40*

*Parents IQs estimated based on educational level attained (Source: Hall, E., Lamb, M. E., & Perlmutter, M. *Child psychology today*. New York: Random House, 1982.)

tions. That is exactly what is found. Identical twins, reared together or apart have the highest IQ correlations. Parents with their children living together or apart, and siblings, including fraternal twins have the same degree of genetic relatedness. All of these correlations are similar and lower than those between identical twins. The genetic relationship between grandparents and grandchildren is the same as that between aunts or uncles and their nephews or nieces, and the IQ correlations are about the same, lower than the above. All the data don't line up perfectly, e.g., that involving first cousins, and it is clear that environment plays a role; e.g., twins reared apart have lower IQ correlations than those reared together. But, of course, that's what heritability less than 100% means—environment plays a role.

The major criticisms involve the lack of certainty about the environments these individuals were reared in (e.g., Kamin, 1974). It is theoretically possible that one could manipulate environments in such a way that heritability of a characteristic would appear high, even if in reality it were close to zero. For example, environments in which identical twins were always treated alike, fraternal twins and siblings were treated similarly but not identically, first cousins less so, and so on, would meet these conditions. It would appear that IQ had a high heritability, but it may have been the environmental manipulation that produced the patterns of correlation found. Recent research has shown, however, that even where fraternal twins have been treated more similarly than identical twins, the IQ correlations were higher for the identical twins (Scarr & Carter-Saltzman, 1979). In addition, how would the environmentalist position explain the correlations involving parents and children, grandparents and children, and uncles or aunts and nephews and nieces, who clearly were treated differently?

Based on our reading of the relevant literature, we share Herrnstein's conclusion that the heritability of IQ is between .50 and .80. This does not mean that racial or ethnic differences in IQ are genetically determined. The statistical techniques for measuring heritability of individual differences are different than those for comparing groups of people. And, there is no convincing evidence that any one group of humans has genetically determined higher IQs than any other. For example, Scarr and Weinberg (1978) have shown that black infants of low SES parents adopted by white middle-class parents have higher IQs in childhood than the national average for white children.

Parental Influences on Early IQ Development

In 1975, Elardo, Bradley, and Caldwell published a study that examined the relationship between children's IQ at age 3 and six qualities of home life. These qualities, called the Home Scale, were measured during a one-hour visit and consisted of the following subscales:

1. Emotional and verbal responsivity of the mother to her child
2. Avoidance of restriction and punishment of the child
3. Organization of child's physical and temporal environment
4. Provision of appropriate play materials for the child
5. Mother's involvement with her child
6. Opportunities for variety in daily stimulation.

The families studied were from lower- and working-class backgrounds. Some were on welfare and in some, the father was not living at home. The results were surprising and important. Each of the subscales and the total Home Scale score were correlated about .5 with subsequent IQ. Correlations are not cause and effect relationships – the different home environments did not necessarily cause the different levels of IQ development. But, they may have. And if so, then parents of young children can be trained to provide the very qualities of home life supportive of their children's intellectual development.

However, before rushing off to train parents to reorganize their family life, several issues must be evaluated. First, it is possible that Home Scale scores are positively correlated with parental IQ, which Elardo et al. did not measure, and thus, primarily reflect genetic influences. We can evaluate this question by examining studies that have assessed parental IQ or education (an indirect measure of IQ) along with Home Scale scores. Second, it is possible that Home Scale scores do not equally predict child's IQ for all social classes. We know for example that middle-class children develop higher IQs than those from lower classes. Further, Elardo et al. noted that Home Scale scores were positively correlated with welfare status and parental occupation, both aspects of SES. Third, infant birth status may either override or accentuate parental influences on early IQ development. That is, premature relative to full-term infants, who are at high risk for a number of developmental deficits, may be either more or less sensitive to the home environment. Finally, powerful interventions, such as full-time day care may override family influences for early IQ development.

Several recent studies deal with the relative contribution of genetics and home environment to IQ development. Ramey, Farran, and Campbell (1979) measured mother's IQ, and Bakeman and Brown (1980), Siegel (1982), and Bee et al. (1982), mother's education, as related to 3- or 4-year-old child's IQ. Longstreth et al. (1981) examined mother's and 12-year-old child's IQ. In all cases Home Scale scores were positively correlated with child's IQ, and where reported, with mother's IQ or education. In the Longstreth et al. study, mother's IQ differences overrode differences in the home environment. In the other four studies, the opposite was true—the IQ of children matched for mother's IQ or education were positively correlated with Home Scale scores. Thus, the family environment affected IQ development over and above possible genetic differences.

The studies by Bee et al. (1982) and Siegel (1982) compared the relative influences of SES and Home Scale scores on children's IQ scores. In Bee et al. nearly all the infants were full-term and primarily from working- and middle-SES families. In Siegel, approximately half were premature and nearly all from lower- and working-class families. In both studies the higher relative to lower SES families had higher Home Scale scores, and their children, higher IQs. In the Bee et al. study, Home Scale scores predicted child's IQ over and above SES level; and in Siegel's study, this was true for only the premature infants. Taken together, these results suggest that parental influences can override SES influences.

The studies by Bakeman and Brown (1980) and Siegel (1982) compared premature and full-term infants. In both, premature infants had lower IQs at 3 years than those born full-term. However, in both studies, Home Scale scores were positively correlated with child's IQ. All the families in Bakeman and Brown were lower SES. In Siegel's study, as noted above, the relationship between Home Scale scores and IQ, over and above SES, was stronger for premature than full-term infants. These results imply that parental influences are especially important for IQ development of premature infants, who are at risk for poor intellectual development.

Finally, Ramey et al. (1979) contrasted two groups of infants from low SES households, many on welfare. In one group, all the children were in a daytime day-care center from age 3 to 36 months. In the other group, none received this treatment. Home scores were measured and correlated with age 3 years IQs. Day care had a dramatic positive effect on IQ development, resulting in a 15-point difference between the two groups. However, for both groups Home scores were positively correlated with IQ development, more strongly in the home-care than the day-care children. Thus, to some effect, day care overrode parental influences.

In summary, the results from these studies indicate that the quality of home life, as measured by the Home Scale, is substantially related to a child's early mental development. These qualities are potent across a range of SES levels, mothers' educational or IQ level, children's IQ levels, infancy birth risk, and the powerful environmental intervention of day care. Although we do not have positive proof that there is a cause and effect relationship between IQ development and home quality, the data are strongly consistent with this conclusion. Should we rush out to train parents to reorganize their home life? Yes, if they want us to.

READING AND READING DISABILITIES

As we noted earlier, spoken language is an evolutionarily old human characteristic, but reading and writing are recent cultural inventions. Although writing dates back 5,000 years, literacy, the ability to read, has become a widespread societal requirement only since the Middle Ages. There are still cultures, however, where no one is literate.

When we started requiring children to learn to read, we opened up for most of them all the marvels of this world and beyond. For some, however, we created a nightmare. These children have an extraordinarily difficult time learning to read, and each year in school finds them slipping further behind their same-age peers. School becomes a place in which they often feel stupid and degraded. They sometimes become behavior problems to teachers and fellow students, play hooky, and drop out as soon as possible. Rutter (1975) estimates that about one third of juvenile delinquents have serious reading disabilities. Although reading disabilities do not cause juvenile delinquency, the school problems associated with these disabilities surely are a contributing factor.

Definition of Reading

Gibson and Levin (1975) define reading as "extracting information from text" (p. 5). The key word here is "information." The ability to name the printed letters of the alphabet, to sound them into phonemes and syllables (consonent-vowel combinations), to combine or blend these into correctly pronounced words, are all important, but don't comprise reading. Nor does the ability to correctly name all the words in a sentence. To read is to read with meaning – to extract information. Furthermore, when people read, they actively direct the way they deal with printed materials and do so with one or more purposes in mind (Gibson & Levin, 1975). The purposes will influence the way we go about reading, which in turn will influence the nature of the information extracted. Typists and proof readers, for example, often have only a vague idea about what they have been reading.

There are enormous differences between reading and listening that make reading a very different, difficult, and unnatural task. These are some of the differences: Speech is auditory, one word at a time, whereas print is visual, with all words presented at once; the rate of speech and hence meaning are controlled by the speaker, whereas the rate of reading, by the reader; the context of speech is usually interpersonal with many nonverbal cues present, whereas that of reading is usually individual without nonverbal cues; speech is often repetitious, whereas print usually is not; interaction is always present in speech, almost never in print; the pauses in speech help clarify semantics and grammar, whereas the spaces between words do neither. The major impact of these differences is that the listener is given many cues over and above the words spoken to help understand what is being said. Printed materials are relatively impoverished. Finally, we know from studies of the brain that different regions are involved in understanding speech and print (text). Those concerned with speech evolved for that purpose. The regions concerned with reading evolved for other purposes. On this basis, we might expect reading to be a difficult enterprise.

Development of Reading Ability

This section is a brief summary of some of the ideas in the following works: Gibson and Levin (1975), Fletcher (1981), Adams (1980) and Menyuk and Flood (1981). Fig. 6.3 indicates some of the major processes that children use and attempt to master while learning to read.

Reading can be divided into two broad categories of processes, those involved with translating printed materials into identifiable words (decoding), and those with making sense out of sentences and paragraphs (comprehending). Once a child starts to try to read a sentence, he simultaneously uses both sets of processes. For example, the word "lead" is pronounced differently (is not the same word) when it refers to a metal, as opposed to showing the way. The sentence "lead" is contained in determines which it is. There is more direct evidence of the effect of comprehending on decoding processes. Most errors beginning readers make are word substitutions. About 90% of these substitutions are grammatically correct and produce a meaningful sentence.

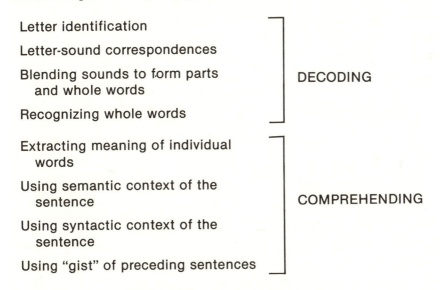

FIG. 6.3   Some major reading processes.

Very few children have difficulty in learning to identify letters. Trouble starts with learning letter-sound correspondences and blending these sounds together. Children usually find it easy to learn to pronounce the initial consonant of a word, but very difficult for a medial vowel, e.g., vowel. A major reason for these difficulties is that there are few consistent rules for pronouncing vowels; moreover, pronunciation of vowels located medially depends on both the preceding and following letters. Initial consonants are nearly always pronounced the same.

The beginning reader typically pays relatively more attention to decoding than to comprehension processes. Often this leads to failures in comprehension, despite accurate pronunciation. On the other hand, children who shift their attention to comprehension before they have mastered decoding make many word substitution errors, ignoring the letters of the unknown word. For example, instead of reading "The boy *went* to the store" they may say "The boy *ran* to the store."

While learning to read, many children come to recognize whole words, without sounding out and blending the component sounds. Some reading specialists have argued that early reading ought to be taught this way. After children have mastered a large sight vocabulary, they can be taught the more fine-grained decoding processes. Research, in fact, shows that many young children have an easier time learning whole words than blending sounds. However, for most children, the long-term gains are greater for the sound-blending approach (Marsh & Sherman, 1970).

Three major changes occur as the child becomes a skilled reader. First, in the decoding processes, she deals with progressively larger units, e.g., from single letters, to regular and irregular letter combinations, to familiar patterns of letter combinations. Second, the decoding processes become automatic, called into consciousness when unfamiliar words are encountered. Third, major emphasis shifts to developing comprehension strategies, which ultimately allow for skimming and other word-skipping devices. During this shift to skilled reading, the child has been developing intellectually and linguistically. The more she knows about the world, the greater is her vocabulary, and the more sophisticated her knowledge of grammar, the more skilled will be her reading. Intellectual and language development ultimately place limits on reading ability.

Definition of Specific Reading Disabilities

The phrase "specific reading disability" is a partial description of *dyslexia*. Dyslexia used to be thought of as a particular pattern of reading difficulties resulting from minimal brain damage or dysfunction (Critchley, 1970). Neurological tests rarely located this dysfunction, but rather identified nonreading behaviors (neurological signs) believed to be associated with it. Although Satz, Friel, and Rudegeair (1974) found evidence of maturational lags of the cerebral cortex of children who subsequently became dyslexic, more recent research (Vellutino, 1979) has failed to confirm either the presence of neurological signs or developmental delays in all reading-disabled children.

Gibson and Levin (1975) define dyslexia as "the condition of failure to master reading at a level normal for age when this failure is not the result of a generally debilitating disorder such as mental retardation, major brain injury, or severe emotional instability" (p. 455). Vellutino (1979) extends this definition to also exclude children who have severe physical disabilities, visual or hearing deficits, and "socioeconomic disadvantages," i.e., reared in environments that provide limited exposure to and motivation for reading. The typical dyslexic child, then, is average or above average in nearly all ways except that he is far behind in reading ability. The latter is usually defined as 2 or more years below grade level, which roughly translates into the bottom 5%–10% of the population.

There is no single type of reading disability. Carr (1981) has summarized much of the recent research on this topic. Dyslexics, relative to normals, show one or more of the following characteristics while reading: difficulty in discriminating letter location and letter order; poor memory for word order; inability to make good use of letter-sound regularities; difficulties in identifying grammatical relations; and poor usage of sentence context to predict forthcoming words and meaning. The end result of any combination of characteristics is that dyslexics have difficulty pronouncing words, defining them, and comprehending them in sentences.

A number of scholars, e.g., Mattis (1981), Satz and Morris (1981), have maintained that there are several independent causes of these deficits. One frequently found set of categories is (a) language disorders; (b) letter-sound dysfunctioning; (c) visual-spatial dysfunctions. Vellutino (1979), however, has argued that what all dyslexics share are deficits in verbal processing. In his view, then, dyslexia is fundamentally a language deficiency.

Vellutino states that "success in learning to read depends, first, upon linguistic ability in general, and second, upon the ability to make one's knowledge of language explicit" (p. 343). By the first, he means that dyslexics have deficiencies in many linguistic characteristics such as vocabulary size, ability to rapidly name things, ability to categorize words into different groupings, and a competent working knowledge of grammar. By the second, he means that dyslexics have difficulty in consciously using their knowledge of language to figure out written materials. For example, good readers, but not dyslexics, learn spelling rules, and spelling-pronunciation rules easily. In attempting to discover the meaning of relatively novel words, conscious knowledge of whether the words are nouns, verbs, or adjectives is very helpful.

Returning to the definition of dyslexia, many children fall behind their peers in reading ability owing to limited intellectual abilities, sensory deficits, severe emotional difficulties, or socioeconomic disadvantages. These children become poor readers, but are not considered to be dyslexic. The group we can be most hopeful about helping are the socioeconomically disadvantaged. What do we know about them?

Social Influences on Learning to Read

Approximately two thirds of black children from low SES families read below the national average (Norman-Jackson, 1982). Norman-Jackson reasoned, consistent with the above discussion, that poor readers are probably deficient in language development. Moreover, she hypothesized that the language deficiencies were related to the nature of children's family interactions.

Norman-Jackson studied a small number of low SES black families each having the following characteristics: There were three or more children under 12 years old; one was in second grade; one was a preschooler between 2 and 3½ years old; and the latter two children had normal IQs. Approximately half the second graders were reading at grade level (good readers), and half were below (poor readers). Family interactions and language development of the preschoolers, and reading ability of the second graders, were measured at this time. Five years later, the reading ability of the former preschoolers, now second graders, was assessed.

The influence of family interactions on reading ability was studied in two ways. In the first (Time 1) the assumption was made that the past and current patterns of family interactions were similar to each other. Specifically, that the present second graders, when younger, were treated much like their preschool siblings. Thus, current family interactions involving the preschoolers were compared with reading ability of the second graders. In the second (Time 2), family interactions and language development involving the preschoolers were compared with their reading ability 5 years later.

Norman-Jackson measured several interaction patterns. She found that at Time 1, parents of good readers tended to interact verbally more with their preschoolers than parents of poor readers did, but the two were equivalent in nonverbal interactions. Parents of good readers encouraged much more than they discouraged verbal interactions initiated by their preschoolers. But, parents of poor readers equally encouraged and discouraged these initiatives. Finally, in families of good, relative to poor, readers, the siblings verbally interacted a great deal with the preschoolers. Thus, children who are currently good readers come from families where language is encouraged and frequently used in their interactions with each other.

At Time 2, 71% of the former preschoolers on reaching second grade attained reading scores similar to their older siblings. When the patterns of previous family interactions were related to good and poor reading ability 5 years later, the findings were essentially the same as those described above. In addition, Norman-Jackson presented the language development data of the poor and good readers. As preschoolers, the children who became good readers used language in more mature ways than those who became poor readers.

In that Norman-Jackson's research involved a small number of families, the conclusions we state are somewhat tentative. The results indicate the following: Low SES black families who frequently interact verbally and encourage verbal exchange with their young children enhance the preschooler's language development. Subsequently, when these children start reading instruction, their language skills are sufficient for grade level reading to be acquired. The implications for low SES black families are clear—talk a lot to your young children and encourage them to initiate talk with you.

Genetic Influences on Learning to Read

At the turn of the century several researchers noted that reading disability runs in families (Lewitter, DeFries, & Elston, 1980). Since that time, others have observed that males are much more likely than females to be dyslexic—the ratio is about 3–4:1. These observations suggested that specific reading disability was an inherited characteristic. This suggestion was strongly supported by data from twin studies. These showed that if an identical twin is dyslexic, there is a 90% chance of the other being so; but if a fraternal twin is dyslexic, there is only a 30% chance of the other being so (Lewitter et al., 1980).

Recent studies have focused on three questions: (1) How many subtypes of dyslexia are inherited? (2) What is the genetic basis of this inheritance? (3) Is the genetic basis the same in males and females? Pennington and Smith (1983) have summarized the research bearing on these questions, giving special emphasis to the Colorado Family Reading Study. The Colorado project involved a large number of dyslexic children, their immediate families, and families matched with them in a variety of ways. In all, more than 1000 people have been evaluated (Lewitter et al., 1980).

Regarding the first question, several experiments have attempted to identify subtypes. The basic procedure is to administer a battery of cognitive and reading tests to dyslexics and normals and note whether patterns of deficits in the dyslexics emerge. Not all researchers employed the same battery, so differences in subtypes would be expected. Generally, however, four subtypes have been identified: (1) children who are deficient (relative to normal readers) in spatial reasoning; (2) children deficient in speed of coding written materials; (3) children deficient in neither; and (4) children deficient in both. The largest group is the third, referred to as "pure" dyslexia. Moreover, this is the only subtype that shows high heritability. That is, dyslexic parents and siblings of these children also tend to be of the pure subtype. For the others, dyslexic parents and siblings may or may not be of same subtype.

The second and third questions concerning the genetic bases and sex differences are answered through the use of elaborate statistical techniques involving comparisons among dyslexic children and their siblings, parents, and other close relatives. This research indicates that dyslexia is generally not transmitted by a single gene, but rather two or more; is not a single entity; instead, there are probably several inherited and noninherited subtypes; is not a sex-linked characteristic. The latter statement means that males and females are as likely to inherit dyslexia from their mothers as from their fathers. Pennington and Smith believe that relatively fewer females are dyslexic because they generally have superior language skills compared to males, which makes reading an easier task to master. Finally, the research implies that females may inherit dyslexia through a recessive gene, located on a non-sex-linked chromosome, but shows no similar pattern for males. Thus, the genetic basis of dyslexia may be different for males and females.

There are several implications of these findings. First, prospective parents who are dyslexic or have close relatives who are dyslexic should be genetically counseled. Second, parents who are likely to have dyslexic children should try to highly develop the language skills of their children, and should attempt to introduce them to reading materials in non-frustrating ways. Third, efforts should be made to identify dyslexic children before they enter school. This will allow for early special training in reading. Fourth, we know little about the psychological development of children who become dyslexics. It is possible that certain types of experiences might diminish or minimize the genetic effects. We need much more research on this issue than is currently being done.

Cross-Cultural Comparisons of Reading Disability

There are two related widespread beliefs among reading specialists: (1) that disabilities are very rare among Chinese and Japanese readers; and (2) that reading disabilities among children reading English and Romance languages are caused by the use of an alphabetic orthography (writing system).

The Chinese orthography consists of characters (logographs) that stand for whole words or parts of them. Each character has a particular sound, and Chinese script involves sequences of these characters, with no space between words. By the end of sixth grade, children have learned about 3000 characters, which allows them to read many more than 3000 words.

The Japanese orthography consists of two different syllable systems, each comprised of about 70 consistently pronounced characters, as well as a large number of Chinese characters. One syllable system, *hiragama*, is used to spell Japanese words, and the other, *katakana*, is for foreign words incorporated into the Japanese language. By the end of first grade, children have learned both syllable systems. By the end of the sixth grade, they have learned about 1850 Chinese characters.

Up until 1982, no research had ever compared reading abilities of these three groups. In that year, Harold Stevenson and his colleagues published the results of such a comparison (Stevenson et al., 1982). Three groups of urban fifth graders—from Japan, Taiwan, and Minneapolis, Minnesota—were evaluated. None were mentally retarded, or attended special schools. Each child was given a reading test comprised of reading single words aloud, reading text aloud, and answering true-false and multiple-choice items of the text material (comprehension). Great care was taken to make this test equivalent across the three cultures.

Testing for each child started at the fifth-grade level, and if all three parts were passed at 75% or better, he or she was moved up one level. Children scoring less than 75% on any part were moved down to the fourth-grade level. They kept moving down one grade level at a time until all three parts were passed at 75% correct. Three months after taking the reading test, the children were tested on 10 cognitive tasks that involved verbal and nonverbal abilities. Some of these were vocabulary, general information, verbal memory, spatial relations, and perceptual speed.

For each culture, the intercorrelations between the three parts of the reading test averaged about .9. This means that these parts were measuring essentially the same ability, and moreover, there were no cross-cultural differences in this pattern. Stevenson et al. presented two measures of reading disability. For the first, they found that 10% of Japanese, 3% of Chinese, and 3.5% of American children scored 2 or more years below grade level in reading. For the second, they found approximately 6% of the children in each country scoring average or higher on the cognitive tasks *and* scoring in the bottom tenth of their group in reading ability. The authors conclude from these results that there is no evidence to support the view that there are more reading-disabled American children than Japanese or Chinese.

Stevenson et al. carried out additional data analyses on the cognitive tasks comparing the 5% poorest readers in each culture with a group of average readers. These comparisons might allow inferences to be made about whether the processes underlying reading disabilities were different in these cultures. For all tasks and all cultures, the average readers performed better than the poor readers. For the Japanese and Chinese the greatest performance differences between the two reading groups involved the general information and verbal memory tasks. For the Americans, these two groups differed most on the general information and the perceptual tasks. The authors conclude from these findings that although the nature of the script may demand somewhat different cognitive processes to be employed in learning to read, the differences are relatively small. The major problem in all cases "is that of abstracting meaning from an abstract set of symbols, and the characteristics of the orthography play a less critical role than has sometimes been proposed" (p. 1179).

MATHEMATICS UNDERSTANDING

Because food sharing is an evolutionarily old human activity, it is likely that at least a primitive concept of numbers and arithmetic understanding evolved along with it. Not all food-sharing activities require an understanding of mathematics. For example, wolves and lions simultaneously eat a recently killed prey rather than divide it up into specific portions. Food sharing seen among contemporary gatherer-hunters, on the other hand, often involves long time delays between the killing or gathering and the division of food. Moreover, the sharing may be very intricate, taking into consideration previous debts and future obligations.

Unlike reading, mathematics can be performed without written materials. Advanced mathematics may require the use of writing, but counting and arithmetic can readily be accomplished in one's head. Because mathematical ability, like language, is an evolved characteristic, children from different societies probably learn it in similar ways. Unfortunately, this hypothesis about the development of mathematical ability can't be tested at the present time due to the lack of detailed cross-cultural analyses.

In the present section we first summarize research dealing with the numerical knowledge of the North American pre-school child. We then discuss the development of the American grade school child's arithmetical abilities. Finally we describe research carried out with the Oksapmin, whose number system differs dramatically from ours. The factor common to all these studies is Piaget's work on cognitive development and number conservation.

The Preschoolers' Concept of Number

Parents of preschool children are often dumbfounded when they watch their child perform the experiment shown in Fig. 6.4. In the first part, two rows with the same number of objects are lined up, one directly above the other. The children are asked (in this case) "Are there as many cups as there are saucers?" Almost all 2- to 5-year-olds say yes. Then, in the second part, while children are watching, the experimenter "stretches" the row of cups so that it is longer than the saucers. The Children are asked again "Are there as many cups as there are saucers?" Nearly all say no. When asked which is more, they say "cups". Piaget devised this procedure, and explains the failure of preschoolers to "conserve number" on the basis of their not yet having developed concrete operations. Between the ages of 5 and 7 nearly all Western industrialized children learn to perform this task correctly.

One major problem with Piaget's explanation is that it doesn't help us understand the number capabilities of preoperational children. Presumably, on the way to acquiring concrete operations they are developing some number schemas. What is needed is a fine-grained analysis of these

Part 1

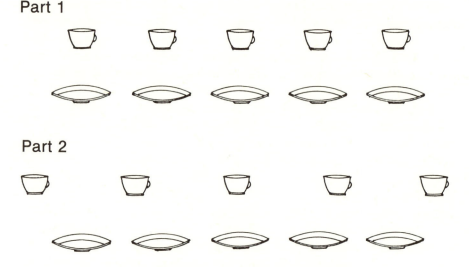

Part 2

FIG. 6.4   Piaget's number conservation experiment.

emerging abilities. Fortunately, two recent studies have accomplished just such an analysis, one by Fuson and Hall (1983) and the other by Gelman and Gallistel (1978). We focus on Gelman and Gallistel's research because it is more closely related to the work on number conservation.

Gelman and Gallistel maintain that between the ages of 2 and 5, children develop an understanding of five counting principles. This does not mean that they can verbalize the principles, but rather they act in ways consistent with them. Two types of research called the "Magic" and "Videotape" experiments bear on the three "how-to-count" principles. In the Magic experiment, children were first shown two plates containing unequal numbers of toys, e.g., three mice and five mice. The experimenter pointed to one of the plates and said, "This is the winner" and to the other, saying, "This is the loser." No mention was made about the different number of toys. The plates were covered and moved around as in the classic shell game, and the children were asked to point to the winner. The plates were uncovered and the children given feedback. This was done several times. Then the experimenter presented some trials in which, unknown to the child, the winner plate was tampered with. In some cases the spatial arrangement of the toys was changed, as in the Piaget experiment, in others, toys were substituted, and in others, toys were added or subtracted. When these plates were uncovered, the children usually showed surprise, and they were asked a series of questions designed to produce counting behaviors.

In the Videotape experiment, the three- to five-year-old child and the experimenter each sat next to a lazy Susan tray, in front of a hidden TV camera. The experimenter held a puppet that helped place and remove between 2 and 19 toys from each tray. The experiment consisted of asking the child (usually the puppet did the asking) how many toys were on the trays.

Most children in both experiments used numbers to count, but some used letters. A typical counting sequence of three toys might be "one, four, six." The first how-to-count principle is called One-to-One. This means that each item being counted is given a unique name. The above sequence obeys this principle, as well as the following two examples: "four, three, eighteen," "A, C, B." The sequence "one, two, one," does not, because two of the items have been given the same name. Children as young as 2 nearly always correctly use the One-to-One principle with small numbers of items. As the number of items to be counted increases from 5 to 19, the performance of all preschoolers gets increasingly worse. Typical errors are double counting and omitting items.

The second how-to-count principle is called Stable-Order. This means that whatever names children use for counting, they use them in the same order each time. For example, if in counting three mice, a child says, "one, four, five" and in counting three trucks, says "one, four, five," the Stable-Order principle has been obeyed. In both experiments, children performed remarkably well in following this principle, irrespective of the number of items to be counted. In the Videotape experiment, however, many of the three-year-olds didn't attempt to count the large collections, but the performance of the four- and five-year-olds was unaffected.

The third how-to-count principle is called Cardinal, which means that the last name given in a counting sequence is equal to the number of items counted. For example, if five toys were counted, the name given to the last toy, e.g., "five," also indicates the total number of toys in all, i.e., the cardinal number. If a child counted three toys as "one, four, five" and said that there were "five" toys in all, this behavior would obey the Cardinal principle. Although this principle seems obvious to us, there is no a priori reason why the last name given in a counting sequence should be used to describe the total number of items. In both experiments all preschool children were very successful in applying the Cardinal principle with small numbers of items. As items increased from 5 to 19 performance worsened for all.

Taken together, these results indicate that children as young as 2 can meaningfully count small collections of objects. With large collections, the Cardinal principle deteriorates earliest, then the One-to-One principle, and lastly, the Stable-Order principle. The major cause for these perform-ance decrements appears to be a faulty memory. Children forget where they are in the sequence and forget which numbers they've already used. Adults also occasionally make these mistakes.

The fourth, Abstraction principle, doesn't refer to how-to-count, but rather *what* to count. The essence of this principle is that any collection of same or different things can be counted. Gelman and Gallistel in reviewing their own and Gelman's earlier research conclude that preschoolers obey this principle. They are as accurate in counting collec-tions of different objects as they are with those all the same. For exam-ple, they showed no tendency to count only similar toys in a collection of similar and dissimilar ones. Also, in the Magic experiments, when a simi-lar toy was replaced by a dissimilar one, though surprised, children indi-cated that cardinal number was unaffected.

The fifth, Order-Irrelevance principle, states that the order in which items are named (counted) is irrelevant provided the above principles are followed. You can start your count anywhere and end up with the same results. This principle emphasizes the arbitrary nature of counting. Experiments dealing with knowledge of this principle ask children to count a group of toys and then either rearrange the toys or ask the chil-dren to start counting from a different toy without rearrangement. Three-year-olds have a fair amount of success on these tasks, but 4- and 5-year-olds do extremely well. Furthermore, these older children can give explanations similar to the principle; e.g., "you give them each a number but not the same number. You can change when you move them." (D.P. age 3 years, 11 months.)

Preschoolers also showed that they could reason about number. Two reasoning principles, Equivalence and Ordering Relations, emerge from the Magic experiments. Two collections are equivalent if their cardinal number is the same, irrespective of the spatial arrangements of the objects or what kind of objects they contain. When the experimenter sub-stituted or rearranged toys on the winner plate, but didn't add or sub-tract any, children said it was still the winner. One child said following a rearrangement, "They moved out. It still wins. It's three now and it was three before." When toys were added or subtracted, the children would "fix" the collection by appropriately reversing what the experimenter did in order to make it a winner. These behaviors indicate that the new collec-tion was equivalent in number to that seen prior to the manipulation.

Two collections are ordered, that is, one is more than the other, if their cardinal numbers are not the same. The Magic experiment by Bullock and

Gelman (1977) clearly shows this understanding. In the first part of a trial the children might be shown one-toy and two-toy plates, with the latter called the winner. In the second part, they would be shown three-toy and four-toy plates. Choosing the four-toy plate as the winner would indicate the use of the ordering relation. This was consistently done by 3- and 4-year-olds, but not by 2-year-olds.

Let's return to preschoolers' performance on Piaget's number conservation task. It would appear, based on the above research that they should not fail on this task. In fact, the Magic experiments show that children do conserve number in certain circumstances. Gelman and Gallistel believe that the key to understanding Piaget's task is that the two collections of objects are lined up in a one-to-one correspondence, as shown in Fig. 6.4. When preschoolers look at these collections they note their equivalence, but don't count the number of objects in each row. When the experimenter "stretches out" one of the rows, the perceptual one-to-one correspondence is destroyed and the preschoolers do not have the algebra reasoning capacity to deal with this situation. They fall back on perceptual evidence.

Gelman and Gallistel make a distinction between numerical reasoning and algebraic reasoning. Preschoolers have the former ability, which means that they can reason about collections having specific cardinal numbers. They do not have algebraic reasoning abilities, that is, they are unable to reason about collections not having specific cardinal numbers. If two collections of four objects each are shown to preschoolers and they count them, they can compare the number four of the first collection with the number four of the second. Changes in the arrangement of the objects don't affect the number four. This is numerical reasoning. Preschoolers need specific numbers to reason about. But when they are shown two equivalent collections, X and Y which are uncounted, they cannot reason about them. To do so would require the cognitive ability to reason about *relationships* between collections. Thus, they do not have the following understanding: "If two collections are equivalent in number, spatial rearrangements do not affect their equivalence." When children develop algebraic reasoning ability, they are able to solve Piaget's number conservation task.

Development of Arithmetic Understanding

Resnick (1983) has summarized recent research on the young schoolchild's abilities to add and subtract. She concludes that the major intellectual achievement that enables children to solve story problems and to make mental computations is their acquiring a "Part-Whole schema." This means that children can now think of numbers as being composed of other numbers; e.g., 9 is composed of 7 and 2, or 7 and 2 are parts of 9 (the whole). The preschooler knows that 9 is greater than 7, which is greater than 2, and that if 2 items are added to 7 items and counted, the total will be 9. He is unable to understand, however, that any 9 can be partitioned into any two parts so long as their combination equals 9.

Stated another way, the Part-Whole schema determines the mathematical relationships between certain sets of three numbers. Given the set of numbers, 6, 4, 2, this schema implies that $6 = 4 + 2$, $6 - 4 = 2$, and so on. The set of numbers 6, 4, 3 does not fulfill the part-whole relationships, and young school-age children can readily observe this.

Figure 6.5 is Resnick's depiction of how the Part-Whole schema underlies number sentences and story problems. In the center the dotted bar represents the whole and the smaller striped and white bars, the parts. When given an arithmetic problem, the child "maps" or transposes the numbers onto some mental representations (the bars), and then solves for the unknown. Several examples are given in the figure.

When young school children solve these problems "in their heads" they adopt efficient counting strategies. Unlike older children and adults who have memorized the answers to simple addition and subtraction problems, these children still count their way to an answer. The nature of these counting strategies can be inferred from reaction time experiments (Groen & Parkman, 1972). The assumption is made that the more they count, the slower will be their reaction time to problem solution. For example, in the problem $7 + 2 = ?$, if children start with 7 and count, "8, 9," their reaction time will be faster than if they start with 2, and count "3, 4, 5, 6, 7, 8, 9." Both will be faster than if they start with 0, and count off 2 and then 7. The data clearly show that children start with the larger of the two numbers whether stated first or second, and count off the smaller.

The strategy used for subtraction problems is more complicated. In the example $7 - 2 = ?$, one strategy would be to start with the 7 and count down two steps, "6, 5," for the answer. Another strategy would be to start with the 2 and count up until the 7 was reached, "3, 4, 5, 6, 7." The number of steps counted up would be the answer. Most children choose the strategy in any problem which leads to the fewest number of steps counted. Thus, in the problem $7 - 2 = ?$ children would count down for the answer, but in the problem $4 - 3 = ?$ they count up.

☐ Peter had some marbles
▨ David brought him 5 more marbles for their game
▨ Now Peter has 7 marbles
How many marbles did Peter have at the start ?

$7 - 5 = \square$
▨ ▨
$5 + \square = 7$
▨ ▨

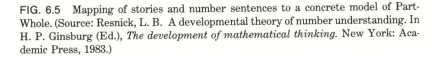

▨ 7 children are skating
▨ 5 are boys
☐ How many are girls ?

▨ Sam had 5 apples
☐ Sarah had 2
▨ How many did they have altogether ?

▨ Carol baked 7 dozen cookies
▨ John baked 5 dozen cookies
☐ How many more did Carol bake than John ?

FIG. 6.5   Mapping of stories and number sentences to a concrete model of Part-Whole. (Source: Resnick, L. B. A developmental theory of number understanding. In H. P. Ginsburg (Ed.), *The development of mathematical thinking.* New York: Academic Press, 1983.)

One of the interesting sidelights of Resnick's research is that her emphasis on the Part-Whole schema parallels Piaget's emphasis (Piaget & Inhelder, 1964) on the class schema in logical development. One of the major difficulties preoperational children have is understanding the distinction between "some" and "all" in problems dealing with class inclusion. When shown 7 blue squares and 2 red squares and asked "Are there more blue squares or more squares?" preoperational children say "More blue squares." In Resnick's terms, they fail to understand that the sum of the parts, 7 + 2, equals the whole, 9. School-age children, who are in the stage of concrete operations, solve part-whole and class inclusion problems. It appears, then, that knowledge of some and all is equivalent to knowledge of the Part-Whole schema.

Arithmetic Development in Papua, New Guinea

Although other studies of mathematical development among non-Western children have been carried out, Saxe's (1981) research with the Oksapmin in Papua New Guinea is particularly interesting. The Oksapmins live in remote villages accessible either by single-engine airplane or by foot. They subsist by raising pigs, cultivating yams, and hunting small game. In recent years they have been intensively studied by anthropologists. Their counting system differs from ours in two primary ways: (1) It does not have a base structure, whereas ours is base-10. (2) Each number is identified with a particular body part, starting with the right-hand thumb (1 in base-10), moving to the nose (14), ending with the small finger of the left hand (27). For numbers greater than 27, the counter loops back around the body. This number system is shown in Fig. 6.6.

In the first experiment Saxe compared two groups of unschooled children, 5 to 9 versus 11 to 16 years old, on three tasks. In the *Comparison*

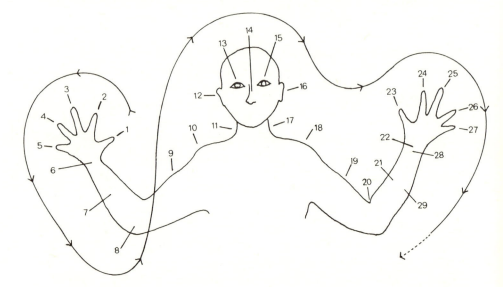

FIG. 6.6 The conventional sequence of body parts used by the Oksapmin. In order of occurrence: (1) tip ʌ na, (2) tipnarip, (3) bumrip, (4) h ʌ tdip, (5) h ʌ th ʌ ta, (6) dopa, (7) besa, (8) kir, (9) tow ʌ t, (10) kata, (11) gwer, (12) nata, (13) kina, (14) aruma, (15) tan-kina, (16) tan-nata, (17) tan-gwer, (18) tan-kata, (19) tan-tow ʌ t, (20) tan-kir, (21) tan-besa, (22) tan-dopa, (23) tan-tip ʌ na, (24) ta-tipnarip, (25) tan-bumrip, (26) tan-h ʌ tdip, (27) tan-h ʌ th ʌ ta. (Source: Saxe, G. B. Body parts as numerals: A developmental analysis of numeration among the Oksapmin in Papau, New Guinea. *Child Development*, 1981, *52*, 306–316. © The Society for Research in Child Development, Inc.)

tasks, they were shown parallel rows of unequal numbers of sticks and stones, with the longer row containing fewer items. They were asked which row contained the most items, and if they did not spontaneously count, were encouraged to do so. In the *Reproduction* tasks, a collection of items was placed behind them, and they were asked to place the same number of items in front of them. In the *Number Conservation* tasks a row of sticks was placed in front of them and they were asked to place the same number of stones next to the sticks. After they did so, the experimenter lined up the rows into a one-to-one correspondence and then stretched out the row of sticks. The children were asked whether there was the same number of sticks and stones.

As might be expected, on all tasks the older group performed more accurately than the younger one. Of interest is the development of counting strategies and the relationship between these strategies and task performance. Saxe identified two strategies, called mediational and premediational. In the former, children counted both collections of items and compared the cardinal numbers. In the latter strategy, children typically either counted only one collection, or counted both together, as if there were only one collection.

For the Comparison and Reproduction tasks fewer than half the younger but all the older children used a mediational strategy. The older children were always accurate on these tasks. On the number conservation tasks, approximately half the children who used a mediation strategy (both groups combined) performed correctly. However, virtually all children who used a premediation strategy erred. Saxe concludes from these results that development of number understanding of the Oksapmin parallels that of Western children in two ways. First, premediational precede mediational strategies in making numerical comparisons and reproductions. Western children, however, acquire mediational strategies at an earlier age. Second, mediational strategies are required for successful number conservation, but they don't guarantee it.

In the second experiment, Saxe studied the nature of children's counting errors with unschooled 7- to 9-year-olds versus 12- to 16-year-olds. He told the children a story about a man counting yams on two different days. On one day he counted to here, pointing to a particular body part, and on the other day he counted to here, pointing to another body part. The story was repeated with six different pairs of pointed-to numbers. Three of the pairs involved symmetrical body parts, e.g., left biceps (19)/ right biceps (9), and three, asymmetrical pairs, e.g., right wrist (6)/ left ear (16), as seen in Fig. 6.6. The children were asked after each story whether the man counted the same or a different number of yams on the 2 days.

When the stories involved asymmetrical body parts, all the older children but only about half the younger ones were always correct. When symmetrical body parts were involved, about half the older and one fourth of the younger children were always correct. In other words, they confused the same body parts located on opposite sides of the body with the same number. Thus, these children have not abstracted fully (in Gelman and Gallistel's sense) the number property of the body part from its bodily identification. Confusion at such late ages seems to be unique to a counting system linked with parts of the body. More generally, this implies that we don't know the extent to which other number developmental findings from Western cultures depend upon the particular experiences of these cultures.

SUMMARY

The starting point of this chapter was the idea that human intelligence was an evolved characteristic that permitted our various forms of cultural adapation. Symboling abilities are at the heart of these adaptations. Premack's research with chimpanzees clearly demonstrates intellectual and linguistic capabilities rarely seen in nonprimates, which parallel accomplishments in young children. Research with American Sign Language taught to chimpanzees and gorillas, and computer symbols taught to chimpanzees, have focused on ape use of words, and the use and understanding of grammar. Their word use is comparable to that of young children, but their grammar seems to be limited to generating two-word sentences. It appears that apes can learn the rudiments of human language, but their use of it reflects both intellectual limitations as well as the unique ways they were taught it.

Recent research in human language development has shifted away from Chomsky's view that development involves the unfolding of a universal innate grammar. Along with this shift has come the realization of previous oversimplifications, such as the notions that young children use grammar and words the same way as adults.

Lenneberg's research on the parallels in motor and language development indicates that certain aspects of language development are canalized. For example, the sequences of motor and language acquisition are the same for normal and Down's syndrome children, except that rate of development is proportionately slower for the latter group.

Prior to learning to speak, the sounds infants produce, as well as those they discriminate, follow a universal pattern. By one year of age, however, cultural differences in these abilities emerge. The first 50 words children acquire are typically of people, animals, or things that move or change in some way. Children will often invent words to convey concepts, and generalize words to other similar things or activities.

Most children start creating two-word sentences once they have a 50-word vocabulary. Nelson has identified two patterns of this development in American children. The referential pattern emphasizes nouns and verbs, whereas the expressive pattern, pronouns and relational terms. Until age 3, children's sentence structure reflects semantic rules and/or more narrow formulas used to convey meanings. After age 3, they develop and use grammatical constructions.

Grammatical understanding continues to develop to adolescence. Two examples were given: use of the passive tense, and ability to detect sentence ambiguity. For the former, active nonreversible sentences were easiest to understand, and passive reversible the most difficult. Regarding sentence ambiguity, phonological confusions were easiest to detect, followed by lexical, then surface and deep-structure confusions.

Speech acts are conversational units designed to have some effect on listeners. Children first acquire the ability to use and understand representatives and directives. Between 5 and 7 they correctly use commissives, and after age 7, expressives and declarations. As children mature they develop the art of speech indirection, which is often important in social interactions.

Most Western definitions of intelligence are tied to academic success. This linkage is a recent historical event attributed to mandatory public education. Three rational approaches to intelligence were discussed: (1) it is species-specific; (2) it is developmental within a species; (3) it differentiates one individual from another. Only the second has received systematic exploration, by Piaget and his collaborators.

The two broad approaches to measuring intelligence focus on abilities and processes, respectively. The major issue for the abilities approach has been whether intelligence is best characterized by a single general factor "g," several less general, more independent factors, or by both. The current evidence favors the general plus more specific factors. The processing approach focuses on how information is internally represented, strategy use in processing it, the component parts of any strategy, and how decisions are made. Recent work has attempted to bridge the gap between these two approaches and Piaget's work.

Intelligence, as measured by IQ, is not a stable characteristic. In normal-bright children it changes, on average, 28 points between the ages of 2½ and 17 years. Year-to-year correlations are also generally low until about age 8, where they average about .8 or higher through adulthood. Despite these great fluctuations, recent work with infants indicates that memory capacity may be a stable predictor of IQ, at least to the extent that IQ depends on it.

The data from dozens of studies have convinced most behavior geneticists that between 50% and 80% of individual differences in IQ can be attributed to genetic differences. There is no convincing evidence, however, that racial differences in IQ are genetically determined. The environmental effects on IQ development can be substantial. Quality of parent-child interactions, as measured by the Home Scale, has been found to be appreciably related to children's early mental development. These relationships were found across a range of SES levels, mothers' IQ, infancy birth risk, and the presence of day care.

Reading is a recent human invention from an evolutionary view. It is defined as "extracting information from text." Sounding out letters, syllables, and words are all important components, but the key element is to read with meaning. There are enormous differences between reading and listening, which make reading a different, difficult, and unnatural task.

Reading can be divided into two broad categories of processes, decoding print into words, and comprehending sentences and paragraphs. Both sets of processes are simultaneously employed, but the beginning reader typically pays more attention to decoding. As children become skilled readers, decoding becomes automatic, and attention shifts to developing comprehension strategies.

Approximately two thirds of black children from low SES families read below grade level. Norman-Jackson's research has suggested that much of this deficit can be prevented in the home. She found that black low SES families with good second-grade readers interact verbally a great deal, and encourage verbal initiatives by their young children. As a consequence, the preschoolers develop good language skills prior to starting reading instruction. Families with poor second-grade readers lack these characteristics.

Dyslexia was defined as failure to master normal grade-level reading when there are no obvious factors producing this retardation. Dyslexics show a variety of reading deficits relative to normals, some of which are probably neurologically based. Vellutino argues that language deficiencies are at the core of all dyslexias. The genetics research indicates that dyslexia is not a single entity, is not sex-linked, and is probably transmitted by two or more genes.

Finally, cross-cultural research comparing reading abilities of urban Chinese, Japanese, and American fifth graders finds few differences in frequency of dyslexia across these cultures. Thus, differences in orthography probably have limited effects on learning to read.

Children's development of number understanding starts by at least age 2. Between 2 and 5 children acquire a good understanding of five counting principles using small collections of objects. They name each counted object uniquely, use the same order of names when counting, and identify the last number in the count sequence as the cardinal number for the collection as a whole. They know that collections made up of different items can be counted and that the order in which they start to count is irrelevant. Furthermore, preschoolers can compare two collections of objects and determine whether their number is equivalent or one is greater than the other. They fail on Piaget's number conservation tasks because they have not yet developed the ability to reason about collections that do not have specific cardinal numbers.

The major arithmetic acquisition of school children is developing an understanding of the Part-Whole schema. This allows them to carry out subtraction and addition among numbers (as opposed to things) and to solve story problems. While carrying out arithmetic problems, they use efficient counting strategies, which differ for addition and subtraction problems. The Part-Whole schema has many parallels to class schema in logical understanding.

Research with the Oksapmin in Papua New Guinea finds parallels and differences in the development of number understanding to Western industrialized children. The Oksapmin counting system does not have a base structure. Moreover each number from 1 to 27 is identified with a particular body part. Like the Western children, premediational counting strategies are used before mediational ones. The mediational strategies are also necessary for successful number conservation. Unlike Western children, many Oksapmin adolescents still have not abstracted number concepts from body parts. This confusion is probably unique to their counting system.

7 Socialization: Schools, Television, and Family

In this chapter we discuss some of the social, emotional, and cognitive effects that schooling, television, and families have on children. These three socialization agents, along with that of peers, are the major influences in the development of children. In several of the preceding chapters we discussed parental and peer influences on development. In most cases, the primary focus was on topics such as personality or social development, and the secondary focus, on the socializing agent. In the present discussion we reverse the emphasis by placing primary focus on the socializing agent. Thus, instead of asking how the development of self-esteem is influenced by television, we now consider the agents, individually, of families, schools, and television, in relation to their effect on children. The major advantage of this approach is that it allows us to gain a broad understanding of these socialization agents. We omit the topic of peer influences in this chapter because that subject has already been extensively dealt with.

Some of the specific issues examined here are as follows. We first discuss the impact of schools on the ability of children to form friendships. This issue is closely connected with children's relationships with the authority figures in their schools. We then look at the long-term consequences of one of the most intensive government intervention programs in existence—a program designed to prepare low SES pre-schoolers for academic achievement. And we also examine the cross-cultural affects of schooling. A major goal of schooling is the student's acquisition of literacy. Sylvia Scribner and Michael Cole (1981) have studied a culture in which literacy and schooling exist independently of one another—e.g., some members of the culture are literate, but have not attended school. Do literacy and schooling have equivalent effects on cognitive development?

The effects of television on children's development are still being widely studied. Some conclusions are controversial: for example, that television violence increases children's aggression. We also examine the consequences of television viewing in relation to the cognitive, social, and emotional functioning of children.

The chapter concludes with a discussion of the child in a family context. The primary data source here is clinical reports by others and my own personal observations of families in family therapy. As was discussed in Chapter 1, the clinical case study method is one among many ways by which we can learn about children's development. Although case studies lack in experimental rigor, they more than make up for this lack by providing a richness of detail in non-laboratory settings.

SCHOOLING

Cusick (1973) argues that schools are typically concerned with two major types of activities, transmitting knowledge and maintaining order. Virtually all schools are arranged so that the teacher has final authority about what goes on in the classroom. The teacher sets the classroom goals, determines activities, and disciplines misconduct. In cases of serious misconduct, the student is sent to a still higher authority, usually a vice-principal, who may have the student beaten (educators refer to this as "paddling") or suspended. Beatings are usually reserved for pre-adolescents and young adolescents, probably because they are smaller, cannot vote, and do not pay taxes.

Cusick maintains that schools operate on the principle that students can't be trusted. If discipline isn't firm they will be disruptive. If homework assignments aren't collected, the work won't be done. If attendance isn't taken, they will skip class. If tests aren't closely monitored, they will cheat. One not-so-subtle message of this process is that the hallway pass is symbolic of the entire set of assumptions educators make about students.

Academic Settings and Friendship Formation

Despite the aura of mistrust generated in schools, most children willingly, even eagerly, go. The major attraction for them is clearly the other students. Although learning can be and often is enjoyable, most primary grade school children will tell you that their favorite times are lunch and recess, sometimes gym, and maybe art.

It is a fair statement that children in school are first interested in making and maintaining friendships, and second in doing well academically. Academic success will usually not produce friendships, but friendships often can lead to academic success. Schools are stressful places. Between the years 1977 and 1979, over 60% of families seeking treatment for a child at the Philadelphia Child Guidance Clinic listed school misbehaviors as a major problem.

Two aspects of classroom settings have been examined in regard to friendship formation. Hallinan (1976, 1979) has compared peer relationships in open and traditional classrooms for children in the primary grades. Classrooms typically differ on how much instruction is individualized, how much the teacher controls student movement, conversation, and assignments, and how closely the teacher supervises student tasks. She found that in open classrooms more children had friends, there were fewer "stars" and isolates, and there was a more equal distribution of friendship choices. There was no difference, however, between the two types of classrooms in terms of the number and size of cliques.

Bossert (1979) studied in a traditional school the effects of teaching style and type of tasks assigned on friendship formation and self-esteem. His was an observational study of four Grade 3 and Grade 4 classes over a period of 2 years. Because of its uniqueness, we describe his results in some detail. In the first year of the study, he selected two Grade 3 classes in a predominantly white upper-middle-class school, whose teachers had very different teaching styles. In the second year, the students moved on to Grade 4 where half were placed in a class whose teacher had a similar style to their Grade 3 teacher, and half were placed with a teacher who had a different style.

The teaching styles were evaluated on the basis of how frequently they used three kinds of classroom activities—recitation, class tasks, and multiple tasks (multitasks). When recitation is used, the teacher controls the flow of activity, selectively calls on different students to "recite," and tries to make sure that all students are paying attention. Class tasks are typically activities that all students carry out at the same time, such as math assignments, silent reading, work sheets, and tests. There is usually one basic task all are working on, there is little choice in task selection, and the teacher is the only person who evaluates and rewards students' performance.

In multitask classrooms, on the other hand, several different activities are going on at the same time, children frequently work in small groups with little direct teacher supervision, and the students have a great deal of choice. One of the third-grade and one of the fourth-grade teachers used recitation about 45% of the time, and the other third- and fourth-grade teachers used it about 20% of the time. The recitation-oriented teachers used multitasks about 10% and the nonrecitation teachers used them about 30% of the time. Bossert makes the important observation that when the four teachers used recitation they reacted to the students in a similar way. The same was true when the teachers used class tasks and multitasks.

Bossert found that all teachers claimed they gave individual assistance to those students who were having the most difficulty. But observation showed that this was true for only the nonrecitation-oriented teachers. The recitation-oriented teachers gave the most assistance to the best students in the class. In addition, they called on these students more frequently during recitation, showing them off for all the students. They also gave the bright students the most privileges. Thus, "the rich get richer" in recitation-oriented classes.

Bossert's second finding is that in the recitation-oriented classes peer associations and friendships were markedly influenced by academic achievement. When children were observed during lunch, free time, recess, and multitask activities, they grouped themselves primarily on the basis of their recitation ability. Even children who had been friends in their third-grade nonrecitation-oriented class stopped associating with each other if they had different achievement levels. Bossert believes that the causes for the phenomenon are the teacher's preferential treatment of the brightest students, the competition created between students for classroom rewards (e.g., giving the correct answer), which leads to bright students supporting each other, and the status differences created by the teacher and the reward system. In the nonrecitation-oriented classrooms there was no evidence of friendships being influenced by academic achievement. Children associated with each other on the basis of shared academic and nonacademic interests, even if they were at different ability levels. Bossert believes that in these classrooms, since recitation takes up such a small portion of class time, the rewards and status that go along with recitation ability are minimized.

Joyce Epstein (1978) carried out a longitudinal study involving several thousand urban middle (Grades 5 to 8) and high school (Grades 9 to 12) students. Like Hallinan, her major focus was the effect of open versus traditional classrooms on friendship selection. Unlike Hallinan, Epstein examined the influences friends exert on each other's attitudes and academic performance.

In general, Hallinan's findings were reproduced for middle, but not high school students. Epstein asked the students to list the names of their three best school friends. Middle school children from open classrooms were more likely to be chosen as a best friend than those from traditional classrooms. There were no appreciable differences for the high school students. However, at all age levels, children in open classrooms chose more varied friends than those from traditional classrooms, e.g., different SES, achievement levels, and gender. Additionally, at all grade levels, friendship choices were more likely to be *reciprocated* in open than traditional classrooms.

Traditional, but not open, classrooms are likely to have stars – students nominated by the teachers as highly independent and achieving. These students are very popular with both peers and teachers. The presence of stars often leads to the opposite – isolates. Epstein, like Bossert, believes that traditional teaching methods foster these discrepancies. She states:

> The "good students" in teachers' eyes in traditional schools are those who can function in school independently and these students are clearly labeled and favored. The label is known to students as well, and those favored by teachers become good all-around students to their peers. In the open schools more students are independent in school and so the "good students" are more numerous or less specifically labeled by teachers. Under such conditions, student choices of peers with positive characteristics will not necessarily match the choices of their teacher, and more (different) students may be selected. (p. 25–26)

One year after their initial choices of best friends, Epstein compared students' current academic attitudes and performances with those of the previous year as a function of two factors: (1) open versus traditional classroom, and (2) the initial scores made by their best friends. Surprisingly, the nature of the classroom had little impact on score changes. However, choice of friends had a substantial influence, for both middle and high school students. In general, selecting high-scoring friends was associated with score increases, and selecting low-scoring friends, with decreases. For example, children whose best friends initially scored high in self-reliance or mathematics had higher scores one year later than those whose best friends initially scored low. These effects were greater for the academic achievement areas than attitudinal ones. Thus, as Epstein points out, friendship choices and academic success are not necessarily antagonistic; in fact, they can, and frequently do, go hand-in-hand.

Friendship Versus Authority in Junior and Senior High Schools

Relative to eighth-grade students, the subjects of Metz's (1978) study, elementary and younger middle school children are docile creatures who accept the values and authority of their teachers. Taking a Piagetian perspective, the younger children tend to believe that rules and laws are enduring facts given from higher up, whereas the older ones realize that almost everything, especially interpersonal dealings, may be negotiable. Eighth graders often have a strong sense of fairness and a weaker tendency to please their elders. Respect must be earned and doesn't necessarily come packaged with the role that an adult is following, e.g., being a teacher.

Metz's observations were of classrooms in two traditional schools that had recently been racially and socially integrated. Prior to desegregation they were almost exclusively white and middle class. They were integrated by a minority of black, low-SES students. Most of the academic classes in the schools were ability tracked into five levels. The upper two levels were almost exclusively white, while the third through fifth were racially mixed, with progressively more blacks appearing in the lower levels. This is a typical pattern in schools comprised of white middle- and black low-SES students. The white students, but not the blacks, tended to share the academic values and expectations of the predominantly white middle-class teachers. These black/white differences influenced the starting positions in authority conflicts between students and teachers.

The two dominant conflict issues for both the students and teachers were control and self-esteem. From the teachers' perspective, it was a given fact that they were in charge and students should be attentive and attempt to learn. From the students' perspective, teachers could control the class if they were clever enough, and should assign tasks that students were competent and interested in performing. From our previous discussion we know that group functioning is improved if goals are shared. The different starting positions of students and teachers in integrated classrooms produced group goals that were not shared, at least not initially. In many cases students and teachers did work together to form common goals, and these classes worked well. In other classes teachers were unable to share authority, and as a consequence, struggles for authority became the primary task for the academic year. The self-esteem of both teachers and students suffered—the teachers couldn't teach and the students couldn't learn.

Both the high- and low-track students challenged the teachers over these issues, but they did so in different ways. The high-track students forced their teachers to prove their intellectual expertise. They would ask teachers about obscure issues, question their grammar and the validity of the rules. Occasionally a teacher was no match for a classroom of honor students. The low-track students forced their teachers to become "con men." Students would behave in disruptive ways that pressed the rules to the limit. For example, one student "seemed" to get his foot stuck in the chair in front of him, and couldn't "seem" to get it out. The teacher had no way of knowing whether his foot was stuck or not. But the whole class became involved in helping him. He won the battle for control and the teacher lost.

Eighth-grade classrooms obviously deal with reading, writing, and arithmetic too. But the context in which academic learning occurs involves struggles for self-esteem and control. Students learn about their abilities to work with authority through these struggles. When both teachers and students win the struggles, mutually accommodating to one another, academic learning can proceed smoothly and enhance the self-esteem of all concerned.

A different set of issues emerges when we look at seniors in a traditional high school, the subjects of Cusick's (1973) study. At the time of data collection Cusick was a young looking man in his early thirties. His intent was to learn about student life in high school from a student perspective. Accordingly, for one academic year he led the life of a senior, going to class, eating in the cafeteria, sneaking a smoke in the lavatory, going to parties during the weekend, and "hanging out" with the boys. With the help of the school administrators, Cusick was eased into membership in a tight group of seven male athletes. Eventually he joined another group made up of six delinquents, and also befriended several members of the music-drama group. All the students knew why he was at the school, but Cusick maintains that within 3 months, that role was unimportant to them.

Cusick, a former high school teacher, was surprised by his observations. It quickly became clear to him that the school consisted of both an official system centered in classes, school work and activities, and an unofficial student group-centered system with its own separate authority. The unofficial system consumed more time, energy, and commitment than the official one. It also provided more rewards. During the entire year, Cusick rarely heard the students discussing any academic activities outside of class. On one occasion a person started to talk about some recent academic issue, and no one present even looked at him to acknowledge that this was a worthwhile topic.

Students who were members of groups, and this includes the overwhelming majority, spent nearly all their out-of-class time, and some in-class time, keeping in close contact with their small circle of friends. School work was almost never demanding and nearly all students learned that they could meet standards with only a minimal amount of work. Since most students planned to go to a state college where acceptance was assured, they engaged in those activities that were the most satisfying. These were not academic work.

In large part Cusick views the problem as being a function of the social structure of the traditional school. Among these he lists the following: Teachers are the experts and students are treated as at best marginally competent; teachers talk and students (at least pretend to) listen; students are treated as a batch, and not as individuals; activities are routine and often mundane; goals are often vague and oriented to a distant future. The primary effects of this structure are infrequent student-teacher interaction; little student choice in classroom activities; weak involvement in academic activities; and students' belief that their major requirement is to follow the rules. The result is that there are relatively few immediate rewards available from academic involvement. Students show up because they are required to. They stay until they graduate, because students need the degree to move on to the next phase in their careers. And along the way they learn that they can best beat the system by "going along."

Based on Cusick's arguments, it might be assumed that more collaborative, mutually satisfying student-teacher relationships would be found in schools with open classrooms. Epstein and McPartland (1978) have provided the relevant data. In their study, thousands of middle, junior, and senior high students from traditional and open schools filled out questionnaires concerning authority relationships, teacher expectations, and various attitudes and perceptions about their school experiences.

In general, there were slight differences on most measures between the two types of schools. For example, students from open schools were no more likely to believe that teachers shared decision making with them than those from traditional schools. Also, students from open schools were only slightly more likely to believe that teachers wanted originality rather than conformity in their classwork. In regard to attitudes and self-perceptions, students from open schools saw themselves as more self-reliant and evaluated their teachers more positively. However, there were essentially no differences between the two types of schools regarding self-esteem, perceived control of the environment, educational aspirations, or academic achievement.

Are Cusick's arguments incorrect? Only partially, for Epstein and McPartland also report that in both types of schools, there are teachers who do share authority with their students. In these cases, students' attitudes, self-perceptions, teacher evaluations and perceptions are all very positive. Thus, the negative effects Cusick and others report are probably caused by the existence of a student-teacher power hierarchy. This hierarchy predisposes both groups to adopt certain roles that are frequently antagonistic. When teachers are able to modify their roles, and encourage students by example to do likewise, the mutual benefits possible in the relationship become realized. Unfortunately, changing the structure of the schools has little impact on this.

Lasting Effects of Early Education

The title of this section is the title of Lazar and Darlington's (1982) monograph, which evaluated the long-term effects of eleven programs designed to prepare low-SES preschoolers (90% black) for academic success. These programs were independently initiated by separate research teams between 1958 and 1968 and were each in operation between 1 and 5 years. None were Head Start programs, but rather had similar clientele and were experimental in nature. The researchers hoped that their efforts, if successful, would influence the ways Head Start and other early education programs would be run.

The eleven programs varied a great deal from each other. Six were based at a preschool, with children attending about 4 hours a day, 5 days a week for an academic year. Two were home based, with a teacher visiting once or twice a week for about an hour, training the mother on how to instruct her child. These programs extended for about 2 academic years. The remaining three programs were combinations of the above two. In all cases, the focus was to develop language and other school-related cognitive skills of the preschoolers.

In 1975, the directors of these projects were contacted by Lazar and Darlington and asked to collaborate on further research designed to measure the academic effects of their programs. The children were then between 8 and 18 years old. Data collection occurred in 1976, with approximately 55% of the original subjects participating. The 1976 research compared these children (treatment subjects) with comparable ones (control subjects) who did not have early education experiences, on four broad areas: (1) school competence; (2) developed abilities; (3) attitudes and values; and (4) impact on the family.

Two measures were used for assessing school competence – whether children were enrolled in remedial special education classes, or repeated a grade. Answers to these questions go to the heart of the study. Children who are adequately prepared for school are enrolled in regular classes, stay in them, and proceed through with their age-mates. The responses to these questions were gratifying. Approximately 29% of the controls, but only 14% of the treatment children, were ever assigned to special education classes. The grade repetition results were not as strong, with 30% of the controls and 25% of the treatment children being retained at least once. When the authors asked what percentage of the two groups were either placed in special classes or repeated a grade, the results were striking: 44% of the controls and 25% of the treatment children fell into this combined category. Thus, the relatively brief early education experiences had important lasting effects.

What might be the basis for these differences? For an answer we turn to the other questions. Although the early education programs did not have raising IQ as a major goal, their focus on language and cognitive skills might have had this effect. When the IQs of treatment and control children were compared immediately at the end of program enrollment, there was a 7.5-point difference favoring the early education children. One and 2 years later the difference was 4.5 points, and 3 and 4 years later, 3 points. From 5 years onward, there were no reliable differences between the two groups. Although a 7.5-point IQ difference might have an impact on school performance, these children were at most in kindergarten at the end of the program. It is very unlikely that the 3 to 4.5-point "advantage" in Grades 1 through 4 could have produced the dramatic differences in school competence.

What about the mathematics and reading achievement levels of the two groups? Lazar and Darlington compared them during Grades 3 through 6 and found that in all programs the treatment children scored higher than the controls in either reading or mathematics. In general, the relative gains in mathematics were higher than those in reading, but in some programs, treatment children scored higher in both. There were no reliable age changes for these patterns. Thus, the superior mathematics and reading skills of the treatment children probably explain their superior school competence. But what accounts for their superior mathematics and reading skills?

The answer appears to be in the children's and parents' attitudes and values. When the children were asked, "Tell me something you've done that made you feel proud of yourself," the treatment children were more likely than the controls to describe an achievement that was school or work related. Treatment and control children, however, did not differ in either occupational or educational aspirations. The mothers of both groups were asked, "Overall, how satisfied are you with how your child has done in school?" Mothers of the treatment children were more satisfied than those of the control children. Finally, they were asked, "What kind of job would you like your child to have later in life?" Mothers of treatment children had higher aspirations than those of control children. Taken together, this pattern of responses indicates that treatment children relative to controls feel greater rewards for school achievement. Moreover, this school achievement orientation is supported by both their mothers' pleasure in their school progress and by their encouragement (push?) to succeed occupationally.

In examining the entire pattern of results, the following scenario is a plausible explanation of the positive lasting effects of early education for low-SES children. While enrolled in these programs, most of the children quickly acquire school-related skills and interests that are obvious to their mothers. Their mothers compare these children to siblings and to children of neighbors, and involve themselves more in the education process. They become hopeful and encouraging of the potential academic success of these children. When the graduates themselves enter kindergarten, they experience success relative to the control children, which reinforces a school achievement orientation. Mothers' encouragement and their own feelings of success mutually influence one another, which keeps the children on a track of steady progress.

Schooling and Cognitive Development:
Cross-Cultural Comparisons

In recent years an extensive literature has accumulated concerning cross-cultural effects of schooling on cognitive development. Barbara Rogoff (1981) has summarized much of it. We subsequently return to her analysis. Two among these studies stand out for special discussion, those by Stevenson and his colleagues (Stevenson et al., 1978) and by Sharp, Cole, and Lave (1979).

Stevenson et al. studied groups of 5- and 6-year-olds from five different geographic/cultural regions of Peru: Quechua Indians living in or near the jungle village of Lamas; Mestizos who are racial mixtures of Indians and Europeans, from Lamas; low-SES Quechuas from Lima, the capital; low-SES Mestizos from Lima; and middle-SES Mestizos and whites from Lima. There were tremendous differences among the parents and the households of these groups. Virtually all the middle-class parents had gone to college, whereas the average low-SES Mestizo parent had 7 years of education and the typical Quechua parent less than 2. All of the middle-class Limans had radios, books, and children's toys, and 88% owned television sets. None of the Quechuas from Lamas had a television, books, or children's toys; but 18% owned radios. The remaining three groups fell in the middle with the Mestizos being more advantaged than the Quechuas. There were also major differences among the groups concerning parents' attempts to teach their children school-related information, e.g., colors, counting, letters, music. The rank ordering here was middle class, Mestizo Lima, Mestizo Lamas, Quechua Lima, and Quechua Lamas.

In Peru, school is mandatory at age 6. However, all the middle-class children, but only about one half of the others attend at that age. Cognitive comparisons began when the children were in their second month of school, and continued until the eighth month. Each child was evaluated once with 15 tests. The tests were designed to measure four clusters of abilities: (1) contextual memory, which tapped the ability to remember information contained in meaningful contexts; (2) spatial representation, which involved several types of spatial responses; (3) serial memory, which tested the ability to remember items or responses presented in serial order; and (4) visual analysis and conceptualization, which included tasks requiring different types of visual thinking.

The first question asked is, do unschooled 6-year-olds perform better on these tasks than 5-year-olds? Generally not. On only 4 of the 15 comparisons was there a reliable performance advantage favoring the older children. Thus, 1 year of age, per se, had little effect on cognitive development. Second, what' is the effect of 2 to 8 months of school on cognitive development? The results were striking with the students performing reliably better than the nonstudents on all 15 tests. Moreover, on most tests, there was less performance variability among the schooled than the unschooled children. These results are amazing when considered in light of the fact that the schooled children were there at most 8 months.

Does social class and geographic/culture have an impact on schooling effects? When the middle-class and Mestizo 5- and 6-year-olds from Lima were compared, the former performed reliably better on 7 of the 15 tests. When the unschooled Quechua children from Lamas and Lima were compared, the Limans performed reliably better on 9 of the tests, and those from Lamas on 3. In a similar comparison among the Mestizos, those from Lamas also performed better on the same three tests—perceptual learning, and placing objects in single or double series. Thus, growing up in a jungle environment leads to particular strengths in seeing similarities and differences in visual stimulation.

The pattern of results from this experiment can be summed up in Fig. 7.1. Along the bottom are 14 of the tests grouped on the basis of the way they cluster. Each of the four panels represents the performance of the group or groups whose results were similar. The three numbers, −1, 0, +1, within each panel represent scores substantially below the overall average (−1), average scores (0), and substantially above average (+1). Looking at the top panel, the two Lamas Quechua groups and the Lamas unschooled Mestizos did poorly or average on all tests, except seriation and perceptual learning. The Lamas schooled Mestizos (second panel) performed above average on everything except the first cluster. In the third panel, the three schooled groups from Lima showed their greatest strength in the first two clusters [through (6)], but were average or above on nearly all the other tests. The Lima unschooled children (fourth panel) showed their greatest strength in the first two clusters, but overall, their performances were average or poor.

Two conclusions stand out from these analyses. Brief exposure to schooling among 6-year-olds has profound effects on their cognitive test performance. Moreover, geographic/cultural experiences differentially predispose certain cognitive abilities to blossom, and others to remain close to the vine.

The research by Sharp et al. (1979) was carried out in the rural Yucatan peninsula of Mexico primarily with Mayan (Indians) and Mestizo subjects ranging in age from about 10 to 15 years. The subjects lived in towns

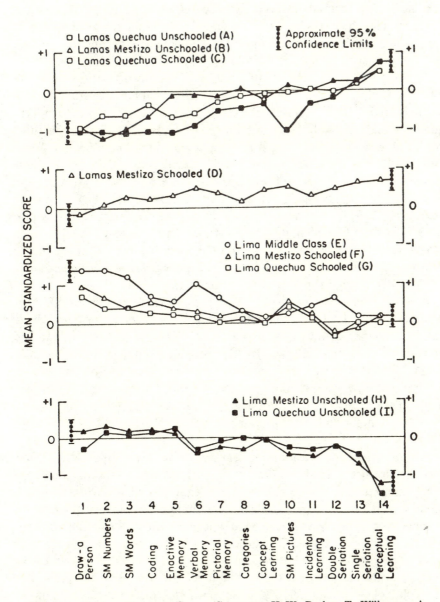

FIG. 7.1 Clusters of groups. (Source: Stevenson, H. W., Parker, T., Wilkonson, A., Bonnevaux, B., & Gonzalez, M. Schooling, environment, and cognitive development: A cross-cultural study. *Monographs of the Society for Research in Child Development*, 1978, *43*, No. 175 © The Society for Research in Child Development, Inc.)

varying in size from about 20 to 200,000 persons. In general, the larger the town, the larger the number of schools, the higher the grades taught, the greater the likelihood of electricity, telephones, telegraph, post office, restaurants, and so on.

At the time of the study (1970–1974) all children were required to attend school, where each received the same curriculum for Grades 1 to 6. During the first year, students started to learn to read and got exposed to numbers and culturally relevant information. By the end of the third year, students had been taught a fair amount of mathematics, e.g., fractions, multiplication, division, geometric figures, and had developed their reading skills. By Grade 6, they had progressed in mathematics to algebra and used their reading to develop detailed knowledge of public health, ecology, human anatomy, and biological classification. They also read essays by Spanish and foreign authors. In secondary school (Grades 7 to 9) students chose either a vocational track leading to skills suitable for careers such as carpenter, electrician, dress designer, or an academic track that provided the groundwork for further study.

The research strategy used by Sharp et al. was to compare different age-groups of school children with adults in their community who have had no schooling or only specified amounts. Thus, the effects of age and amount of schooling on cognitive development could be independently evaluated. Three types of cognitive tasks were used, those dealing with categorization, memory, and problem solving. Different groups of students and adults were used in these studies. The students were referred to as "students" whether they were Mayan or Mestizo. The adults were identified by their ethnic group.

Several types of categorization tasks were used. In some of these, correct classification required that the subject attend to and use the structural characteristics of the stimuli. For example, when presented with cards showing different sizes, colors, and numbers of kernels of corn, correct classification into two piles would place all the large (or red, or cards with two kernels) in one pile, and the rest in the other pile. Sharp et al. refer to this cognitive ability as *taxonomic*. In other tasks, correct classification could be based on either taxonomic or *functional* abilities. For example, when presented with cards containing pictures of a chicken, an egg, and a horse, correct classification of two of them might be taxonomic; i.e., horse and chicken because they're animals; or functional, i.e., egg and chicken because the chicken lays eggs.

On these tasks, when only taxonomic classifications could be used, correct performance was directly related to how much schooling subjects had, independent of age. When functional classification was called for, correct performance was directly related to age, with amount of schooling largely irrelevant. Where both taxonomy and function could be employed, the unschooled used function, and the schooled usually used taxonomy.

Two types of memory tasks were employed: free recall and paired associates. In the free recall experiment, the subjects (all adults) were read common nouns in random order, which could be classified into four categories: animals, utensils, food, and clothing. They were asked to recall the words in any order they wished. In general, there were slight performance differences among the groups who had 6 or fewer years of schooling. However, those who had 7 or more years performed the best because they semantically clustered the nouns that were taxonomically related.

Two paired-associate tasks were used with different sets of school children and adults. In one task, each pair was of the same category, e.g., root-branch, plate-bowl. In the second task, the same words were used, but each pair contained words from different categories, e.g., root-sheep, plate-crocodile. For both lists, the greater the number of years of schooling, the fewer the errors made. All the groups had trouble with the second task, but this was especially the case for the unschooled Mayan adults. Thus, as in the free recall experiment, "educational effects will appear most strongly in those cases where the task allows, but does not require, the subject to apply his semantic knowledge" (p. 48).

The major experiment of problem solving used 10 distinctive logic problems; e.g., "A dog and horse are always together; the horse is here now; where do you think the dog might be now?" The subjects were asked to provide an answer and a justification for it. In general, accuracy of performance and of justifications was related to amount of schooling, age playing no part. However, unschooled urban Mayan adults performed better than barely schooled (less than a year) rural Mayan adults. Thus exposure to commercial settings seems to improve problem solving.

One of the conclusions Sharp et al. reach from this research is the following:

> More highly educated subjects more readily engage in intellectual activities which are not rigidly predetermined by the structure of the task and which promote efficient performance. It is not differences in the information about the stimuli per se but differences in what people do with commonly available information that is critical ... differences between educated and uneducated subjects will depend on the extent to which the task permits or requires such activities, and the difficulty of the required behaviors. (p. 77)

How do we explain these often dramatic effects of schooling on cognitive abilities? Rogoff (1981) discusses three methodological problems. First, in nearly all studies where schooled and unschooled children have been compared, the schooled typically come from social environments that developed school-related skills, e.g., emphasis on language development. Thus, the schooled children have "one leg up" by the time they enroll in school. Stevenson (1982) has recently examined the Stevenson et al. (1978) study from this point of view and confirms the preschool advantage of those children who subsequently were enrolled. However, he, like Rogoff, concludes that schooling has positive effects over and above this initial advantage.

Second, in nearly all studies comparing schooled and unschooled persons, those in school probably have greater familiarity with testing materials and with the demands of the testing situation. Thus, they have an initial performance advantage. The argument weakens somewhat when the variable of interest is number of years of school, with adults and children being compared.

Third, the tests that schooled and unschooled (or less schooled) persons are compared on nearly always tap the cognitive skills being taught and used in school. It shouldn't be surprising, then, that the more practice you've had with the cognitive skills, the better you'll perform on tests of them. As has often been pointed out, the reason IQ tests work so well in predicting academic success is that they're made up of tests like those used in schools. In a sense, this issue goes to the heart of the question whether the effects of schooling are context specific (to school-like situations) or whether the education received is more generalized. No one has a satisfactory answer to this dilemma.

Finally, Rogoff speculates on four possible mechanisms of schooling's influence on cognition. First, schooling may induce students to search for general rules that will apply across a variety of situations. Most, but not all, of the data are consistent with this view. Second, schooling instructs verbally, and out of the context to which the instruction applies. Informal teaching relies less on language, but mostly involves observations in context, e.g., the tailor shop. This language use out of context probably increases the likelihood of abstract thinking and mental manipulations. Third, specific skills and strategies are taught in school as goals in themselves, e.g., memory strategies, but they are applicable to other classes of problems taught in school. Finally, learning to read, literacy, may carry with it special cognitive developments. We expand this issue in the next section.

Rogoff concludes that the evidence is strongest for the relationship between schooling and the development of specific cognitive skills, and weakest for their generalizability. She ends her chapter with the following 1744 quotation from the leaders of the Indians of Five Nations in response to the request of the Commissioners of Virginia to send their boys to William and Mary College:

> You who are wise must know, that different nations have different conceptions of things; and you will therefore not take it amiss, if our ideas of this kind of education happen not to be the same with yours. We have had some experience of it: several of our young people were formerly brought up at colleges of the northern provinces; they were instructed in all your sciences; but when they came back to us . . . [they were] ignorant of every means of living in the woods . . . neither fit for hunters, warriors, or counsellors; they were totally good for nothing. We are, however, not the less obliged by your kind offer . . . and to show our grateful sense of it, if the gentlemen of Virginia will send us a dozen of their sons, we will take great care of their education, instruct them in all we know, and make "men" of them. (Drake, 1834, Book I, Chapter III, p. 27)

Literacy

During the middle 1970s, Sylvia Scribner, Michael Cole, and a large number of collegues (Scribner & Cole, 1981) took advantage of a unique opportunity – they studied a small cultural group who had invented their own written language. The Vai people lived in very secluded regions of Liberia, mostly farming for subsistence, but also engaging in various crafts. The largest town in Vai country has about 2500 people, but most Vai live in hamlets ranging from 20 to 200 inhabitants. The official language of Liberia is English, and American style schools taught in English exist throughout the country. However, only a small portion of the Vai have ready access to them.

All adults speak Vai, some speak English, and some Arabic. Among the adults, literacy is largely restricted to males (though there is apparently no official policy for this). Approximately 20% are literate in Vai, 15% in Arabic, and 6% in English. While Arabic and English are relatively old alphabetic written languages, the Vai syllabary is about 150 years old. Following a dream in which the man Dualu Bukele was shown a number of written signs, he enlisted the aid of several friends, and together they invented the written language. It consists of 210 syllables and several free-floating vowels, and cannot be compared to any other written languages.

Learning to read and write English, Arabic, and Vai takes three different forms. English is taught in schools and is part of an educational curriculum. Arabic is taught by village Qur'an teachers to children in small groups. Most students learn to read and write Arabic sufficiently to recite the Qur'an, but without comprehension. About 15% ultimately carry their Qur'an studies further and become literate in Arabic. There are no formal Vai schools. Rather one adult will ask a literate friend to teach him. The friend apparently always complies, and Vai literacy is usually attained within several months. Written Vai is primarily used for correspondence, personal and town records. The primary use for Arabic is religious. And English is mainly used in correspondence, personal record keeping, and religion.

Does literacy substitute for schooling? If the major effect from schooling on cognitive development is through the acquisition of literacy, then all literate groups should perform about the same on cognitive tasks. If literacy is only part of the cause for cognitive gains, then differences among various literate groups should emerge. Scribner and Cole used three sets of tasks to evaluate the above question. The first set was comprised of a large number of cognitive tests that had previously been shown to differentiate schooled from unschooled children (Rogoff, 1981; Sharp et al., 1979). These tests included sorting geometric shapes, memorizing, placing familiar objects into categories, solving verbal logic problems, and giving explanations for their solutions to the categorizing and logic problems. The subjects in this experiment were five groups of Vai men and women: nonliterate, Vai literate, Arabic literate, literate in Vai and Arabic, and schooled in English.

The results from this experiment were surprising. The adults schooled in English performed better than other literate or nonliterate adults in only two ways: solving syllogisms, and giving verbal explanations for the syllogism and categorizing problems. There were no systematic differences between any of the groups on any of the other tests. Thus, among Vai adults neither schooling nor literacy had profound effects on cognitive development as reflected by these tests.

The second set of tasks dealt with adults' Vai grammatical knowledge and understanding of Vai word meaning and use. Some of the tests involved interchanging words, defining words, segmenting sentences into words, detecting and explaining grammatical errors, and solving verbal syllogisms. The subjects comprised the same five groups noted above. In this experiment, the only systematic difference found between any of the groups was the superior performance of the Vai literate and English-schooled groups in giving explanations for grammatical errors. In all other tests, the groups performed similarly. These results suggested to Scribner and Cole that literacy per se produces no general effects on cognitive development. Rather, any effects are probably specific to two factors: (1) the psychological processes required in learning to read and write a specific language; and (2) the ways in which the literacy is practiced or used. Thus, becoming literate in Vai might result in different cognitive gains than becoming literate in Arabic or English.

The third set of tasks were designed to evaluate this hypothesis. The complete listing of these tests can be seen in the two left-hand columns of Fig. 7.2. Most of the tests had been used in previous experiments. The new ones are incremental recall, which involves memorizing lists by starting with one item and adding one at a time; rebus reading and writing; integrating words and syllables, which involves listening to syllables and words read at a slow pace and trying to comprehend their meaning; and the communication game, which involves explaining the rules of a game to a person unfamiliar with it. For this experiment, five groups of adult subjects were compared: nonliterate, English schooled, Vai literate, Arabic literate, and those who could read but not understand the Qur'an. The last group is referred to as Qur'anic literate in Fig. 7.2.

The summary of results is shown in this figure. A shaded box indicates that a particular group performed better than the nonliterate group on that test. For example, both the Qur'anic and Arabic groups, but not the English-schooled or Vai groups, performed better than the nonliterate group on the incremental recall tests.

As can be seen from Fig. 7.2, English schooling, overall, has the most widespread effects on cognitive development. This result is partially a function of schooling, and partially on the ways English is learned and used. Most importantly, as can be seen, each form of literacy produces unique patterns of cognitive development, consistent with Scribner and Cole's hypothesis. For example, the sole superiority of the Vai literate in integrating syllables is explained by the fact that the Vai writing system is based on syllables, whereas English and Arabic are alphabetic. The superior incremental recall of the Qur'anic and Arabic groups is explained by the observation that Qur'anic learning involves processes highly similar to incremental recall.

Considering their results as a whole, Scribner and Cole conclude that the powerful effects of schooling on cognitive development are not primarily produced through learning to read and write. Rather, the cognitive activities that are called upon in school are the major vehicles for

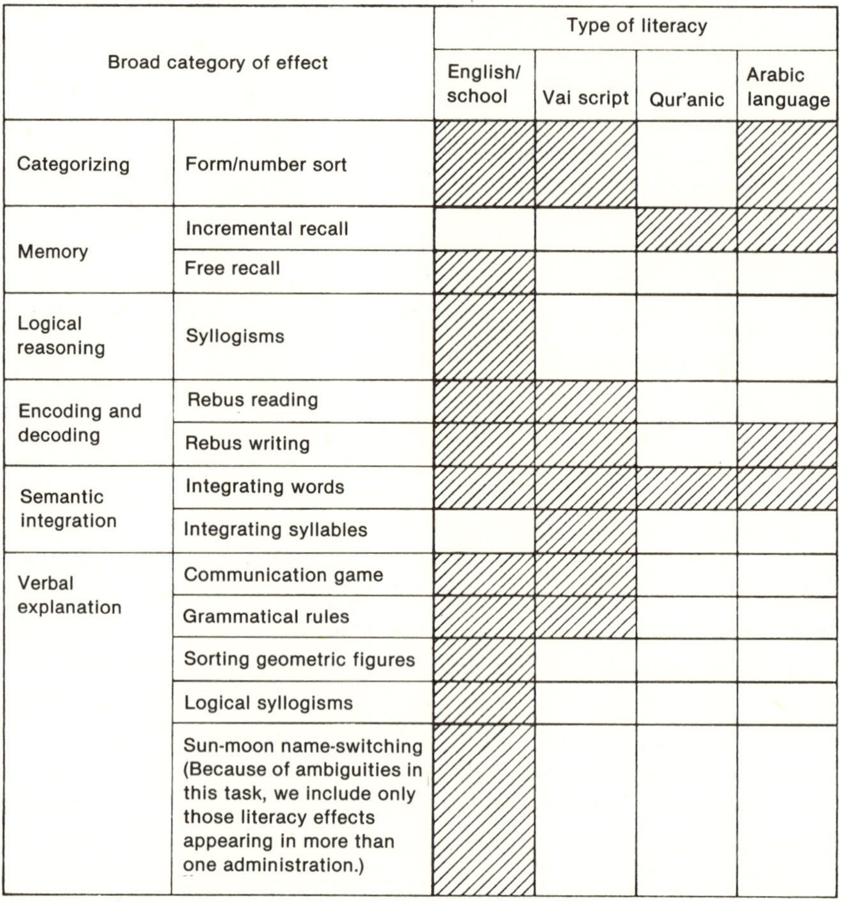

Broad category of effect		Type of literacy			
		English/ school	Vai script	Qur'anic	Arabic language
Categorizing	Form/number sort	▨	▨		▨
Memory	Incremental recall			▨	▨
	Free recall	▨			
Logical reasoning	Syllogisms	▨			
Encoding and decoding	Rebus reading	▨	▨		
	Rebus writing	▨	▨		▨
Semantic integration	Integrating words	▨	▨	▨	▨
	Integrating syllables		▨		
Verbal explanation	Communication game	▨	▨		
	Grammatical rules	▨	▨		
	Sorting geometric figures	▨			
	Logical syllogisms	▨			
	Sun-moon name-switching (Because of ambiguities in this task, we include only those literacy effects appearing in more than one administration.)	▨			

FIG. 7.2   Schematic representation of effects associated with each literacy. (Source: Scribner, S. & Cole, M. *The psychology of literacy.* Cambridge: Havard University Press, 1981.)

growth. Though literacy is an important cognitive attainment, and opens enormous avenues of communication, its key impact on cognitive development stems from the ways it is practiced. Moreover these practices, e.g., writing a letter, vary with the particular cultural context in which they are employed. It is the use of cognitive processes that leads to cognitive development, and not literary per se.

The preceding discussion of the socialization process as it takes place in North American schools can be summarized in the following manner. In relation to the child, the social context of schools involves a tension and interplay between academic requirements, the child's response to authority, his ability to make and maintain friendships and to establish self-esteem. As children move through the primary grades, junior high, and then senior high school, their obedience to and respect for school teachers and principals undergo a dramatic change. More and more, as they progress through school, children challenge the legitimacy of authority figures, and their choice of friends is progressively less influenced by the behavior of their teachers. Academic performance, at least in traditional classrooms, becomes less of a basis for the child's choice of friends and his maintenance of self-esteem. A child's reasons for meeting academic requirements also shift during these years. Children in the early grades are more likely to work hard in order to please teachers and gain classroom rewards, whereas children in the later grades tend to gear their performance toward pleasing their friends and fulfilling their future nonschool expectations.

The process of the academic socialization of low-SES predominantly black preschool children has often been highly successful. Children who have completed as little as 1 year in programs such as Head Start have generally performed better in school than children who have not had these experiences. The success of the preschool programs appears to depend on the following factors: children's acquisition of academic skills that help them in their first-grade learning; greater involvement of mothers in their children's school progress; and the development of positive school attitudes by the children and their mothers.

The cross-cultural comparisons focused on the cognitive developmental influences of both schooling and literacy. The Peruvian research led to two major conclusions: (1) Several months of schooling have dramatic effects on children's performance of cognitive tasks; (2) schooling has differential cognitive effects on children, depending upon the culture in which they have been reared. One major conclusion of the Mexican research is that schooling increases the likelihood that children will use a variety of cognitive abilities to solve intellectual problems. In general, research indicates that schooling strengthens those cognitive abilities closely related to academic tasks, but does not increase the more generalized cognitive skills of children.

The research on the influences of literacy versus the effects of schooling clearly shows that the two are not equivalent. Schooling affects the cognitive development of children well beyond the point of mere literacy. Moreover, the psychological processes and practices involved with each type of literacy produce unique effects on children's development of cognitive skills.

TELEVISION

Between 3 and 12 years of age the average North American, British, and Australian child increases his television viewing from 1.5 to 4 hours a day. Younger children watch less often. These patterns are observed in other European and in Japanese cultures as well (Murray, 1980). However, in all societies, teenagers and young adults decrease their daily viewing time to about 3 hours. When children watch television they are choosing it rather than other activities. The activities that suffer most are listening to the radio, going to the movies, reading comic books, and "hanging out" or in Murray's words "unstructured outdoor activities." The data on book reading are inconsistent, but it is clear that spending time with friends and participating in sports, hobbies, and pursuing personal interests are unaffected.

Psychologists, public officials, and others have been deeply concerned about the effects of television viewing. By 1982 approximately 3,000 articles, chapters, and books had been written about this issue. In that year, the report sponsored by the National Institute of Mental Health, *Television and Behavior*, was published (Pearl, Bouthilet, & Lazar, 1982). This work contains original chapters by leading scholars who reviewed 24 different areas of research. In addition, other excellent works have recently appeared that present new findings, e.g., Singer and Singer (1981), Bryant and Anderson (1983) or summarize previous research, e.g., Murray (1980), Huston and Wright (1982). This is an enormous amount of material, covering a wide range of topics. Much of it focuses on children.

As will become clear, psychologists have learned a lot about the effects of television on children. However, there is a great deal we don't know. For example, some studies found heavy viewing associated with extensive book reading, others with limited reading and some with no effect (Murray, 1980). The topics we'll discuss are those that have been highly researched and for which at least tentative conclusions can be reached.

Children's Attention to and Comprehension of Television.

Some people refer to television as the "boob tube" or "idiot box." One implication is that when you watch it, you put aside all judgment and reasoning and react to whatever is presented in a passive way. The opposite position is that children and adults bring to the situation active thought processes oriented toward uncovering the meaning of their experiences.

In this view, if television is idiotic, it's the content of the programs and not the persons watching it. Yet, television is designed to grab and hold our attention. When this happens, we may put aside higher level thinking and stay plugged in. Which view is correct?

Wright and Huston (1983) have evaluated the attention-getting (*perceptually salient*) properties of television and measured their impact on different-aged children. Some of these are animation, rapid movement of characters, fast scene changes, rapid cuts as opposed to slower zooms, loud music, laugh tracks, special effects, and peculiar sounding voices. Saturday morning commercially produced programs are generally highly salient, much more so than afternoon educational programs and prime-time shows. The educational programs such as *Sesame Street* tend to emphasize long zooms, moderate character movement, and singing. Less use is made of animation and special effects. Prime-time shows rely much more than others on adult dialogue. Unlike programs designed for children, this dialogue is often oriented to the future or the past.

Wright and Huston summarize research concerning age changes in sensitivity to perceptual salience. Between 1 and 4, children become increasingly attentive to these features. This probably accounts for the dramatic increase in television viewing during these years. However, there are essentially no differences in attentiveness between ages 4 and 10. Highly salient properties grab and hold children's attention. From about 8 onwards, people become increasingly interested in human dialogue, a nonsalient feature. This finding indicates that after 8 years story and content become a very strong focus for attention.

Anderson and Lorch (1983) have closely examined preschoolers' television behavior, focusing primarily on programs such as *Sesame Street*. In their work, 2- to 5-year-old children are brought into a comfortably furnished room containing a variety of interesting toys and a television set. In all experiments, their mother is present, and in some cases, other children, too. The television is turned on to *Sesame Street*, and the children are observed. One of the most striking findings is that preschoolers are not glued to the television. Rather, on the average, they look at and away from it about 150 times an hour. During this time they play with toys and talk with their mother or peers. When the program ends, they devote most of their time to play. The quality of this play is equivalent to that which occurs after listening to a parent reading a story. It seems clear that young children integrate their viewing with other available attractive activities. When the television is turned off, they merely shift attention to those activities without any impairment in functioning.

Anderson and Lorch believe that children's television viewing is an active process guided by their comprehension of what they are attending to. When children look away from the television they are often still listening to what is going on, but dividing their attention with other activities. Importantly, these shifts do not appreciably affect their understanding of the program. Anderson and Lorch verified this idea by comparing two groups of 5-year-olds watching *Sesame Street*. One group was allowed to play with attractive toys, whereas no toys were available for the others. The latter group spent twice as much time looking at the program as those with toys. When tested for comprehension after the program ended, however, there were no differences between the groups. Other research using different techniques confirmed the position that children's attention to television is usually guided by their understanding, and not by its perceptual saliency.

There is another side to the story, which Anderson and Lorch refer to as "attentional inertia." This refers to the observation that the longer a person has been looking at a program, the longer he will continue to keep on looking, without turning away for 1 or 2 minutes. Attentional inertia has been observed in 1-year-olds, children, adolescents, and adults. The critical looking duration is about 15 seconds. If you've not turned away by then you'll keep on looking for a relatively long while thereafter. Research with preschoolers shows that this inertia is not linked with attempts to understand specific content. For example, when content shifts in *Sesame Street*, which it does up to 40 times an hour, children in a state of attentional inertia keep on watching. These data strongly suggest that states of inertia are passive responses to television, not guided by comprehension.

The above research indicates that television viewing by preschool and grade school children is generally guided by higher level thought processes. These processes guide their attention to and away from it. Although perceptually salient features can grab their attention, they can't hold it. Occasionally, children and adults enter a passive viewing state in which their attention seems to get locked in. These states comprise a minority of viewing time.

We conclude the present section by discussing Collins' research (1983) concerning developmental trends in understanding program content. A typical dramatic program has a basic story plot, put presents a number of cognitive challenges to its young viewers. For example, material irrelevant to understanding the plot is shown; some of the relevant information is implied by the action as contrasted with being explicit; and material presented early in the program may be crucial for understanding scenes occurring later. These and other factors require the viewer to remember a lot of information and to make a number of inferences about the content. Young children often get hopelessly lost in the process.

In one set of experiments Collins showed television dramas and then asked children and adolescents questions testing recall of two important specific incidents and an inference based upon the two. For example, John saw Bill steal money (Incident 1). Bill subsequently shot John (Incident 2). Why did Bill shoot John (Inference)? Regarding recall, second graders remembered far less than either fifth or eighth graders, who performed near adult levels. The inference questions were scored if the children had answered both recall questions correctly. The second graders were correct about half the time, fifth graders about two thirds, and eighth graders, three fourths of the time. Thus not only do 8-year-olds forget crucial story information, but even when they remember it, incorrect inferences are frequently made.

In other studies Collins showed second and fifth graders one of two versions of an adventure drama in which most of the irrelevant-to-plot information was edited out. In the first version, the scenes containing the chief character's motives and attempts to kill his wife were shown 4 minutes apart. In the second, the scenes were shown with no time separation. At the end of the program children were asked why the man tried to kill his wife. The fifth-grade children were correct about three fourths of the time for both versions. The second graders responded at a chance level in the 4 minutes, and about 50% correctly in the no-separation version. These results indicate that the memory capacities of 8-year-olds place severe limitations on their understanding. They do not accurately recall or infer motives if the motive and action are separated by only 4 minutes. Moreover, when there is no separation, they still make many comprehension errors. These and the above results strongly imply that children under 8 years have a very incomplete understanding of television drama.

Television Viewing and Academic Skills

In this section we describe research concerning the impact of television viewing on the development of school-related skills. The first studies, by Ball and Bogatz (1970) and Bogatz and Ball (1971), evaluate *Sesame Street*, a program explicitly designed to teach 3- to 5-year-olds numbers, letters, geometric forms, and various problem-solving skills. In the research dealing with the first season of the program, a large group of low- and middle-SES children were initially given a battery of tests. These were designed to assess the above cognitive skills targeted by the program. At the end of the television season the children were retested. The researchers compared gains in cognitive skills as a function of how frequently the children watched the program.

The results were clear and consistent. Children who watched *Sesame Street* three to five times a week showed greater cognitive gains than those who watched two or fewer times. Three-year-olds gained more than 5-year-olds, and low-SES children as much as middle-SES if they watched often. However, for the infrequent viewers, middle-SES children gained more than the low-SES children. The latter findings suggest that middle-relative to low-SES families provide greater opportunities for development of cognitive skills, but that frequent watching of *Sesame Street* can overcome these differences.

In the study focused on the second season, two low-SES groups were selected from a city in which *Sesame Street* was only available through cable. One of the groups was given cable and encouraged to have its preschoolers watch the program. The children were tested before and after the television season. Those given cable television showed cognitive gains almost twice as great as those without cable, confirming the direction of the first-year results. Thus, *Sesame Street* has powerful effects on the development of the cognitive skills toward which it is targeted.

A second set of experiments are concerned with the impact of the introduction of television into a community. We rely on Murray's (1980) summary of Corteen's (1977) and Harrison and Williams' (1977) papers, which were orally presented at the 1977 meetings of the Canadian Psychological Association. Corteen studied second, third, and eighth graders, and Harrison and Williams, second and third graders in three Canadian towns that differed in television access. In the first part of the study, Notel (the names are fictitious) had no television, Unitel had access to only one public television channel, and Multitel had access to several public and commercial television channels. The children in Corteen's research were tested in reading skills, and those in Harrison and Williams' research were tested in vocabulary, visual-spatial ability, and creative language use. For reading skills, second- and third-grade children in Notel scored higher than those in Unitel, who in turn scored higher than those in Multitel. There were no differences among the eighth graders. For creative language use, Notel children performed better than those in the other two towns, but there were no effects in either vocabulary or visual-spatial ability.

The second part of the study compared second- and third-grade children in these towns 2 years after television came to Notel. The children from the first part were retested, as well as a new group of second and third graders. No performance differences were found at this time. Children from Notel, previously superior in reading ability and creative language use, experienced relative performance decreases. And the new groups of second and third graders all tested at about the same level, comparable to that of the first part. These findings show that the introduction of television into a community has a negative impact on reading skills and some language abilities of primary grade school children. Corteen's data indicate, however, that the early depressed reading skills are overcome by eighth grade. It is likely that other cognitive skills, on the average, also catch up by this age.

A third group of studies deals with the relationship between amount of daily television viewing and both IQ and academic achievement. The findings fit nicely with those described above. We follow Morgan and Gross' (1982) review of the available research. Regarding IQ, a consistent result is that prior to about age 13, children with high IQs (greater than 115) watch more television than those with low IQs (less than 100). After age 13, the reverse holds. Morgan and Gross (1980), for a large sample of sixth through tenth graders, found the correlation between IQ and self-reported daily television viewing to be $-.27$. Close examination of their data further showed that heavy viewers infrequently had high IQs, whereas light viewers had a wide range of IQs. Although correlation is not the same as cause and effect, this suggests that heavy viewing indirectly leads to a relative lowering of IQ. We know from Chapter 6 that children's IQs can change tremendously prior to adulthood. Early in development, television viewing may positively accelerate IQ. Later in development, too heavy viewing may exclude intellectually stimulating activities, and thus reduce the potential for further growth.

The results concerning academic achievement are more complicated. A number of studies have found for children up to about age 13 that those who watch from 1 to 2 hours daily score higher in reading and mathematics than those who watch *less* or *more*. After age 13, however, these scores are negatively correlated with amount of daily viewing, paralleling the IQ results.

Finally, Morgan and Gross (1980) report seven separate achievement-television viewing correlations for boys and girls of low, medium, and high IQ. For low-IQ boys, reading, vocabulary and mathematics, and for high-IQ boys, reading, spelling, and mathematics were negatively correlated with amount of viewing. For low-IQ girls, reading and vocabulary were *positively* correlated, but for high-IQ girls, *negatively* correlated with amount of viewing. For middle-IQ boys and girls, no systematic positive or negative correlations were found. Does heavy television viewing interfere with academic achievement? It depends on gender, IQ, and area of achievement.

The fourth set of results is a longitudinal study by Singer and Singer (1983) concerning the combined effects of family characteristics and television viewing on several cognitive abilities. The importance of this research stems from the fact that children's television viewing occurs within a family context. The impact of television is probably influenced by parental values and beliefs as well as their own involvement with viewing.

The Singers extensively studied a group of 4-year-old nursery school children and their parents in 1977, and again observed and interviewed them in 1980, 1981, and 1982. The parental interviews covered such aspects as their own self-described values, child-rearing techniques, beliefs about the world, and daily life-style. They were also asked about their own and their children's television viewing behaviors. When the children were in second and third grade, their comprehension of television drama, reading ability, language use, and imaginativeness were evaluated. As might be expected the results were complex.

For comprehension of dramas and reading ability, children perform poorly if they come from families who frequently watch and highly value television, whose mothers are self-reportedly not imaginative, and who use force rather than reason in their discipline. For language usage, highly effective children come from families who watch relatively little television, who are flexible in house routines, and whose fathers are self-reportedly imaginative. For imagination, those who score high watched relatively little television as preschoolers, currently watch little realistic action-adventure programming, have parents who self-describe themselves as imaginative, and who use reason rather than force in discipline. As can be seen, the development of these cognitive abilities in 8- and 9-year-olds jointly depends on characteristics of the parents and the nature and frequency of children's television viewing. The two, of course, are intimately related; e.g., parents who frequently watch television also encourage their children (by role modeling) to do the same.

In looking at this section as a whole, we can conclude that television programs directed toward enhancing the cognitive skills of preschoolers can be successful. But television viewing by young children in general seems to have a positive effect on their cognitive growth, provided that they live in communities with established programming. For teenagers, extensive viewing is usually associated with lower IQs and poorer academic achievement. Within this set of results, parental attitudes and values play an important role.

Social Beliefs and Social Behavior

In this section we closely follow the reviews of Greenberg (1982) concerning the impact of television on social beliefs, and of Rushton (1982) dealing with positive social behaviors. The next section considers aggression and violence.

Greenberg selected for analysis five social roles – family, sex, race, job, and age – and presented a content analysis of how these roles are portrayed during prime time and Saturday mornings. He then evaluated research relating amount of children's viewing to their beliefs about these roles. In only a few cases did the research connect viewing a specific program to a shift in social beliefs. Thus the assumption is made that children who watch a great deal of television will likely be exposed to and influenced by the typical social portrayals. Owing to the fact that there are few studies dealing with the impact of the effects of job and age role portrayals on children's beliefs, we will not consider these further.

Family. The research about beliefs emphasizes how children perceive family interactions. Television families are typically portrayed very positively, with about 90% of their interactions being helpful, mutually supportive, and cooperative. Conflict occurs only about 10% of the time, but is higher in broken families than intact ones, and with teenagers than with younger children. In one major study, fourth, sixth, and eighth graders filled out questionnaires that assessed their viewing habits and beliefs about both television and real-life families. It was found that (a) frequency of watching dramas and/or shows featuring small children was correlated with the belief that real-life families typically had positive interactions; (b) frequency of watching dramas featuring teenagers and/or broken families was correlated with the belief that real-life families are typically conflictual; (c) children's perceptions of how television families interacted were correlated with perceptions of real-family interactions; and (d) when parents watched and favorably commented to their children about the portrayals, this increased the correlation between viewing and beliefs.

Sex roles. In general, sex roles are heavily stereotyped on television. During the 1970s males in major roles outnumbered females by at least two to one. Women are typically married and are parents, whereas with about one half the men, marital and parental status are uncertain. Men nearly always have jobs, but about two thirds of the women are not employed outside the home. About 90% of doctors, lawyers, ministers, and business owners are men, whereas women are typically secretaries, teachers, nurses, journalists, and entertainers. About 90% of supervisors are men—thus women nearly always report to them. Men overwhelmingly have the prestigious jobs.

Not surprisingly, these consistent male-oriented messages influence children's beliefs and attitudes. When grade school children were asked which "characters they would like to be like when they grow up" boys chose many more characters than girls, and almost never chose women. About one fourth of the girls chose at least one man. Further, preschool and primary grade school children who were heavy watchers had stronger sex stereotypes than light watchers. However, girls who watched programs in which women portrayed counter-stereotype sex roles, e.g., police officer, school principal, accepted these occupations as appropriate for women.

Race. During the 1970s, between 10% and 15% of all prime-time characters were blacks. They were the only minority portrayed in significant numbers on television. Blacks typically appear in situation comedies and Saturday morning programs often with no white characters. Blacks under 23 are the most frequent characters portrayed, whereas the majority of whites are older. Blacks are usually unemployed or have lower prestige jobs than whites. In situation comedies blacks are dominant over whites, but in crime shows the reverse holds.

In general, the portrayal of blacks on television has had positive effects on both white and black children. For black children, there is a correlation between frequency of watching shows featuring black characters and cultural pride and self-confidence. Further, black children have more positive perceptions about the black characters than the white characters depicted, despite the opposite bias in television content. White children who have little contact with blacks state that their basic knowledge about blacks comes from television. In addition, they display very positive racial attitudes. Other research shows that white children who watched *Sesame Street* for 2 years developed more positive racial attitudes than those who watched for a shorter time span. Interestingly, *All in the Family* had no consistent impact on the racial views of white primary grade school children.

We can conclude from the above that television can and does help to shape the social beliefs of children. In nearly all cases the correlations between extent of viewing and beliefs were about .25, not strong, but consistent. We saw in the case of sex and race beliefs that these effects were often socially desirable. Some were not. One of the most important findings is that when parents watch and favorably comment about the portrayals, beliefs are strengthened. Other research, summarized by Huston and Wright (1982) has shown that parents' unfavorable comments can also counteract the effects of these portrayals. The implication is that parents should watch television with their children and discuss content with them.

Rushton's (1982) analysis includes laboratory studies and naturalistic observations concerning the behavioral effects of showing altruistic, friendly, self-controlled, or fear-coping behaviors on television. Nearly all these studies were carried out since 1970. Most used materials from public and commercial television, and some developed special videotapes designed to produce given effects. The results with all procedures and situations were highly consistent with each other.

Altruism.   In a typical laboratory study of altruism 5- to 10-year-old children watched a short videotape of a child playing a game and winning gift certificates. In one condition the child donated some of the certificates to charity, and in the other condition, acted selfishly. The viewers then played the same game themselves and won gift certificates, which they could donate to charity. The children who had watched the generous child donated more than those who watched the selfish child. Parallel results were found in other research for selected commercial television programs.

The majority of naturalistic studies of altruism were situated in preschool and kindergarten classrooms. Children were shown anywhere from 4 to 20 half-hour segments of programs showing an abundance of positive social interactions, e.g., *Mister Rogers' Neighborhood*, neutral content, or aggressive interactions. In some studies, teachers and children also role-played the positive interactions. The children's classroom behavior was then observed for several weeks thereafter, and compared with their pre-watching experience. Generally, for 1 to 2 weeks after viewing, children who saw the positive interaction programs were more cooperative and helpful during free play than those who saw the other programs. These effects were more dramatic if role playing had occurred. However, by 4 weeks post-viewing, virtually all group differences had disappeared. This implies that consistent altruistic effects require persistent viewing of altruistic-oriented programs.

Friendliness. Rushton reports two laboratory experiments dealing with friendly behaviors. In the first, nursery school children watched either a brief segment showing an adult demonstrating affectionate behavior toward a toy clown, or a neutral segment. When given an opportunity to play with a group of toys, including the clown, those who saw the affectionate behavior acted more affectionately toward the clown than the other group. In the second, nursery school children watched either segments of *Sesame Street* containing nonwhite children, or neutral segments. Subsequently, the first group showed a stronger preference than the "neutral" group to play with nonwhites.

Several of the naturalistic studies dealt with the use of television to help socially isolated nursery school children to interact positively with their peers. In these experiments, special videotape segments were created that graphically showed similar-age children successfully interacting in a nursery school setting. Children watched either these brief segments or nature films over a period of 1 to 8 days. Those who watched the successful interactions markedly improved their social behavior, and these changes lasted throughout the school year. Those who saw the nature films evidenced no changes. Thus, unlike altruistic behaviors, which apparently have little payoff for young children, changes in friendly behavior are sustained for long time periods. These are important results that should be further evaluated in a variety of settings.

Self-control. Several laboratory studies have dealt with the effects of televised self-control. In the typical experiment children between 5 and 8 years old are presented with a collection of toys to play with, but forbidden to touch them. They are then shown a videotape of a child with a similar collection of toys. The child either plays with the forbidden toys or does not touch them. The experimenter then leaves the room and through a one-way mirror observes the child with the toys. Children who saw the obedient child, relative to those who watched the transgressor, showed more self-control. They waited longer before touching the forbidden toys and played with them for a shorter time period. However, when tested one month later, without any intervening television experience, these differences washed out. Thus, like altruism, self-control requires frequent exposure.

Friedrich and Stein (1973) showed nursery school children three segments a week for 4 weeks of *Mister Rogers' Neighborhood,* aggressive programs such as *Batman* and *Superman,* or neutral nature-type programs. During this time and 2 weeks post-viewing, three categories of self-control behavior were noted during free play: tolerance of delay, obedience to rules, and task persistence. Although there was some variation across categories, the children who watched *Mister Rogers* showed the most self-control and those who watched the aggressive programs, the least.

Fear coping. In three laboratory studies dealing with fear coping, subjects were 3- to 9-year-old children afraid of either dogs or snakes. Over a 2- to 8-day period they were shown either brief videotapes of children enjoyably interacting with the dreaded animal, or neutral films. Those who saw the successful children were much more likely than those who saw the neutral films to approach and interact with the animal they feared, e.g., a 4-foot-long boa constrictor. These positive effects lasted between 2 and 4 weeks post-viewing.

The naturalistic studies have used videotapes to help children overcome fear in either dental or hospital settings. In one of these experiments, by Melamed and Siegel (1975), 4- to 12-year-old children about to receive elective surgery were shown a short videotape of a child undergoing surgery or a neutral film. The group who saw the surgery videotape experienced less fear both preoperatively and postoperatively than the other group. Moreover, these effects lasted at least 4 weeks after surgery.

On the whole, the experiments dealing with the behavioral effects of television indicate that children can be positively influenced by their viewing experiences. If the social environment does not provide rewards for these behavioral changes, they quickly trail off to pre-viewing levels. If the environment does reward the changes, then they are maintained for long time periods. These results are consistent with the theories of Albert Bandura (1973, 1977) whose thinking has been of major importance in laying the groundwork for much of this research.

Violence and Children's Aggression

North American television, especially during prime time and Saturday mornings, is filled with portrayals of violence. More than 80% of all programs show at least one violent encounter, with the average being 7.5 acts per hour. Most characters are either on the giving or receiving end of violence. Importantly, Saturday morning commercial programs portray the highest levels of all (Gerbner, et al., 1980).

A distinction is made between "aggression" and "assertiveness." Violence is an extreme form of aggression. Aggression involves the intentional physical or psychological harm to others. Assertiveness involves personal striving, achievement, or self-confidence. Assertiveness may be directed in relation to others as in sports competition, or in relation to noninterpersonal activities as in making art. In the popular literature, aggressiveness and assertiveness are often confused, e.g., "Irving is not an aggressive salesman." The present discussion is restricted to aggression, as defined above.

Most researchers and reviewers of the literature dealing with the effects of television on children and adolescents have concluded that viewing violence does increase aggression, e.g., Huston and Wright (1982); Pearl, Bouthilet, and Lazar (1982); Singer and Singer (1981). However, the ABC television network, in their own analysis of the data, has challenged that conclusion (ABC Social Research Unit/Broadcast Standards and Practices Department, 1983), as have the authors of a recent large-scale study (Milavsky et al., 1983).

The key issue in this disagreement hinges on the concept of *causation*. To show that watching violence and acting aggressively are *correlated* does not prove that watching *caused* the aggression. It's possible that aggression caused the watching; e.g., highly aggressive people seek out violent programs, or that a third factor caused preference for both violent programs and aggressiveness. Laboratory studies similar to those discussed by Rushton (1982) overcome the causal problem. We will summarize this research. However, to show that watching *Batman* and *Superman* in nursery school increases short-term aggressiveness in that setting does not prove that long-term preferences for violent programs cause long-term aggression.

In a dilemma like this, most researchers adopt the strategy of examining findings from various settings with a variety of procedures and looking for converging or compatible results. If a consistent pattern is found, then one is in a strong position to infer causation. Fortunately, such a variety of settings and procedures exists. We presently describe four different types: laboratory findings, naturalistic field studies, short-term and long-term correlational research.

Laboratory studies. Dozens of laboratory investigations have been carried out relating exposure to violent programs with children's and adolescents' immediate aggressiveness. Three of the major researchers have been Bandura (1973), Berkowitz (1973), and Liebert (1974). In a typical experiment, preschoolers through adolescents were shown a videotape depicting aggression or a commercial television program containing a large number of violent acts, e.g., *The Untouchables,* or a neutral program. Immediately thereafter, they were given opportunities to interact with toys or peers. In the overwhelming majority of experiments, children who viewed the violent program acted more aggressively than those who watched neutral programs (Murray, 1980). For example, in Liebert and Baron's (1972) study, children who watched violent segments of *The Untouchables* were more likely to hurtfully interfere with the play of another child than those who watched a track race.

Naturalistic field studies. Large numbers of these studies have been carried out with preschool and young grade school children. In the typical experiment children are shown either 1 to 12 violent or neutral programs while at school, and their peer behavior observed thereafter. As an example, in the Friedrich and Stein (1973) experiment, preschoolers' behavior was first observed for 3 weeks. They were then shown 12 violent, neutral or positive social programs over a 4-week period, and observed for an additional 3 weeks. Children who were initially highly aggressive were most affected by viewing violent television. Their peer aggressiveness increased substantially during the 4-week viewing period and stayed high for the following 2 weeks. The behavior of children initially low in aggression was unaffected by viewing the violent programs. As with the laboratory work, the overwhelming majority of field studies have found that in-school exposure to violent programs increases subsequent interpersonal aggressiveness.

Short-term correlational studies. This category includes all the experiments in which current television viewing habits and preferences were related to current levels of interpersonal aggression. For preschoolers and kindergartners, television viewing was typically observed by the parents. The older children reported on their own viewing. Current levels of aggression were assessed in one of three ways, depending upon the study: self-reports, reports by peers and teachers, observations by experimenters. In addition to older studies, several relatively large-scale experiments have recently been published, i.e., Belson (1978) with English 12- to 17-year-old boys; Singer and Singer (1981) with North American preschoolers; Huesmann (1982) briefly summarizing results with first- through fourth-grade Finnish and Polish children; and Eron et al. (1983) with first- through fifth-grade children from the United States. There is striking agreement across all these studies despite substantial differences in how television viewing and aggression were observed. For the boys, amount of violent television watched correlated about .20 with aggresivenesss. For girls from the United States, the correlations were about the same, but for Finnish and Polish girls, the correlations were generally at a chance level. Thus, viewing of violence on television is consistenly associated with level of aggressive activity, especially among American children.

Long-term correlational studies.   Three large-scale experiments with North Americans fall into this category: Eron et al.(1972); Huesmann (1982); and Milavsky et al. (1983). In these experiments children's previous levels of watching violent television were evaluated with subsequent levels of interpersonal aggression. In two cases television viewing was measured by self-report, and in one case by the child's parents. In all three, aggression was measured by the reports of their peers. In the Eron et al. (1972) study, television viewing preferences at ages 8 and 9 were correlated with reported aggression at ages 18 and 19, a 10-year lag. In the Huesmann (1982) study, television viewing at ages 7 and 9 years and in the Milavsky et al. study, television viewing at ages 7 to 16 were correlated with aggression during each of the next 3 years. Finally, Eron et al. and Huesmann analyzed their data with cross-lagged correlations and Milavsky et al. with regression coefficients. (See Chapter 1 for a discussion of these techniques).

In all three studies, present levels of viewing violent television were found to be correlated with current levels of aggressive behavior. In the Eron et al. and Huesmann experiments previous viewing was also found to be correlated with subsequent aggression levels, but in the Milavsky et al. experiment they correlated at a chance level. It's not clear whether the various statistical techniques used by these researchers produced their different findings.

In the cross-lagged technique, television viewing of violence at Time 1, e.g., 1977, is correlated with aggression at Time 2, e.g., 1978, and compared with the correlation between aggression at Time 1 with viewing at Time 2. If viewing violence causes subsequent aggression then the first correlation should be higher than the second. If aggression causes subsequent viewing of violence then the second correlation should be higher than the first. In both the Eron et al. and Huesmann studies, the cross-lagged correlations were consistent with the conclusion that viewing television violence causes subsequent aggression. The results of the Huesmann study are shown in Fig. 7.3. However, as we noted earlier, it's possible that a third unknown factor produced the pattern of correlations.

Where do we stand on this issue? The data linking television violence to aggression are stronger than those relating viewing positive programs to social behaviors. All four types of studies converge on one conclusion— heavy viewing of televised violence increases the likelihood of acting aggressively toward others. Although the correlations are not large, owing to the fact that millions of children and adolescents are involved, even a very small increment in aggressiveness can have striking negative effects. Additionally, there is no convincing evidence that watching violence has any positive effects, such as reducing subsequent aggression (the catharsis hypothesis).

Huesmann (1982) has analyzed the reseach from the perspective of understanding the psychological processes that underlie the relationship between television violence and aggression. He concludes that two of the major processes are observational learning and attitude change. Through observing television characters engage in violent acts, especially those that bring rewards, children develop a model for aggressive behavior. When they find themselves in situations even minimally similar to those depicted on television, aggression gets activated. Further, persistent

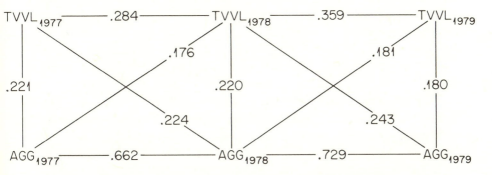

FIG. 7.3   Cross-lagged correlations between peer-nominated aggression and television violence viewing obtained in the currrent U.S. data. (Source: Huesmann, L. R. Television violence and aggressive behavior. In D. Pearl, L. Bouthilet, & J. Lazar (Eds.), *Television and behavior* (Vols. 1 & 2). Washington, D.C.: U.S. Government Printing Office, 1982.)

viewing of violence shapes their attitudes toward aggression, making it a more acceptable mode of behavior.

Given the above conclusion that heavy viewing of television violence at least partially causes increased aggressiveness, our view is (others may disagree) that parents have a strong responsibility to take action. At a minimum they should closely monitor their children's viewing choices and prevent extensive viewing of violence. With slight effort they can urge commercial networks to decrease the amount of violence shown. Also, they can attempt to influence members of government to place severe restrictions on programs aimed toward children. We live in violent times that require positive, not negative, social messages.

The Impact of Commercials

The business of commercial television is commercials. The typical American child who watches television 4 hours a day is exposed to approximately 15,000 of them a year. The time, care, and money expended on commercials frequently exceed that of the programming itself. Thus, commercials are often more perceptually compelling than the programs. Saturday morning commercials are primarily targeted for children, during which time they are encouraged to eat candy, sugared cereals, snack foods, and at fast-food restaurants. Sandwiched between these sugared and fried oral activities, children are shown the delights of a wide array of toys, records, and movies (Huston & Wright, 1982).

Not surprisingly mothers strongly dislike commercials directed toward children, especially those in kindergarten (Ward, Wackman, & Wartella, 1977). In this study working- and middle-SES kindergarten, third- and sixth-grade children and their mothers were interviewed about commercials, products, and purchasing. Many of the results parallel those discussed in the section dealing with children's comprehension. For example, recall of commercials is related to age, with older children remembering more of the content and in a more coherent fashion than the younger ones. Similarly, older children more clearly distinguish commercials from programs and understand that the point of the former is to motivate people to buy products. In these and other results, a major shift in beliefs and understanding occurs between kindergarten and third grade, as in the comprehension research.

Kindergartners are much more gullible than the older children. About half of them believe that commercials are always truthful, as contrasted with 12% of third and 3% of sixth graders. They are far more likely to believe that you can tell how good something is from watching television. Regarding actual experiences, far fewer kindergartners than third and sixth graders reported getting something they saw on television that didn't work as well as shown. Despite the older children's skepticism, about half of them say that they would "like to have most things they show on TV commercials." This finding points up the compelling aspects of commercials.

In that children have little money they can call their own, they have to ask their parents to buy things for them. Based on self-reports, there were no consistent differences as a function of age or SES in the frequency with which they did so. Nearly all the children interviewed made a lot of requests. The parents' responses to these requests (based on interviews with the mothers) varied considerably with child's age and SES. Middle-class relative to working-class mothers are much more likely to negotiate with their children. There were no SES differences in mothers either yielding to or rejecting children's requests without an explanation. Sixth graders fared better than the younger children— mothers were more likely either to buy the products they asked for, or to negotiate with them.

The study by Ward et al. is nicely complemented by a paper by Atkin (1982), one of the major researchers in this area. Atkin reports that there are substantial correlations between the extent to which children are exposed to commercials and (a) their desire for frequently advertised foods; (b) requests to parents to purchase such advertised items, including those at fast-food restaurants; and (c) the extent to which they consume the items. Recall that a huge proportion of the consumables are heavily sugared or fried. Nutritional value typically carries little weight on commercials, and as a consequence, little weight in the minds of children.

Cereals are among the most heavily advertised items on Saturday mornings. Many offer premiums. Mothers report that the premiums are a major factor in their children's requests, more so for heavy than light watchers. When 6- to 10-year-olds were given a choice between cereals with high nutrition versus those with premiums, the majority chose premiums. Similarly, good taste was chosen over nutrition. In general, the extent to which children judge the non-nutritional aspects of food as important for their preferences is related to the extent of their television viewing.

Finally, young children have distorted views of the adults shown in commercials. They believe that like the circus strong man lifting a playhouse while eating a particular brand of cereal, they too will become strong if they eat that cereal. They believe that the adults shown are experts about the products they are advertising. They believe that Fred and Barney Flintstone know a lot about nutrition. Again, these effects are correlated with extent of viewing.

There's a saying in English common law "Let the buyer beware." This means that in transactions among adults, the buyer should use reasonable and proper caution because the seller is not required to disclose all. In television, the results of the above studies indicate "Let the viewer beware." The difficulty is that young viewers do not have the cognitive, emotional, or social capacities to use reasonable and proper caution. Even the appropriately skeptical sixth graders want what they see and urge their parents to get it for them.

There are no easy answers to the problems associated with commercials aimed toward children. Apparently one major government committee suggested banning them, whereupon congressmen threatened to abolish the committee. At this time, our suggestion (which others may disagree with) is almost the same as that regarding television violence: Parents should closely monitor the commercials and write advertisers to emphasize the positive social and/or nutritional aspects of their products.

Research has shown that television produces both positive and negative effects on the socialization of children. However, these effects were often complexly related to children's age, as well as to parental behaviors and values. The research dealing with children's attention to and comprehension of television found vast age-related effects. Children under age 8, for example, apparently are very limited in their ability to comprehend story lines that extend longer than 4 minutes. Children's cognitive and academic performance have usually benefited from television viewing. Programs specifically designed to stimulate cognitive growth in preschoolers have been found to do so successfully. These effects are usually greater for low- than for middle-SES children. It has been found that IQ development in grade school children is positively correlated with the amount of viewing they do. However, after children reach the age of 13, their IQs are negatively correlated with the amount of television viewing in which they engage. The relationships between the amount of children's viewing and various academic performances are influenced by age, sex, parental involvement, as well as when television was introduced into the community.

Television viewing has also been found to have positive effects on children's social and emotional behavior, as reflected in their attitudes toward women and minority groups. Family life, however, is usually portrayed in unrealistically positive ways, such as the absence of conflict, which may be inconsistent with the actual daily experiences most children have. The selective viewing of programs having positive social content like *Mr. Rogers' Neighborhood* generally produces positive social behaviors in children, such as altruism and friendliness. However, if the home or school environments don't support these positive social behaviors, children stop engaging in them. On the negative side of the picture is the finding that extensive watching of televised violence leads to increased aggressiveness in children of all ages. Another negative effect is that commercials aimed at children encourage them to eat sugared foods and fast foods at the expense of good nutrition. Our view is that parents should take a more active role in combating these negative influences.

FAMILIES IN FAMILY THERAPY

There are a number of ways in which to observe the social interactions that take place in families. Among these are observing families in their homes; viewing them on vacations and away from home; testing them in a laboratory setting, where they carry out structured tasks; noting their performance on questionnaires; and studying them in family therapy, where they have sought help for one or more of their family members. In the discussion of attachment between family members, we described studies in which families were observed both in the home and in a laboratory setting. These studies provided valuable information, but were limited by the procedures employed. Every method of obtaining information has its limitations, however—a point that was discussed in Chapter 1.

In this section, we describe results based on the following method—the observation of families in family therapy. The family therapist makes two types of observations: (1) behaviors observed in the therapy session, and (2) behaviors reported by the family members about themselves. Reliability is an obvious problem with both types of observations, but frequently the therapist can check with schools and relatives for confirmation of the information provided to him during the session. From these types of observations, the therapist is often able to construct a scenario depicting how the family is organized and how it functions in its usual activities. Most importantly, these observations help us to make some generalizations about how the interactions between family members help to shape the emotional and intellectual development of the children. Family therapy is a relatively recent form of treatment, but the use of the clinical method in developmental psychology, as depicted in the works of Freud, Erikson, and Piaget, is a method of longer standing and value.

The Family Therapy Context

The contrast between individual psychotherapy and family psychotherapy is enormous. Three of the major differences are that the family therapist works with a family system and actively tries to change it, whereas the individual therapist works in a relatively passive way trying to help a single person to change. The family therapist generally views the emotional symptom of one of its members as being a family symptom, whereas the individual therapist views the symptom as an individual one. Although the goal of helping the symptomatic child is the same, family and individual therapists pursue very different tactics in reaching it.

There are three recent studies that summarize research evaluating family therapy (Dewitt, 1978; Gurman & Kniskern, 1978; Wells & Dezen, 1978). The conclusions from these studies were all very similar. In general, family therapy results in positive outcomes for about 70% of all treated families, in negative outcomes (worsening of symptoms) for about 3%, and has no measurable effect on approximately 27% of all treated families. These figures are comparable to those obtained measuring the results of individual psychotherapy. About one third of untreated families (or individuals) eventually improve without any external intervention.

In the remainder of this section I draw heavily on the following material: my 6 years of experience as a family therapist; the observations of other therapists' family therapy sessions; discussions with more than two dozen therapists at the Philadelphia Child Guidance Clinic from 1977–1979; books by Minuchin (1974), Napier and Whitaker (1978), Guerin (1976), and Papp (1977). Most of the families seen at the Philadelphia Child Guidance Clinic were black, single-parent, and from low-SES classes. Most of the families that I have worked with are white, two-parent, and from working- and middle-SES classes. Some have been stepfamilies – e.g., one of the parents is not the biological parent – and a small percentage have involved children adopted when they were 5 years of age or older. The case studies discussed in the above books include the effects of therapy on single- and two-parent families – black, white, step, adoptive, and traditional types of families. Since we have previously discussed the effects of divorce on children, our present discussion is limited to the effects of family therapy on two-parent families.

There are a variety of reasons that prompt a family to seek help for one or more of its children. Usually the problems the parents are concerned about have been long-standing, as opposed to an immediate crisis. This implies at least two things: (1) that the parents believe that given either enough time or a change in circumstances the problems will disappear, e.g., the child will "grow out of it," the school difficulties are related to the child's teacher; and (2) that psychotherapy is a last-ditch effort, to be avoided if possible. They finally seek outside help when the problems persist and their efforts have not been successful.

Some parents are quite surprised when they are asked to bring everyone living in the household to the first session. They assume that the therapist is going to, in some way, "cure" their child. In setting up the appointment, and in the first session, a therapist tries to make the following points to them: (1) The best people to help their child are the family, and not a stranger the child may see for an hour a week. (2) The word "abnormal" is rarely useful when talking about individuals or families. Rather, therapists use the more neutral terms of functional and dysfunctional, implying that areas of an individual's or family's life are not working well. All of us, and our families, are occasionally dysfunctional— it's normal to be that way sometimes. (3) No one—not the child having problems, siblings, nor parents—is to blame for those problems. Rather, the therapy will focus on how the family members are dealing with each other, and try to find alternative ways for them to do so. In some families there is an agreed-upon scenario—"Jimmy's having a problem. We can't imagine why. We'd like you to help." In other families, Mom or Dad will say, "Jimmy's having a problem. I think we're to blame. We want you to help." The children often say, "We don't know why we're here," or essentially repeat what their parents say. They also make it clear that they'd rather not be here at all. The therapist tells them that everyone is in the same boat; no one wants to be here.

In this meeting the therapist tries to accomplish several goals that form the basis for future sessions. By seeking everyone's view she tries to engage them all in the process. At the same time the therapist looks for disagreements and lack of involvement between family members. When obvious, these are pointed out to the family and an attempt is made to get them to talk; e.g., "You know, Mom and Dad, when Jimmy was talking, Sue was looking out the window, not paying attention. Is this what usually goes on?" Or, "Mom and Dad, you have different views about what's going on. Can you discuss this with each other?" The therapist also tries to spread the problem—point out difficulties others have—in order to reduce the pressure on the identified patient (IP), and to underline the necessity for the whole family to work together. If there are multiple problems, perhaps many of the family members will be open to seeing their part, and hence try to produce change.

The therapy continues until the major problems the family is concerned with are substantially improved, they give up, or the therapist does. By the nature of the business, therapists have to be optimists, so when improvement has been very slight, the family typically gives up first. On the average, family therapy lasts between 10 and 20 sessions. In families where there is substantial conflict between the parents, and in some stepfamilies and adoptive-families, they give up after a few sessions, but others who want to work for change, stay with the process longer, often with success.

Some research-oriented therapists try to combine theoretical research and psychotherapy in the sessions. This approach usually fails, leading to bad research and poor therapy. The theoretical questions asked usually have little direct bearing on the specific issues with which the family is struggling. And when answers to those particular questions are sought, the therapist often does not pay sufficient attention to the theoretically relevant ones. The researcher and therapist have to put on blinders—you can't observe everything—and in trying to combine both approaches, one stumbles blindly.

In another sense, however, the therapist is a researcher as well as a therapist. Her tasks are to try to understand the dynamics of each family and what roles the symptoms play in these dynamics. Given this understanding, she tests hypotheses concerning the effects certain changes in family interactions would have on the symptoms. One of the great problems a therapist has in this process is trying to be an objective observer seeking understanding, while at the same time being an active agent for change. This is not an easy task, but when she succeeds, the results are gratifying.

The Child in a Family Context

In the following pages we restrict our discussion to families in which the IP is 12 years old or younger. Older children occasionally present somewhat different problems, demonstrating the greater influence of peers—e.g., sexuality, drug abuse. In dealing with older teenagers therapists often prefer to see them on an individual basis, depending upon the nature of the problems and the family dynamics involved in the situation. In addition to focusing on preadolescents we emphasize situational contexts in which the children live with both biological parents.

In Table 7.1 is a list, in approximate frequency of occurrence, of the major problems parents present in relation to their children. As noted earlier school difficulties are by far the most common type of problem. When children receive poor grades, the therapist usually asks that these children be evaluated for learning disabilities and IQ. If these evaluations show that the child can perform better, therapists work with the teachers and parents to closely monitor the homework and to arrange for tutoring. Once in a while, it becomes clear that the school is not suitable for this particular child, and the parents and therapist agree that she should transfer to another one.

Only infrequently are school problems the only ones a child has. If he is misbehaving at school, he's probably doing so at home. If he is not doing homework, he may also be unhappy or withdrawn at home. However, in many of these cases, if the child were not having school problems, the parents would not bring her into therapy. Where the school problems are large, the home problems seem small.

There are two important lessons to be learned from these observations. First, the school is a different social system from the family, with its own unique rules, customs, and roles. People of all ages frequently have

TABLE 7.1
Major Symptoms/Problems of Families Seeking Help
(In Decreasing Frequence)

School Related:
    Poor grades
    Not doing homework, not handing homework in on time
    Misbehavior in class, inattentive
    Fighting with other children
Talks back to parents, disobedient, doesn't do chores
Fights with siblings
Peer problems, no friends
Angry towards family members, verbally abusive
Lying to parents, stealing from family members
Unhappy, depressed, withdrawn in family
Cries with criticized, or when angry
Headaches, stomachaches

trouble when they move from one social system to another. The rules of the family are often in conflict with those of the school, and children have to learn to adapt to both systems. Second, parents often feel powerless to have any impact on the schools. They place their child into the care of strangers, under an authority structure in which they are outsiders. In part, they seek the help of an outside professional who may exert some influence on their behalf.

Returning to Table 7.1, most of the remaining symptoms occur in combination with others. It's the rare family, for example, whose only concern is their child's lying or stealing. Usually that child is also unhappy, or has peer problems. In looking through this list, it's obvious that nearly all families occasionally experience some of these problems with at least one of their children. Are the problems worse in families who seek psychotherapy than those who don't? In general, I don't think so. In fact, the reverse may be true. It's possible that the families who seek help are more sensitive to their children's needs and development than those who don't do so. Obviously, in many families the problems are minimal and there is no point in getting involved with family therapy. In a few cases where these families come in, therapists see them once or twice and send them on their way with blessings and reassurance that all is well.

In Table 7.2 is a list of the key parental factors involved with their children's problems. Again, this list is approximate. Notice that we used the phrase "involved with" and not "caused" their children's problems. The point here is that children and parents are part of a changing open system (the family) in which everybody is mutually influencing and being influenced by everybody else and by the nonfamilial environment. Think about two siblings having a fight. Ask them who started it. Usually both will point to the other and give good reasons to justify their response.

There are always large numbers of factors involved in producing and maintaining any problem behaviors, including the characteristics of the child himself. However, despite our reluctance to say that the parents caused the child's problem, interventions in therapy often deal with having the parents change these behaviors. If they're inconsistent the therapist asks them to become more consistent. If they're overcontrolling, they are asked to loosen up. The implication is that in a social system, if any member changes her behavior, everybody interacting with that person will be affected, and forced to accommodate to the change. In our judgment these "key parental factors" often have detrimental effects on children's development.

TABLE 7.2
Key Parental Factors Involved With Children's Symptoms

Inability to negotiate with each other or their children
Inconsistency in upholding family rules or following through
Too intrusive in social or emotional life of their children
Overcontrolling of their children's decisions or behaviors
Too rigid in upholding family rules and maintaining role differences
Excessive, unresolved parental conflict
One parent too uninvolved in the social or emotional life of the family
Too critical of their children without sufficient praise
Not enough structure is provided for the children
Undercontrolling of their children's decisions or behaviors
One parent is too needy of the affection and involvement of the children
A grandparent is allowed to be too influential concerning the children

Four additional comments should be made about this table. First, it is too static, and not related to children's age. Parental behavior may be appropriate for young children but not older ones. For example, parents should be somewhat intrusive and overcontrolling with their preschoolers but not middle grade school children. Additionally, young children may be less sensitive to some of these factors than older ones, e.g., a too powerful grandparent. Second, not all children in a family are affected by these factors. Some children manage to develop and behave in age-appropriate ways despite their parents' dysfunctional behavior. Psychologists need to know more about this phenomenon. In the extreme, for example, one identical twin may become schizophrenic while the other becomes a successful parent, husband, and worker. As noted above, many factors affect children, and some may compensate for and balance others. Third, the presence of any of these factors does not lead to the same symptoms. Inconsistent, rigid parents may have verbally abusive or withdrawn children who have trouble with their teachers or with peers. The relationship between parental factors and symptoms is very complex. Finally, children may develop symptoms despite the absence of these parental factors. Again, they move in and out of a variety of systems, and the difficulty may lie elsewhere than with the family.

A question therapists always ask themselves in working with families is, "Why is this particular child (the IP) having difficulties?" Certainly circumstances change such that the stresses presently operating on a family are different or greater than those at earlier times. Many therapists have been impressed, however, in a minority of the cases that the IP is often vulnerable, physiologically or anatomically. Table 7.3 gives examples of some of the most typical ones encountered. We believe that some of these are genetically based, only partially under environmental control. In essentially all cases, parents will say that from infancy onwards their child has been slow, awkward, hyperactive, or shy. When there are siblings without these vulnerabilities, the parents state that they were always different from the IP. Children vulnerable in these ways have a more difficult time coping with family stresses, but especially those involved with school and peer systems.

We do not want to imply that all or even most children with these vulnerabilities will develop psychological symptoms. With sensitive and caring family and school environments, most will not. Also, we do not want to imply that the genetically based vulnerabilities are more powerful than those produced by the child's social environment. Both are influential. What is impotant is that we can have a large impact by changing the social environment (family, school, community) but none on the child's genetics. Family therapy can help to bring about those changes.

Concluding Observations

The most difficult families to work with are those where the parents have a great deal of unresolved conflict, stepfamilies, and families who have adopted an older child. In these families, one or more children are symptomatic, and both parents are usually under a great deal of stress. In the case of extensive parental conflict, the parents typically have coped with this situation either by avoiding each other or their areas of conflict–by one parent withdrawing and becoming a peripheral family member–or by bringing in the children on their side of the conflict (continuous arguing usually leads to divorce, which is another means of coping). When

TABLE 7.3
Physiological and Anatomical Vulnerabilities of Children

Easily excitable, hyperactive
Shy, withdrawn
Learning disabled
Awkward, poor motor coordination
Obese
Physically unattractive
Speech and/or hearing difficulties
Low IQ

the family comes into therapy, every member brings with him or her all the current modes of coping with each other, and moreover, they use these modes with the therapist, e.g., try to pull him in on their side. When the therapist presses them to attempt new ways of coping, such as bringing the conflict into the open and negotiating, tension rapidly mounts. In that it takes practice to change old patterns, the early sessions are often quite tense, and progress is frequently slow. For some families, the stress in therapy is more uncomfortable than the stresses at home. This often leads to their terminating the therapy.

For stepfamilies, the major problem involves clarifying the stepparent's (usually stepfather) role in the family. He is a husband first, and even if his wife wants him to parent the children, they usualy resent his efforts. Further, no matter how competent a parent he is, his wife will often object to those methods which are different from hers. An additional difficulty stems from the children's loyalty to their natural father (Boszormenyi-Nagy & Spark, 1973). As they become emotionally closer to stepfather they may feel disloyal to father, and hence be in considerable conflict.

The process of integrating him into the family involves the mutual accommodation of all family members to each other. It is unrealistic to assume that only the stepparent has to change. One rule many therapists have discovered is that this process will tend to have a favorable outcome if stepfather takes the role of supporting mother's rules, and not asserting his own. Mother has primary responsibility for her children, and has to assert that responsibility. Attempts to share it equally with stepfather, or turn it over to him, will lead to an unsuccessful outcome.

Couples who have adopted an older child or children (two adoptive siblings are often involved) are faced with three major problems. First they have to learn to parent a relative stranger, who has a developmental history unknown to them (the records of the adoption agency can't begin to provide a detailed history). Second, the child or children usually come from a different family culture and social class, which have instilled different values and standards. These values are frequently in conflict with those of the adoptive parents. Third, older adoptive children require a tremendous amount of time, care, and understanding, which often emotionally fatigues the parents. This fatigue has a negative effect on the marital relationship. Add to these all the usual problems with family life, and you can wind up in a grim situation.

Therapists generally recommend that couples who have no children of their own not adopt an older child. Those who have children the same age or older than the adoptive child may have sufficient experience and knowledge to cope well with the new situation. Of course, couples who have previously adopted older children will probably be successful. The process of integrating the adoptive child into the family requires mutual accommodation by all members. Therapists tell the parents to try to develop both great patience, and expectations compatible with the difficult task they have taken on. They should not expect their new child to quickly or easily take on the characteristics, standards, and behaviors they wish for him.

For nearly every child seen in family therapy the two most recurring issues are control and responsibility. By control we mean the child's ability to make decisions for herself without unreasonable parental influence. Sometimes the parents give the child too much control over her life as well as theirs. Most typically, the parents have been consistently and continuously influencing their child's choices in ways inappropriate to her developmental level, e.g., for sixth graders, setting homework times and locations, not allowing them to sleep over at friends' houses, telling them how to spend their allowances. The issue of responsibility is closely related and is often brought about by the parents either being too intrusive, e.g., sitting with fourth graders while they are doing homework, or not following through on expectations, e.g., taking the garbage cans in when the children forget to.

For both issues, any given situation seems small and insignificant to the child's development. The long-term accumulation, however, often has strong negative effects. Some children choose to perform poorly at school as their way of asserting personal control in relation to their parents. This choice may not always be conscious, but it is effective. And the harder the parents try to control their children's academic performance, the poorer the grades. As the struggle for academics escalates, the children discover that their poor performance is an aggressive weapon, against which their parents' distress more than compensates for failing grades. The turning point in therapy with these families often comes when the child and parents fight over another area of control, and the child wins. As the family works out more age-appropriate levels of control, the child starts to perform better academically.

My experience as a family therapist leaves me optimistic about the process of therapy, especially where the IP is a preadolescent. In that these families have sought help, therapists rarely encounter bad-intentioned, uncaring, or unloving parents. In most families lack of affection is not often an important factor. Although all members are involved in therapy, the parents who have legitimate power and authority are primarily responsible for initiating change. Where they are flexible and willing to see their own role in helping their child, the outcome is nearly always positive.

SUMMARY

Classroom settings exert a powerful influence on children's ability to form friendships and develop self-esteem. Hallinan, in a study for primary graders, and Epstein, in a study for middle and high school students, compared peer relationships in open and traditional classrooms. For the primary and middle schools, children in open classrooms had more friends, there were fewer "stars," and fewer were isolated. In high school, these differences between classroom types did not emerge. However, for all ages, children in open classrooms had friends from more varied backgrounds. In Bossert's study of third- and fourth-grade traditional classes, it was found that teachers who primarily rely on recitation methods unconsciously bias the students to favor those who perform the best.

According to Metz and Cusick, in junior and senior high schools authority becomes a pressing issue. Students do not willingly acknowledge the teachers' control, but challenge them to both prove their competence and negotiate agreed-upon authority relationships. Maintaining friendships is a primary motivation for students, and in high school it successfully competes with academic concerns. A key issue here appears to be students' and teachers' difficulties in modifying their roles in the traditional power hierarchy. Where a mutual accommodation can be worked out, academic priorities get strengthened.

Lazar and Darlington headed a team that evaluated the long-term effects of 11 programs similar to Head Start. In comparisons of overall school competence, reading, and mathematics achievement, children who participated in these programs performed better than those who didn't. There were essentially no effects on IQ. The superior performance of the program participants appears to be related to the more positive attitudes they and their mothers developed towards academic achievement.

The effects of schooling on cognitive development was examined for five different cultural groups of 5- and 6-year-olds in Peru (Stevenson et al.), and two different cultural groups of 10- to 15-year-olds in Mexico (Sharp et al.). In all cases the cognitive abilities of the schooled children were superior to those of the unschooled children. However, for some tasks, schooled children and adults performed equivalently to unschooled adults. Thus, life experiences can occasionally compensate for lack of formal schooling. This is consistent with the conclusion that schooling tends to develop those cognitive skills closely related to academic achievement, and not more generalizable attainments.

Literacy is the ability to read. The Vai, a cultural group in Liberia, invented their own written language, which a minor portion of adult males can read. They are taught to read on a one-to-one basis by other men. In addition, many Vai males receive formal schooling in English. In a variety of cognitive tasks, schooled Vai adults performed better than literate and nonliterate Vai adults in two ways: giving verbal explanations to problems and solving verbal syllogisms. For both these and other tasks, neither schooling nor literacy had marked effects on the cognitive development of adults.

North American school children watch television for about one third of their waking hours. This extraordinary time involvement has prompted considerable concern and substantial research efforts to study viewing impact. Although children appear to be grabbed by the perceptually salient features of television—e.g., rapid movement and cuts, loud music—their watching is actually a more active process guided by comprehension. Five-year-olds have no difficulty in dividing attention between a program and peer play; i.e., understanding is relatively unaffected. However, comprehension of story plots markedly improves between ages 4 and 8. Children under age 8 have a very limited understanding of story line and character motivation, which leads to substantial confusion on their part.

Television programs, such as *Sesame Street*, designed to teach cognitive skills to young children, are very successful in accomplishing this goal. When commercial television is introduced into a community, it initially has a negative impact on the reading skills and language abilities of second and third graders. However, by eighth grade, these negative effects disappear. Age and gender are both important in assessing the impact of amounts of daily watching on IQ development and academic achievement. Extensive viewing is often beneficial to preadolescents, but usually detrimental to teenagers. For low-IQ girls, amount of watching is positively correlated with reading ability and vocabulary. Finally, all these effects are probably influenced by the nature of the involvement of parents with their children's viewing.

Television viewing shapes the social beliefs of children. Despite the presence of some sex and race role stereotyping, heavy viewers develop more positive beliefs about women and blacks than light viewers. Parents' comments about social portrayals also influence their children's beliefs. Laboratory studies and naturalistic observations show that positive social behaviors such as altruism and self-control are effected by watching programs with positive social interactions. If the child's usual social environment does not provide rewards for these behavior changes, however, they quickly drop off to pre-viewing levels.

Four lines of research concerning the relation between television violence and children's and adolscents' aggression were discussed: (1) laboratory studies; (2) naturalistic field studies; (3) short-term correlational; and (4) long-term correlational. In all cases results of most of the research showed that heavy viewers of televised violence were more aggressive than light viewers, indicating a causal relationship. Although the correlations were small, the cultural impact could be large. Parents and others should take action to decrease the amount of violence shown.

The typical American child is exposed to about 15,000 televised commercials a year. Commercials targeted toward children encourage them to eat heavily sugared and fast foods, which frequently have limited nutritional value. Younger children are much more gullible than older ones about the truthfulness of commercials, but all children make demands on their parents to purchase the advertised products. Cereals receive special emphasis on Saturday mornings. As a consequence, children prefer sugared cereals that offer premiums. Children place little value on nutrition.

Many children have difficulty adjusting to their family and school. When their children's problems continue for long periods, some parents seek professional help, often family therapy. In family therapy an attempt is made to reorganize family functioning in such a way that the symptomatic child can find more mature ways of interacting. The therapist acts as a researcher by attempting to understand family dynamics and testing hypotheses concerning the effects of change on the child's symptoms.

Most symptomatic children (IPs) in family therapy have school difficulties that are often produced because the rules of the school social system are different from those of the family. Nearly all IPs have multiple symptoms involving family, peers, and/or school life. Although parents don't *cause* the IP's symptoms, their mode of interacting with children and with each other is often *heavily involved* with those symptoms. Some parental modes of interaction are appropriate at one age level but not at other age levels. The IPs themselves also contribute to the development of their symptoms. Many children have physiological or anatomical vulnerabilities that make them sensitive to social stresses.

The most difficult families to work with are those in which the parents have much unresolved conflict, stepfamilies, and families who have adopted an older child. In the first group, all members bring to the therapy session their current ways of failing to resolve conflict, and actively resist change. A therapist's attempts to get them to negotiate produce considerable stress, which may lead to termination of therapy. For stepfamilies, the major problem involves clarifying the stepparent's role. Therapy outcome will usually be favorable if the stepparent supports the biological parent's rules, and does not take primary responsibility for the children. There are several major problems couples face when adopting an older child, relating to the different family culture an adoptive child has experienced. A major goal of therapy is to encourage parents to develop considerable patience and appropriate expectations.

Finally, the two most recurring issues for the IP in family therapy are control and responsibility. Most typically, the parents have been consistently influencing their child's decisions in ways inappropriate to the child's developmental level. Any given incident may seem insignificant, but the long-term effects of a number of incidents can be substantial. Where parents are flexible and willing to acknowledge their role in helping their child, the outcome of family therapy is nearly always positive.

8 Recapitulation

When we are discussing an article or book chapter I usually ask my students, "What's the punchline, what's the author trying to tell you?" Often there are several punchlines, depending upon the scope of the work. In the present book there are many which I've divided into two categories: general and specific. The general points refer to the principles upon which this book is based. The specific points are some of the basic findings about human psychological development.

MAJOR GENERAL POINTS

Evolution sets the plan, culture provides the framework, socialization determines the enactment.

Evolution

Evolution is an unplanned experiment in species design. Those members of a species who best fit their social and physical environments throughout their development will generally reproduce the most (or their close relatives will do so). Over many generations the species as a whole will come to resemble these members. Evolutionary designs are conservative in the sense that new phenotypic characteristics, e.g., behaviors, anatomical structures, are either added on to or are modifications of the old characteristics. Canalization processes, which involve gene-phenotype interactions, are part of the basis for this conservatism. Canalization is a complex buffering system which protects the developing individual from minor environmental and genetic abnormalities so that the normal developmental targets will be reached. It is likely that nearly all evolutionarily important phenotypic characteristics are canalized.

In order to understand human development we must first understand the nature of the human design. It was argued that there are three broad components of this design: mammalian, primate, and hominid. All of these components are canalized, from relatively stronger to relatively weaker, respectively. The most important mammalian psychological characteristic is the bonding which occurs between an infant and its primary caretaker. The most important primate psychological characteristic is an individual's life-long involvement with a subsistence group. In these groups, the core is formed by mothers and their pre-adolescent offspring. Adult males and adolescents of both sexes are drawn to each other and to the mother-offspring units. Socialization occurs primarily through play, imitation, and observation. The most important hominid psychological characteristic is an individual's life-long involvement in families. In gatherer-hunter families, females gather food, males hunt, they share and cooperate with each other, and fathers and grandparents participate in the care of young children.

Culture

In relation to methods of subsistence and variability of habitat, humans are by far the most flexible species. People live and work in climates that range from very cold to very hot, from dry to wet, from forest to desert, from mountain to plains. The extensive development of diverse cultures has permitted these adaptations. All cultures, however, are limited by our evolutionary design. As an example, families hold a central place in each culture, but the nature of the family varies with the type of culture in which it lives. Despite this great diversity, some general principles concerning the social structures of a culture have been identified. One important principle is that the typical subsistence modes of a culture have a large impact on its social structure. This principle is illustrated by the following three examples: (1) Societies which are nomadic, don't store food, live in small subsistence groups, and have little role differentiation; (2) Societies which store food and live in permanent settlements have many social status differences; (3) Societies in which economic survival depends upon the continuous cooperation of several adults generally have non-nuclear families. It should be obvious that the type of culture into which an infant is born will dramatically influence its developmental possibilities.

Although the social structures of cultures may resemble one another, they will differ among themselves in relation to "contents"–their standards for deciding what is, how one feels about it, what to do about it, and how to go about doing it. No general principles have been identified which allow one to predict the contents of any culture. There seems to be a strong element of chance here, but it is clear that nearby cultures influence each other more than distant ones, and that in the long run essentially all contents serve some adaptive function. There are cultural differences within most complex societies. One of the most useful within-society distinctions is based on social class (SES). For example, child rearing values and practices are related to SES membership.

Socialization

Socialization consists of all the influences that people, institutions, and media have on individuals and groups. For North American children the most important socializing agents are their families, peers, schools, and television. In cultures which Eisenstadt refers to as "familistic," peers may have relatively little influence on children. In some of these cultures, neither schools nor television exist. Therefore, the child's family is the most significant factor in controlling and influencing her psychological development.

Cultures differ considerably in the nature of their families, and hence, in the types of influence families have on their children's development. The nuclear family consisting of mother, father, and their offspring, residing in a single separate household, is the ideal of relatively few cultures. The two most common ideal family constellations are the "joint" and the "stem" types. Joint families consist of parents, their married sons and sons' families, and their unmarried sons and daughters. Most stem families consist of parents, their eldest married son and his family, and their unmarried sons and daughters. Thus, in nuclear families, sons and daughters are reared (socialized) to leave the home at marriage (or before) and set up an independent household. In joint families, the sons are reared to remain with their parents and household, but the daughters to leave at marriage. In stem families, all children except the oldest son are reared to leave the family and household at marriage.

In the United States the socializing influences of schools have increased in importance over the past 100 years. More children are attending schools for longer time periods than ever before. Schools influence the cognitive, social, and emotional development of children. Denzin argues that schools teach middle class political values, as well as sex and race roles. Ogbu maintains that one major function of schools is to prepare people to become taxpayers. The ways in which schools carry out their functions, and the impact that they have on children is strongly dependent upon their social context–e.g., how wealthy a school is, the extent of community support and involvement, the racial and SES mixture of the students, and the racial and SES mixture of the staff.

Over a 12-month-period, North American children spend as much time watching television as they do sitting in classrooms. Most of the programs viewed by children have been designed to entertain, and ultimately to sell products. The gatekeepers to commercial television programming–the people who determine what will be shown–are typically white middle and upper class people who have limited accountability to anyone. The primary criterion for showing a program is the probable size of its viewing audience. Although designed to entertain and sell products, television educates, babysits, fills time, and to some extent takes the place of other activities which are valued by many people. It can be a highly positive tool for socializing the young, but it can also have detrimental effects. Our view is that responsbile citizens should take an active role in determining its content.

Methods and Approaches

There are a variey of methods and approaches to the study of psychological development. These range from rigorous, highly structured, narrow-in-scope laboratory procedures to highly fluid, relatively unstructured, open-ended family therapy sessions. Each approach provides a window through which to view the developing child. Any one window, however, gives us an incomplete picture. The collection of methods and approaches is likely to give us a more complete understanding. In general, our developmental conclusions are most secure when they are based on converging evidence from several kinds of studies, used with many kinds of populations.

The easiest and most frequently employed approach is the cross-sectional design–simultaneously studying children of different ages. With this design, we assume that all the age groups follow the same developmental pathway. The more difficult, but more useful approach is the longitudinal design–studying the same group of children over months or years. With this design, we assume that the socializing influences are unchanged over the time span covered. A combination of the two approaches which allows one to evaluate the above assumptions, is the preferred approach.

Developmental research utilizes a variety of statistical methods. Many of these are correlational in nature—they show what behaviors co-vary, and the direction of this co-variation. Correlation is not the same as cause and effect. Thus, we often don't know what produces the developmental changes observed in our research. Although correlational techniques have this built-in limitation, their use does not necessarily undercut the merits of the research. The science of astronomy is built on correlational methods, and ultimately led to our ability to land people on the moon. This ability was based on the construction of elaborate and testable theories. Developmental psychology is sorely in need of this type of theory in its research procedures.

MAJOR SPECIFIC POINTS

Prenatal and Postnatal Physical Development

Canalization processes play a substantial role in children's physical development. During the first 2 weeks of prenatal development, canalization seems to work in an all or none fashion—the zygote either dies or develops normally. During the embryonic period—the third through the seventh weeks of pregnancy—failures of canalization usually lead to major anatomical abnormalities. This is the period during which most major organ systems are being formed. During the fetal period—the eighth through the thirty-eighth weeks—failures of canalization can be observed in only the slowest growing structures such as the brain, eyes, and external genitals. Postnatally, canalization processes maintain sex-related growth differences, which are seen in all primates. In humans, girls reach physical maturity about 2 years earlier than boys. Disease, severe malnutrition and serious hormonal deficiencies early in life may not be guarded against by canalization, leading to severely stunted growth in children.

It is highly likely that behavioral development is closely linked to the maturation of the brain. Of all the organ systems, the brain grows the most postnatally. Brain size is 75% adult levels at age 3, 90% at age 6, and 95% at age 10. However, not all regions mature at the same rate. In a rough, approximate way, the evolutionary old regions mature faster than the evolutionary new ones. Thus, those neocortex areas involved with movement, touch, hearing, and vision mature the fastest. The newer interpretive areas which connect various brain regions to each other, and the language areas are the slowest to mature.

It is important to emphasize that physical development does not occur in a piecemeal fashion. We are fully integrated systems, each anatomical structure and region intimately tied to the others. Moreover, our physical development is also determined by our social environment. In evolution, changes in physical development which did not fit with other physical changes, or with the social environment, did not survive.

Attachment

The mutual attachment of an infant to her primary caretakers is the beginning of the infant's personality development. The sense of self (personality) primarily develops through a child's interactions with other people. Through the attachment process, the infant starts to develop a sense of competence or incompetence, and by early childhood, to learn the rudiments of several social roles.

For both human and non-human primates, an infant's attachment has these characteristics: an intense emotional tie with caretakers, the use of caretakers as a secure base for exploration of her environment, and receiving comfort from caretakers when she is frightened. Laboratory research with monkeys indicates that the social structure of the group has profound effects on the development and maintenance of the attachment behaviors of infants and their mothers. Although comparable fine-grain analyses have not been carried out with humans, the cross cultural research suggests that group social structure has relatively little impact on human attachment behaviors. In the human studies, mothers who are affectionate, enjoy interacting with their infants, and are responsive to their needs and desires, have securely attached infants. Anxiously attached infants have mothers who lack these characteristics.

The nature of a human infant's attachment to mother or father is strongly related to his future social competence in childhood. Two-year-olds who were securely attached infants, in contrast to those anxiously attached, are more compliant and cooperative with adults, play more imaginatively and are more task-oriented. Three-to five-year-olds who were securely attached infants, in comparison with those anxiously attached, are more competent with peers, more resilient in problem solving situations, have greater ego strength, and greater curiosity.

Development of Personal Identity

The most basic criterion for establishing self-identity involves the distinction between one's body and the bodies of others. Body self-recognition, as an evolutionary characteristic, is apparently restricted to the great apes and humans. Monkeys show no evidence of this capacity. In humans, body self-awareness starts to emerge in children at about 9 months of age and continues to develop until they are 2 years old, at which time this concept begins to stabilize.

By age 2½ children correctly label themselves as either boys or girls. However, their self-labels do not become stable until they are about 4½ years old. And it is not until children are about age 6½ that they understand that gender differences are based on genital differences between the sexes. Although the acquisition of sex-role stereotypes, e.g., girls but not boys like to play with dolls, is apparent in 2½-year-olds, knowledge of them slowly grows during childhood. This knowledge is still incomplete, however, at the beginning of adolescence. Cross-cultural research shows that societies differ in the extent to which sex-roles are stereotyped. Nevertheless, in nearly all societies girls are more likely than boys to be trained to be nurturant and responsible, and boys are more likely than girls to be trained to be self-reliant and achievement-oriented.

Self-descriptions are a very common way of assessing the development of personal identity. Children between ages 3 and 8 primarily use external characteristics, e.g., personal possessions, to define themselves; secondarily, they employ behavioral characteristics such as hobbies; and finally, they use internal characteristics such as self-evaluations for self-descriptive purposes. Children aged 10 and older primarily use behavioral self-descriptions, then internal characteristics, and use external traits the least of all.

Self-Esteem

Relatively litle psychological research has been done concerning the development of self-esteem. Self-esteem is usually assessed through the use of questionnaires, and is seen by most researchers as comprised of both broad and narrow characteristics of the self. Rosenberg defines self-esteem as "self-acceptance, self-respect, feelings of self-worth."

Self-esteem develops as a result of our experiences with other people in a variety of situations. If others react to us in positive ways or we perceive that others believe we are worthy, our self-esteem is enhanced.

Another factor influencing the development of self-esteem is the positive or negative results of our comparisons of self with others, especially for attributes that are psychologically central to us.

Children with high self-esteem, in contrast to those with low self-esteem are academically more successful, have more internal academic motivation, and are more likely to take leadership roles in class. They are not more popular with classmates than children with low self-esteem, but they feel that they have an easier time making friends.

Developmentally, the children's self-esteem decreases between the ages of 8 and 12, stabilizes, and then increases from the ages of 13 to 18. The greatest negative change occurs during their transition into junior high school. This decline is produced by environmental effects rather than the physiological changes accompanying the onset of puberty.

The specific environmental and interpersonal factors influencing the development of self-esteem are complex. One consistent finding is that mothers of children with high self-esteem are generally emotionally stable, and feel competent and unburdened by motherhood. Peers, siblings, teachers, and one's own competencies all contribute to the development of self esteem, but their effects depend upon a child's developmental level.

Play, Aggression, and Dominance

Play is the major vehicle through which young human and non-human primate peers socialize one another. Infants and juveniles of all primate species spend extraordinary amounts of time in peer play. Adolescents and adults spend progressively less time doing so. Play seems to be one of the major ways in which monkeys, apes and children learn the skills required for establishing dominance relationships. For non-human primates and young children aggression is the primary route by which they establish dominance over each other. Once established, one's dominance over another is maintained through the threat of aggression.

Children from ages 4 to 8 increasingly use verbal aggression rather than physical methods, to assert their dominance. During the latter part of these years and into early adolescence, aggression towards others diminishes as the basic means of establishing dominance. For children in this age range, aggression is largely replaced by athletic ability, physical maturation, and leadership qualities. Dominance relations in young children and non-human primates are rigid, but those of 12 to 14 year olds are flexible.

Cross-cultural research indicates that patterns of aggression among children are highly similar, wherever they occur. An examination of the biology of sex differences in the expression of aggression strongly suggests the existence of a biological base for the greater aggressiveness of boys. However, socialization practices are also quite influential in determining these differences, and there is great overlap between boys and girls in their expression of aggression.

Cognitive Aspects of Play

Human play is a creative process in which the infant and child attempt to gain new perspectives and new understandings of their physical and social environments. Piaget maintains that there are three types of play associated with three stages of cognitive development: practice play, symbolic play, and games with rules. Each type of play has as a focus a different objective to be mastered. In practice play, the infant attempts to master his own sensory-motor activities. In symbolic play, the child tries to master her understanding and use of symbols. In games with rules, children attempt to master their understanding of social relationships. In evaluating reseach concerned with testing aspects of Piaget's theory of play we concluded that age should be used as a rough guideline only for determining the emergence of certain psychological functions.

Sociodramatic play, a form of symbolic play, has been extensively studied with nursery school children by Garvey and Schwartzman. Central to the research of both is the idea that children use their cognitive capacities to adopt an "as if" or hypothetical relationship to persons, situations, and actions, e.g., "Let's pretend I'm the father and you're my son." Garvey shows us that this form of play allows children to test out a variety of the social roles which they experience in their daily lives. These experiences lead to their learning how to better control their own social behavior as well as how to influence the behavior of others. Schwartzman points out that play allows players to comment on, interpret, and perhaps test out new ways of dealing with authorities. These comments and interpretations are enacted in the various roles of children's play dramas.

A Cross-Cultural View of Games

Competitive games apparently do not exist in some cultures. In general people in these cultures discourage competition among themselves and with members of neighboring cultures. They place little pressure on children to achieve relative to their peers. Cultures which engage only in games requiring physical skill are very similar to the cultures previously discussed. The major differences between these two types are that the gaming cultures have greater sex-role differentiation than the non-gaming cultures, as well as a greater percentage of nuclear, as opposed to extended, families. Cultures which engage in strategy games are generally highly complex societies. They incorporate substantial social stratification and role differentiation. Most scholars agree that the types of games children play reflect cultural values as well as instill those values in the players. "Gaming" knowledge is seen as important for future success in life.

The relationship between cultural values and children's game behavior is clearly seen in the Madsen "cooperation-competition games." In most cultures, families in rural areas are engaged in agriculturally-related work. Family members must cooperate with each other in order to attain at least a minimal standard of living. This level of cooperation is rare among families in urban settings. In cities, competition and personal gain are the norm, even if this is done at the expense of others. In the Madsen games there is much more cooperation among children from rural areas than among children from urban areas. Futher, recent immigrants from rural to urban areas cooperate with each other more than do second and third generation urban dwellers. Also, young children cooperate more than older children from the same culture. Three major factors influence children's level of cooperation: (1) how much their culture emphasizes competition; (2) how much their culture emphasizes strong ties and commitments to others; (3) the extent to which urban living has weakened those ties.

Development of Altruism

In general, experiments show the following: (1) Older children are more altruistic than younger children (2) Boys and girls are equally altruistic at each age level; (3) Children are only moderately consistent in their level of altruism across situations; (4) Children's level of altruism is positively related to their level of moral development; but (5) The reasons children give for helping reflect a higher level of altruistic thinking than their altruistic acts—they talk a better game than they play.

Parental Influences on Peer Behavior

Baumrind studied child rearing practices of parents of 4-year-old and 8½-year-old children and related these to children's peer interactions in a school setting. She found that the same parenting behaviors frequently had very different effects on son's than daughter's behavior. This phenomenon was more marked with the younger than with the older children. Generally, however, children with parents who were authoritarian and restrictive, had difficulty with peers. Children with parents who were authoritative and appropriately demanding had good peer relationships. Children whose parents encouraged autonomy and were emotionally supportive also had good peer relationships.

Hetherington, Cox and Cox studied the impact of divorce on young children living with their mothers. Two months following the divorce boys and girls played with peers in immature and disruptive ways. They were more often observed in solitary play than were children from intact families. One year following the divorce, their play became more constructive, especially for the girls. Two years after the divorce, girls' play, but not boys' play, was indistinguishable from that of children from intact families. In general, the negative impact of divorce is longer lasting for boys than for girls.

Piaget's Theory of Cognitive Development

For Piaget, cognitive development is synonymous with the development of intelligence. His concern is with creating a theory to understand how the mind works in its attempts to make sense out of experience. According to this theory, each of us constructs a world view by applying our schemas—the mental tools for acquiring knowledge—in our interactions with the environment. Each time we apply our schemas, we are said to assimilate or fit interactions to them. In that each interaction is different from all preceeding ones, we must modify or accommodate our schemas in order to make them fit. Thus, with repetition the schemas progressively change in such a way that more of our interactions can be interpreted (made sense out of), and our interpretations become more complex.

Cognitive development is seen as an evolved canalized process. The small changes which occur through repetitive use of schemas always culminate in more dramatic changes in how the schemas are organized. These dramatic changes are grouped into four stages. In the first, sensory-motor stage, the schemas consist of actions, such as reflexes and habits. Cognitive development during this stage is highly similar for monkeys, gorillas, and humans. In the second, preoperational stage, the child is able to symbolically represent her world. She can extend her experiences by carrying out mental experiments. In the third, concrete operational stage, the previously limited logical abilities are overcome through the emergence of two new mental operations – inversion and reciprocity. Both involve the ability to mentally reverse observed actions. The existence of this sequence of three stages is found in childen of all cultures, and at approximately the same ages. In Western cultures, the fourth, formal operational stage, emerges at about age 12. Children can now perform inversion and reciprocity simultaneously. This stage is apparently related to formal schooling in the respect that is is not often observed in unschooled children and adolescents.

Development of Attention and Memory

Attention and memory processes always operate together. We must attend to an object or event in order to remember it, but the extent to which we attend to it is determined by whether or not we remember having had an experience of it. From birth to about 3 months, infants are "captured" by stimuli, having virtually no memory for them. Between 3 and 12 months they progressively improve in their attentional abilities to clarify and explore stimuli. During this age range, short-term memory in children dramatically improves. Between 1 and 3 years of age, children increasingly use symbolic activities involving both attention and memory, resulting in marked improvement in both.

The exploratory and selective aspects of attention change systematically in children between ages 3 and 12. From ages 3 to 5, children's exploration of objects is incomplete and uneconomical. From 5 to 7 their exploratory activities are more extensive, task-relevant, and economical. In children from 7 to 12 these abilities slowly improve and stabilize. Children's capacity to selectively attend to relevant versus irrelevant stimuli shows a progressive increase in the 3 to 12 age range.

Three topics in memory development were discussed. When asked to remember objects or events, some 4-year-olds can use memory strategies, such as rehearsal. But it is not until after age 7 that nearly all children spontaneously do so. At about age 7, the capability to accurately evaluate one's own memory abilities emerges. As this capability develops, so does the mature use of memory strategies. At about age 7, children start to employ a variety of means for organizing their memories, which leads to superior recall. From age 7 and older, children's organizational abilities progressively increase. Finally, the development of acquistion, storage, and retrieval processes was compared. Children's acquisition and storage capabilities stabilize at about age 12, but their retrieval capabilities progressively develop between ages 3 and 20.

Social Cognition

Social cognition refers to one's knowledge of situations involving the interactions of two or more people. Based on an evolutionary perspective, knowledge about reciprocal obligations and moral judgments is at the core of social cognition. The two psychologists who have most extensively elaborated on and studied this view are Piaget and Kohlberg. Piaget defines morality as a system of rules. Moral development involves the respect people acquire for them. Through the use of games and stories with children of varying ages, Piaget has found that between ages 4 and 10, children base their judgments primarily on obedience to rules handed down by elders. Children are inflexible and they estimate degree of wrongdoing by the amount of damage done.After age 10, they progressively view themselves and their peers as rule-givers. Rules are seen as flexible, depending on circumstances and ongoing mutual agreement as to what these rules are. Estimates of wrongdoing are largely detemined by one's intentions, as opposed to external consequences. Peers become the primary teachers of morality.

Recent research on intentions and consequences in relation to children's moral judgments has led to revisions of Piaget's conclusions. Three-year-olds are able to consider another's motive in their making of moral judgments, and by age 5, children are able to consider intentions. From about age 6 onwards they are able to simultaneously consider damage, intentions, and another's rationale in making moral decisions. Contrary to Piaget's analysis, external consequences continue to be a factor in children after age 10.

Kohlberg's research utilizes stories which emphasize moral dilemmas. A child is asked to make a moral decision and to give his reasons for this decision. By studying these reasons, Kohlberg has evolved a stage theory of moral development, consisting of three levels (two stages in each). The Preconventional level is characteristic of the moral reasoning of 4- to 10-year-olds. Moral acts are interpreted in terms of either their physical consequences or whether they are consistent with roles set by those with superior physical power, such as parents. Depending upon the particular culture, the Conventional level emerges in children during the age range of 10 to 20. Conventional thinking is conformist–individuals engaged in this type of thinking seek to support and maintain the social order as it is. The Postconventional level emerges in adults after the age of 18. Morality is viewed as a set of principles which apply to essentially all societies and individuals. Few people in any culture attain this level. Cross-cultural research supports the sequential nature of these stages.

Turiel has questioned Piaget's and Kohlberg's assumption that moral issues comprise a single category of social understanding. Rather, he provides evidence that there are at least two categories of social rules: (1) morality and (2) social convention. These two categories are concerned with different issues, develop in different ways, and are distinguished as such by young children.

One of the oldest moral rules is the Biblical statement, "Do unto others as you would have them do unto you." The qualities of empathy and self-awareness comprise the underlying psychology of this form of reciprocity. Research on the development of empathy indicates that it does not generalize across situations. Moreover, there are at least two forms of empathy, simple and flexible. The golden rule, stated above, is based on simple empathy—predict that another person will respond as you do. This form emerges in children by the age of 3 and starts to stabilize at the age of 5. Flexible empathy involves the ability to simultaneously relate differing viewpoints of the same objective events. This ability emerges in children age 5, and continues to develop after age 12. Juvenile delinquents are deficient in flexible empathy. Training which improves this ability leads to decreases in criminal behavior.

Intelligence and Language of Apes

Intelligence is closely related to information-processing capacity, language, and symbol use. It is virtually impossible to study language developed in apes, or any species, without simultaneously studying the development of intelligence. Through the use of symbols, apes have been found to understand cause and effect relationships, intentions, higher order linquistic relationships, and to have a highly elaborated memory. Apes acquire very rich concepts involving word symbols. They use words novelly and metaphorically, and make errors in generalization comparable to those of young children. There is good evience that apes use grammar in forming two-word sentences, but there is no evidence of consistent word order for three- and four-word statements. Generally, apes' language use is different from that of young children. However, considering the fact that apes and children receive different kinds of language training, these differences in word usage are not surprising.

Human Language Development

There is good evidence from analyses of the pre-linguistic sounds infants produce and understand, as well as from Lenneberg's research on the parallels in motor and speech development, that human language development is a canalized process. For example, children with Down's Syndrome and normal children acquire speech and motor skills in the same sequence, despite great differences in rate of acquisition.

In all languages studied by researchers, when children acquire a 50-word vocabulary, they start using two-word sentences. These first words are generally ones representing things that move or change in some way, such as toys. The structures of sentences created by children under age 3 are determined by their semantic intentions, as opposed to their knowledge of syntax. After that age, syntax plays an increasing role in sentence structure. A child's grammatical understanding continues to develop well into her adolescence.

Language is typically used to converse with, and thereby, to influence others. "Speech acts" (conversational units) can be divided into five major categories. The speech of children under age 5 is largely restricted to representatives (assertions or representations) and directives (directions to listeners). By about that age, children have also learned the act of indirection, a form of hinting which is useful in social interactions.

Development of Intelligence

Western definitions of intelligence are linked to academic success. There are two broad approaches to defining and measuring intelligence. The Psychometric or abilities approach views intelligence as a collection of mental characteristics which underlie performance on all cognitive tasks. Intelligence is measured by evaluating performance on these tasks and statistically determining the type and nature of the factors underlying performance. Currently most researchers conclude that intelligence is based on one general and several more narrow factors. The second, Processes approach, focuses on identifying the underlying processes people use in solving cognitive problems. One person may be more intelligent than another because she uses the processes more quickly or more efficiently.

Most behavioral geneticists estimate the heritability of IQ to range from .50 to .80. Thus, between 20% and 50% of IQ differences between individuals of the same race are produced by environmental influences. The most potent of these is the quality of home care children receive during the first three years of life. Several of the most important factors influencing a child's IQ development are the mother's involvement with and emotional responsiveness to her child, variety in play materials, and daily stimulation.

Reading and Reading Disabilities

Reading is defined as extracting information from printed text. It can be divided into two categories—decoding print into words, and comprehending sentences and paragraphs. Children use both sets of processes simultaneously, but as they become skilled readers, decoding becomes automatic.

There are a variety of forms or types of reading disability, and a variety of causes for it. Vellutino argues that language deficiences are common to all forms. The genetics research indicates that various types of reading disabilities are inherited characteristics. The underlying genetic mechanisms appear to be different for boys and girls. The socio-cultural influences on reading disabilities can be powerful. Approximately two thirds of black children from low SES families read below the national average. The one third who are good readers apparently come from families that encourage verbal interactions. As a consequence, these children develop good language skills before the start of reading instruction.

Cross-cultural research comparing reading ability in Chinese, Japanese, and North American children concluded that the nature of the script has little impact on learning to read. Moreover, the proportion of reading disabled children is approximately the same in each of these cultures. This suggests that neither race nor culture influences reading development, provided that equivalent reading instruction is provided.

Mathematics Understanding

Unlike reading, mathematics can be performed without written materials. Gellman and Gallistel have shown that preschoolers have a rather sophisticated understanding of numbers. They know that each counted object should have a unique name, that the names should be used in the same order, and that the last name used in a counting sequence is the cardinal number of the set of objects counted. Although preschoolers can successfully compare the cardinal numbers of two collections of objects which they have counted, they fail on Piaget's number conservation tasks because they have not developed the ability to reason about uncounted collections.

The major arithmetic acquisition of school children is developing an understanding of the Part-Whole schema. The development of this schema parallels and is comparable to the class schema in logical development. With the Part-Whole and class schemas, children can solve addition and substraction problems as well as make correct distinctions between "some" and "all" in problems dealing with class inclusion.

Arithmetic development depends largely upon the nature and type of numerical system used. Americans use an abstract base 10 system, whereas the Oksapmins of New Guinea use a non-base system tied to 28 distinct body parts. Thus the Oksapmin children confuse numbers that correspond to similar body parts, e.g., left versus right wrist, and many adolescents still have not fully abstracted number concepts from body parts. These discrepancies in comprehension place severe limitations on their numerical capabilities.

Socialization Through Schools

Schools are one of the four major socializing agents of children. In a school setting, children attempt to balance the focus generated by academic requirements, authority figures, friends, and self-esteem motives. As children progress through school, they increasingly challenge the legitimacy of teachers and principals, and their choice of friends is increasingly based on non-academic concerns. In the primary grades teachers exert a marked influence on both friendship choices and a child's development of self-esteem. By the time children reach senior high school, teachers have virtually no influence on either of these two factors. The behavior of adolescents in schools seems primarily motivated by their desire to maintain friendships, and secondarily, by academic concerns. The type of classroom structure used—open versus closed—has a far greater effect on children in primary than secondary schools, especially in relation to their forming of friendships.

The academic socialization of low-SES black children can be dramatically influenced by their enrollment in Head Start type programs. These programs have essentially no lasting impact on IQ development. Rather the academic success of children previously enrolled in these programs depends upon the more positive attitudes they and their mothers have developed towards academic achievement.

The Peruvian research concerning the impact of school on 5- and 6-year-olds showed that even a few months of schooling could have marked effects on children's cognitive performance. However, these effects vary with the culture in which the children are reared. The Mexican research indicated that the one major effect of schooling is to increase the likelihood that children will use a variety of cognitive abilities to solve intellectual problems.

Schooling and learning to read and write do not have equivalent effects on cognitive development. The effects of schooling are generally more profound, but both influences depend upon the teaching methods employed, and how the education is put into practice.

Socialization Through Television

During the course of a year children spend as much time watching television as they do sitting in classrooms. Research has shown that this intensive involvement of children with television viewing has both positive and negative effects on them. The type and degree of these effects are determined by a child's age and parental values. In the cognitive realm, children's viewing behavior is determined to a greater degree by their understanding of the T.V. material seen than it is by the perceptually salient features of the programs. Children under age 8 have a very limited understanding of programs which have a story line and require analysis of the motivation of the characters portrayed.

Programs such as *Sesame Street* designed to teach cognitive skills to preschoolers are successful in doing so. The development of academic skills in older children is complexly related to amount of daily television viewing engaged in, as well as to age, IQ, and parental values. IQ development, however, is positively correlated with amount of viewing for grade school children, but negatively correlated for children age 13 or older.

Television viewing shapes children's social beliefs, usually in positive ways. For example, amount of viewing is positively correlated with positive attitudes towards women and minority groups. Selective viewing of programs having positive social content such as *Mr. Rogers' Neighborhood* generally enhances positive social behaviors such as altruism and friendliness. However, if the home or school environments don't support these changes, children revert to their old patterns of behavior.

On the negative side, it has been shown that extensive viewing of violence leads to increased aggressiveness. Although the correlations between the two variables are small, the cultural impact from slight increases in aggressiveness can be very destructive. Another negative result that was found is that commercials aimed at children have the effect of encouraging poor nutrition preferences and eating habits. Our view is that parents should take an active role in combating these experiences.

Socialization by the Family

Children move in and out of variety of social contexts—schools, peer groups, stores, and families. Each context can be viewed as having a somewhat unique culture with its own set of rules and social roles. As children mature they expect to play different roles in each of these contexts, but their expectations may not be matched by those of parents, peers, and other adults. As a consequence, there is often conflict between the participants in these different contexts. For example, young children can take candy at home without paying for it, but they cannot do this in a store. School age children can sometimes "talk back" to their parents with impunity, but are punished for talking back to their teachers. They can curse at their peers but not at their parents or teachers. Often these conflicts are easily resolved, but when they are not, the parents sometimes bring their children into family therapy. Family therapy is a unique laboratory for studying child development in the family context.

Control and responsibility are the two major recurring issues in family therapy. As children mature, they progressively wish to control their own destiny, and sometimes that of their parents and siblings as well. Parents resent being controlled, and become fearful when their children are out of control. They also feel responsible for their children's development and behavior. They want their children to be responsible for themselves and to the family, and to accept parental rules and parental controls. These different values and motivations invariably lead to child-parent conflicts. Such conflicts are normal and to be expected, but they must be negotiated. Most families can successfully do so, and most families involved in family therapy succeed also. Failures to resolve these conflicts often lead to poor social and emotional development in children.

References

Abravanel, E. The development of intersensory patterning with regard to selected spatial dimensions. *Monographs of the Society for Research in Child Development*, 1968, *33*, No. 18.

Achenbach, T. M. *Research in developmental psychology*. New York: Free Press, 1978.

Adams, M. J. Failures to comprehend and levels of processing in reading. In R. J. Spiro, B. C. Bruce & W. F. Brewer (Eds.), *Theoretical issues in reading comprehension*. Hillsdale, NJ: Lawrence Erlbaum Associates, 1980.

Ainsworth, M. D. The development of mother-infant interaction among the Ganda. In B. M. Foss (Ed.), *Determinants of infant behavior* (Vol. 2). New York: Wiley, 1963.

Ainsworth, M. D., Blehar, M., Waters, E., & Wall, S. *Patterns of attachment*. Hillsdale, NJ: Lawrence Erlbaum Associates, 1978.

Als, H., Tronick, E., Lester, B. M., & Brazelton, T. B. Specific neonatal measures: The Brazelton Neonatal Behavior Assessment scale. In J. Osofsky (Ed.), *Handbook of infant development*. New York: Wiley, 1979.

ABC Social Research Unit/Broadcast Standards and Practices Department. *A research perspective on television and violence*. New York: American Broadcasting Companies, 1983.

Amsterdam, B. K. Mirror self-image reactions before age two. *Developmental Psychology*, 1972, *5*, 297–305.

Anderson, D. R., & Lorch, E. P. Looking at television: Action or reaction? In J. Bryant & D. R. Anderson (Eds.), *Children's understanding of television: Research on attention and comprehension*. New York: Academic Press, 1983.

Arend, R., Gove, F. L., & Sroufe, L. A. Continuity of individual adaptation from infancy to kindergarten: A predictive study of ego-resiliency and curiosity in preschoolers. *Child Development*, 1979, *50*, 950–959.

Atkin, C. K. Television advertising and socialization to consumer roles. In D. Pearl, L. Bouthilet, & J. Lazar (Eds.), *Television and behavior* (Vols. 1 & 2). Washington, DC: U.S. Government Printing Office, 1982.

Bakeman, R., & Brown, J. V. Early interaction: Consequences for social and mental development at three years. *Child Development*, 1980, *51*, 437–447.

Ball, S., & Bogatz, G. A. *The first year of Sesame Street: An evaluation*. Princeton, NJ: Educational Testing Service, 1970.

Baltes, P. B., Reese, H. W., & Nesslreoade, J. R. *Life span developmental psychology*. Monterey, CA: Brooks Cole, 1977.

Baltes, P. B., & Schaie, K. W. (Eds.). *Life span developmental psychology: Personality and socialization.* New York: Academic Press, 1973.

Bandura, A. *Aggression: A social learning analysis.* Englewood Cliffs, NJ: Prentice Hall, 1973.

Bandura, A. Behavior theory and the models of man. In A. Wandersman, P. Poppen & D. F. Ricks (Eds.), *Humanism and behaviorism: Dialogue and growth.* New York: Pergamon Press, 1976.

Bandura, A. *Social learning theory.* Englewood Cliffs, NJ: Prentice-Hall, 1977.

Bane, M. J. *Here to stay.* New York: Basic Books, 1977.

Barber, J. D. *The presidential characters: Predicting performance in the white house.* Englewood Cliffs, NJ: Prentice-Hall, 1972.

Barry, H. III, Bacon, M. K., & Child, I. L. A cross-cultural survey of some sex differences in socialization. *Journal of Abnormal and Social Psychology,* 1957, *55,* 327–332.

Bar-Tal, D., Raviv, A., Leiser, T. The development of altruistic behavior: Empirical evidence. *Developmental Psychology,* 1980, *16,* 516–524.

Baumrind, D. The development of instrumental competence through socialization. In A. D. Pick (Ed.), *Minnesota Symposia on Child Psychology* (Vol. 7). Minneapolis: University of Minnesota Press, 1973.

Baumrind, D. Current patterns of parental authority. *Developmental Psychology Monographs,* 1971, *4,* No. 1, Pt. 2.

Baumrind, D. *Childrearing effects.* Unpublished manuscript., 1982.

Baxter, P. J. W., & Almagor, U. Observations about generations. In J. S. LaFontaine (Ed.), *Sex and age as principles of social differentiation.* New York: Academic Press, 1978.

Bayley, N., & Schaefer, E. S. Correlations of maternal and child behaviors with the development of mental abilities: Data from the Berkeley Growth Study. *Monographs of the Society for Research in Child Development,* 1964, *29,* 1–50.

Beck, A. T. *Cognitive therapy and the emotional disorders.* New York: International Universities Press, 1976.

Bee, H. L., Barnard, K. E., Eyres, S. J., Gray, C. A., Hammond, M. A., Spietz, A. L., Snyder, C., & Clark, B. Prediction of IQ and language skill from perinctal status, child performance, family characteristics, and mother-infant interaction. *Child Development,* 1982, *53,* 1134–1156.

Bell, S. M., & Ainsworth, M. D. S. Infant crying and maternal responsiveness. *Child Development,* 1972, *43,* 1171–1190.

Berkowitz, L. The control of aggression. In B. Caldwell & H. Ricciuti (Eds.), *Review of Child Development Research* (Vol. 3). Chicago: University of Chicago Press, 1973.

Belson, W. A. *Television violence and the adolescent boy.* Westmead, England: Saxon House, 1978.

Berndt, T. J., & Berndt, E. G. Children's use of motives and intentionality in person perception and moral judgment. *Child Development,* 1975, *46,* 904–912.

Berry, J. W. *Human ecology and cognitive style.* New York: Wiley, 1976.

Bertrand, M. Rough and tumble play in stumptails. In J. S. Bruner, A. Jolly, & K. Sylva (Eds.), *Play.* New York: Basic Books, 1976.

Bertrand, M. The behavior repertoire of the stumptail macaque. *Biblioteca Primatologica II,* S. Karger, Basle, 1976.

Birch, H. G. Methodological issues in the longitudinal study of malnutrition. In D. F. Ricks, A. Thomas, & M. Roff (Eds.), *Life history research in psychopathology* (Vol. 3). Minneapolis: University of Minnesota Press, 1974.

Blanchard, M., & Main, M. Avoidance of the attachment figure and social-emotional adjustment in day care infants. *Developmental Psychology,* 1979, *14,* 445–446.

Bloch, J. H. Conceptions of sex role. *American Psychologist,* 1973, *28,* 512–526.

Block, J. *Lives through time*. Berkeley, CA: Bancroft, 1971.

Bloom, B. S. *Stability and change in human characteristics*. New York: Wiley, 1964.

Bloom, L. Language development. In F. G. Horowitz (Ed.), *Review of child development research* (Vol. 4). Chicago: University of Chicago Press, 1975.

Blumberg, R. L., & Winch, R. Societal complexity and familial complexity: Evidence for the curvilinear hypothesis. *American Journal of Sociology*, 1973, *77*, 898-920.

Bogatz, G. A., & Ball, S. *The second year of Sesame Street: A continuing evaluation*. Princeton, NJ: Educational Testing Service, 1971.

Bogin, B., & MacVean, R. B. The relationship of socioeconomic status and sex to body size, skelatal maturation, and cognitive status of Guatemala City schoolchildren. *Child Development*, 1983, *54*, 115-128.

Borke, H. Interpersonal perception of young children. *Developmental Psychology*, 1971, *5*, 263-269.

Borman, K. M., & Lippincott, N. J. Cognition and culture: Two perspectives on "free play." In K. M. Borman (Ed.), *The social life of children in a changing society*. Hillsdale, NJ: Lawrence Erlbaum/Ablex, 1982.

Bossert, S. *Tasks and social relationships in classrooms*. Cambridge, England: Cambridge University Press, 1979.

Boszormenyi-Nagy, I., & Spark, G. *Invisible loyalties: Reciprocity in intergenerational family therapy*. New York: Hoeber-Harper, 1973.

Bower, T. G. R. *A primer of infant development*. San Francisco: W. H. Freeman, 1977.

Bower, T. G. R. *Development in infancy*. (2nd Edition). San Francisco: W. H. Freeman and Company, 1982.

Bowlby, J. *Maternal care and mental health*. (2nd ed. Monograph Series, No. 2). Geneva: World Health Organization, 1952.

Bowlby, J. *Attachment and loss* (Vol. I). *Attachment*. New York: Basic Books, 1969.

Bowlby, J. *Attachment and loss* (Vol. II). *Separation*. New York: Basic Books, 1973.

Braidwood, R. J. *Prehistoric man* (7th ed.). Glenview, IL: Scott, Foresman, 1967.

Braine, M. D. S. The ontogeny of English phrase structure: The first phase. *Language*, 1963, *39*, 1-14.

Braine, M. D. S. Children's first word combinations. *Monographs of the Society for Research in Child Development*, 1976, *41*, No. 164.

Brandt, M. M. Relations between cognitive role-taking performance and age, task presentation and response requirements. *Developmental Psychology*, 1978, *14*, 206-213.

Brazelton, T. B., Koslowsky, B., & Tronek, E. Neonatal evaluation of urbanizing blacks in Lusaka. Paper presented at the Society for Research in Child Development. Minneapolis, MN, 1971.

Brody, L. R. Visual short-term cued recall memory in infancy. *Child Development*, 1981, *52*, 242-250.

Bronfenbrenner, V. Socialization and social class through time and space. In E. E. Maccoby, T. M. Newcomb & E. L. Hartley (Eds.), *Readings in social psychology*. New York: Holt, Rinehart, & Winston, 1958.

Brookhart, J., & Hock, E. The effects of experimental context and experiential background on infants' behavior toward their mothers and a stranger. *Child Development*, 1976, *47*, 333-340.

Brown, P., & Elliot, R. The control of aggression in a nursery school class. *Journal of Experimental Child Psychology*, 1965, *2*, 103-107.

Brown, R. *A first language*. Cambridge, MA: Harvaard University Press, 1973.

Bruner, J. S., Jolly, A., & Sylva, K. (Eds.) *Play*. New York: Basic Books, 1976.

Bryant, J., & Anderson, D. R. (Eds.) *Children's understanding of television: Research on attention and comprehension*. New York: Academic Press, 1983.

Bullock, M., & Gellman, R. Numerical reasoning in young children: The ordering principle. *Child Development,* 1977, *48,* 427–434.

Carr, T. H. Building theories of reading ability: On the relation between individual differences in cognitive skills and reading comprehension. *Cognition,* 1981, *9,* 73–114.

Cattel, R. B. Factor analysis: An introduction to essentials I. The purpose and underlying models. *Biometrics,* 1965, *21,* 190–215.

Chandler, J. J., Greenspan, S., & Barenboim, C. Assessment and training of role-taking and referential communication skills in institutionalized emotionally disturbed children. *Developmental Psychology,* 1974, *10,* 546–553.

Chandler, M. J. Egocentricism and antisocial behavior: The assessment and training of social perspective-taking skills. *Developmental Psychology,* 1973, *9,* 326–332.

Charlesworth, W. R. Human intelligence as adaptation: An ethological approach. In L. B. Resnick (Ed.), *The nature of intelligence.* Hillsdale, NJ: Lawrence Erlbaum Associates, 1976.

Chechile, R. A., Richman, C. L., Topinka, C., & Ehrensbeck, K. A developmental study of the storage and retrieval of information. *Child Development,* 1981, *52,* 251–259.

Chomsky, N. *Language and mind.* New York: Harcourt, Brace & World, 1968.

Clark, H. H., & Clark, E. V. *Psychology and language.* New York: Harcourt, Brace & Jovanovich, 1977.

Clark, R. Theory and method in child-language research: Are we assuming too much? In S. A. Kuczaj II (Ed.), *Language development* (Vol. 1). *Syntax and semantics,* Hillsdale, NJ: Lawrence Erlbaum Associates, 1982.

Clarke-Stewart, A. K. Interactions between mothers and their young children: Characteristics and consequences. *Monographs of the Society for Research in Child Development,* 1973, *38,* Serial No. 153.

Cohen, L. B. Our developing knowledge of infant perception and cognition. *American Psychologist.* 1979, *34,* 894–899.

Cohen, L. J., & Campos, J. J. Father, mother, and stranger as elicitors of attachment behavior in infancy. *Developmental Psychology,* 1974, *10,* 146–154.

Cohen, M. B., Baker, G., Cohen, R. A., Fromm-Reichmann, F., & Weigert, E. V. An intensive study of twelve cases of manic-depressive psychosis. *Psychiatry,* 1954, *17,* 103–137.

Collins, W. A. Interpretation and inference in children's television viewing. In J. Bryant & D. R. Anderson (Eds.), *Children's understanding of television: Research on attention and comprehension.* New York: Academic Press, 1983.

Conel, J. L. *The postnatal development of the human cerebral cortex.* Vols. 1–8. Cambridge: Harvard University Press, 1939–1967.

Connell, D. B. *Individual differences in attachment: An investigation into stability, implications, and relationships to structure of early language development.* Unpublished doctoral dissertation, Syracuse University, 1976.

Conrad, R. The chronology of the development of covert speech in children. *Developmental Psychology,* 1971, *5,* 398–405.

Constanzo, P. R., Coie, J. D., Grumet, J. F., & Farnill, D. Reexamination of the effects of intent and consequence on children's moral judgments. *Child Development,* 1973, *44,* 154–161.

Coopersmith, S. *The antecedents of self-esteem.* San Francisco: W. H. Freeman, 1967.

Cordua, G. D., McGraw, K. O., & Drabman, R. S. Doctor or nurse: Children's perception of sex typed occupations. *Child Development,* 1979, *50,* 590–593.

Corteen, R. S. Television and reading skills. Paper presented at the annual meeting of the Canadian Psychological Association. Vancouver, B. C., June, 1977.

Critchley, M. *The dyslexic child.* Springfield, IL: Charles C. Thomas, 1970.

Cusick, P. A. *Inside high school.* New York: Holt, Rinehart, & Winston, 1973.

Dasen, P. R. A contribution to cross-cultural Piagetian psychology. In N. Warren (Ed.), *Studies in cross-cultural psychology* (Vol. 1). London: Academic Press, 1977.

Denzin, W. K. *Childhood socialization.* San Francisco: Jossey-Bass, 1977.

Dewitt, K. N. The effectiveness of family therapy: A review of outcome research. *Archives of General Psychology,* 1978, *35,* 549–561.

Dickstein, E. Self and self-esteem: Theoretical foundations and their implications for research. *Human Development,* 1977, *20,* 129–140.

Dolhinow, P. At play in the fields. *Natural History.* Special Supplement, December, 1971.

Drake, S. G. *Biography and history of the Indians of North America.* Boston: O. L. Perkins and Hilliard, Gray & Co., 1834.

Eaton, W. O., & Von Bargen, D. Asynchronous development of gender understanding in preschool children. *Child Development,* 1981, *52,* 1020–1027.

Edelbrock, C., & Sugawara, A. I. Acquisition of sex-typed preferences in preschool-aged children. *Developmental Psychology,* 1978, *14,* 614–623.

Eifermann, R. R. Social play in childhood. In R. E. Herron & B. Sutton-Smith (Eds.), *Child's play.* New York: John Wiley, 1971.

Eimas, P. D., & Tartter, V. C. On the development of speech perception: Mechanisms and analogies. In H. W. Reese & L. P. Lipsett (Eds.), *Advances in child development and behavior* (Vol. 13). New York: Academic Press, 1979.

Eisenberg, N. Social development. In C. B. Kopp & J. B. Krakow (Eds.), *The child: Development in a social context.* Reading, Mass.: Addison-Wesley, 1982.

Eisenberg, N., Cameron, E., Tyron, K., & Dodez, R. Socialization of prosocial behavior in the preschool classroom. *Developmental Psychology,* 1981, *17,* 773–782.

Eisenberg-Berg, N., & Hand, M. The relationship of preschoolers' reasoning about prosocial moral conflicts to prosocial behavior. *Child Development,* 1979, *50,* 356–363.

Eisenberg-Berg, N., & Neal, C. Children's moral reasoning about their own spontaneous prosocial behavior. *Developmental Psychology,* 1979, *15,* 228–229.

Eisenstadt, S. N. *From generation to generation.* Glencoe: Free Press, 1956.

Elardo, R., Bradley, R., & Caldwell, B. The relation of infants' home environments to mental test performance from six to thirty-six months: a longitudinal analysis. *Child Development,* 1975, *46,* 71–76.

Epstein, J. L. *Friends in school: Patterns of selection and influence in secondary schools.* Report No. 266, Baltimore: The Johns Hopkins University Center for Social Organization of Schools, 1978.

Epstein, J. L., & McPartland, J. M. *Authority structures and student development.* Report No. 246, Baltimore: The Johns Hopkins University Center for Social Organization of Schools, 1978.

Erikson, E. H. *Childhood and society* (2nd ed.), New York: W. W. Norton, 1963.

Eron, L. D., Huesmann, L. R., Brice, P., Fischer, P., & Mermelstein, R. Age trends in the development of aggression, sex typing, and related television habits. *Developmental Psychology,* 1983, *19,* 71–77.

Eron, L. D., Huesmann, L. R., Lefkowitz, M. M., & Walder, L. O. Does television violence cause aggression? *American Psychologist,* 1972, *27,* 253–263.

Fagan, J. F. III, & McGrath, S. K. Infant recognition memory and later intelligence. *Intelligence,* 1981, *5,* 121–130.

Feldman, S. S., & Ingham, M. E. Attachment behavior: A validation study in two age groups. *Child Development,* 1975, *46,* 319–330.

Finley, G. E., Kagan, J., & Layne, O., Jr. Development of young children's attention to normal and distorted stimuli: A cross-cultural study. *Developmental Psychology,* 1972, *6,* 288–292.

Fishbein, H. D. *Evolution, development, and children's learning.* Pacific Palisades, CA: Goodyear, 1976.

Fisher, B. A. *Small group decision making* (2nd ed.). New York: McGraw-Hill, 1980.

Flavell, J. H. *Cognitive development.* Englewood Cliffs, NJ: Prentice-Hall, 1977.

Flavell, J. H., Beach, D. R., & Chinsky, J. M. Spontaneous verbal rehearsal in a memory task as a function of age. *Child Development,* 1966, *37*, 283–299.

Fletcher, J. M. Linguistic factors in reading acquisition. In F. J. Pirozzolo & M. C. Wittrock (Eds.), *Neuropsychological and cognitive processes in reading.* New York: Academic Press, 1981.

Ford, M. E. The construct validity of egocentricism. *Psychological Bulletin,* 1979, *86*, 1169–1188.

Fouts, R. S. Ameslan in *Pan.* In G. H. Bourne (Ed.), *Progress in ape research.* New York: Academic Press, 1977.

Fox, N. Attachment of kibbutz infants to mother and metapelet. *Child Development,* 1977, *48*, 1228–1239.

Friedrich, L. K., & Stein, A. H. Aggressive and pro-social television programs and the natural behavior of preschool children. *Monographs of the Society for Research in Child Development.* 1973, *38*, No. 151.

Freud, A. *Normality and pathology in childhood.* New York: International Universities Press, 1965.

Frisch, H. L. Sex stereotypes in adult-infant play. *Child Development,* 1977, *48*, 1671–1675.

Fuson, K. C., & Hall, J. W. The acquisition of early number word meanings: A conceptual analysis and review. In H. P. Ginsburg (Ed.), *The development of mathematical thinking.* New York: Academic Press, 1983.

Gallup, G. G., Jr. Self-recognition in primates: A comparative approach to the bidirectional properties of consciousness. *American Psychologist,* 1977, *32*, 329–338.

Gallup, G. G., Jr. Self-awareness in primates. *American Scientist,* 1979, *67*, 417–421.

Gardner, R. A., & Gardner, B. T. Teaching sign language to a chimpanzee, *Science,* 1969, *165*, 664–672.

Gardner, B. T., & Gardner, R. A. Evidence for sentence constituents in the early utterances of child and chimpanzee. *Journal of Experimental Psychology: General,* 1975, *104*, 244–267.

Garvey, C. Some properties of social play. *Merrill-Palmer Quarterly,* 1974, *20*, 163–180.

Garvey, C. Communicational controls in social play. In B. Suttom-Smith (Ed.), *Play and learning.* New York: Gardner Press, 1979.

Garmezy, N. Children at risk: The search for the antecedents of schizophrenia: II On going research programs, issues, and interaction. *Schizophrenia Bulletin,* 1974, *1*, (9), 55–125.

Gecas, V. The influence of social class on socialization. In W. R. Burr, R. Hill, F. I. Nye, & I. L. Reiss (Eds.), *Contemporary theories about the family.* Vol. 1. New York: Free Press, 1979.

Gelman, R. S. Conservation acquisition: A problem of learning to attend to relevant attributes. *Journal of Experimental Child Psychology,* 1969, *7*, 167–187.

Gelman, R., & Gallistel, C. R. *The child's understanding of numbers.* Cambridge, MA: Harvard University Press, 1978.

Gerbner, G., Gross, L., Morgan, M., & Signorelli, N. The "mainstreaming" of America: Violence profile No. 11, *Journal of Communication,* 1980, *30*, 10–29.

Geschwind, N. Language and the brain. *Scientific American,* 1972, *226*, 76–83.

Gibson, E. J., & Levin, H. *The psychology of reading.* Cambridge, MA: The MIT Press, 1975.

Gilligan, C. In a different voice: Women's conceptions of self and of morality. *Harvard Educational Review,* 1977, *47*, 481–517.

Glick, P. C. Children of divorced parents in demographic perspective. *Journal of Social Issues,* 1979, *35*, 170–182.

Globerson, T. Mental capacity and cognitive functioning: Developmental and social class differences. *Developmental Psychology*, 1983, *19*, 225–230.

Goffman, E. *Frame analysis*. New York: Harper & Row, 1974.

Gold, D., & Andres, D. Developmental comparisons between ten-year-old children with employed and non-employed mothers. *Child Development*, 1978, *49*, 75–84.

Goodenough, W. H. *Cooperation in change*. New York: Russel Sage Foundation, 1963.

Goodenough, W. H. *Culture, language, and society*. Reading, MA: Addison-Wesley, 1970.

Gove, F. L., & Keating, D. P. Empathic role-taking precursors. *Developmental Psychology*, 1979, *15*, 594–600.

Greenberg, B. S. Television and role socialization: An overview. In D. Pearl, L. Bouthilet, & J. Lazar (Eds.), *Television and behavior* (Vols. 1 & 2). Washington, DC: U.S. Government Printing Office, 1982.

Groen, G. J., & Parkman, J. M. A chronometric analysis of simple addition. *Psychological Review*, 1972, *79*, 329–343.

Guerin, P. J., Jr. *Family therapy: Theory and practice*. New York: Gardner Press, 1976.

Gurman, A. S., & Kniskern, D. P. Research on marital and family therapy: Progress, perspective, and prospect. In S. L. Garfield & A. E. Bergin (Eds.), *Handbook of psychotherapy and behavior change* (2nd ed.). New York: Wiley, 1978.

Hagen, J. W., & Hale, G. A. The development of attention in children. In A. D. Pick (Ed.), *Minnesota Symposium on Child Psychology* (Vol. 7). Minneapolis: University of Minnesota Press, 1973.

Hale, G. A., & Piper, R. A. Developmental trends in children's incidental learning. *Developmental Psychology*, 1973, *8*, 327–335.

Hale, G. A., Taweel, S. S., Green, R. Z., & Flaugher, J. Effects of instructions on children's attention to stimulus components. *Developmental Psychology*, 1978, *14*, 499–506.

Haley, J. *Uncommon therapy*. New York: W. W. Norton, 1973.

Hall, E., Lamb, M. E., & Perlmutter, M. *Child psychology today*. New York: Random House, 1982.

Hallinan, M. Friendship patterns in open and traditional classrooms. *Sociology of Education*, 1976, *49*, 254–264.

Hallinan, M. Children's friendships and cliques. *Social Psychology Quarterly*, 1979, *42*, 43–54.

Harlow, H. F. The formation of learning sets. *Psychological Review*, 1949, *56*, 51–65.

Harlow, H. F. Age-mate or peer affectional system. In D. S. Lehrman, R. A. Hinde, & E. Shaw (Eds.), *Advances in the study of behavior* (Vol. 2). New York: Academic Press, 1969.

Harlow, H. F., & Mears, C. *The human model: Primate perspectives*. Washington, DC: V. H. Winston & Sons, 1979.

Harrison, L. F., & Williams, T. M. Television and cognitive development. Paper presented at the annual meeting of the Canadian Psychological Association. Vancouver, B. C., June, 1977.

Harter, S. A new self-report scale of intrinsic versus extrinsic orientation in the classroom: Motivational and informational components. *Developmental Psychology*, 1981, *17*, 300–312.

Harter, S. The perceived competence scale for children. *Child Development*, 1982, *53*, 87–97.

Harter, S. Developmental perspectives on the self-system. In M. Hetherington (Ed.), *Carmichael's manual of child psychology, Volume on social and personality development*. New York: Wiley, 1983.

Hartup, W. W. Aggression in childhood: Developmental perspectives. *American Psychologist*, 1974, *29*, 220–226.

Herrnstein, R. J. The evolution of behaviorism. *American Psychologist*, 1977, *32*, 593–603.

Herrnstein, R. J. IQ testing and the media. *The Atlantic Monthly*, August, 1982, pps. 68–74.

Hess, E. H. Ethology: An approach toward the complete analysis of behavior. In R. Brown, E. Galanter, E. H. Hess, & G. Mandler (Eds.), *New Directions in Psychology*. New York: Holt, Rinehart, and Winston, 1962.

Hetherington, E. M., Cox, M., & Cox, R. Stress and coping in divorce: A focus on women. In J. E. Gullahorn (Ed.), *Psychology and women: In transition*. Washington, DC: V. H. Winston & Son, 1979. (a)

Hetherington, E. M., Cox, M., & Cox, R. Play and social interaction in children following divorce. *Journal of Social Issues*, 1979, *35*, 26–49. (b)

Hinde, R. A. Mother-infant separation and the nature of inter-individual relationships: Experiments with rhesus monkeys. *Proceedings Royal Society: London B.* 1977, *196*, 29–50.

Hoffman, L. W. Changes in family roles, socialization, and sex differences. *American Psychologist*, 1977, *32*, 644–657.

Hoffman, M. L. Empathy, its development and prosocial implications. In *Nebraska Symposium on Motivation, 1977* (Vol. 25). Lincoln: University of Nebraska Press, 1978.

Holloway, R. L. The evolution of the primate brain: Some aspects of quantitative relations. *Brain Research*, 1968, *7*, 121–172.

Huesmann, L. R. Television violence and aggressive behavior. In D. Pear, L. Bouthilet, & J. Lazar (Eds.), *Television and behavior* (Vols. 1 & 2). Washington, DC: U.S. Government Printing Office, 1982.

Hunt, E. On the nature of intelligence. *Science*, 1983, *219*, 141–146.

Huston, A. C., & Wright, J. C. Effects of communication media on children. In C. B. Kopp & J. B. Krakow (Eds.), *The child: Development in a social context*. Boston: Addison-Wesley, 1982.

Jencks, C., Smith, M., Acland, H., Bane, M. J., Cohen, D., Gintis, H., Heyns, B., & Michelson, S. *Inequality: A measurement of the effect of family and schooling in America*, New York: Basic Books, 1972.

Jensen, A. R. *Bias in mental testing*. New York: Free Press, 1980.

Jerison, H. J. *Evolution of the brain and intelligence*. New York: Academic Press, 1973.

Jerison, H. J. The evolution of biological intelligence. In R. J. Sternberg (Ed.), *Handbook of human intelligence*. New York: Cambridge University Press, 1982.

Jordaan, J. P., & Super, D. E. The prediction of early adult vocational behavior. In D. F. Ricks, A. Thomas, & M. Roff (Eds.), *Life history research in psychopathology*. (Vol. 3). Minneapolis: University of Minnesota Press, 1974.

Kagan, J. The determinants of attention in the infant. *American Scientist*, 1970, *58*, 298–306.

Kagan, J. *The second year*. Cambridge: Harvard University Press, 1981.

Kagan, J., & Klein, R. E. Cross-cultural perspectives on early development, *American Psychologist*, 1973, *28*, 947–961.

Kagan, J., & Moss, H. A. *Birth to maturity*. New York: Wiley, 1962.

Kagan, S., Knight, G. P., Martinez, S., & Santana, P. E. Conflict resolution style among Mexican children. *Journal of Cross-Cultural Psychology*, 1981, *12*, 222–232.

Kagan, S., & Madsen, M. C. Cooperation and competition of Mexican, Mexican-American, and Anglo-American children of two ages under four instructional sets. *Developmental Psychology*, 1971, *5*, 32–39.

Kail, R. *The development of memory in children*. San Francisco: W. H. Freeman, 1979.

Kamara, A. I. *Cognitive development among school-age Themne children of Sierra Leone*. Ph.D. dissertation, University of Illinois, 1971.

Kamara, A. I., & Easley, J. A., Jr. Is the rate of cognitive development uniform across cultures? – A methodological critique with new evidence from Themne children. In P. R. Dasen (Ed.), *Piagetian psychology*. New York: Gardner Press, 1977.

Kamin, L. J. *The science and politics of IQ*. New York: Wiley, 1974.

Karniol, R. Children's use of intention cues in evaluating behavior. *Psychological Bulletin*, 1978, *85*, 76–85.

Kasden, L. Family structure, migration, and the entrepreneur. *Comparative Studies in Society and History*, 1965, *7*, 345–357.

Keasey, C. B. Children's developing awareness and usage of intentionality and motives. In *Nebraska Symposium on Motivation, 1977* (Vol. 25). Lincoln: University of Nebraska Press, 1978.

Keeney, J. T., Cannizzo, S. R., & Flavell, J. H. Spontaneous and induced verbal rehearsal in a recall task. *Child Development*, 1967, *38*, 953–966.

Kellam, S. G. First-grade antecedents of teenage drug use and psychological well being: A ten-year community-wide prospective study. In D. F. Ricks & B. S. Dohrenwend (Eds.), *Origins of psychopathology: Problems in research and public policy*. New York: Cambridge University Press, 1983.

Keller, A., Ford, L. H., Jr., & Meachan, J. A. Dimensions of self-concept in preschool children. *Developmental Psychology*, 1978, *14*, 483–489.

Kiminyo, D. M. A cross-cultural study of the development of conservation of mass, weight, and volume among Kamba children. In P. R. Dasen (Ed.), *Piagetian psychology*. New York: Gardner Press, 1977.

Knight, G. P., & Kagan, S. Acculturation of prosocial and competitive behaviors among second and third generation Mexican-American children. *Journal of Cross-Cultural Psychology*, 1977, *8*, 273–284.

Kobasigawa, A. Utilization of retrieval cues by children in recall. *Child Development*, 1974, *45*, 127–134.

Kohlberg, L. Stage and sequence: The cognitive-developmental approach to socialization. In D. A. Goslin (Ed.), *Handbook of socialization theory and research*. Chicago: Rand McNally, 1969.

Kohlberg, L. From is to ought: How to commit the naturalistic fallacy and get away with it in the study of moral development. In T. Mischel (Ed.), *Cognitive development and epistomology*. New York: Academic Press, 1971.

Kohn, M. L. *Class and conformity: A study in values* (2nd ed.). Chicago: University of Chicago Press, 1977.

Kokenes, B. Grade level differences in factors of self esteem. *Developmental Psychology*, 1974, *10*, 954–958.

Konner, M. J. Relations among infants and juveniles in comparative perspective. *Social Science Information*, 1976, *15*, 371–402.

Kotelchuck, M. The infant's relationship to the father: Experimental evidence. In M. E. Lamb (Ed.), *The role of the father in child development*. New York: Wiley, 1976.

Kuhn, D., Nash, S. C., & Brucken, L. Sex role concepts of two and three year olds. *Child Development*, 1978, *49*, 445–451.

Kurtines, W., & Grief, E. B. The development of moral thought: Review and evaluation of Kohlberg's approach. *Psychological Bulletin*, 1974, *81*, 453–470.

LaFontaine, J. S. Introduction. In J. S. LaFontaine (Ed.), *Sex and age as principles of social differentiation*. New York: Academic Press, 1978.

Lakoff, R. T. Questionable answers and answerable questions. In B. B. Kachru, R. B. Lees, Y. Malkiel, A. Pietrangeli, & S. Saporta (Eds.), *Papers in linguistics in honor of Henry and Renee Kahane*, Edmonton, IL: Linguistic Research, 1973.

Lamb, M. E. Effects of stress and cohort on mother-and-father-infant interaction. *Developmental Psychology*, 1976, *12*, 435–443. (a)

Lamb, M. E. Twelve-month-olds and their parents: Interaction in a laboratory playroom. *Developmental Psychology*, 1976, *12*, 237–244. (b)

Lamb, M. E. Father-infant and mother-infant interaction in the first year of life. *Child Development*, 1977, *48*, 167–181. (a)

Lamb, M. E. The development of mother-infant and father-infant attachments in the second year of life. *Developmental Psychology*, 1977, *13*, 637–648. (b)

Lamb, M. E., Easterbrooks, M. A., & Holden, G. W. Reinforcement and punishment among preschoolers: Characteristics, effects and correlates. *Child Development*, 1980, *51*, 1230–1236.

Lambert, W. W. Promise and problems of cross-cultural exploration of children's aggressive strategies. In W. W. Hartup & J. deWit (Eds.), *Origins of aggression*. The Hague: Mouton, 1978.

Lancaster, J. B. *Primate behavior and the emergence of human culture*. New York: Holt, Rinehart, & Winston, 1975.

Lane, D. M. Incidental learning and the development of selective attention. *Psychological Review*, 1980, *87*, 316–319.

Langlois, J. H., & Downs, A. C. Mothers, fathers, and peers as socialization agents of sex-typed play behaviors in young children. *Child Development*, 1980, *51*, 1237–1247.

Lasky, R. E., Klein, R. E., Yarbrough, C., Engle, P. L., Lechtig, A. & Mortorell, R. The relationship between physical growth and infant behavioral development in rural Guatemala. *Child Development*, 1981, *52*, 219–226.

Lazar, I., & Darlington, R. Lasting effects of early education: A report from the consortium for longitudinal studies. *Monographs of the Society for Research in Child Development*, 1982, *47*, No. 195.

Lee, R. B., & DeVore, I. (Eds.). *Man the hunter*. Chicago: Aldine, 1968.

Lehman, E. B. Selective strategies in children's attention to task-relevant information. *Child Development*, 1972, *43*, 197–209.

Lehman, E. B., & Goodnow, J. Memory for rhythmic series: Age changes in accuracy and number coding. *Developmental Psychology*, 1972, *6*, 363.

Lenneberg, E. H. The natural history of language. In F. Smith & G. A. Miller (Eds.), *The genesis of language*. Cambridge: MIT Press, 1966.

Lenneberg, E. H. *Biological foundations of language*. New York: Wiley, 1967.

Leon, M. Rules in children's moral judgments: Integration of intent, damage, and rationale information. *Developmental Psychology*, 1982, *18*, 835–842.

Leroi-Gourhan, A. The evolution of Paleolithic art. *Scientific American*, 1968, *218*, 58–68.

Lester, B. M., Kotelchuck, M., Spelke, E., Sellers, M. J., & Klein, R. E. Separation protest in Guatemalan infants: Cross-cultural and cognitive findings. *Developmental Psychology*, 1974, *10*, 79–85.

Levinson, D. J., Darrow, C. N., Klein, E. B., Levinson, M. H., & McKee, B. *The seasons of a man's life*. New York: Alfred A. Knopf, 1978.

Lewis, M. Infants response to facial stimuli during the first year of life. *Developmental Psychology*, 1969, *2*, 75–86.

Lewis, M., & Brooks-Gunn, J. *Social cognition and the acquisition of self*. New York: Plenum Press, 1979.

Lewis, M., & Brooks-Gunn, J. Visual attention at three months as a predictor of cognitive functioning at two years of age. *Intelligence*, 1981, *5*, 131–140.

Lewitter, F. I., DeFries, J. C., & Elston, R. C. Genetic models of reading disability. *Behavior Genetics*, 1980, *10*(1), 9–30.

Liben, L. S., & Posnansky, J. J. Inferences on inference: The effects of age, transitivity ability, memory load, and lexical factors. *Child Development*, 1977, *48*, 1490–1497.

Lieberman, P. On the evolution of language: A unified view. *Cognition*, 1973, *2*, 59–94.

Liebert, R. M. Television violence and children's aggression: The weight of the evidence. In J. DeWit & W. W. Hartup (Eds.), *Determinants and origins of aggressive behavior*. The Hague: Mouton, 1974.

Liebert, R. M., & Baron, R. A. Some immediate effects of televised violence on children's behavior. *Developmental Psychology*, 1972, *6*, 469–475.

Livesley, W. J., & Bromley, D. B. *Person perception in childhood and adolescence.* London: Wiley, 1973.

Longstreth, L. E., Davis, B., Carter, L., Flint, D., Owen, J., Rickert, M., & Taylor, E. Separation of home intellectual environment and maternal IQ as determinants of child IQ. *Developmental Psychology*, 1981, *17*, 532–541.

Lorenz, K. Z. Innate bases of learning. In K. Pribram (Ed.), *On the biology of learning.* New York: Harcourt, Brace & World, 1969.

Lorenz, K. Z. Comparative behaviorology. In J. M. Tanner & B. Inhelder (Eds.), *Discussions on child development* (Vol. 1). London: Tavistock Publications, 1956.

Louderville, S., & Main, M. Security of attachment, compliance, and maternal training methods in the second year of life. *Developmental Psychology*, 1981, *17*, 289–299.

Maccoby, E. E., & Jacklin, C. N. Sex differences in aggression: A rejoinder and reprise. *Child Development*, 1980, *51*, 964–980.

MacLean, P. D. The brain in relation to empathy and medical education. *Journal of Nervous and Mental Disorders*, 1967, *144*, 374–382.

MacLean, P. D. Clarence M. Hincks Memorial Lectures, 1969. In T. J. Boag and D. Campbell (Eds.), *A triune concept of the brain and behavior.* Toronto: University of Toronto Press, 1973.

Madsen, M. C., & Connor, C. Cooperative and competitive behavior of retarded and nonretarded at two ages. *Child Development*, 1973, *44*, 175–178.

Madsen, M. C., & Lancy, D. F. Cooperative and competitive behavior. *Journal of Cross-Cultural Psychology*, 1981, *12*, 389–408.

Madsen, M. C., & Shapira, A. Cooperative and competitive behavior of urban Afro-American, Mexican-American, and Mexican village children. *Developmental Psychology*, 1970, *3*, 16–20.

Mahler, M., Pine, F., & Bergman, A. *The psychological birth of the human infant.* New York: Basic Books, 1975.

Mandler, J. M., & Robinson, C. A. Developmental changes in picture recognition. *Journal of Experimental Child Psychology*, 1978, *26*, 122–133.

Marantz, S. A., & Mansfield, A. F. Maternal employment and the development of sex-role stereotyping in five-to-eleven-year-old girls. *Child Development*, 1977, *48*, 668–673.

Marcus, D. E., & Overton, W. F. The development of cognitive gender constancy and sex role preferences. *Child Development*, 1978, *49*, 434–444.

Marsh, G., & Sherman, M. *Transfer from word components to words and vice versa in beginning reading.* Southwest Regional Laboratory for Educational Research and Development, March, 1970.

Maslow, A. H. *Motivation and personality.* New York: Harper & Row, 1954.

Matas, L., Arend, R. A., & Sroufe, L. A. Continuity of adaptation in the second year: The relationship between quality of attachment and later competence. *Child Development*, 1978, *49*, 547–556.

Mattis, S. Dyslexia syndromes in children: Toward the development of syndrome-specific treatment programs. In F. J. Pirozzolo and M. C. Wittrock (Eds.), *Neuropsychological and cognitive processes in reading.* New York: Academic Press, 1981.

McCall, R. B., Appelbaum, M. I., & Hogarty, P. S. Developmental changes in mental performance. *Monographs of the Society for Research in Child Development*, 1973, *38*, No. 150.

McCarver, R. B. A developmental study of the effect of organizational cues on short-term memory. *Child Development*, 1972, *43*, 1317–1328.

McConaghy, M. J. Gender permanence and the genital basis of gender: Stages in the development of constancy of gender identity. *Child Development*, 1979, *50*, 1223–1226.

Mednick, S. A., & Schulsinger, F. Factors related to breakdown in children at high risk. In

M. Roff & D. F. Ricks (Eds.), *Life history research in psychopathology*. Minneapolis: University of Minnesota Press, 1970.

Melamed, B. G., & Siegel, L. J. Reduction of anxiety in children facing hospitalization and surgery by use of filmed modeling. *Journal of Consulting and Clinical Psychology*, 1975, *43*, 511–521.

Menyuk, P. Language development. In C. B. Kopp and J. B. Krakow (Eds.) *The child: Development in a social context*. Reading, MA: Addison-Wesley, 1982.

Menyuk, P., & Flood, J. Linguistic competence, reading, writing problems and remediation. *Bulletin of the Orton Society*, 1981, *31*, 13–28.

Metz, M. M. *Classrooms and corridors*. Berkeley: University of California Press, 1978.

Meyer, B. The development of girl's sex-role attitudes. *Child Development*, 1980, *51*, 508–514.

Milavsky, J. R., Kessler, R. C., Stipp, H. H., & Rubens, W. S. *Television and aggression*. New York: Academic Press, 1983.

Milgram, S. The experience of living in cities. *Science*, 1970, *167*, 1461–1468.

Miller, A. G. Integration and acculturation of cooperative behavior among Blackfoot Indian and Non-Indian Canadian children. *Journal of Cross-Cultural Psychology*, 1973, *4,*, 374–380.

Minuchin, S. *Families and family therapy*. Cambridge, MA: Harvard University Press, 1974.

Modell, J., Furstenberg, F. F., Jr., & Hershberg, T. Social change and transitions to adulthood in historical perspective. *Journal of Family History*, 1977, *2*, 7–32.

Mohr, D. M. Development of attributes of personal identity. *Developmental Psychology*, 1978,, *14*, 427–428.

Money, J., & Ehrhardt, A. A., *Man and woman: Boy and girl*. Baltimore: Johns Hopkins University Press, 1972.

Moore, K. L. *The developing human* 3rd Edition, Philadelphia. W. B. Saunders, 1983.

Morgan, M., & Gross, L. Television viewing, IQ, and academic achievement. *Journal of Broadcasting*, 1980, *24*, 117–133.

Morgan, M., & Gross, L. Television and educational achievement and aspiration. In D. Pearl, L. Bouthilet, & J. Lazar (Eds.), *Television and behavior* (Vols. 1 & 2). Washington, DC: U.S. Government Printing Office, 1982.

Morioka, K. Life cycle patterns in Japan, China, and the United States. *Journal of Marriage and the Family*. 1967, *29*, 595–606.

Moskowitz, D. S., Schwarz, J. C., & Corsini, D. A. Initiating day care at three years of age: Effects on attachment. *Child Development*, 1977, *48*, 1271–1276.

Murray, H. A. *Explorations in personality*. New York: Oxford University Press, 1938.

Murray, J. P. *Television and youth*. Boys Town, Nebraska: The Boys Town Center for the study of youth development, 1980.

Mussen, P. H., & Eisenberg-Berg, N. *Roots of caring, sharing and helping*. San Francisco: Freeman, 1977.

Napier, A. Y., & Whitaker, C. A. *The family crucible*. New York: Harper & Row, 1978.

Neale, J. M., & Oltmanns, T. F. *Schizophrenia*. New York: John Wiley, 1980.

Neisser, U. *Cognition and reality*. San Francisco: W. H. Freeman, 1976.

Nelson, K. Structure and strategy in learning to talk. *Monographs of the Society for Research in Child Development*. 1973, *38*, No. 149.

Nelson, K. Concept, word and sentence: Interrelations in acquisition and development. *Psychological Review*, 1974, *81*, 267–285.

Nelson, K. Individual differences in language development: Implications for development and language. *Developmental Psychology*, 1981, *17*, 170–187.

Niemark, E., Slotnick, N. A., & Ulrich, T. Development of memorization strategies. *Devel-*

opmental Psychology, 1971, *5*, 427–432.

Noller, P. Sex differences in the socialization of affectionate expression. *Developmental Psychology*, 1978, *14*, 317–319.

Norman-Jackson, J. Family interactions, language development, and primary reading achievement of Black children in families of low income. *Child Development*, 1982, *53*, 349–358.

Nucci, L. P., & Nucci, M. S. Children's social interactions in the context of moral and conventional transgressions. *Child Development*, 1982, *53*, 403–412. (a)

Nucci, L. P., & Nucci, M. S. Children's responses to moral and social conventional transgressions in free-play settings. *Child Development*, 1982, *53*, 1337–1342. (b)

Nucci, L. P., & Turiel, E. Social interactions and the development of social concepts in preschool children. *Child Development*, 1978, *49*, 400–407.

Nyiti, R. M. The development of conservation in the Meru children of Tanzania. *Child Development*. 1976, *47*, 1122–1129.

Nyiti, R. M. The validity of "cultural differences explanations" for cross-cultural variation in the rate of Piagetian cognitive development. In D. A. Wagner & H. W. Stevenson (Eds.), *Cultural perspectives in child development*. San Francisco: W. H. Freeman, 1982.

Ogbu, J. U. *The next generation: An ethnography of education in an urban neighborhood*. New York: Academic Press, 1975.

Olsen, N. J. The role of grandmothers in Taiwanese family socialization. *Journal of Marriage and the Family*, 1976, *38*, 363–372.

Olweus, D. *Aggression in the schools*. New York: Halsted Press, 1978.

Olweus, D. Stability of aggressive reaction patterns in males: A review. *Psychological Bulletin*, 1979, *86*, 852–875.

Omark, D. R., Omark, M., & Edelman, M. Formation of dominance heirarchies in young children. In T. R. Williams (Ed.), *Psychological anthropology*. The Hague: Mouton, 1975.

Palermo, D. S., & Molfese, D. L. Language acquisition from age five onward. *Psychological Bulletin*, 1972, *78*, 409–428.

Papp, P. (Ed.) *Family therapy: Full-length case studies*. New York: Gardner Press, 1977.

Pascuel-Leone, J. A mathematical model for the transition rule in Piaget's developmental stages. *Acta Psychologica*, 1970, *32*, 301–345.

Pastor, D. L. The quality of mother-infant attachment and its relationship to toddler's initial sociality with peers. *Developmental Psychology*, 1981, *17*, 326–335.

Patterson, G. R., Littman, R. A., & Bricker, W. Assertive behavior in young children: A step toward a theory of aggression. *Monographs of the Society for Research in Child Development*, 1967, *35*, (4).

Patterson, F. G. Innovative uses of language by a gorilla: A case study. In K. E. Nelson (Ed.) *Children's language* (Vol. 2). New York: Gardner Press, 1980.

Pearl, D., Bouthilet, L., & Lazar, J. (Eds.) *Television and behavior*. (Vols. 1 & 2). Washington, DC: U.S. Government Printing Office, 1982.

Pennington, B. F., & Smith, S. D. Genetic influences on learning disabilities and speech and language disorders. *Child Development*, 1983, *54*, 369–387.

Perlmutter, M., & Myers, N. A. Development of recall in 2- to 4-year old children. *Developmental Psychology*, 1979, *15*, 73–83.

Piaget, J. *The moral judgment of the child*. Glencoe, Illinois: Free Press, 1948 (originally published in 1932).

Piaget, J. *Play, dreams and imitation in childhood*. New York: Norton, 1962.

Piaget, J. *The origins of intelligence in children*. New York: W. W. Norton, 1963.

Piaget, J., & Inhelder, B. *The early growth of logic in the child*. London: Routledge & Kegan Paul, 1964.

Piaget, J. *Psychology of intelligence*. Totowa, NJ: Littlefield, Adams, 1966.

Piaget, J. Piaget's theory. In P. H. Mussen (Ed.), *Carmichael's manual of child psychology* (3rd ed.) New York: Wiley, 1970.

Piaget, J. *Biology and knowledge.* Chicago: University of Chicago Press, 1971.

Portnoy, F. C., & Simmons, C. H. Day care and attachment. *Child Development,* 1978, *49,* 239–242.

Premack, D. *Intelligence in ape and man.* Hillsdale, NJ: Lawrence Erlbaum Associates, 1976.

Pressley, M. Elaboration and memory development. *Child Development,* 1982, *53,* 296–306.

Ragozin, A. S. Attachment behavior of day-care children: Naturalistic and laboratory observations. *Child Development,* 1980, *51,* 409–415.

Ramey, G. T., Farran, D. C. & Campbell, F. A. Predicting IQ from mother-child interactions. *Child Development,* 1979, *50,* 804–814.

Ramey, G. T., Stedman, D. J., Borders-Patterson, A., & Mengel, W. Predicting school failure from information available at birth. *American Journal of Mental Deficiency,* 1978, *82,* 525–534.

Reichenback, H. *Experience and prediction.* Chicago: University of Chicago Press, 1938.

Renshaw, M. A. Cognitive development in human and gorilla infants. *Journal of Human Evolution,* 1978, *7,* 133–141.

Resnick, L. B. A developmental theory of number understanding. In H. P. Ginsburg (Ed.) *The development of mathematical thinking.* New York: Academic Press, 1983.

Rest, J. *Developmental hierarchy in preference and comprehension of moral comprehension of moral judgment.* Unpublished doctoral dissertation. University of Chicago, 1968.

Rest, J. *Development of judging moral issues.* Minneapolis: University of Minnesota Press, 1979.

Ricks, D. F. Dimensions in life space: Factor analytic case studies. In S. R. Brown & D. J. Brenner (Eds.), *Science, psychology and communication.* New York: Teachers College Press, 1972.

Ristau, C. A., & Robbins, D. Language in the great apes: A critical review. In J. S. Rosenblatt, R. A. Hinde, C. Beer, and M. C. Busnel (Eds.) *Advances in the study of behavior* (Vol. 12). New York: Academic Press, 1982.

Roberts, J. M., Sutton-Smith, B., & Kendon, A. Strategy in games and folktales. *Journal of Social Psychology,* 1963, *61,* 185–199.

Roff, M. Childhood antecedents of adult neurosis, severe bad conduct, and psychological health. In D. F. Ricks, A. Thomas, & M. Roff (Eds.), *Life history research in psychopathology* (Vol. 3). Minneapolis: University of Minnesota Press, 1974.

Roff, M., Sells, S. B., & Golden, M. M. *Social adjustment and personality development in children.* Minneapolis: University of Minnesota Press, 1972.

Rogoff, B. Schooling and the development of cognitive skills. In H. C. Triandis & A. Heron (Eds.) *Handbook of cross-cultural psychology: Developmental Psychology.* Vol. 4, Boston: Allyn & Bacon, 1981.

Rosenberg, M. *Conceiving the self.* New York: Basic Books, 1979.

Rosenblum, L. A. Infant attachment in monkeys. In H. R. Schaffer (Ed.) *The origins of human social relations.* London: Academic Press, 1971.

Rosenblum, L. A., & Plimpton, E. H. The effects of adults on peer interactions. In M. Lewis and L. A. Rosenblum (Eds.), *The child and its family.* New York: Plenum, 1979.

Rossi, A. S. A biosocial perspective on parenting. In A. S. Rossi, J. Kagan, & T. K. Hareven (Eds.), *The family.* New York: W. W. Norton, 1977.

Rubenstein, J. L., & Howes, C. Caregiving and infant behavior in day care and in homes. *Developmental Psychology,* 1979, *15,* 1–24.

Ruble, D. N., Balaban, R., & Cooper, J. Gender constancy and the effects of sex-typed televised toy commercials. *Child Development,* 1981, *52,* 667–673.

Rumbaugh, D. M. (Ed.) *Language learning by a chimpanzee: The LANA project.* New York: Academic Press, 1977.

Runyan, W. M. *Life histories and psychobiography.* New York: Oxford University Press, 1982.

Rushton, J. P. Socialization and the altruistic behavior of children, *Psychological Bulletin,* 1976, *83,* 898–913.

Rushton, J. P. Television and prosocial behavior. In D. Pearl, L. Bouthilet, & J. Lazar (Eds.) *Television and behavior* (Vols. 1 & 2). Washington, D.C.: U.S. Government Printing Office, 1982.

Rutter, M. *Helping troubled children.* Middlesex, England: Penguin, 1975.

Satz, P., Friel, J., & Rudegeair, F. Differential changes in the acquisition of developmental skills in children who later become dyslexic. In D. G. Stein, J. J. Rosen, and N. Butters (Eds.), *Plasticity and recovery of function in the central nervous system.* New York: Academic Press, 1974.

Satz, P., & Morris, R. Learning disability subtypes: A review. In F. J. Pirozzolo and M. C. Wittrock (Eds.), *Neuropsychological and cognitive processes in reading.* New York: Academic Press, 1981.

Savage-Rumbaugh, E. S. & Rumbaugh, D. M. Language analogue project, phase II: Theory and tactics. In K. E. Nelson (Ed.) *Children's language* (Vol. 2). New York: Gardner Press, 1980.

Savin-Williams, R. C. Dominance hierarchies in groups of early adolescents. *Child Development,* 1979, *50,* 923–935.

Saxe, G. B. Body parts as numerals: A development analysis of numeration among the Oksapmin in Papua, New Guinea. *Child Development,* 1981, *52,* 306–316.

Saxén, L., & Rapola, J. *Congenital defects.* New York: Holt, Rinehart & Winston, 1969.

Scarr, S., & Carter-Saltzman, L. Twin-method: Defense of a critical assumption. *Behavior Genetics,* 1979, *9,* 527–542.

Scarr, S., & Weinberg, R. A. Attitudes, interests, and IQ. *Human Nature,* 1978, *1,* 29–36.

Schaie, K. W. A general model for the study of developmental problems. *Psychological Bulletin,* 1965, *64,* 92–107.

Schaie, K., & Strother, C. A cross-sequential study of age changes in cognitive behavior. *Psychological Bulletin,* 1968, *70,* 671–680.

Schlesinger, I. M. Production of utterances and language acquisition. In D. J. Slobin (Ed.), *The ontogenesis of grammar.* New York: Academic Press, 1971.

Schrag, P., & Divoky, D. *The myth of the hyperactive child.* New York: Pantheon books, 1975.

Schulsinger, F., Mednick, S. A., & Knop, J. (Eds.) *Longitudinal research.* Boston: Martinus Nijhoff Publishing, 1981.

Schultz, T. R., & Pilon, R. Development of the ability to detect linguistic ambiguity. *Child Development,* 1973, *44,* 728–733.

Schutz, W. C. *Firo: A three dimensional theory of interpersonal behavior.* New York: Holt, Rinehart, and Winston, 1960.

Schwartzman, H. *Transformations.* New York: Plenum Press, 1978.

Schwartzman, H. The sociocultural context of play. In B. Sutton-Smith (Ed.), *Play and learning.* New York: Gardner Press, 1979.

Scribner, S., & Cole, M. *The psychology of literacy.* Cambridge: Harvard University Press, 1981.

Searle, J. R. A taxonomy of illocutionary acts. In K. Gunderson (Ed.) *Minnesota studies in the philosophy of language.* Minneapolis: University of Minnesota Press, 1975.

Selman, R. L., & Byrne, D. F. A structural-developmental analysis of levels of role taking in middle childhood. *Child Development,* 1974, *45,* 803–806.

Selman, R. L., & Jaquette, D. Stability and oscillation in interpersonal awareness: A clinical-developmental analysis. In *Nebraska Symposium on Motivation, 1977* (Vol. 25). Lincoln: University of Nebraska Press, 1978.

Shantz, C. The development of social cognition. In E. M. Hetherington (Ed.), *Review of child development research* (Vol. 5). Chicago: University of Chicago Press, 1975.

Shapira, A. Developmental differences of competitive behavior of kibbutz and city children in Israel. *Journal of Social Psychology*, 1976, *98*, 19–26.

Sharp, D., Cole, M., & Lave, C. Education and cognitive development: The evidence from experimental research. *Monographs of the Society for Research in Child Development*, 1979, *44*, No. 178.

Siegel, L. S. Reproduction, perinatal, and environmental factors as predictors of the cognitive and language development of preterm and full-term infants. *Child Development*, 1982, *53*, 963–973.

Simpson, E. L. Moral development research: A case of scientific cultural bias. *Human Development*, 1974, *17*, 81–106.

Simpson, G. G. *The meaning of evolution*. New Haven: Yale University Press, 1949.

Sinclair-deZwart, H. Language acquisition and cognitive development. In T. E. Moore (Ed.), *Cognitive development and the acquisition of language*. New York: Academic Press, 1973.

Singer, J. L., & Singer, D. G. *Television, imagination, and aggression*. Hillsdale, NJ: Lawrence Erlbaum Associates, 1981.

Singer, J. L., & Singer, D. G. Psychologists look at television: Cognitive, developmental, personality, and social policy implications. *American Psychologist*, 1983, *38*, 826–834.

Skinner, B. F. *Particulars of my life*. New York: Knopf, 1976.

Slobin, D. I. Grammatical transformations and sentence comprehension in childhood and adulthood. *Journal of Verbal Learning and Verbal Behavior*. 1966, *5*, 219–227.

Slobin, D. I. *Psycholinguistics*. New York: Scott, Foresman. 1971.

Smith, D. W., & Bierman, E. L. *The biologic ages of man*. Philadelphia: Saunders, 1973.

Smith, P. K., & Daglish, L. Sex differences in parent and infant behavior in the home. *Child Development*, 1977, *48*, 1250–1254.

Sokolov, E. N. Neuronal models and the orienting reflex. In M. A. B. Brazier (Ed.), *The central nervous system and behavior*. New York: Josiah Macy Foundation, 1960.

Sommerlad, E. H., & Bellingham, W. P. Cooperation-competition: A comparsion of Australian and European and Aboriginal school children. *Journal of Cross-Cultural Psychology*, 1972, *3*, 149–157.

Spearman, C. *The abilities of man*. London: Macmillan, 1927.

Staub, E. *Positive social behavior and morality: Socialization and development*. New York; Academic Press, 1979.

Stephenson, W. The study of behavior: *Q technique and its methodology*. Chicago: University of Chicago Press, 1953.

Sternberg, R. J. The nature of mental abilities. *American Psychologist*, 1979, *34*, 214–230.

Stevenson, H. W. Influences of schooling on cognitive development. In D. A. Wagner, & H. W. Stevenson (Eds.), *Cultural perspectives in child development*. San Francisco: W. H. Freeman, 1982.

Stevenson, H. W., Parker, T., Wilkonson, A., Bonnevaux, B., & Gonzalez, M. Schooling, environment, and cognitive development: A cross-cultural study. *Monographs of the Society for Research in Child Development*, 1978, *43*, No. 175.

Stevenson, H. W., Stigler, J. W., Lucker, G. W., Lee, S., Hsu, C. & Kitamura, S. Reading disabilities: The case of Chinese, Japanese, and English. *Child Development*, 1982, *53*, 1164–1181.

Stierlin, H. *Separating parents and adolescents*. New York: Quadrangle, 1974.

Strayer, F. F., & Strayer, J. An ethological analysis of social agonism and dominance relations among preschool children. *Child Development*, 1976, *47*, 980–989.

Suomi, S. J. Differential development of various social relationships by Rhesus monkey infants. In M. Lewis & L. A. Rosenblum (Eds.) *The child and its family*. New York: Plenum, 1979.

Sutton-Smith, B., & Roberts, J. M. The cross-cultural and psychological study of games. In G. Luschen (Ed.), *The cross-cultural analysis of games*. Champaign, IL: Stipes, 1970.

Tanner, J. M. *Growth at adolescence* (2nd ed.). Oxford: Blackwell Scientific Publications, 1962.

Tanner, J. M. *Fetus into man*. Cambridge: Harvard University Press, 1978.

Tanner, N. M. *On becoming human*. Cambridge: Cambridge University Press, 1981.

Tauber, M. A. Sex differences in parent-child interaction styles during a free-play session. *Child Development*, 1979,40 50, 981–988.

Terman, L. M., & Merrill, M. A. *Measuring intelligence: A guide to the administration of the new revised Stanford-Binet Tests*. Boston: Houghton Mifflin, 1937.

Terman, L. M., & Oden, M. H. *Genetic studies of genius V: The gifted group at midlife*. Stanford, CA: Stanford University Press, 1959.

Terrace, H. S., Petitto, L. A., Sanders, R. J., & Bever, T. G. On the grammatical capacity of apes. In K. E. Nelson (Ed.), *Children's language* (Vol. 2), New York: Gardner Press, 1980.

Thomas, L. *The lives of a cell*. New York: Viking Press, 1974.

Thompson, S. K. Gender labels and early sex role development. *Child Development*, 1975, *46*, 339–347.

Thurstone, L. L. *Multi-factor analysis*. Chicago: University of Chicago Press, 1947.

Tieger, T. On the biological basis of sex differences in aggression. *Child Development*, 1980, *51*, 943–963.

Tobias, P. V. *The brain in hominid evolution*. New York: Columbia University Press, 1970.

Trow, M. The second transformation of American secondary education. *International Journal of Comparative Sociology*, 1961, *2*, 144–165.

Tulving, E. Cue-dependent forgetting, *American Scientist*, 1974, *62*, 74–82.

Turiel, E. Domains and categories in social cognitive development. In W. Overton (Ed.), *The relationship between social and cognitive development*. Hillsdale, NJ: Lawrence Erlbaum Associates, 1983.

Turiel, E. Distinct conceptual and developmental domains: Social convention and morality. *Nebraska Symposium on Motivation, 1977* (Vol. 25). Lincoln: University of Nebraska Press, 1978.

Turner, E. A., & Rommetveit, R. The acquisition of sentence voice and reversibility. *Child Development*, 1967, *38*, 649–660.

Underwood, B., & Moore, B. Perspective-taking and altruism. *Psychological Bulletin*, 1982, *91*, 143–173.

Ungerer, J. A., Zelazo, P. R., Kearsley, R. B., & O'Leary, K. Developmental changes in the representation of objects in symbolic play from 18 to 34 months of age. *Child Development*, 1981, *52*, 186–195.

Vaughn, B. E., Egeland, B., Sroufe, L. A., & Waters, E. Individual differences in infant-mother attachment at 12 and 18 months: Stability and change in families under stress. *Child Development*, 1979, *50*, 971–975.

Vaughn, B. E., Gove, F. L., & Egeland, B. The relationship between out-of-home care and the quality of infant-mother attachment in an economically disadvantaged population. *Child Development*, 1980, *51*, 1203–1214.

Vellutino, F. R. *Dyslexia: Theory and research*. Cambridge, MA: The MIT Press, 1979.

Vernon, P. E. *The structure of human abilities*. London: Methuen, 1950.

Voyat, G., Personal communication, 1983.

Vurpillot, E. The development of scanning strategies and their relation to visual differentiation. *Journal of Experimental Child Psychology*, 1968, *6*, 622–650.

Waddington, C. H. *The strategy of genes*. London: Allen & Unwin, 1957.

Ward, S., Wackman, D. B., & Wartella, E. *How children learn to buy*. Beverly Hills, CA: Sage, 1977.

Washburn, S. L., & Hamburg, D. A. The study of primate behavior. In I. deVore (Ed.), *Primate behavior: Field studies of monkey and ape*. New York: Holt, Rinehart, and Winston, 1965.

Waters, E. The reliability and stability of individual differences in infant-mother attachment. *Child Development*, 1978, *49*, 483–494.

Waters, E., Wippman, J., & Sroufe, L. A. Attachment, positive affect, and competence in the peer group: Two studies in construct validation. *Child Development*, 1979, *50*, 821–829.

Weisfeld, G. E., Omark, D. R., & Cronin, C. L. A longitudinal and cross-sectional study of dominance in boys. In D. R. Omark, F. F. Strayer, & D. C. Freedman (Eds.), *Dominance Relations*. New York: Garland STPM Press, 1980.

Wells, R. A., & Dezen, A. E. The results of family therapy revisited: The nonbehavioral methods. *Family Process*, 1978, *17*, 251–274.

Werner, E. E. *Cross-cultural child development*. Monterey, CA: Brooks/Cole, 1979.

Wessman, A., & Ricks, D. F. *Mood and personality*. New York: Rinehart and Winston, 1966.

Weston, D. R., & Turiel, E. Act-rule relations: Children's concept of social rules. *Developmental Psychology*, 1980, *16*, 417–424.

Wheeler, R. J., & Dusek, J. B. The effects of attentional and cognitive factors on children's incidental learning. *Child Development*, 1973, *44*, 253–258.

White, C. B., Bushnell, N., & Regnemer, J. L. Moral development in Bahamian school children: A three year examination of Kohlberg's stages of moral judgment. *Developmental Psychology*, 1978, *14*, 58–65.

White, L.A. *The evolution of culture*. New York: McGraw-Hill, 1959.

White, R. W. Competence and the psychosexual stage of development. In M. R. Jones (Ed.), *Nebraska symposium on motivation*. Lincoln: University of Nebraska Press, 1960.

Whiting, B., & Edwards, C. P. A cross-cultural analysis of sex differences in the behavior of children aged three through eleven. *Journal of Social Psychology*, 1973, *91*, 171–188.

Wilson, E. D. *Sociobiology: The abridged edition*. Cambridge, MA: Harvard University Press, 1980.

Wilson, R. S. Concordance in physical growth for monozygotic and dizygotic twins. *Annals of Human Biology*, 1976, *3*, 1–10.

Wilson, R. S. Synchronies in mental development: An epigenetic perspective. *Science*, 1978, *202*, 939–948.

Wise, K. L., Wise, L. A., & Zimmerman, R. R. Piagetian object permanence in the rhesus monkey. *Developmental Psychology*, 1974, *10*, 429–437.

Woodruff, G. & Premack, D. Intentional communication in the chimpanzee: The development of deception. *Cognition*, 1979, *7*, 333–362.

Wright, J. C., & Huston, A. C. A matter of form: Potentials of television for young viewers. *American Psychologist*, 1983, *38*, 835–843.

Young, J. Z. *An introduction to the study of man*. New York: Oxford University Press, 1971.

Zinchenko, V. P., Chzhi-tsin, V., & Tarakanov, V. V. The formation and development of perceptual activity. *Soviet Psychology and Psychiatry*, 1962, *2*, 3–12.

Author Index

Subject Index